MARKOV PROCESSES
AND LEARNING MODELS

This is Volume 84 in
MATHEMATICS IN SCIENCE AND ENGINEERING
A series of monographs and textbooks
Edited by RICHARD BELLMAN, *University of Southern California*

The complete listing of the books in this series is available from the Publisher upon request.

MARKOV PROCESSES AND LEARNING MODELS

M. FRANK NORMAN

Department of Psychology
University of Pennsylvania
Philadelphia, Pennsylvania

 ACADEMIC PRESS   New York and London   1972

ACADEMIC PRESS, INC.
111 Fifth Avenue, New York, New York 10003

United Kingdom Edition published by
ACADEMIC PRESS, INC. (LONDON) LTD.
24/28 Oval Road, London NW1

LIBRARY OF CONGRESS CATALOG CARD NUMBER: 70-182638

AMS (MOS) 1970 Subject Classifications: 60B10, 60F05,
60J05, 60J20, 60J70, 92A25; 60J35, 60J60, 62M05, 62M10,
62M15, 92A10

PRINTED IN THE UNITED STATES OF AMERICA

To Sandy

○ Contents

8 Transient Behavior in the Case of Large Drift

9 Transient Behavior in the Case of Small Drift

10 Steady-State Behavior

11 Absorption Probabilities

Part III SPECIAL MODELS

12 The Five-Operator Linear Model

13 The Fixed Sample Size Model

14   Additive Models

15   Multiresponse Linear Models

16   The Zeaman–House–Lovejoy Models

17   Other Learning Models

18   Diffusion Approximation in a Genetic Model and a Physical Model

○ Preface

This monograph presents some developments in probability theory that were motivated by stochastic learning models, and describes in considerable detail the implications of these developments for the models that instigated them. No attempt is made to establish the psychological utility of these models, but ample references are provided for the reader who wishes to pursue this question. In doing so he will quickly become aware that the difficulty of deriving predictions from these models has prevented them from developing to their full potential, whatever that may be. Since I am more a probabilist than a psychologist, I am in a position to regard this difficulty as a challenge rather than a nuisance.

The book has four main parts: Introduction (Chapter 0), Distance Diminishing Models (Part I), Slow Learning (Part II), and Special Models (Part III). Parts I and II and Chapter 14 in Part III (Additive Models) constitute the theoretical core. From the mathematical point of view, Part I develops a theory of Markov processes that move by random contraction of a metric space. Transition by random translation on the line is considered in Chapter 14. Part II presents an extensive theory of diffusion approximation of discrete time Markov processes that move "by small steps." Parts I and II are practically independent, so it would be almost as natural to read them in reverse order. Chapters 12–16 of Part III consider the various special models described in the Introduction in the light of Parts I and II. In addition, some special properties of these models are obtained by ad hoc calculation. Chapter 17 takes up a number of other learning models briefly, and Chapter 18 spells out the implications of Part II for a population genetic model of S. Wright and for the Ehrenfest model for heat exchange. The chapters of Part III are almost independent, except that Chapter 13 depends heavily on Chapter 12. Open mathematical problems are easily visible throughout the book, but especially in Chapters 14–16.

The mathematical prerequisites for close reading of Parts I and II are analysis (integration, metric topology, functional analysis) and probability at about the first-year graduate level. The texts of Royden (1968) and Breiman (1968) would be excellent preparation. An acquaintance with the language and notation of these subjects will suffice if the reader is willing to skip most of the proofs. The prerequisites for Part III (excepting Chapter 14) are less stringent, and it can be used for reference purposes without studying Parts I and II systematically.

No previous exposure to mathematical learning theory is assumed, though it would be useful. The glimpse of this subject in Chapter 0 is adequate preparation for the rest of the book. The reader is referred to Atkinson, Bower, and Crothers (1965) for a balanced and thorough introduction. Those who are familiar with mathematical learning theory will notice that the emphasis on "continuous state models" in this book, at the expense of "finite state models," is the reverse of the emphasis in the psychological literature. In particular, the book makes no contribution to the analysis of models with very few states of learning. These models are quite well understood mathematically, and they have been extremely fruitful psychologically.

Concerning the numbering of formal statements, Theorem 5.2.3 is the third theorem of Section 5.2. Within Chapter 5, it is referred to as Theorem 2.3. Equations, lemmas, and definitions are numbered in the same way. The symbol ∎ signifies the end of a proof.

I have not attempted to reconstruct the history of the topics treated. In most cases, only the main source or immediate antecedent of a development is cited in the text. These sources often give additional information concerning prior and complementary results. The publications of the following individuals deserve special mention in connection with the parts indicated: C. T. Ionescu Tulcea (Part I), A. Khintchine (Part II), and R. R. Bush and F. Mosteller (Part III).

Much of the research reported in this volume is my own, and a significant portion appears here for the first time. My work has been generously supported by the National Science Foundation under grants GP-7335 and GB-7946X to the University of Pennsylvania. Most of the writing was done in particularly pleasant circumstances at Rockefeller University on a Guggenheim Fellowship.

It is a pleasure to acknowledge the encouragement and assistance of a number of my teachers and colleagues, especially R. C. Atkinson, K. L. Chung, W. K. Estes, M. Kac, S. Karlin, and P. Suppes. I am also much obliged to R. Bellman for suggesting that I write a book for this series. The manuscript was expertly typed by Mrs. Maria Kudel and Miss Mary Ellen O'Brien. Finally, the book is dedicated to my wife, Sandy, in gratitude for her inexhaustible affection and patience.

0 ○ Introduction

0.1. Experiments and Models

In this section we describe a few more or less standard experimental paradigms, and certain special models for subjects' behavior in such experiments. These models have stimulated and guided the development of the general mathematical theories presented in Parts I and II of this volume. In addition, they are of substantial psychological and mathematical interest in their own right. The implications of Parts I and II for these models, as well as numerous results of a more specialized character, are collected in Part III.

All but one of the experiments to be described consist of a sequence of *trials*. On each trial the subject is presented with a *stimulus* configuration, makes a *response*, and an *outcome* ensues. There are at least two response alternatives, and there may be infinitely many. The outcome or payoff typically has obvious positive or negative value to the subject, and would be expected to influence future responses accordingly. If an outcome raises, or at least does not lower, the probability of a response in the presence of a stimulus, it is said to *reinforce* the association between stimulus and response. The probabilities of different stimuli, and the conditional probabilities of

1

various outcomes, given the stimulus and response, are prescribed by the experimenter and are constant throughout the experiment. *Simple learning* experiments are those in which only one stimulus configuration is ever presented. The complementary case of two or more stimulus configurations is called *discrimination* or *identification learning*, since the subject must distinguish between stimuli if he is to be able to make appropriate responses (i.e., responses that yield preferred outcomes) to each.

A. SIMPLE LEARNING WITH TWO RESPONSES

Three of the six models described in this section relate to experiments of this type. The two responses are denoted A_1 and A_0, and, in the most general case considered, response A_i can be followed by either of two outcomes, O_{i1} or O_{i0}, where O_{ij} reinforces A_j. The reinforcement probability parameters are

$$\pi_{ij} = P(O_{ij}|A_i).$$

Of course, if there is no outcome O_{ij} in a particular experiment, we take $\pi_{ij} = 0$, and, conversely, if $\pi_{ij} = 0$, we need not include O_{ij} in the description of the experiment.

The notation O_{ij} emphasizes that the outcome O_{11} that follows A_1 and reinforces A_1 (perhaps presentation of food or money) may be of a totally different character than the outcome O_{01} that follows A_0 and reinforces A_1 (perhaps no food or loss of money). However, it is convenient, for most purposes, to redefine the outcomes in terms of their supposed reinforcing effects. Thus we introduce the new outcomes O_1 and O_0, where O_j indicates reinforcement of A_j, irrespective of the preceding response. Thus $A_i O_j$ ("A_i is followed by O_j") means the same thing as $A_i O_{ij}$.

The trial number is indicated by a subscript. Thus A_{in} or O_{jn} denotes occurrence of A_i or O_j on trial n. We always call the first trial "trial 0," so $n = 0, 1, 2, \ldots$. This is slightly more convenient mathematically than beginning the trial numbers with 1.

EXPERIMENTS. (i) *Paired-associate learning* (see Kintsch, 1970). A human subject is required to learn a "correct" response to each of a sequence of stimuli presented repetitively, as when a student learns the vocabulary of a foreign language from a deck of cards. Though this is basically a complex discrimination learning experiment with multiple responses, as a first approximation we may focus on successive presentations of the same item, ignoring interitem interactions, and code the subject's responses on that item as "correct" (A_0) or "incorrect" (A_1). If the subject is told the correct response after each of his responses, then O_0 is the only outcome, $\pi_{00} = \pi_{10} = 1$, and we have an example of *continuous reinforcement*.

(ii) *Prediction experiments* (see Estes, 1964; Myers, 1970). A human subject is asked to predict which of two lights, 0 and 1, will flash on each trial. Response A_i is prediction of light i, and outcome O_j is flashing of light j. Monetary payoffs are sometimes used (with, of course, a larger prize for a correct prediction), but more often they are not.

The special case of *noncontingent outcomes*, where the outcome probabilities do not depend on the response made ($\pi_{11} = \pi_{01} = \pi$), has received most attention experimentally. After performance has stabilized, it is often found that the proportion of A_1 responses is very close to the probability π that A_1 is reinforced, at least when the average of several subjects' data is considered. This *probability matching* is somewhat surprising, since frequency of correct prediction is maximized by always predicting the light which flashes most frequently. As one might expect, experiments with monetary payoffs tend to produce behavior closer to this optimal strategy.

The condition

$$P(A_{1n}) - P(O_{1n}) \to 0$$

as $n \to \infty$ defines a form of probability matching that is applicable to arbitrary outcome probabilities. Since

$$P(O_{1n}) = \pi_{11} P(A_{1n}) + \pi_{01}(1 - P(A_{1n})),$$

we have

$$P(A_{1n}) - P(O_{1n}) = (\pi_{01} + \pi_{10}) P(A_{1n}) - \pi_{01}.$$

Therefore, if $\pi_{01} + \pi_{10} > 0$, probability matching in the above sense is equivalent to $P(A_{1n}) \to l$, where

$$l = \pi_{01}/(\pi_{01} + \pi_{10}).$$

Hence we refer to l as the *probability matching asymptote*. It is a useful reference point for asymptotic performance.

(iii) *T-Maze experiments* (see Bitterman, 1965; Weinstock, North, Brody, and LoGuidice, 1965). On each trial a rat is placed at the bottom of a T-shaped alley, and proceeds to the end of the right or left arm (response A_1 or A_0, respectively), where he may or may not find food. Finding food reinforces the response just made, and finding no food reinforces the other response, though in some variants of this experiment it appears that the effect of not finding food may be nil or almost nil. Rats show no tendency to match response to outcome probability. Practically all of them develop a decided preference for the response with the highest probability of yielding food.

(iv) *Avoidance learning* (see Bush and Mosteller, 1959; Theios, 1963; Hoffman, 1965). A dog or rat may avoid an electric shock if he jumps over a barrier (A_1) shortly after a warning signal. Otherwise (A_0) he must clear the barrier to escape the shock. The only possible outcomes are avoidance and shock, and both appear to reinforce jumping, so $\pi_{01} = \pi_{11} = 1$.

MODELS. All of the models presented below allow for the possibility that an outcome will have no effect on response probability on some trials. This state of affairs is called ineffective conditioning and denoted C_0; otherwise, conditioning is *effective* (C_1). The probability of effective conditioning is a function only of the preceding response and outcome:

$$c_{ij} = P(C_1 | A_i O_j).$$

In all three models, the effects of a subject's experience before trial n are summarized by a random variable that represents his probability of making response A_1 on trial n. In the linear and stimulus sampling models, this random variable is denoted X_n. In additive models, this variable is called p_n, and X_n is a certain transform of p_n that is more useful for most purposes.

(i) *A stimulus sampling model.* Stimulus sampling theory was introduced by Estes in 1950. Atkinson and Estes (1963) gave a unified presentation of the theory, and Neimark and Estes (1967) collected many relevant papers. In the models considered here, it is postulated that the stimulus configuration consists of a *population* of N *stimulus elements*, each of which is conditioned to either A_1 or A_0. The subject *samples* s of these without replacement, and makes response A_1 with probability m/s if the sample contains m elements conditioned to A_1. If A_j is effectively reinforced, everything in the sample becomes conditioned to A_j. If conditioning is ineffective, no element changes its state of conditioning.

Various sampling mechanisms have been considered, but it is usually assumed that the sample size s is fixed throughout the experiment, and all elements are equally likely to be sampled. We will restrict our attention to this *fixed sample size model*. In the special case $s = 1$, each "stimulus element" may be interpreted as a *pattern* of stimulation, and this special case is consequently referred to as the *pattern model*.

Let X_n be the proportion of elements in the stimulus population conditioned to A_1 at the beginning of trial n. It is easy to compute the conditional probability, given X_n, of any succession of occurrences on trial n. For example, the probability of obtaining a sample with m elements conditioned to A_1, making A_1, and having A_0 effectively reinforced, is

$$\frac{\binom{NX_n}{m}\binom{N(1-X_n)}{s-m}}{\binom{N}{s}} \frac{m}{s} \pi_{10} c_{10}.$$

This event produces the decrement $\Delta X_n = -m/N$ in X_n. The variable X_n gives the subject's A_1 response probability before sampling, in the sense that

$$P(A_{1n}|X_n) = \sum_{m=0}^{s} \frac{m}{s} \frac{\binom{NX_n}{m}\binom{N(1-X_n)}{s-m}}{\binom{N}{s}} = X_n.$$ (1.1)

(ii) *A linear model.* Linear models were introduced by Bush and Mosteller in 1951, and reached a high degree of development in a treatise published soon thereafter (Bush and Mosteller, 1955). The effectiveness of conditioning mechanism was first used in conjunction with linear models by Estes and Suppes (1959a). The *five-operator linear model* postulates a linear transformation

$$x' = (1-\theta)x + \theta\lambda \qquad (0 \leqslant \theta, \lambda \leqslant 1)$$ (1.2)

of A_1 response probability x for each response–outcome–effectiveness sequence. Rewriting this as

$$x' - x = \theta(\lambda - x),$$

we see that the change in x is a proportion θ of the distance to the fixed point λ. If conditioning is ineffective, then $\theta = 0$ and λ is immaterial. If $O_1 C_1$ occurs, then $x' - x \geqslant 0$ for all $0 \leqslant x \leqslant 1$, so that, if $\theta > 0$, we must have $\lambda = 1$. Similarly $\lambda = 0$ for $O_0 C_1$. Thus

$$\Delta X_n = \begin{cases} \theta_{i1}(1-X_n) & \text{if } A_{in}O_{1n}C_{1n}, \\ -\theta_{i0}X_n & \text{if } A_{in}O_{0n}C_{1n}, \\ 0 & \text{if } C_{0n}. \end{cases}$$

The conditional probabilities that various operators are applicable are given by expressions like

$$P(A_{1n}O_{0n}C_{1n}|X_n) = X_n\pi_{10}c_{10},$$

that are common to all three of the models discussed here.

If $\theta_{ij} = 1$, $A_{in}O_{jn}C_{1n}$ produces complete learning, in the sense that $X_{n+1} = j$, irrespective of X_n. This fact permits us to regard certain "all-or-none" models as linear models. Norman (1964) has given an example in which this point of view is rather natural.

It is shown in Chapter 13 that the linear and stimulus sampling models are quite closely related. For example, predictions of the stimulus sampling model converge, as $N \to \infty$ and $s/N \to 0$, to those of the linear model with $\theta_{ij} = \theta$ for all i and j.

(iii) *Additive models.* Luce (1959) proposed that the A_1 response probability variable p be represented

$$p = v_1/(v_1+v_0)$$

in terms of the *strength* $v_i > 0$ of A_i. In terms of the relative strength $v = v_1/v_0$ or $x = \ln v$, this becomes

$$p = v/(v+1) = e^x/(e^x+1). \tag{1.3}$$

Beta models postulate that a learning experience multiplies each v_i by a positive constant β_i. Thus v is multiplied by $\beta = \beta_1/\beta_0$, and $b = \ln \beta$ is added to x. If the experience reinforces A_1, then $\beta \geqslant 1$ or $b \geqslant 0$; if it reinforces A_0, then $\beta \leqslant 1$ or $b \leqslant 0$. For the *five-operator beta model*, the value X_n of x on trial n thus satisfies

$$\Delta X_n = b_{ij} \quad \text{if} \quad A_{in}O_{jn}C_{1n}, \tag{1.4}$$

where $b_{i1} \geqslant 0$ and $b_{i0} \leqslant 0$. Alternatively,

$$v_{n+1} = \beta_{ij}v_n \tag{1.5}$$

or

$$p_{n+1} = \frac{\beta_{ij}p_n}{\beta_{ij}p_n + 1 - p_n} \tag{1.6}$$

if $A_{in}O_{jn}C_{1n}$, where $\beta_{i1} \geqslant 1$ and $\beta_{i0} \leqslant 1$. Of course, ΔX_n, Δv_n, and Δp_n are all 0 if C_{0n}.

Generalizing slightly, we may consider *additive models*, in which a learning experience effects a change $x' = x+b$ in the variable x (equivalently $v' = \beta v$, where $v = e^x$ and $\beta = e^b$), just as in the beta model, but the A_1 response probability variable $p = p(x)$ need not be of the form (1.3). It is natural to assume that p is continuous and strictly increasing with $p(-\infty) = 0$ and $p(\infty) = 1$, though some of our results require less. Given such qualitative restrictions, the precise form of p has remarkably little influence on those aspects of these models' behavior that are considered in Chapter 14. *Five-operator additive models* satisfy (1.4) and (1.5). If p is strictly increasing, there will also be an equation analogous to (1.6).

SYMMETRY. Symmetries in the experimental situation permit us to reduce the number of distinct parameters in these models. One type of symmetry is especially prevalent. In prediction experiments, and in T-maze experiments where the same amounts of food are used to reward left and right choices, it is natural to assume that the response–outcome pairs A_1O_1 and A_0O_0 that involve "success" are equally effective for learning, and that the same is true of the "failure" pairs A_1O_0 and A_0O_1. To say that they are equally effective means, first, that they have equal probabilities of producing effective conditioning, thus

$$c_{11} = c_{00} = c \qquad \text{and} \qquad c_{01} = c_{10} = c^*. \tag{1.7}$$

In the linear and beta models, equal effectiveness of two response–outcome pairs also implies that the corresponding operators u and $\tilde{u}$ on A_1 response probability x are *complementary*. This means that the new value

$$1 - \tilde{u}(x) = 1 - \tilde{u}(1 - (1 - x))$$

of $1 - x$ produced by $\tilde{u}$ is the same function of $1 - x$ that u is of x:

$$u(x) = 1 - \tilde{u}(1 - x).$$

If $\tilde{u}(x) = (1 - \theta)x$, then

$$u(x) = 1 - (1 - \theta)(1 - x) = (1 - \theta)x + \theta,$$

while if

$$\tilde{u}(p) = \frac{\beta p}{\beta p + 1 - p},$$

then

$$u(p) = \frac{p}{\beta(1 - p) + p} = \frac{(1/\beta)p}{(1/\beta)p + 1 - p}.$$

Thus complementarity of the success operators and complementarity of the failure operators reduce, respectively, to

$$\theta_{11} = \theta_{00} = \theta \qquad \text{and} \qquad \theta_{01} = \theta_{10} = \theta^* \tag{1.8}$$

in the linear model, and

$$\beta_{11} = 1/\beta_{00} = \beta \qquad \text{and} \qquad \beta_{01} = 1/\beta_{10} = \beta^*$$

or, alternatively,

$$b_{11} = -b_{00} = b \qquad \text{and} \qquad b_{01} = -b_{10} = b^* \tag{1.9}$$

in the beta model. This characterization of complementarity is valid for all additive models with p strictly increasing and $p(-x) = 1 - p(x)$.

The further condition that success and failure be equally effective, an extremely stringent symmetry condition, would take the form $c = c^*$ and, also, $\theta = \theta^*$ in the linear model and $b = b^*$ in additive models.† These assumptions are sometimes convenient mathematically, but most of our results do not require them.

† The pattern model is exceptional, since success has no effect and c_{ii} has no role.

B. Simple Learning with Many Responses

As in the experiments described previously, the subject confronts the same stimulus configuration on every trial. But on trial n he makes a choice Y_n from a set Y of alternatives that may have more than two elements, perhaps even a continuum of elements. This is followed by an outcome Z_n from a set Z of possibilities. The conditional probability distribution

$$\Pi(Y_n, A) = P(Z_n \in A | Y_n)$$

of Z_n given Y_n is normally specified by the experimenter, and, at any rate, it does not vary over trials.

Linear models for such experiments take the following form. Let X_n be a subject's choice distribution on trial n; i.e.,

$$P(Y_n \in A | X_n) = X_n(A),$$

where A is any (measurable) subset of Y. For every response–outcome pair $e = (y, z)$, there is a $0 \leqslant \theta_e \leqslant 1$ and a probability λ_e on Y such that, if $Y_n = y$ and $Z_n = z$, then

$$X_{n+1} = (1 - \theta_e) X_n + \theta_e \lambda_e.$$

If $\theta_e > 0$, λ_e represents the asymptote of X_n under repeated occurrence of e. In typical experimental situations, one has enough intuition about this asymptote to place some restrictions on the form of λ_e.†

A continuous prediction experiment.   Suppes (1959) considered a situation in which a subject predicts where on the rim of a large disk a spot of light will appear. Here Y_n is the subject's prediction and Z_n is the point subsequently illuminated on trial n. Suppes assumed that $\theta_e = \theta$ does not depend on e and $\lambda_e = \lambda(z, \cdot)$ does not depend on y. In addition, the distribution $\lambda(z, \cdot)$ is symmetric about z and has mode at z. Suppes and Frankmann (1961) and Suppes, Rouanet, Levine, and Frankmann (1964) report experimental tests of this model and a closely related stimulus sampling model, also due to Suppes (1960), that is described in Section 17.1.

Free-responding.   A pigeon pecks a lighted "key" in a small experimental chamber (or "Skinner box"). Occasional pecks are reinforced by brief presentation of a grain hopper. In the experiments considered here, the experimenter specifies the probability $u(y)$ that a peck y seconds after the last one (that is, a y-second interresponse time or IRT) is reinforced. Such experiments do not have trials in the usual sense, but one can consider each response as a choice of an IRT from $Y = (0, \infty)$. In Norman's (1966) linear

---

† A different type of multiresponse linear model has been considered by Rouanet and Rosenberg (1964).

model, Y_0 is the time until the first response, Y_n is the nth IRT for $n \geqslant 1$, X_n is a subject's distribution of Y_n, and

$$Z_n = \begin{cases} 1 & \text{if } Y_n \text{ is reinforced,} \\ 0 & \text{otherwise.} \end{cases}$$

Clearly, $\Pi(y, \{1\}) = u(y)$.

It is assumed that the entire effect of nonreinforcement is to decrease the rate of responding. Thus

$$X_{n+1} = (1 - \theta^*) X_n + \theta^* \tau^*$$

if $Z_n = 0$, where τ^* has a very large expectation. Reinforcement of a y-second IRT is supposed to result in a compromise between two effects: an increase in the rate of responding, and an increase in the frequency of approximately y-second IRT's. If τ is a probability on Y with a very small expectation, $\Lambda(y, \cdot)$ is a probability on Y with mode near y, and $0 \leqslant \alpha \leqslant 1$, then this compromise is represented by the assumption that

$$X_{n+1} = (1 - \theta) X_n + \theta [(1 - \alpha) \tau + \alpha \Lambda(y, \cdot)],$$

if $Y_n = y$ and $Z_n = 1$. The case where y is a scale parameter of $\Lambda(y, \cdot)$ [i.e., $\Lambda(y, A) = \eta(A/y)$ for some probability η on Y] is especially interesting. Comparison of this model with data from some standard schedules of reinforcement indicates that realistic values of θ and θ^* have θ^*/θ extremely small.

C. DISCRIMINATION LEARNING

One of the lateral arms of a T-maze is white, the other is black, and the positions of the two are interchangeable. The black arm is placed to the left on a randomly chosen half of the trials. This stimulus configuration is denoted (B, W), the other, (W, B). The rat's choice of arms may be described either with respect to brightness (B or W) or position (L or R). Reward could be correlated with either brightness or position, but let us consider an experiment in which *the rat is fed if and only if he chooses the black arm*. In many experiments of this type, training is continued until performance meets some criterion, and then the correct response is reversed, that is, switched to W. An interesting question is the effect of extra trials before reversal on the number of errors in the new problem. Though such overtraining leads to more errors early in reversal, it sometimes produces fewer total errors in reversal—*the overlearning reversal effect*.

Clearly the rat must learn to *observe* or *attend to* brightness, the relevant stimulus dimension, if he is to be fed consistently. And, in so far as perceptual learning of this type takes place in overtraining, an overlearning reversal effect is a possibility. The concept of attention to a stimulus dimension is central to the model described below. This model is a specialization, to the case of two stimulus dimensions, of a theory proposed by Zeaman and House (1963) in the context of discrimination learning in retarded children. See Estes (1970, Chapter 13) for a full discussion of the model in that context.

The animal is supposed to attend to either brightness (br) or position (po), and v denotes the probability of the former. If he attends to brightness, he chooses black with probability y. If he attends to position, his probability of going left is z. To summarize:

$$v = P(br), \qquad y = P(B|br), \qquad \text{and} \qquad z = P(L|po).$$

The values of v, y, and z on trial n are V_n, Y_n, and Z_n.

Trial-to-trial changes in these variables are determined by the same considerations that govern changes in response probability in simple learning with two responses. The probability v of attending to brightness increases if the rat attends to brightness and is fed, or does not attend to brightness and is not fed. Otherwise it decreases. The conditional response probabilities y and z change only if the rat attends to the corresponding dimension. Since food is always associated with B, $y = P(B|br)$ increases whenever the rat notices brightness. If he attends to position on a (B,W) trial, $z = P(L|po)$ increases, since food is (fortuitously!) on the left. On (W, B) trials, z decreases. These changes are summarized in Table 1, which also gives the conditional probabilities of various events, given $V_n = v$, $Y_n = y$, and $Z_n = z$. Choices are specified only as B or W, but, since stimulus configurations are given, laterality is implicit.

TABLE 1

Event Effects and Probabilities in a Discrimination Learning Model[a]

Event	v	y	z	Probability
$(B,W)\,br\,B$	+	+	0	$vy/2$
$(B,W)\,br\,W$	−	+	0	$v(1-y)/2$
$(W,B)\,br\,B$	+	+	0	$vy/2$
$(W,B)\,br\,W$	−	+	0	$v(1-y)/2$
$(B,W)\,po\,B$	−	0	+	$(1-v)z/2$
$(B,W)\,po\,W$	+	0	+	$(1-v)(1-z)/2$
$(W,B)\,po\,B$	−	0	−	$(1-v)(1-z)/2$
$(W,B)\,po\,W$	+	0	−	$(1-v)z/2$

[a] Notation: + indicates an increase, − a decrease, 0 no change.

Zeaman and House stipulated that all of these changes are effected by linear operators like those in two-choice simple learning models, and, further, that there are only two learning rate parameters, one for v and one for y and z. We will forego the latter restriction at this juncture. Thus the first two entries under v in Table 1 mean that

$$\Delta V_n = \begin{cases} \phi_1(1-V_n) & \text{if} \quad (B,W)_n \, br_n \, B_n, \\ -\phi_2 V_n & \text{if} \quad (B,W)_n \, br_n \, W_n, \end{cases}$$

where $0 \leqslant \phi_1, \phi_2 \leqslant 1$.

This rather complex model describes the rat's choices with respect to both brightness and position. For example,

$$P(B|v,y,z) = P(B|br)v + P(B|po)(1-v)$$
$$= yv + \tfrac{1}{2}(1-v),$$

and, similarly,

$$P(L|v,y,z) = z(1-v) + \tfrac{1}{2}v,$$

so that

$$P(B_n) = E(Y_n V_n) + E(1-V_n)/2$$

and

$$P(L_n) = E(Z_n(1-V_n)) + E(V_n)/2.$$

Note that the probability of a black (hence correct) response depends only on v and y. There is a simpler description of the transitions of these variables than that given in Table 1. Collapsing the pair of rows corresponding to each attention–response specification, we obtain the reduced model of Table 2. This reduction presupposes a natural lateral symmetry condition: The operators on v (and y) in the rows to be combined must have the same learning rate parameter, as well as the same limit point.

TABLE 2

EVENT EFFECTS AND PROBABILITIES FOR THE REDUCED MODEL

Event	v	y	Probability
br B	+	+	vy
br W	−	+	$v(1-y)$
po B	−	0	$(1-v)/2$
po W	+	0	$(1-v)/2$

This model was proposed by Lovejoy (1966, Model I) as an explanation of the overlearning reversal effect. Though he noted that his theory was "quite close" to that of Zeaman and House, the precise nature of the relationship seems to have eluded him, since he later faulted his model for having "... completely disregarded the fact that sometimes an animal chooses one side and sometimes the other..." (Lovejoy, 1968, p.17). This was held to be a serious omission because of the frequent occurrence of strong lateral biases or "position habits" early in acquisition. Within the full model of Table 1, these would be reflected in values of v near zero and values of z near zero or one. Henceforth we will refer to both the full and reduced models described in this subsection as *Zeaman–House–Lovejoy* (or *ZHL*) *models.* The merits and limitations of these models are discussed in Sutherland and Mackintosh's (1971) treatise on discrimination learning in animals.

The experimental situation that we have considered is an example of a *simultaneous* discrimination procedure, since both values of the relevant brightness dimension are present on each trial. In the comparable *successive* procedure, food would be available on the left, say, if both lateral arms are black, and on the right if both are white. A model for successive discrimination, due to Bush (1965) and built on the same psychological base as the ZHL models, is presented in Section 17.2.

0.2. A General Theoretical Framework

All of the examples given in the preceding section have the following structure. At the beginning of trial n, the subject is characterized by his *state of learning* X_n, which takes on values in a *state space* X. On this trial, an *event* E_n occurs, in accordance with a probability distribution

$$p(X_n, G) = P(E_n \in G | X_n)$$

over subsets G of an *event space* E. This, in turn, effects a transformation

$$X_{n+1} = u(X_n, E_n)$$

of state. In all of the examples, the subject's response is one coordinate of the event E_n, and, in the simple learning models, its outcome is another. Additional coordinates are as follows: number of elements in the stimulus sample conditioned to A_1 (fixed sample size model), effectiveness of conditioning (two-choice simple learning models), state of attention (ZHL models), and stimulus configuration (full ZHL model).

In all of the two-choice simple learning models, X_n can be taken to be a subject's A_1 response probability, though we prefer a certain transform of this variable for additive models. Thus X_n is one dimensional. In the multi-choice models, X_n is the choice distribution on trial n. Even though X_n is multidimensional in this case, all of its "coordinates" $X_n(A)$ are of the same type—probabilities of sets of responses. Thus all of our examples of simple learning models are considered *uniprocess models*. The coordinates of the state variables

$$X_n = (V_n, Y_n, Z_n) \quad \text{and} \quad X_n = (V_n, Y_n)$$

of the ZHL models, on the other hand, do not possess this homogeneity. One of them, V_n, describes a perceptual learning process, while the others describe response learning, but under the influence of different stimuli. These are, therefore, examples of *multiprocess models*. Though there has been a tendency for uniprocess and multiprocess models to be used in conjunction with simple and discrimination learning, respectively, the association is not inevitable. For an example of a multiprocess simple learning model, see Bower (1959). In Sections 17.3 and 17.4, we consider the uniprocess models of Atkinson and Kinchla (1965) and Kac (1962, 1969) for signal detection experiments with two stimulus conditions.

Intermediate in generality between the various special models introduced in Section 0.1 and the general framework described above are two classes of models that will play a prominent role in subsequent developments. The *finite state models* are those whose state spaces have only a finite number of elements. In the fixed sample size model, for example,

$$X = \{j/N : j = 0, ..., N\}.$$

In *distance diminishing models*, X is a metric space with metric d. Typically, all of the event operators $u(\cdot, e)$ are nonexpansive:

$$d(u(x, e), u(y, e)) \leqslant d(x, y) \quad \text{for all} \quad x \text{ and } y,$$

and some are contractive:

$$d(u(x, e), u(y, e)) < d(x, y) \quad \text{if} \quad x \neq y.$$

The precise definition of this class of models is given in Section 2.1. For example, the operators (1.2) of the five-operator linear model satisfy

$$|x' - y'| = (1 - \theta)|x - y|.$$

Such an operator is nonexpansive, and contractive if $\theta > 0$. Given slight restrictions on their parameters, all of the uniprocess linear models discussed above, as well as the reduced ZHL model, are distance diminishing.

0.3. Overview

In the general theoretical framework described at the beginning of the last section, the sequence X_n of states is a Markov process. The event process E_n is not Markovian, but the sequence $X_n' = (E_n, X_{n+1})$ of event-state pairs is. When E_n includes a specification of the subject's response Y_n on trial n, as is usually the case, we may consider Y_n as a function either of E_n, $Y_n = g(E_n)$, or of the Markov process X_n', $Y_n = f(X_n')$. Thus the study of learning models quickly leads to Markov processes.

Most of this volume is given over to the systematic investigation of Markov processes arising in or suggested by learning models. Considerations specific to events and responses provide a closely related secondary focus. Some of our results are rather general, and this generality has been emphasized in order to heighten mathematical interest and facilitate use in areas other than learning theory. But applications of general theorems to particular learning models and specific psychological problems are not neglected, and we have not hesitated to include results applicable only to special models. In addition to this multiplicity of levels of abstraction, a variety of different mathematical techniques and viewpoints are employed. We have been quite impressed by the range of analytic and probabilistic tools that yield important insights into the behavior of a few simple models.

Here is a brief survey of the contents of the book. Part I is concerned with distance diminishing models and the much simpler finite state models. Chapter 1 gives background material on Markov processes in abstract spaces and on our general theoretical framework. Chapter 2 provides preliminary results for distance diminishing models, and for a class of Markov processes in metric spaces—*Doeblin–Fortet processes*—that includes their state sequences X_n. The ergodic theory of *compact Markov processes*, that is, Doeblin–Fortet processes in compact state spaces, is presented in Chapter 3. This theory is completely analogous to the theory of finite Markov chains, which is a special case. Some comparable results for distance diminishing models in noncompact state spaces are given in Chapter 4. Chapter 5 contains a law of large numbers, a central limit theorem, and some estimation techniques for certain bounded real valued functions $f(X_n)$ of *regular* Markov processes X_n. This theory is applied in Chapter 6 to the processes $X_n' = (E_n, X_{n+1})$ in distance diminishing and finite state models for which X_n is regular.

Part II deals with slow learning, to which Chapter 7 gives a full introduction. To study learning *by small steps*, we consider a family X_n^θ of Markov processes indexed by a parameter θ such that $\Delta X_n^\theta = O(\theta)$, and take limits as $\theta \to 0$. Diffusion approximations to the distribution of X_n^θ for the *transient* phase of the process, when n is not too large, are obtained in Chapters 8 and 9. Approximations to stationary distributions and absorption probabilities are considered in Chapters 10 and 11, respectively. The form of these approximations is determined by the *drift* $E(\Delta X_n^\theta | X_n^\theta = x)$, and by the conditional variance (or covariance matrix in higher dimensions) of ΔX_n^θ, given $X_n^\theta = x$. Some special considerations apply to the case of small ($O(\theta^2)$) drift.

In Part III the methods of Parts I and II and some special techniques are applied to various special models. In order to gain a definite impression of the types of results obtained in Part III (and, therefore, in Parts I and II as well), let us consider some examples pertaining to the symmetric case of the five-operator linear model. In this model, A_1 response probability satisfies the stochastic difference equation

$$\Delta X_n = \begin{cases} \theta(1 - X_n), & \text{with probability} \quad X_n \pi_{11} c, \\ -\theta^* X_n, & \text{with probability} \quad X_n \pi_{10} c^*, \\ \theta^*(1 - X_n), & \text{with probability} \quad (1 - X_n) \pi_{01} c^*, \quad (3.1) \\ -\theta X_n, & \text{with probability} \quad (1 - X_n) \pi_{00} c, \\ 0 & \text{otherwise.} \end{cases}$$

First, there is a slow learning approximation to the mean learning curve

$$x_n = P(A_{1n}) = E(X_n).$$

Suppose that $X_0 = x$ and that θ and θ^* approach zero along a line $\theta^*/\theta = k$. Note that the quadratic function

$$w(x) = E(\Delta X_n/\theta | X_n = x)$$

does not depend on θ. Let $f(t)$ be the solution of the differential equation

$$\frac{df}{dt}(t) = w(f(t)),$$

for which $f(0) = x$. Then

$$x_n - f(n\theta) = O(\theta),$$

as long as $n\theta$ remains bounded. Furthermore,

$$\text{var}(X_n) = O(\theta),$$

and the distribution of

$$(X_n - f(n\theta))/\sqrt{\theta}$$

approaches normality as $\theta \to 0$.

The results that follow require certain restrictions on the model's parameters. Suppose, for simplicity, that success is effective, in the sense that $\theta c > 0$, and that either outcome can follow either response ($\pi_{ij} > 0$ for all i and j). The cases of effective failure ($\theta^* c^* > 0$) and ineffective failure ($\theta^* c^* = 0$) must be distinguished. The former arises more frequently in practice.

When $\theta^*c^* > 0$, the process X_n has no absorbing states and is regular, so that the distribution of X_n converges (weakly) to a limit μ that does not depend on $X_0 = x$. Let x_∞ be the expectation of μ:

$$x_\infty = \lim_{n\to\infty} x_n = \int_0^1 y\mu(dy),$$

and let $\bar{A}_{1n}$ be a subject's proportion of A_1 responses in the first n trials. Then $\bar{A}_{1n}$ is asymptotically normally distributed as $n\to\infty$, with mean x_∞ and variance proportional to $1/n$. The proportionality constant σ^2 can be consistently estimated on the basis of a single subject's data.

The asymptotic A_1 response probability x_∞ is bounded by the probability matching asymptote $l = \pi_{01}/(\pi_{01}+\pi_{10})$ and the unique root λ in $(0,1)$ of the quadratic equation $w(\lambda) = 0$. In fact, if A_1 is the "better" response, in the sense that $\pi_{11} > \pi_{00}$ (or, equivalently, $\pi_{01} > \pi_{10}$), and if $\theta^* < 1$, then

$$l < x_\infty < \lambda \quad \text{if} \quad \theta c > \theta^*c^*,$$

$$l = x_\infty = \lambda \quad \text{if} \quad \theta c = \theta^*c^*,$$

$$l > x_\infty > \lambda \quad \text{if} \quad \theta c < \theta^*c^*.$$

The quantity λ is an appropriate approximation to x_∞ when θ and θ^* are small. For w and thus λ are independent of θ along any line $\theta^*/\theta = k$, and $x_\infty \to \lambda$ as $\theta\to 0$. In addition, the asymptotic distribution μ of X_n is approximately normal with variance proportional to θ when θ is small.

The behavior of X_n is radically different when $\theta^*c^* = 0$. Both 0 and 1 are absorbing states, and

$$P_x(\lim_{n\to\infty} X_n = 0 \text{ or } 1) = 1$$

for any initial state x. The probability

$$\phi(x) = P_x(\lim_{n\to\infty} X_n = 1)$$

that the process is attracted to 1 is fundamental. When $\pi_{00} = \pi_{11}$, $\phi(x) = x$. We now describe an approximation to ϕ that is valid when θ is small and $\pi_{00} - \pi_{11} = O(\theta)$.

Suppose that π_{11} is fixed and that π_{00} approaches it along a line

$$((\pi_{00}/\pi_{11})-1)/\theta = k,$$

where $k \neq 0$. This constant is a measure of the relative attractiveness of A_0 and A_1. It follows that

$$E(\Delta X_n | X_n = x) = \theta^2 a(x)$$

and

$$E((\Delta X_n)^2|X_n = x) = \theta^2 b(x) + O(\theta^3),$$

where $b(x) = \pi_{11} cx(1-x)$ and $a(x) = -kb(x)$. As $\theta \to 0$, $\phi(x) \to \psi(x)$, where $\psi(x)$ is the solution of the differential equation

$$\frac{1}{2} b(x) \frac{d^2\psi}{dx^2}(x) + a(x) \frac{d\psi}{dx}(x) = 0$$

with $\psi(0) = 0$ and $\psi(1) = 1$; i.e.,

$$\psi(x) = (e^{2kx} - 1)/(e^{2k} - 1).$$

Note that

$$\psi(\tfrac{1}{2}) = 1/(e^k + 1),$$

which is very small when k is large. Thus, if a subject has no initial response bias, and learning is slow, it is very unlikely that he will be absorbed on A_1 when A_0 is much more attractive. This is, of course, just what we would expect intuitively.

Part I ○ **DISTANCE DIMINISHING MODELS**

1 ○ Markov Processes and Random Systems with Complete Connections

1.1. Markov Processes

Our starting point is a measurable space $(X, \mathscr{B})$, and a *stochastic kernel K* defined on $X \times \mathscr{B}$. For every $x \in X$, $K(x, \cdot)$ is a probability on $\mathscr{B}$, while for every $B \in \mathscr{B}$, $K(\cdot, B)$ is $\mathscr{B}$-measurable. A sequence $\mathscr{X} = \{X_n\}_{n \geqslant 0}$ of random vectors on a probability space $(\Omega, \mathscr{F}, P)$, with values in $(X, \mathscr{B})$, is a *Markov process with* (*stationary*) *transition kernel K* if

$$P(X_{n+1} \in B | X_n, \ldots, X_0) = K(X_n, B) \qquad (1.1)$$

almost surely (a.s.), for each $n \geqslant 0$ and $B \in \mathscr{B}$. The process has *state space* $(X, \mathscr{B})$ and *initial distribution* $\mu_0(B) = P(X_0 \in B)$.

For any $(X, \mathscr{B})$, K, and μ_0, there exists a corresponding $(\Omega, \mathscr{F}, P)$ and $\mathscr{X}$ (Neveu, 1965, V.2). Moreover the distribution of such a process, which is the probability Q on $\mathscr{B}^\infty = \mathscr{B} \times \mathscr{B} \times \cdots$ given by

$$Q(B) = P(\mathscr{X} \in B),$$

is completely determined by μ_0 and K. In fact, Q is the only probability on

$\mathscr{B}^\infty$ such that

$$Q\left(\prod_{n=0}^{\infty} B_n\right) = \int_{B_0} \mu_0(dx_0) \int_{B_1} K(x_0, dx_1) \cdots \int_{B_k} K(x_{k-1}, dx_k)$$

for any sequence B_n in $\mathscr{B}$ such that $B_n = X$ for $n > k$. We sometimes write $Q_x(B)$ or $P_x(\mathscr{X} \in B)$ when $\mu_0 = \delta_x$ [the probability concentrated at x, also denoted $\delta(x, \cdot)$] and we wish to call attention to x.

For a (real or complex) scalar valued function f on X, let $|f|$ be its supremum norm, $H(f)$ the closed convex hull of its range, and osc(f) the diameter of its range or, equivalently, the diameter of $H(f)$. Thus

$$|f| = \sup_{x \in X}|f(x)|,$$

$$H(f) = \overline{\text{co}}(\text{range } f),$$

and

$$\text{osc}(f) = \sup_{x,y \in X}|f(x) - f(y)| = \text{diam } H(f).$$

Let $B(X)$ be the Banach space of bounded $\mathscr{B}$-measurable scalar valued functions on X under the supremum norm. Let $M(X)$ be the Banach space of finite signed measures on $\mathscr{B}$, under the norm

$$|\mu| = \text{total variation of } \mu,$$

and let $P(X)$ be the probability measures on $\mathscr{B}$. If $\mu \in P(X)$ and $f \in B(X)$, then

$$\int f \, d\mu \in H(f). \tag{1.2}$$

If $\mu \in M(X)$ with $\mu(X) = 0$, then

$$\sup_{B \in \mathscr{B}}|\mu(B)| = \tfrac{1}{2}|\mu| \tag{1.3}$$

and

$$\left|\int f \, d\mu\right| \leqslant \tfrac{1}{2}|\mu| \text{ osc}(f) \tag{1.4}$$

for $f \in B(X)$.

The *transition operators*

$$Uf(x) = \int K(x, dy) f(y) \tag{1.5}$$

and

$$T\mu(B) = \int \mu(dx) K(x, B) \tag{1.6}$$

on $B(X)$ and $M(X)$, respectively, generalize left and right multiplication by the transition matrix in the theory of finite Markov chains. The second is the *adjoint* of the first, in the sense that

$$(\mu, Uf) = (T\mu, f), \tag{1.7}$$

where

$$(\mu, f) = \int f \, d\mu$$

for $\mu \in M(X)$ and $f \in B(X)$. Both U and T are positive ($Uf \geqslant 0$ if $f \geqslant 0$, $T\mu \geqslant 0$ if $\mu \geqslant 0$) and both are contractions ($|U|, |T| \leqslant 1$). In addition, $T\mu \in P(X)$ if $\mu \in P(X)$, and $Uf = f$ if f is constant. More generally, $Uf(x) \in H(f)$ by (1.2); hence,

$$H(Uf) \subset H(f). \tag{1.8}$$

It follows that $\mathrm{osc}(Uf) \leqslant \mathrm{osc}(f)$.

The powers of the transition operators satisfy

$$U^n f(x) = \int K^{(n)}(x, dy) f(y) \tag{1.9}$$

and

$$T^n \mu(B) = \int \mu(dx) K^{(n)}(x, B), \tag{1.10}$$

where $K^{(n)}$ is the *n-step transition kernel*, defined recursively by

$$K^{(0)}(x, \cdot) = \delta_x$$

and

$$K^{(n+1)}(x, B) = \int K(x, dy) K^{(n)}(y, B).$$

The probabilistic significance of $K^{(j)}$, U^j, and T^j is clear from the formulas

$$P(X_{n+j} \in B | X_n, \ldots, X_0) = K^{(j)}(X_n, B) \qquad \text{a.s.,}$$

$$E(f(X_{n+j}) | X_n, \ldots, X_0) = U^j f(X_n) \qquad \text{a.s.,}$$

and

$$\mu_{n+j} = T^j \mu_n,$$

where $\mathcal{X} = \{X_n\}_{n \geqslant 0}$ is any Markov process with transition kernel K, and μ_n is the distribution of X_n. The first equation is obtained by applying the second to the *indicator function* $I_B(x)$ of B:

$$I_B(x) = \begin{cases} 1 & \text{if} \quad x \in B, \\ 0 & \text{if} \quad x \in' B. \end{cases}$$

A set $B \in \mathscr{B}$ is *stochastically closed* if $B \neq \varnothing$ and $K(x, B) = 1$ for all $x \in B$. Thus $P(X_{n+1} \in B | X_n) = 1$ a.s. when $X_n \in B$. If a stochastically closed set contains a single element a, we say that a is an *absorbing state*.

A probability μ is *stationary* if $T\mu = \mu$. If the initial distribution μ_0 of $\mathscr{X}$ is stationary, then $\mu_n = \mu_0$ for all n. In fact, $\mathscr{X}$ is a strictly stationary stochastic process.

1.2. Random Systems with Complete Connections

In this section we begin with two measurable spaces $(X, \mathscr{B})$ and $(E, \mathscr{G})$, a stochastic kernel p on $X \times \mathscr{G}$, and a transformation u of $X \times E$ into X that is measurable with respect to $\mathscr{B} \times \mathscr{G}$ and $\mathscr{B}$. Following Iosifescu (1963; see Iosifescu and Theodorescu, 1969), we call the system $((X, \mathscr{B}), (E, \mathscr{G}), p, u)$ a (homogeneous) *random system with complete connections*. A sequence $\mathscr{S} = X_0, E_0, X_1, E_1, \ldots$ of random vectors on a probability space $(\Omega, \mathscr{F}, P)$ is an *associated stochastic process* if X_n and E_n take on values in $(X, \mathscr{B})$ and $(E, \mathscr{G})$, respectively,

$$X_{n+1} = u(X_n, E_n) \tag{2.1}$$

and

$$P(E_n \in A | X_n, E_{n-1}, \ldots) = p(X_n, A) \tag{2.2}$$

a.s., for each $A \in \mathscr{G}$. The processes $\mathscr{X} = \{X_n\}_{n \geq 0}$ and $\mathscr{E} = \{E_n\}_{n \geq 0}$, are, respectively, *state* and *event sequences*, $(X, \mathscr{B})$ is the *state space*, and $(E, \mathscr{G})$ is the *event space*. The distribution μ_0 of X_0 is the *initial distribution* of an associated stochastic process.

The concept of a random system with complete connections may be regarded as a generalization and formalization of the notion of a stochastic learning model. Thus we will often call such a system a *learning model* or simply a *model*.[†] In this context, the *state of learning* X_n characterizes a subject's response tendencies on trial n, and the *event* E_n specifies those occurrences on trial n that affect subsequent behavior. Typically E_n includes a specification of the subject's response and its observable outcome or payoff. When the subject is in state x, the event has distribution $p(x, \cdot)$, and the transformation of state associated with the event e is $u(\cdot, e)$. Three classes

---

† This terminology is slightly at variance with that in Chapter 0. For example, "the five-operator linear model" of Chapter 0 is a *family* of models indexed by the parameters θ_{ij}, c_{ij}, and π_{ij} according to the present terminology.

of learning models with which we will be especially concerned are the distance diminishing models defined in the next section, the additive models discussed in Chapter 14, and the finite state models.

DEFINITION 2.1. A *finite state model* is a learning model for which X is a finite set and $\mathscr{B}$ contains all its subsets.†

There is a stochastic process $\mathscr{S}$ associated with any random system with complete connections and any initial distribution μ_0 (Neveu, 1965, V. 1). The distribution Q of any such process is the unique extension to $\mathscr{B} \times \mathscr{G} \times \mathscr{B} \times \cdots$ of the measure on cylinder sets given by

$$Q\left(\prod_{n=0}^{\infty} B_n \times A_n\right)$$

$$= \int_{B_0} \mu_0(dx_0) \int_{A_0} p(x_0, de_0) \int_{B_1} \delta(u(x_0, e_0), dx_1) \cdots \int_{A_k} p(x_k, de_k),$$

$$(2.3)$$

where $B_n \in \mathscr{B}$ and $A_n \in \mathscr{G}$ for $n \leqslant k$, and $B_n = X$ and $A_n = E$ for $n > k$.

Let $p_1 = p$, and, for $k \geqslant 1$, let

$$p_{k+1}(x, A) = \int p(x, de_0) \int p_k(u(x, e_0), d(e_1, \ldots, e_k)) I_A(e_0, \ldots, e_k)$$

for $x \in X$ and $A \in \mathscr{G}^{k+1}$. Then p_k is a stochastic kernel on $X \times \mathscr{G}^k$, and the equation

$$P((E_n, \ldots, E_{n+k-1}) \in A | X_n, E_{n-1}, \ldots) = p_k(X_n, A) \qquad (2.4)$$

generalizes (2.2).

Let $p_\infty(x, \cdot)$ be the distribution of $\mathscr{E} = \{E_n\}_{n \geqslant 0}$ when X_0 has distribution δ_x; i.e.,

$$p_\infty(x, A) = P_x(\mathscr{E} \in A)$$

for $A \in \mathscr{G}^\infty$. Then p_∞ is a stochastic kernel on $X \times \mathscr{G}^\infty$ which extends p_k in the sense that, if $A \in \mathscr{G}^k$,

$$p_\infty(x, A \times E^\infty) = p_k(x, A). \qquad (2.5)$$

If S is the shift operator in $E^\infty : S\{e_n\}_{n \geqslant 0} = \{e_{n+1}\}_{n \geqslant 0}$, and $\mathscr{E}^N = S^N \mathscr{E} = \{E_{N+n}\}_{n \geqslant 0}$, then, a.s.,

$$P(\mathscr{E}^N \in A | X_N, E_{N-1}, \ldots) = p_\infty(X_N, A). \qquad (2.6)$$

One of our prime objectives is to study state sequences from various classes of learning models. Such sequences are interesting in their own right, and

---

† Similarly, when E is finite, we always assume that all subsets are in $\mathscr{G}$.

provide an indispensable tool for the study of event sequences. The following simple observation is fundamental.

THEOREM 2.1. *An associated state sequence $\mathscr{X}$ of a random system with complete connections is Markovian, with transition operator*

$$Uf(x) = \int p(x, de) f(u(x, e)).$$

In finite state models, $\mathscr{X}$ is a finite Markov chain.

Proof. As a consequence of (2.1),

$$E(f(X_{n+1})|X_n, X_{n-1}, \ldots) = E(f(u(X_n, E_n))|X_n, X_{n-1}, \ldots)$$

for $f \in B(X)$, thus

$$E(f(X_{n+1})|X_n, X_{n-1}, \ldots) = Uf(X_n)$$

by (2.2). ▮

A useful representation of the powers of the transition operator U is

$$U^n f(x) = \int p_n(x, de^n) f(u(x, e^n)), \tag{2.7}$$

where $e^n = (e_0, \ldots, e_{n-1})$ and $u(x, e^n)$ is defined iteratively:

$$u(u(x, e^n), e_n) = u(x, e^{n+1}). \tag{2.8}$$

Joint measurability of $u(x, e)$ ensures that $u(x, e^n)$ is measurable with respect to $\mathscr{B} \times \mathscr{G}^n$, so the integral on the right in (2.7) makes sense and defines a measurable function of x. For any $A \in \mathscr{G}^\infty$,

$$p_\infty(x, S^{-N}A) = P_x(\mathscr{E}^N \in A) = E_x(P(\mathscr{E}^N \in A|X_N))$$

$$= E_x(p_\infty(X_N, A))$$

$$= U^N p_\infty(x, A). \tag{2.9}$$

The sequence $X_n' = (E_n, X_{n+1})$ is also Markovian, and the application of an appropriate Markov process theory to this process in Section 6.1 yields additional information about event sequences in distance diminishing and finite state models. The Markov process $X_n'' = (X_n, E_n)$ can be used in the same way for finite state models. In finite state models with finite event spaces, both X_n' and X_n'' are finite Markov chains. Let $\mathscr{X}' = \{X_n'\}_{n \geq 0}$ and $\mathscr{X}'' = \{X_n''\}_{n \geq 0}$.

THEOREM 2.2. *The process $\mathscr{X}'$ is Markovian, with transition operator*

$$U'f(e, x) = \int p(x, de') f(e', u(x, e')) = f'(x) \tag{2.10}$$

and initial distribution

$$\mu_0'(B) = \int \mu_0(dx) I_B'(x),$$

where μ_0 is the distribution of X_0.

Proof. By (2.1)

$$E(f(X_{n+1}')|X_n', X_{n-1}', \dots) = E(f(E_{n+1}, u(X_{n+1}, E_{n+1}))|X_{n+1}, E_n, X_{n-1}', \dots)$$
$$= f'(X_{n+1})$$

by (2.2). Similarly

$$E(f(X_0')) = E(E(f(X_0')|X_0))$$
$$= E(f'(X_0)) = \int \mu_0(dx) f'(x). \quad \blacksquare$$

Note that, if $f \in B(X')$ depends only on x, $U'f(e, x) = Uf(x)$. Thus, for any $f \in B(X')$,

$$U'^n f(e, x) = U'^{n-1} f'(x, e)$$
$$= U^{n-1} f'(x). \tag{2.11}$$

THEOREM 2.3. *The process $\mathscr{X}''$ is Markovian with transition operator*

$$U''f(x, e) = \bar{f}(u(x, e))$$

and initial distribution

$$\mu_0''(B) = \int \mu_0(dx) \bar{I}_B(x),$$

where

$$\bar{f}(x) = \int p(x, de) f(x, e).$$

The simple proof is omitted. It is easily shown that

$$U''^n f = (U^{n-1} \bar{f}) \circ u \tag{2.12}$$

for $f \in B(X'')$ and $n \geqslant 1$, where $\circ$ indicates composition of functions; i.e., $g \circ u(x, e) = g(u(x, e))$.

REDUCTION. An important tool in the study of learning models with multi-dimensional state and event spaces is the reduction procedure that was applied to the full ZHL model in Section 0.1. Here we describe this procedure in abstract terms and note its properties.

The starting point is a learning model $((X, \mathscr{B}), (E, \mathscr{G}), p, u)$, with which are associated state and event sequences X_n and E_n. In addition, there are measurable spaces $(X^*, \mathscr{B}^*)$ and $(E^*, \mathscr{G}^*)$, and measurable transformations Φ and Ψ of X and E onto X^* and E^*, respectively. Intuitively, $x^* = \Phi(x)$ and $e^* = \Psi(e)$ represent simplified state and event variables. In the full ZHL model, they are projections:

$$\Phi(v, y, z) = (v, y)$$

and

$$\Psi(s, a, r) = (a, r),$$

where $s = (B, W)$ or (W, B), $a = br$ or po, and $r = B$ or W. We now give conditions under which $X_n^* = \Phi(X_n)$ and $E_n^* = \Psi(E_n)$ are state and event sequences for a learning model.

Suppose that $\Phi(u(x, e))$ depends only on x^* and e^*, and that, for any $A^* \in \mathscr{G}^*$, $p(x, \Psi^{-1}(A^*))$ depends only on x^*. In other words, there are functions u^* on $X^* \times E^*$ and p^* on $X^* \times \mathscr{G}^*$ such that

$$u^*(\Phi(x), \Psi(e)) = \Phi(u(x, e)) \tag{2.13}$$

and

$$p^*(\Phi(x), A^*) = p(x, \Psi^{-1}(A^*)). \tag{2.14}$$

Since Φ and Ψ are onto, these functions are unique and $p^*(x^*, \cdot)$ is a probability.

THEOREM 2.4. *If u^* and $p^*(\cdot, A)$ are measurable, so that $((X^*, \mathscr{B}^*), (E^*, \mathscr{G}^*), u^*, p^*)$ is a learning model, then $X_n^* = \Phi(X_n)$ and $E_n^* = \Psi(E_n)$ are associated state and event sequences.*

Proof. Substituting X_n and E_n for x and e in (2.13) and (2.14) we obtain

$$u^*(X_n^*, E_n^*) = \Phi(X_{n+1}) = X_{n+1}^*$$

and

$$p^*(X_n^*, A^*) = P(E_n \in \Psi^{-1}(A^*) | X_n, E_{n-1}, \ldots)$$
$$= P(E_n^* \in A^* | X_n, E_{n-1}, \ldots)$$

a.s. And it follows from the latter equation that

$$p^*(X_n^*, A^*) = P(E_n^* \in A^* | X_n^*, E_{n-1}^*, \ldots). \qquad \blacksquare$$

The significance of this is that the *reduced model* of Theorem 2.4 may be far simpler than the model with which we began, and hence may yield useful information about X_n^* and E_n^*. This is certainly the case for the ZHL models, since, as we shall see in Chapter 16, the reduced model is distance diminishing while the full model is not. It is not difficult to verify that the conditions for applicability of Theorem 2.4 are satisfied by the ZHL models. The most important of these conditions are (2.13) and (2.14).

2 ○ Distance Diminishing Models and Doeblin–Fortet Processes

This chapter begins our study of a class of random systems with complete connections with metric state spaces, and a class of Markov processes in metric spaces that includes their state sequences.

2.1. Distance Diminishing Models

Roughly speaking, a distance diminishing model is a random system with complete connections with a metric d on its state space X, such that the distance $d(x', y')$ between $x' = u(x, e)$ and $y' = u(y, e)$ tends to be less than the distance $d(x, y)$ between x and y. It might be assumed, for example, that the event operators $u(\cdot, e)$ are uniformly distance diminishing:

$$d(u(x, e), u(y, e)) \leqslant rd(x, y)$$

for some $r < 1$ and all $x, y \in X$. A more general condition, first suggested by Isaac (1962) in a more restricted context, is

$$\int p(x, de) \, d(u(x, e), u(y, e)) \leqslant rd(x, y).$$

Let

$$r_j = \sup_{x \neq y} \int p_j(x, de^j) \frac{d(u(x, e^j), u(y, e^j))}{d(x, y)}, \qquad (1.1)$$

where $e^j = (e_0, \ldots, e_{j-1})$. The definition given below uses the more general condition $r_1 < \infty$ and $r_k < 1$ for some $k \geq 1$. In addition, the functions $p(\cdot, A)$ are assumed to satisfy the same Lipschitz condition:

$$|p(x, A) - p(y, A)| \leq C d(x, y).$$

For $1 \leq j \leq \infty$, let

$$\delta p_j(x, y, \cdot) = p_j(x, \cdot) - p_j(y, \cdot)$$

and

$$
\begin{aligned}
R_j &= \frac{1}{2} \sup_{x \neq y} \frac{|\delta p_j(x, y, \cdot)|}{d(x, y)} \\
&= \sup_{A \in \mathscr{G}^j} \sup_{x \neq y} \frac{|\delta p_j(x, y, A)|}{d(x, y)}, \qquad (1.2)
\end{aligned}
$$

by (1.1.3) with $\mu = \delta p_j(x, y, \cdot)$. Since $p_{j+1}(x, A \times E) = p_j(x, A)$, $R_{j+1} \geq R_j$, and taking $j = 1$ in (1.2) we see that the uniform Lipschitz condition on $p(\cdot, A)$ given above is equivalent to $R_1 < \infty$.

DEFINITION 1.1. A random system with complete connections $((X, \mathscr{B}), (E, \mathscr{G}), p, u)$ is a *distance diminishing model* (*with metric d*) if (X, d) is a metric space with Borel sets $\mathscr{B}$, $r_1 < \infty$, $r_k < 1$ for some $k \geq 1$, and $R_1 < \infty$.

A more restrictive notion of a distance diminishing model was introduced by Norman (1968a).

Implicit in Definition 1.1 is the assumption that $d(u(x, e^j), u(y, e^j))$ is measurable in e^j for each $x, y \in X$ and $j \geq 1$, so that r_j is well defined. If (X, d) is separable, $d(\cdot, \cdot)$ is jointly measurable and this condition is satisfied. Separability has other uses in this connection. If (X, d) is separable, a sufficient condition for joint measurability of u, part of the definition of a random system with complete connections, is that $u(x, \cdot)$ be measurable for each $x \in X$ and $u(\cdot, e)$ be continuous for each $e \in E$. Separability is not a very restrictive condition in applications.

Lemmas 1.1 and 1.2 give basic properties of the r_j and R_j.

LEMMA 1.1. For all $i, j \geq 1$, $R_{i+j} \leq r_i R_j + R_i$.

LEMMA 1.2. For all $i, j \geq 1$, $r_{i+j} \leq r_i r_j$.

Proof of Lemma 1.1.   Writing $p_{i+j}(x, A)$, $A \in \mathscr{G}^{i+j}$, as

$$p_{i+j}(x, A) = \int p_i(x, de^i) h(x, e^i),$$

where

$$h(x, e^i) = \int p_j(u(x, e^i), de^j) I_A(e^i, e^j),$$

we have

$$\delta p_{i+j}(x, y, A)$$
$$= \int p_i(x, de^i) \left(h(x, e^i) - h(y, e^i) \right) + \int \delta p_i(x, y, de^i) h(y, e^i). \quad (1.3)$$

It follows from Inequality (1.1.4) that

$$|h(x, e^i) - h(y, e^i)| \leqslant \tfrac{1}{2} |\delta p_j(u(x, e^i), u(y, e^i), \cdot)|$$
$$\leqslant R_j d(u(x, e^i), u(y, e^i)) \qquad (1.4)$$

and

$$\left| \int \delta p_i(x, y, de^i) h(y, de^j) \right| \leqslant R_i d(x, y). \qquad (1.5)$$

Combination of (1.3), (1.4), and (1.5) yields

$$|\delta p_{i+j}(x, y, A)| \leqslant R_j \int p_i(x, de^i) d(u(x, e^i), u(y, e^i)) + R_i d(x, y)$$
$$\leqslant (R_j r_i + R_i) d(x, y),$$

from which Lemma 1.1 follows.   ∎

Proof of Lemma 1.2.   Clearly

$$q = \int p_{i+j}(x, de^{i+j}) d(u(x, e^{i+j}), u(y, e^{i+j}))$$
$$= \int p_i(x, de^i) \int p_j(x', de^j) d(u(x', e^j), u(y', e^j)),$$

where $x' = u(x, e^i)$ and $y' = u(y, e^i)$. The inner integral is at most $r_j d(x', y')$, and

$$\int p_i(x, de^i) d(x', y') \leqslant r_i d(x, y),$$

so $q \leqslant r_i r_j d(x, y)$.   ∎

Taking $i = 1$ in Lemmas 1.1 and 1.2, and recalling our assumption that $R_1 < \infty$ and $r_1 < \infty$, we see that $R_j < \infty$ and $r_j < \infty$ for all $j \geq 1$ in a distance diminishing model. The assumption that $r_k < 1$ permits us to say more.

THEOREM 1.1

$$r^* = \lim_{j \to \infty} r_j^{1/j} < 1$$

and

$$R_\infty = \sup_{j \geq 1} R_j < \infty.$$

Proof. By Lemma 1.2, for any $n \geq j \geq 1$, $r_n \leq r_j^q r_m$, where $q = [n/j]$ and $m = n - jq < j$. Thus

$$\limsup_{n \to \infty} r_n^{1/n} \leq r_j^{1/j}$$

for all $j \geq 1$. Therefore the limit r^* exists and

$$r^* \leq r_j^{1/j} \tag{1.6}$$

for all $j \geq 1$. Taking $j = k$ we see that $r^* < 1$.

Since $R_{j+1} \geq R_j$, $\sup R_j = \lim R_j$, and

$$(1 - r_i) R_{i+j} \leq R_i$$

by Lemma 1.1. If $r_i < 1$ (e.g., $i = k$) we obtain

$$\sup R_j \leq R_i/(1 - r_i) < \infty \tag{1.7}$$

on letting $j \to \infty$.

It remains to show that $R_\infty = \sup R_j$. As a consequence of (1.2.5), $R_\infty \geq R_j$ for all $j \geq 1$; hence, $R_\infty \geq \sup R_j$. To obtain the converse, let $A \in \mathcal{G}^\infty$, $x, y \in X$, and $\varepsilon > 0$ be given. Since $\mathcal{G}^\infty$ is generated by the algebra $\mathcal{G}' = \bigcup_{j=1}^\infty \mathcal{G}^j$ (here we identify $A \in \mathcal{G}^j$ and $A \times E^\infty \in \mathcal{G}^\infty$), there is an $A' \in \mathcal{G}'$ such that

$$p_\infty(x, A \, \Delta A') + p_\infty(y, A \, \Delta A') \leq \varepsilon$$

(Halmos, 1950, Theorem 13.D). Then

$$|\delta p_\infty(x, y, A)| \leq |p_\infty(x, A) - p_\infty(x, A')|$$
$$+ |\delta p_\infty(x, y, A')| + |p_\infty(y, A') - p_\infty(y, A)|,$$

and $|\delta p_\infty(x, y, A')| \leq \sup R_j d(x, y)$ by (1.2.5), so

$$|\delta p_\infty(x, y, A)| \leq \varepsilon + \sup R_j d(x, y).$$

Since ε is arbitrary, $|\delta p_\infty(x, y, A)| \leq \sup R_j d(x, y)$. Thus $R_\infty \leq \sup R_j$, so that $R_\infty = \sup R_j$. ∎

The key to understanding the state sequence in a distance diminishing model is to restrict the transition operator U to bounded Lipschitz functions. The following notation will be needed. For $f \in B(X)$,

$$m(f) = \sup_{x \neq y} \frac{|f(x) - f(y)|}{d(x, y)}$$

and

$$\|f\| = m(f) + |f|.$$

Let

$$L(X) = \{f : \|f\| < \infty\}$$

be the set of bounded Lipschitz functions. In terms of m, (1.2) becomes

$$R_j = \sup_{A \in \mathscr{G}^j} m(p_j(\cdot, A)).$$

A few important properties of $L(X)$ will now be noted. First, $L(X)$ is a normed linear space with respect to both $|\cdot|$ and $\|\cdot\|$. Also, if $f_n \in L(X)$, $f \in B(X)$, and $|f_n - f| \to 0$ as $n \to \infty$, then $m(f) \leqslant \liminf m(f_n)$, so that

$$\|f\| \leqslant \liminf_{n \to \infty} \|f_n\|. \tag{1.8}$$

In particular, $f \in L(X)$ and $\|f\| \leqslant C$ if $\|f_n\| \leqslant C$ for all n. Another consequence of (1.8) [together with the completeness of $B(X)$ and the inequality $|f| \leqslant \|f\|$] is that $(L(X), \|\cdot\|)$ is complete. The inequality

$$m(fg) \leqslant |f| \, m(g) + |g| \, m(f),$$

valid for $f, g \in B(X)$, implies that $L(X)$ is closed under multiplication, with $\|fg\| \leqslant \|f\| \, \|g\|$. Thus $L(X)$ is a Banach algebra with unit 1.

We now establish some elementary results concerning the action of U on $L(X)$.

LEMMA 1.3.   For all $f \in L(X)$ and $j \geqslant 1$

$$|U^j f(x) - U^j f(y)| \leqslant r_j m(f) d(x, y) + \tfrac{1}{2} |\delta p_j(x, y, \cdot)| \operatorname{osc}(f).$$

Proof.   This follows directly from

$$U^j f(x) - U^j f(y) = \int p_j(x, de^j) \left(f(u(x, e^j)) - f(u(y, e^j)) \right)$$

$$+ \int \delta p_j(x, y, de^j) f(u(y, e^j)). \quad \blacksquare$$

DEFINITION 1.2.   A transition operator U for a metric state space (X, d) is a *Doeblin–Fortet operator* if U maps $L(X)$ into $L(X)$ boundedly with respect to $\|\cdot\|$, and if there are $k \geqslant 1$, $r < 1$, and $R < \infty$ such that

$$m(U^k f) \leqslant rm(f) + R|f| \qquad (1.9)$$

for all $f \in L(X)$. A corresponding Markov process is a *Doeblin–Fortet process*.

A special case of Theorem 1.2 was proved by Doeblin and Fortet (1937, see (3), p. 143) using computations similar to our own.

THEOREM 1.2.   *The transition operator for state sequences of a distance diminishing model is a Doeblin–Fortet operator.*

Proof.   It follows immediately from Lemma 1.3 that

$$m(U^j f) \leqslant r_j m(f) + 2R_j |f| \qquad (1.10)$$

for all $j \geqslant 1$. Taking $j = 1$ and adding $|Uf| \leqslant |f|$ we obtain

$$\|Uf\| \leqslant r_1 m(f) + (2R_1 + 1)|f| \leqslant \max(r_1, 2R_1 + 1)\|f\|.$$

Thus U is bounded on $L(X)$. Putting $j = k$ in (1.10) we obtain (1.9) with $r = r_k < 1$ and $R = 2R_j < \infty$. ∎

It follows immediately from (1.9) and $|Uf| \leqslant |f|$ that

$$\|U^k f\| \leqslant r\|f\| + R'|f|, \qquad (1.11)$$

where $R' = R + 1$. This inequality, in a slightly different setting, is one of the main hypotheses of the Ionescu Tulcea–Marinescu theorem (Theorem 3.2.1), which is, in turn, the cornerstone of the theory of Doeblin–Fortet processes in compact state spaces ("compact Markov processes") presented in Chapter 3.

COMPACT STATE AND FINITE EVENT SPACES.   Both the five-operator linear model and the reduced ZHL model have compact state spaces and finite event spaces. Proposition 1 gives a relatively simple criterion for such a model to be distance diminishing. If w maps X into X, let

$$\iota(w) = \sup_{x \neq x'} \frac{d(w(x), w(x'))}{d(x, x')}.$$

PROPOSITION 1.   A model with compact state space and finite event space is distance diminishing if $m(p(\cdot, e)) < \infty$ and $\iota(u(\cdot, e)) \leqslant 1$ for all $e \in E$, and if, for every $x \in X$, there are $j \geqslant 1$ and $e^j \in E^j$ such that

$$\iota(u(\cdot, e^j)) < 1 \qquad \text{and} \qquad p_j(x, e^j) > 0.$$

Proof. Clearly

$$R_1 \leqslant \sum_{e \in E} m(p(\cdot, e)) < \infty$$

and

$$r_1 \leqslant \sup_{e \in E} \iota(u(\cdot, e)) \leqslant 1.$$

Thus it remains only to find a k for which $r_k < 1$.

Since $\iota(v \circ w) \leqslant \iota(v)\iota(w)$,

$$\iota(u(\cdot, e^n)) \leqslant 1, \tag{1.12}$$

and

$$\iota(u(\cdot, e^{n+1})) \leqslant \iota(u(\cdot, e^n)) \tag{1.13}$$

if $e^{n+1} = (e_0, \ldots, e_n)$ and $e^n = (e_0, \ldots, e_{n-1})$. Let

$$g(y, n) = \sum_{E^n} p_n(y, e^n) \left(1 - \iota(u(\cdot, e^n))\right).$$

Then $g(\cdot, n)$ is continuous, $g(y, n+1) \geqslant g(y, n)$ by (1.13), and, if $j = j(x)$ and $e^j = e^j(x)$ are as in the statement of the proposition,

$$g(x, j) \geqslant p_j(x, e^j) \left(1 - \iota(u(\cdot, e^j))\right)$$

by (1.12). Thus $g(x, j) > 0$, and

$$x \in \{y : g(y, j) > g(x, j)/2\} = T(x).$$

But $T(x)$ is open, and X is compact, so there is a finite subset X' of X such that

$$X = \bigcup_{x \in X'} T(x).$$

Let

$$k = \max_{x \in X'} j(x)$$

and

$$g = \min_{x \in X'} g(x, j) > 0.$$

If $y \in X$, there is an $x \in X'$ such that $y \in T(x)$. Thus

$$g(y, k) \geqslant g(y, j) > g(x, j)/2 \geqslant g/2.$$

Therefore

$$r_k \leqslant 1 - g/2 < 1. \quad \blacksquare$$

2.2. Transition Operators for Metric State Spaces

We begin our study of transition operators for Markov processes in metric spaces by introducing some terminology concerning the asymptotic behavior of U^n or

$$\overline{U}^n = (1/n) \sum_{j=0}^{n-1} U^j$$

as $n \to \infty$, where U is a bounded linear operator on a Banach space $(L, \| \cdot \|)$.

DEFINITION 2.1. The operator U is *orderly* if there is a bounded linear operator U^∞ on L such that $\| \overline{U}^n - U^\infty \| \to 0$ as $n \to \infty$. It is *aperiodic* if $\| U^n - U^\infty \| \to 0$ as $n \to \infty$. An orderly operator is *ergodic* if $U^\infty L$ is one dimensional. And an aperiodic, ergodic operator is *regular*.

If U is a transition operator for a measurable space $(X, \mathscr{B})$ and $L \subset B(X)$, we apply the same terminology to corresponding Markov processes. If $1 \in L$, then $U^\infty 1 = 1$, so that ergodicity is equivalent to constancy of $U^\infty f$ for each $f \in L$. The Markov processes considered in the next chapter are all orderly. They are ergodic when there is a unique "ergodic kernel," in which case there is a unique stationary probability μ, and $U^\infty f = \int f d\mu$. They are aperiodic if each ergodic kernel has "period" one, as is the case if each ergodic kernel is an absorbing state.

An aperiodic operator is clearly orderly.

The following simple lemma is very informative.

LEMMA 2.1. If U is aperiodic, and $V = U - U^\infty$, then

$$U^\infty U^\infty = U^\infty, \tag{2.1}$$

$$VU^\infty = U^\infty V = 0, \tag{2.2}$$

$$U^n = U^\infty + V^n, \tag{2.3}$$

for all $n \geq 1$, and

$$r(V) = \lim_{n \to \infty} \| V^n \|^{1/n} < 1. \tag{2.4}$$

In the case of complex scalars, the quantity $r(V)$ is V's spectral radius (Dunford and Schwartz, 1958, Lemma VII.3.4). It follows from (2.4) that for any $r(V) < \alpha < 1$ there is a $D = D_\alpha$ such that

$$\| V^n \| \leq D\alpha^n \tag{2.5}$$

for all $n \geq 0$.

Proof. Since U^{n+1} converges to $U^\infty U$, UU^∞, and U^∞, we have

$$U^\infty U = UU^\infty = U^\infty. \tag{2.6}$$

Thus $U^n U^\infty = U^\infty$, by iteration of the second equality. Equation (2.1) follows on letting $n \to \infty$, and (2.2) follows from (2.1) and (2.6). The case $n = 1$ of (2.3) is the definition of V, and the general case follows by induction using (2.1) and (2.2). Since $\|V^{m+n}\| \leq \|V^m\| \|V^n\|$, the argument in the first paragraph of the proof of Theorem 1.1 shows that the limit $r(V)$ exists, and

$$r(V) \leq \|V^n\|^{1/n}$$

for all $n \geq 1$. By (2.3) and aperiodicity, $\|V^n\| < 1$ for n sufficiently large; hence, $r(V) < 1$. ∎

If K is a transition kernel with operator U, the kernel

$$\bar{K}^n = (1/n) \sum_{j=0}^{n-1} K^{(j)}$$

corresponds to $\bar{U}^n$. If U is orderly (or aperiodic) with respect to $L = B(X)$,[†] the question arises whether U^∞ is the transition operator of any stochastic kernel K^∞, and, if so, what can be said concerning the convergence of $\bar{K}^n(x) = \bar{K}^n(x, \cdot)$ [or $K^{(n)}(x)$] to $K^\infty(x)$. Let $K^\infty(x, B) = U^\infty I_B(x)$. Since

$$\bar{K}^n(x, B) = \bar{U}^n I_B(x) \to K^\infty(x, B)$$

for *all* x and $B \in \mathscr{B}$, the Vitali–Hahn–Saks theorem (Neveu, 1965, Corollary 1 of Proposition IV.2.2) ensures that K^∞ is a stochastic kernel. It then follows from the linearity and continuity of U^∞ that U^∞ is the transition operator with kernel K^∞. Furthermore, the equality

$$
\begin{aligned}
|U - U'| &= \sup_{|f| \leq 1} \sup_{x \in X} |Uf(x) - U'f(x)| \\
&= \sup_{x \in X} \sup_{|f| \leq 1} \left| \int (K(x, dy) - K'(x, dy)) f(y) \right| \\
&= \sup_{x \in X} |K(x) - K'(x)|,
\end{aligned}
$$

for arbitrary transition operators U and U' with kernels K and K', enables us to translate statements concerning the rate at which $|\bar{U}^n - U^\infty|$ (or $|U^n - U^\infty|$) converges to 0 in terms of convergence of $\bar{K}^n(x)$ [or $K^{(n)}(x)$] to $K^\infty(x)$.

When (X, d) is a metric space and U is a transition operator that is orderly (or aperiodic) on $L(X)$, e.g., an orderly Doeblin–Fortet operator, such questions lead to consideration of weak convergence in the space $P(X)$ of probability measures on the Borel subsets $\mathscr{B}$ of (X, d) (Parthasarathy, 1967, is a good general reference on this subject). A sequence μ_n in $P(X)$ *converges*

---

† This means that $|\bar{U}^n - U^\infty| \to 0$ as $n \to \infty$. Regularity with respect to $B(X)$ is of some importance in subsequent chapters.

weakly to $\mu \in P(X)$ if $\int f d\mu_n \to \int f d\mu$ for all real valued bounded continuous functions f $(f \in C^r(X))$. Equivalently

$$\mu(\mathring{B}) \leqslant \liminf_{n \to \infty} \mu_n(B) \quad \text{and} \quad \limsup_{n \to \infty} \mu_n(B) \leqslant \mu(\bar{B})$$

for all $B \in \mathscr{B}$, where $\mathring{B}$ is the interior and $\bar{B}$ is the closure of B. This is the most natural notion of convergence for probability measures on a metric space. For $\omega \in M(X)$, let

$$\|\omega\| = \sup_{\substack{f \in L^r(X) \\ \|f\| = 1}} \left| \int f d\omega \right|.$$

Then $\|\omega\| = 0$ [i.e., $\int f d\omega = 0$ for all $f \in L^r(X)$] implies that $\omega = 0$, and $\|\cdot\|$ is a norm on $M(X)$. The corresponding metric

$$\Delta(\mu, v) = \|\mu - v\|$$

on $M(X)$ and $P(X)$ has been carefully studied by Dudley (1966). If (X, d) is separable, weak convergence in $P(X)$ is equivalent to Δ convergence. Furthermore, if (X, d) is complete as well as separable, $P(X)$ is complete with respect to Δ.

Let U and U' be transition operators, bounded on $L(X)$, corresponding to stochastic kernels K and K'. Then

$$\|U - U'\| \geqslant \sup_{\|f\| = 1} |Uf - U'f| \tag{2.7}$$

and

$$\|U - U'\| \geqslant \sup_{\|f\| = 1} m(Uf - U'f) \tag{2.8}$$

for $f \in L(X)$. Interchanging the f and x suprema on the right in (2.7), and the f and $x \neq y$ suprema on the right in (2.8), and restricting to $L^r(X)$, we obtain the inequalities

$$\|U - U'\| \geqslant \sup_{x \in X} \Delta(K(x), K'(x)) \tag{2.9}$$

and

$$\|U - U'\| \geqslant \sup_{x \neq y} \Delta\left(\frac{K(x) - K(y)}{d(x, y)}, \frac{K'(x) - K'(y)}{d(x, y)}\right). \tag{2.10}$$

If U^∞ is the transition operator for a stochastic kernel K^∞, (2.9) and (2.10) permit us to translate statements about the rate at which $\|\bar{U}^n - U^\infty\|$ (or $\|U^n - U^\infty\|$) converges to 0 into comparable statements about

$$\sup_{x \in X} \Delta(\bar{K}^n(x), K^\infty(x)),$$

etc.

We can now give sufficient conditions for U^∞ to be a transition operator.

THEOREM 2.1.   *If U is a transition operator that is orderly on $L(X)$, and if (X, d) is complete and separable, then U^∞ is the transition operator for a stochastic kernel K^∞. For any $x \in X$ and $B \in \mathcal{B}$,*

$$\int K^\infty(x, dy) K(y, B) = \int K(x, dy) K^\infty(y, B) = K^\infty(x, B). \qquad (2.11)$$

If U is ergodic, $K^\infty(x, \cdot) = K^\infty(\cdot)$ does not depend on x and is the unique stationary probability of the adjoint T of U.

The last two sentences also apply if U is orderly on $B(X)$, where $(X, \mathcal{B})$ is an arbitrary measurable space.

Proof.   Since U is orderly, $\|\overline{U}^n - \overline{U}^m\| \to 0$ as $m, n \to \infty$; hence, by (2.9), $\Delta(\overline{K}^m(x), \overline{K}^n(x)) \to 0$ as $m, n \to \infty$. Since $P(X)$ is complete with respect to Δ, there is a $K^\infty(x) \in P(X)$ to which $\overline{K}^n(x)$ converges weakly. Clearly

$$U^\infty f(x) = \int K^\infty(x, dy) f(y) \qquad (2.12)$$

for each $f \in L(X)$ and $x \in X$. This representation, and the fact that $U^\infty f \in B(X)$ for each $f \in L'(X)$, imply that $K^\infty(\cdot, B) \in B(X)$ for each $B \in \mathcal{B}$, so that K^∞ is a stochastic kernel. We omit the proof. (Theorem 2.2 gives a much stronger result for Doeblin–Fortet operators.)

Clearly

$$U\overline{U}^n = \overline{U}^n U = \overline{U}^n + n^{-1} U^n - n^{-1} I.$$

Applying this to $f \in L(X)$, and noting that $U\overline{U}^n f$, $\overline{U}^n U f$, and $\overline{U}^n f$ converge to $UU^\infty f$, $U^\infty U f$, and $U^\infty f$, respectively, in $L(X)$, hence in $B(X)$, while $|U^n f| \leqslant |f|$, we obtain

$$UU^\infty f = U^\infty U f = U^\infty f,$$

from which (2.11) follows.

If U is ergodic, $U^\infty f(x) = U^\infty f(y)$ for all $f \in L(X)$, so that $K^\infty(x, \cdot) = K^\infty(y, \cdot)$ for all $x, y \in X$. The outer equality in (2.11) says that $K^\infty(x, \cdot)$ is stationary, so, in the ergodic case, $K^\infty(\cdot)$ is stationary. If μ is a stationary probability,

$$(\mu, f) = (\overline{T}^n \mu, f) = (\mu, \overline{U}^n f)$$

$$\to (\mu, U^\infty f) = U^\infty f = (K^\infty, f)$$

as $n \to \infty$, for all $f \in L(X)$. Hence $\mu = K^\infty$.   ∎

The next result gives a rather special property of Doeblin–Fortet operators.

THEOREM 2.2. *If U is an orderly Doeblin–Fortet operator, and if, for every $x \in X$, $K^\infty(x, \cdot)$ is a probability that satisfies (2.12) for all $f \in L(X)$, then*

$$\sup_{B \in \mathscr{B}} m(K^\infty(\cdot, B)) < \infty.$$

For the proof we need this lemma.

LEMMA 2.2. Let A and B be nonempty subsets of X with

$$d(A, B) = \inf_{x \in A, y \in B} d(x, y) > 0.$$

Let

$$\rho(x) = \rho(x, A, B) = \frac{d(x, A)}{d(x, A) + d(x, B)},$$

where $d(x, A) = d(\{x\}, A)$. Then $\rho \in L(X)$, $\rho(x) = 0$ on A, $\rho(x) = 1$ on B, and $0 \leqslant \rho(x) \leqslant 1$ for all $x \in X$.

Proof of lemma. By direct computation

$$(\rho(x) - \rho(y)) d(x) d(y)$$

$$= (d(x, A) - d(y, A)) d(y, B) + d(y, A)(d(y, B) - d(x, B)),$$

where $d(x) = d(x, A) + d(x, B)$. But $m(d(\cdot, A)) \leqslant 1$, so

$$|\rho(x) - \rho(y)| \leqslant d(x, y)/d(x),$$

and $d(x) \geqslant d(A, B)$, so $m(\rho) \leqslant 1/d(A, B)$. ∎

Proof of theorem. It follows from (1.9) that

$$m(U^{nk}f) \leqslant r^n m(f) + R^* |f|,$$

where $R^* = R/(1 - r)$. Replacing f by $U^i f$, $0 \leqslant i \leqslant k - 1$, we obtain

$$m(U^j f) \leqslant C r^{\lfloor j/k \rfloor} \|f\| + R^* |f|,$$

where $C = \max \{\|U^i\| : 0 \leqslant i \leqslant k - 1\}$. Therefore

$$m(\overline{U}^n f) \leqslant O(n^{-1}) \|f\| + R^* |f|,$$

from which

$$m(U^\infty f) \leqslant R^* |f| \tag{2.13}$$

follows on letting $n \to \infty$. This holds for all $f \in L(X)$.

Suppose that B is closed and $B \neq X$ or $\varnothing$. Then

$$A^n = \{x : d(x, B) \geqslant 1/n\}$$

is not empty for n sufficiently large, and $d(A^n, B) \geq 1/n > 0$; thus $\rho_n(x) = \rho(x, A^n, B) \in L(X)$. Also $\rho_n(x) \to I_B(x)$ for all $x \in X$; thus $U^\infty \rho_n(x) \to K^\infty(x, B)$ for each $x \in X$. Therefore

$$|K^\infty(x, B) - K^\infty(y, B)| = \lim_{n \to \infty} |U^\infty \rho_n(x) - U^\infty \rho_n(y)|$$

$$\leq R^* d(x, y) \qquad (2.14)$$

by (2.13). The inequality (2.14) holds trivially for $B = X$ and $B = \varnothing$; hence it is valid for all closed sets B and $x, y \in X$.

If A is an arbitrary element of $\mathcal{B}$, then, by the regularity of $K^\infty(x, \cdot) + K^\infty(y, \cdot) = \Sigma(\cdot)$, there is a closed subset $B = B_{\varepsilon, x, y}$ of A such that $\Sigma(A - B) < \varepsilon$. Thus

$$|K^\infty(x, A) - K^\infty(y, A)|$$

$$\leq |(K^\infty(x, A) - K^\infty(y, A)) - (K^\infty(x, B) - K^\infty(y, B))|$$

$$+ |K^\infty(x, B) - K^\infty(y, B)|$$

$$\leq \Sigma(A - B) + |K^\infty(x, B) - K^\infty(y, B)| \leq \varepsilon + R^* d(x, y)$$

by (2.14). Since ε is arbitrary, we conclude that

$$m(K^\infty(\cdot, A)) \leq R^*$$

for all $A \in \mathcal{B}$. ∎

We close this section with a lemma that will be needed shortly. A real valued function f on X is *upper semicontinuous* if $\{x : f(x) < y\}$ is open for all y. Clearly continuity implies this.

LEMMA 2.3.   If U is a transition operator for a metric state space such that Uf is upper semicontinuous for all $f \in L'(X)$, then $K(\cdot, B)$ is upper semicontinuous for all closed sets B.

Proof.   The sequence $\{A_n\}$ defined in the second paragraph of the preceding proof is increasing, so $\{\rho_n\}$ is decreasing. Thus the sequence $\{U\rho_n\}$ of upper semicontinuous functions decreases to $K(\cdot, B)$. But upper semicontinuity is preserved under decreasing pointwise limits. ∎

3 ○ The Theorem of Ionescu Tulcea and Marinescu, and Compact Markov Processes

The material in this chapter and the next gives information about certain Doeblin–Fortet operators and corresponding Markov processes, thus for state sequences in certain distance diminishing models. The results in Section 3.1 are applicable to all Doeblin–Fortet operators, while those in later sections of this chapter require compactness of (X, d), so that corresponding Markov processes are compact according to Definition 3.1. Chapter 4 treats distance diminishing models whose state spaces satisfy weaker conditions such as boundedness.

3.1. A Class of Operators

Generalizing the situation in Chapter 2, we consider two complex Banach spaces $(B, |\cdot|)$ and $(L, \|\cdot\|)$ with $L \subset B$. B is not necessarily a function space, though we use the notation f for one of its elements. It is assumed that

(a) if $f_n \in L$, $f \in B$, $\lim_{n \to \infty} |f_n - f| = 0$, and $\|f_n\| \leqslant C$ for all n, then $f \in L$ and $\|f\| \leqslant C$.

43

A linear operator U from L into L is bounded with respect to both $\|\cdot\|$ and $|\cdot|_L$, where the latter is the restriction of $|\cdot|$ to L. In addition,

(b) $H = \sup_{n \geqslant 0} |U^n|_L < \infty$; and

(c)   there is a $k \geqslant 1$, an $r < 1$, and an $R < \infty$ such that

$$\|U^k f\| \leqslant r\|f\| + R|f| \tag{1.1}$$

for all $f \in L$.

Only (b) and (c) are needed for the next lemma.

LEMMA 1.1.   For all $m \geqslant 0$ and $f \in L$,

$$\|U^{mk} f\| \leqslant r^m \|f\| + R'|f|, \tag{1.2}$$

where $R' = (1-r)^{-1} RH$. Furthermore, $J = \sup_{n \geqslant 0} \|U^n\| < \infty$.

Proof. Equation (1.2), which is obtained by iterating (1.1), implies that $\sup_m \|U^{mk} f\| < \infty$ for each $f \in L$. By the uniform boundedness principle, the supremum D of $\|U^{mk}\|$ is finite (Dunford and Schwartz, 1958,† Corollary II.3.21). The lemma then follows from

$$\sup_{n \geqslant 0} \|U^n\| \leqslant D \max_{0 \leqslant i \leqslant k-1} \|U^i\|. \quad \blacksquare$$

Definition 2.2.1 is applicable in the present context. The following useful condition for aperiodicity generalizes Lemma 1 of Norman (1970a).

THEOREM 1.1.   *If there is a sequence δ_n with limit 0, and, for each $f \in L$, there is a $U^\infty f \in B$ such that*

$$|U^n f - U^\infty f| \leqslant \delta_n \|f\| \tag{1.3}$$

for all $n \geqslant 1$, then U is aperiodic.

Proof. By Lemma 1.1, $\|U^n f\| \leqslant J\|f\|$ for all n; hence, $U^\infty f \in L$ and $\|U^\infty f\| \leqslant J\|f\|$ by (a). The operator U^∞ is clearly linear.

By means of arguments similar to those in the proof of Lemma 2.2.1, but using (1.3) instead of $\|U^n - U^\infty\| \to 0$, we obtain (2.2.1), (2.2.2), and (2.2.3).

Replacing f by $V^n f$, $n \geqslant 1$, in (1.2), and noting that $UV = V^2$, we get

$$\|V^{mk+n} f\| \leqslant r^m \|V^n f\| + R'|V^n f|$$

$$\leqslant r^m 2J\|f\| + \delta_n R'\|f\|.$$

Therefore

$$\|V^{mk+n}\| \leqslant r^m 2J + \delta_n R'.$$

---

† This convenient reference on functional analysis is cited repeatedly in this chapter.

For arbitrary $j \geqslant 1$ let $m = [j/2k]$ and $n = j - mk$, so that $j = mk + n$. Then $m, n \to \infty$ as $j \to \infty$, so $\|V^j\| \to 0$. ∎

3.2. The Theorem of Ionescu Tulcea and Marinescu

To the conditions (a), (b), and (c) of the last section, we now add

(d) if L' is a bounded subset of $(L, \|\cdot\|)$, then $U^k L'$ has compact closure in $(B, |\cdot|)$.

Under these hypotheses, Ionescu Tulcea and Marinescu (1950) obtained the representation of U^n given in the important theorem that follows. For any complex number λ, let

$$D(\lambda) = \{f \in L : Uf = \lambda f\},$$

so that λ is an eigenvalue of U if and only if $D(\lambda) \neq \varnothing$.

THEOREM 2.1. *The set G of eigenvalues of U of modulus 1 has only a finite number p of elements. For each $\lambda \in G$, $D(\lambda)$ is finite dimensional. There are bounded linear operators U_λ, $\lambda \in G$, and V on L such that*

$$U^n = \sum_{\lambda \in G} \lambda^n U_\lambda + V^n, \tag{2.1}$$

$$U_\lambda U_{\lambda'} = 0 \quad \text{if} \quad \lambda \neq \lambda', \quad U_\lambda^2 = U_\lambda, \tag{2.2}$$

$$U_\lambda V = V U_\lambda = 0, \tag{2.3}$$

$$U_\lambda L = D(\lambda), \tag{2.4}$$

$$r(V) < 1. \tag{2.5}$$

The operator $\sum_{\lambda \in G} \lambda^n U_\lambda$ has a finite-dimensional range, hence is strongly compact. Since $\|V^n\| < 1$ for n sufficiently large, it follows that U is quasi-strongly compact (see Loève, 1963, Section 32.2).

The proof of the theorem is broken down into a number of lemmas.

LEMMA 2.1. *If $|\lambda| = 1$, $D(\lambda)$ is finite dimensional.*

LEMMA 2.2. *There are only a finite number of eigenvalues of modulus 1.*

Note that $U' = U^k$ satisfies (b), (c), and (d) with $k' = 1$. Furthermore, $Uf = \lambda f$ implies that $U'f = \lambda^k f$, and $|\lambda^k| = |\lambda|$. Thus $D(\lambda) \subset D'(\lambda^k)$, so the former is finite dimensional if the latter is. Also $G^k \subset G'$, so G is finite if G' is. Hence it suffices to prove these lemmas for $k = 1$.

Proof of Lemma 2.1. If $f \in D$, where

$$D = D(\lambda) \cap \{f : |f| \leqslant 1\},$$

then

$$\|f\| = \|Uf\| \leqslant r\|f\| + R,$$

so that

$$\|f\| \leqslant R/(1-r).$$

Thus D is bounded, and, by (d), UD has compact closure in $|\cdot|$. But $D \subset \lambda^{-1}UD$, so $D = \bar{D}$ is compact. It follows that $D(\lambda)$ is finite dimensional (Dunford and Schwartz, 1958, Theorem IV.3.5). ∎

Proof of Lemma 2.2. Suppose not. Let $\lambda_1, \lambda_2, \ldots$ be a sequence of distinct elements of G and let $f_n \in D(\lambda_n)$, $f_n \neq 0$. The f_n are linearly independent. Let $S(n)$ be the linear span of $f_1, f_2, \ldots, f_n$. Then $S(n-1)$ is a proper subspace of $S(n)$, so that there is a sequence g_n such that $g_n \in S(n)$, $|g_n| = 1$, and $|g_n - f| \geqslant \frac{1}{2}$ for all $f \in S(n-1)$ (Dunford and Schwartz, 1958, Lemma VII.4.3).

If $f = \sum_{i=1}^{m} a_i f_i \in S(m)$, it is easy to see that $zU^n f \in S(m)$ for all complex z and $n \geqslant 0$, and that $\lambda_m^{-n} U^n f - f \in S(m-1)$ for all $n \geqslant 0$.

By Lemma 1.1

$$\|\lambda_j^{-n} U^{n-1} g_j\| \leqslant r^{n-1} \|g_j\| + R' \leqslant 1 + R'$$

for n sufficiently large. Thus (d) implies that there is an increasing sequence j_i and a sequence n_i such that

$$h_i = \lambda_{j_i}^{-n_i} U^{n_i} g_{j_i}$$

converges in B. However,

$$\Delta_i = |h_{i+1} - h_i| = |h_{i+1} - g_{j_{i+1}} - h_i + g_{j_{i+1}}|,$$

$$h_{i+1} - g_{j_{i+1}} \in S(j_{i+1} - 1) \qquad \text{and} \qquad h_i \in S(j_i) \subset S(j_{i+1} - 1).$$

Thus $\Delta_i \geqslant \frac{1}{2}$. This contradiction establishes the lemma. ∎

LEMMA 2.3. If $|\lambda| = 1$ and λ is not an eigenvalue of U^k, then $(\lambda I - U^k)L = L$.

Proof. Again it suffices to consider $k = 1$. Since $\|U^n\|$ is bounded, $r(U) \leqslant 1$, and so $(\lambda' I - U)L = L$ for $|\lambda'| > 1$. For $g \in L$ we seek an $f \in L$ such that $(\lambda I - U)f = g$. If $g = 0$, let $f = 0$. If $g \neq 0$, let $|\lambda_n| > 1$, $\lambda_n \to \lambda$, and $f_n \in L$ with $(\lambda_n I - U)f_n = g$. Clearly $f_n \neq 0$, so we may put $f_n' = f_n/|f_n|$. Then

$$f_n' = \lambda_n^{-1} U f_n' + \lambda_n^{-1} g/|f_n|, \qquad (2.6)$$

so that

$$\|f_n'\| \leqslant \|Uf_n'\| + \|g\|/|f_n|$$

$$\leqslant r\|f_n'\| + R + \|g\|/|f_n|.$$

Therefore

$$\|f_n'\| \leqslant (R + \|g\|/|f_n|)/(1-r). \tag{2.7}$$

Suppose now that $|f_n| \to \infty$. By (2.7), $\|f_n'\|$ is bounded, so that, for some subsequence $f_{n'}'$, $Uf_{n'}'$ converges in B. By (2.6), $f_{n'}'$ does too, and the limit f' belongs to L by (a). Since $|U|_L < \infty$, $Uf_{n'}' \to Uf'$, and (2.6) yields $f' = \lambda^{-1} Uf'$. Now $1 = |f_{n'}'| \to |f'|$, so $f' \neq 0$, and λ is an eigenvalue of U. This contradicts our assumption, and rules out the possibility that $|f_n| \to \infty$. Applying this result to subsequences of f_n, we see that $d = \sup_n |f_n| < \infty$.

Multiplication of (2.7) by $|f_n|$ then yields

$$\|f_n\| \leqslant (Rd + \|g\|)/(1-r).$$

Consequently Uf_n has a subsequence $Uf_{n'}$ that converges in B, and $f_{n'} = \lambda_{n'}^{-1}(Uf_{n'} + g)$ converges in $|\cdot|$ to an element f of L. Then $Uf_{n'} \to Uf$ in $|\cdot|$, and $f = \lambda^{-1}(Uf + g)$. ∎

If $|\lambda| = 1$ let

$$U_\lambda^n = (1/n) \sum_{j=0}^{n-1} \lambda^{-j} U^j.$$

LEMMA 2.4. For every $|\lambda| = 1$ and $f \in L$ there is a $U_\lambda f \in L$ to which $U_\lambda^n f$ converges in B. The linear operators U_λ have $|U_\lambda|_L \leqslant H$ and $\|U_\lambda\| \leqslant J$, and satisfy (2.1)–(2.4) where

$$V = U - \sum_{\lambda \in G} \lambda U_\lambda.$$

This operator has no eigenvalues of modulus 1.

Proof. Let L' be the closure of L in B. Then $(L', |\cdot|_{L'})$ is a Banach space, and the unique continuous extension U' of U to L' is a bounded linear operator on $(L', |\cdot|_{L'})$ with $|U'^n|_{L'} \leqslant H$ for all $n \geqslant 0$. Furthermore, for any $f \in L$, the sequence $U_\lambda'^n f = U_\lambda^n f$ is strongly compact. For note first that

$$\|U_\lambda^n f\| \leqslant J \|f\|. \tag{2.8}$$

Also, for any $n \geqslant m \geqslant 1$,

$$U_\lambda^n f = \lambda^{-m} U^m U_\lambda^n f + \varepsilon_n, \tag{2.9}$$

where

$$\varepsilon_n = n^{-1} m (I - \lambda^{-n} U^n) U_\lambda^m f$$

converges to 0 in B as $n \to \infty$. Compactness follows from (2.8), (2.9) with $m = k$, and (d).

As a consequence of a standard strong ergodic theorem (Dunford and Schwartz, 1958, Corollary VIII.5.3), $U_\lambda'^n f$ converges in L' for every $f \in L'$. When $f \in L$ we denote the limit $U_\lambda f$. Thus

$$\lim_{n \to \infty} |U_\lambda^n f - U_\lambda f| = 0 \qquad (2.10)$$

for all $f \in L$.

By (2.10), (2.8), and (a), $U_\lambda f \in L$ and $\|U_\lambda f\| \leqslant J \|f\|$. Thus $\|U_\lambda\| \leqslant J$. And it follows from (2.10) and (b) that $|U_\lambda|_L \leqslant H$.

Taking $m = 1$ in (2.9) and letting $n \to \infty$ we obtain

$$\lambda U_\lambda f = U U_\lambda f. \qquad (2.11)$$

Thus

$$U_{\lambda'}^n \, U_\lambda f = (1/n) \sum_{j=0}^{n-1} \lambda'^{-j} U^j U_\lambda f$$

$$= \left[(1/n) \sum_{j=0}^{n-1} (\lambda/\lambda')^j \right] U_\lambda f.$$

The left side converges to $U_{\lambda'} U_\lambda f$ and the right to $U_\lambda f$ if $\lambda = \lambda'$, and to 0 if $\lambda \neq \lambda'$. This yields (2.2).

Equation (2.11) also implies that $U_\lambda L \subset D(\lambda)$. If, on the other hand, $f \in D(\lambda)$, then $f = U_\lambda^n f$ for all n, so that $f = U_\lambda f$ and $f \in U_\lambda L$. Thus (2.4) obtains for all $|\lambda| = 1$.

The fact that $V U_\lambda = 0$ is a consequence of (2.2) and (2.11), and $U_\lambda V = 0$ follows similarly from $\lambda U_\lambda = U_\lambda U$, which is, in turn, obtained from the case $m = 1$ of (2.9) on commuting U and U_λ^n. This establishes (2.3), and (2.1) follows from (2.2) and (2.3) by induction.

Suppose now that $|\lambda| = 1$, $f \in L$, and $Vf = \lambda f$. Then

$$Uf = \lambda^{-1} U V f = \lambda^{-1} V^2 f = \lambda f.$$

Therefore

$$f = U_\lambda f = \lambda^{-1} U_\lambda V f = 0,$$

and λ is not an eigenvalue of V. ∎

LEMMA 2.5. If $|\lambda| = 1$ and $\nu \geqslant 1$, then λ is an eigenvalue of U^ν only if some νth root of λ is an eigenvalue of U.

Proof. Let $\lambda_0^\nu = \lambda$ and $\omega = \exp(i2\pi/\nu)$, so that the νth roots of λ are $\lambda_\mu = \omega^\mu \lambda_0$, $\mu = 0, 1, \ldots, \nu - 1$. Then

$$\sum_{\mu=0}^{\nu-1} (1/m\nu) \sum_{j=0}^{m\nu-1} \lambda_\mu^{-j} U^j = (1/m\nu) \sum_{j=0}^{m\nu-1} \left[\sum_{\mu=0}^{\nu-1} (\omega^{-j})^\mu \right] \lambda_0^{-j} U^j,$$

and the quantity in brackets is v or 0, depending on whether or not j is a multiple of v, so

$$\sum_{\mu=0}^{v-1} (1/mv) \sum_{j=0}^{mv-1} \lambda_\mu^{-j} U^j = (1/m) \sum_{k=0}^{m-1} \lambda^{-k} W^k,$$

where $W = U^v$. Now W satisfies (b), (c), and (d) with $k_W = k$ [see Lemma 1.1 for (c)]; thus Lemma 2.4 is applicable to W. Letting $m \to \infty$ in the above equation we obtain

$$\sum_{\mu=0}^{v-1} U_{\lambda_\mu} = W_\lambda.$$

If λ is an eigenvalue of W, (2.4) gives $W_\lambda \neq 0$. Thus $U_{\lambda_\mu} \neq 0$ for some λ_μ, and, again by (2.4), this λ_μ is an eigenvalue of U. ∎

LEMMA 2.6. The operator V satisfies (b), (c), and (d) with $k_V = k$.

Proof. First, (2.1), (b), and Lemma 2.4 give

$$|V^n|_L \leqslant |U^n|_L + \sum_{\lambda \in G} |U_\lambda|_L \leqslant (p+1) H,$$

so V satisfies (b).

Let $F = \sum_{\lambda \in G} U_\lambda L$. Then F is a finite-dimensional linear space by Lemma 2.1 and (2.4). Thus there is a constant K such that $\|f\| \leqslant K|f|$ for all $f \in F$. Hence

$$\|V^k f\| \leqslant \|U^k f\| + \left\| \sum_{\lambda \in G} \lambda^k U_\lambda f \right\|$$

$$\leqslant r \|f\| + R|f| + K \left| \sum_{\lambda \in G} \lambda^k U_\lambda f \right|$$

$$\leqslant r \|f\| + (R + KHp)|f|,$$

and (c) is satisfied.

Finally, (d) follows from

$$V^k = U^k \left(I - \sum_{\lambda \in G} U_\lambda \right). \quad \blacksquare$$

LEMMA 2.7. $r(V) < 1$.

Proof. Since $r(V) = r(V^k)^{1/k}$ (Dunford and Schwartz, 1958, Theorem VII.3.11), it suffices to show that $r(V^k) < 1$. By Lemma 2.4, V has no eigenvalues of modulus 1. Lemma 2.6 permits us to apply Lemma 2.5 to V, from which we conclude that V^k has no eigenvalues of modulus 1. Application of Lemma 2.3 to V then shows that the spectrum $\sigma(V^k)$ of V^k is disjoint from the unit circle, hence from $\{z : |z| \geqslant 1\}$. Since $\sigma(V^k)$ is compact, $r(V^k) < 1$. ∎

All of the assertions of Theorem 2.1 have now been established.

3.3. Compact Markov Processes: Preliminaries

In the remaining sections of this chapter we will consider a class of Markov processes whose transition operators satisfy the hypotheses of Theorem 2.1. As in Chapter 2, let (X, d) be a metric space with Borel sets $\mathscr{B}$, bounded measurable (complex valued) functions $B(X)$, supremum norm $|\cdot|$, and norm $\|\cdot\| = m(\cdot) + |\cdot|$ on the bounded Lipschitz functions $L(X)$. Let K be a stochastic kernel in $(X, \mathscr{B})$ and let U be the corresponding transition operator (1.1.5) restricted to $L(X)$.

DEFINITION 3.1.   A Markov process $\mathscr{X} = \{X_n\}_{n \geqslant 0}$ with state space (X, d) and transition kernel K is *compact* if (X, d) is compact and U is a Doeblin–Fortet operator.

This terminology was introduced and the theory of such processes outlined by Norman (1968b).

It was observed in Section 2.1 that (a) of Section 3.1 is satisfied by $L = L(X)$ and $B = B(X)$, whether or not (X, d) is compact. Since U is a transition operator, (b) of Section 3.1 holds with $H = 1$. A Doeblin–Fortet operator is assumed to satisfy (c) of Section 3.1. Finally, if $L' \subset L(X)$ is bounded in $\|\cdot\|$, the same is true of $U^k L'$. Thus this set is bounded in $B(X)$ and equicontinuous. Since (X, d) is compact, the Arzelà–Ascoli theorem (Dunford and Schwartz, 1958, IV.6.7) implies that its closure with respect to $|\cdot|$ is compact, and (d) of Section 3.2 obtains. Therefore U satisfies all of the hypotheses of Theorem 2.1.

THEOREM 3.1.   *Theorem 2.1 is applicable to the transition operator of a compact Markov process.*

As a consequence of Theorem 2.1.2 we have the following important class of examples of compact Markov processes.

PROPOSITION 1.   If the state space of a distance diminishing model is compact, then any state sequence is a compact Markov process.

In addition, all finite Markov chains are compact Markov processes.

PROPOSITION 2.   A Markov process in a finite set X is compact with respect to any metric d on X.

Proof.   The metric space (X, d) is obviously compact, and $B(X) = L(X)$ contains all complex valued functions on X. Clearly $\|f\| \leqslant R|f|$, where

$$R = 1 + 2/\min_{x \neq x'} d(x, x').$$

Thus

$$\|Uf\| \leqslant R|Uf| \leqslant R|f|,$$

so that $\|U\| \leqslant R$, and (c) of Section 3.1 holds with $k = 1$ and $r = 0$. ∎

For any compact Markov process, $\{U^n f\}_{n \geqslant 0}$ is equicontinuous whenever f is continuous. For by Lemma 1.1 this is certainly true if $f \in L(X)$, and $L(X)$ is dense in the space $C(X)$ of continuous functions by the Stone–Weierstrass theorem (Dunford and Schwartz, 1958, IV.6.17). If $f \in C(X)$, let $g \in L(X)$ with $|f - g| < \varepsilon/3$, and let δ be so small that $d(x, y) \leqslant \delta$ implies

$$|U^n g(x) - U^n g(y)| \leqslant \varepsilon/3$$

for all n. Then

$$|U^n f(x) - U^n f(y)| \leqslant |U^n f(x) - U^n g(x)|$$
$$+ |U^n g(x) - U^n g(y)| + |U^n g(y) - U^n f(y)|$$
$$\leqslant \varepsilon$$

for all $n \geqslant 0$ and $d(x, y) \leqslant \delta$, as required. The theory of transition operators having this property (see Jamison, 1964, 1965; Jamison and Sine, 1969; Rosenblatt, 1964a, b, 1967) has guided our development at a number of junctures below. However, our stronger assumptions sometimes yield stronger results or permit simpler methods, and the theory that emerges is completely analogous to that of finite Markov chains.

Since $U1 = 1, 1$ is an eigenvalue of U, and all constant functions are corresponding eigenvectors. Clearly

$$U_1^n = \frac{1}{n} \sum_{j=0}^{n-1} U^j = \frac{1}{n} \sum_{j=1}^{n} U^j + \frac{1}{n} I - \frac{1}{n} U^n$$

$$= U_1 + \frac{1}{n} \sum_{\substack{\lambda \in G \\ \lambda \neq 1}} \frac{\lambda - \lambda^{n+1}}{1 - \lambda} U_\lambda + \frac{1}{n} \sum_{j=0}^{n} V^j - \frac{1}{n} U^n,$$

so that

$$\|U_1^n - U_1\| = O(1/n).$$

Thus U is orderly in the sense of Definition 2.2.1. When, and only when, 1 is the only eigenvalue of modulus 1, U is aperiodic and $\|U^n - U_1\| \to 0$ geometrically.

Since compactness implies completeness and separability, Theorem 2.2.1 is applicable to U. Theorem 2.2.2 is also. Theorem 3.2 summarizes some of these results in our present notation.

THEOREM 3.2. *The operator U_1 is the transition operator for a stochastic kernel K_1. For any $B \in \mathscr{B}$, $K_1(\cdot, B) \in D(1)$, and, for any $x \in X$, $K_1(x, \cdot)$ is stationary.*

3.4. Ergodic Decomposition

The key concept in the analysis of compact Markov processes is that of an *ergodic kernel*. A subset F of X is an ergodic kernel if it is stochastically and topologically closed, and if it has no stochastically and topologically closed proper subsets.

LEMMA 4.1. Any stochastic kernel defined on the Borel subsets $\mathscr{B}$ of a compact metric space (X, d) possesses an ergodic kernel. Any two distinct ergodic kernels are disjoint.

Proof. If F_1 and F_2 are ergodic kernels and $F = F_1 \cap F_2 \neq \varnothing$, then F is a stochastically and topologically closed subset of F_1 and F_2. Thus $F_1 = F = F_2$.

The ergodic kernels are clearly the minimal elements of the collection $\mathscr{P}$ of stochastically and topologically closed subsets of X under the natural ordering $\subset$. Zorn's lemma (Dunford and Schwartz, 1958, Theorem I.2.7) implies that there is at least one such minimal element. For since $X \in \mathscr{P}$, $\mathscr{P}$ is not empty. If $\mathscr{A}$ is a totally ordered subset of $\mathscr{P}$, it has the finite intersection property; hence $A = \cap \mathscr{A} \neq \varnothing$. The Lindelöf theorem (Dunford and Schwartz, 1958, I.4.14) implies that $A = \cap \mathscr{A}'$ for some countable subcollection $\mathscr{A}'$ of $\mathscr{A}$, from which it follows that A is stochastically closed. It is obviously topologically closed; hence $A \in \mathscr{P}$. Clearly A is a lower bound for $\mathscr{A}$. ∎

If $F \in \mathscr{B}$ is stochastically closed, then $K_1^{\,n}(x, F) = 1$ for all $x \in F$, so that $K_1(x, F) = 1$ if F is also topologically closed. It follows that the functions $K_1(\cdot, F)$, for different ergodic kernels F, are linearly independent. By Theorem 3.2, all such functions belong to $D(1)$, so the number i of ergodic kernels does not exceed the dimension d of $D(1)$. Let $F_1, F_2, \ldots, F_i$ be the ergodic kernels, $F = \bigcup_{j=1}^{i} F_j$, and

$$g_j(x) = K_1(x, F_j).$$

THEOREM 4.1. *The functions g_j are a basis for $D(1)$, so there are d ergodic kernels. A compact Markov process is ergodic if and only if there is a unique ergodic kernel.*

The second statement follows from the first. There is a unique ergodic kernel if and only if $D(1) = U_1 L(X)$ is one dimensional, i.e., contains only constants. Our proof of the first statement is based on a corollary to the following lemma.

LEMMA 4.2.   *If f is upper semicontinuous and $f(x) \leqslant Uf(x)$ for all $x \in X$, then f is constant on each ergodic kernel, and f attains its maximum on F.*

Proof.   Let

$$C_j = \{x \in F_j : f(x) = \max_{y \in F_j} f(y)\}.$$

Since f restricted to F_j is upper semicontinuous and F_j is compact, C_j is a nonempty topologically closed subset of F_j. If $x \in C_j$ we have

$$\max_{y \in F_j} f(y) = f(x) \leqslant \int_{F_j} K(x, dy) f(y),$$

since F_j is stochastically closed. Hence $K(x, C_j) = 1$, and C_j is stochastically closed. But F_j is an ergodic kernel, so $C_j = F_j$, and f is constant on F_j.

Similarly, if

$$A = \{x : f(x) = \max_{y \in X} f(y)\},$$

A is stochastically and topologically closed. Lemma 4.1 implies that there is an ergodic kernel for the compact metric space (A, d) and the restriction to A of the kernel K, and it is easily seen that this set is an ergodic kernel for (X, d) and K unrestricted. Hence $A \supset F_j$ for some j, and f attains its maximum on F. ∎

COROLLARY.   *If $f \in D(1)$, f is constant on each ergodic kernel. If $|\lambda| = 1$ and $f \in D(\lambda)$, then $|f(\cdot)|$ is constant on each ergodic kernel, and $f(x) = 0$ for all $x \in X$ if $f(x) = 0$ for all $x \in F$.*

Proof.   If $f \in D(1)$, then $\mathrm{re} f \in D(1)$ and $\mathrm{im} f \in D(1)$, so both are constant on each ergodic kernel by Lemma 4.2. If $|\lambda| = 1$ and $f \in D(\lambda)$, then $g = |f(\cdot)|$ is continuous and satisfies $g \leqslant Ug$. ∎

Proof of Theorem 4.1.   Suppose that $f \in D(1)$. Let ϕ_j be the value of f on F_j and let $\delta = f - \sum_{j=1}^{i} \phi_j g_j$. Then $\delta \in D(1)$ and δ vanishes throughout F. Thus $\delta = 0$; that is, $f = \sum_{j=1}^{i} \phi_j g_j$. Therefore the linearly independent functions g_j span $D(1)$. ∎

The expansion of $K_1(\cdot, B)$ in terms of the g_j turns out to be especially interesting. For any probability μ on the Borel subsets of a separable metric space, there is a smallest closed set with probability 1. This set, called the *support* of μ, is the set of points x such that $\mu(O) > 0$ for all open sets O containing x (Parthasarathy, 1967, Theorem 2.1 of Chapter II).

THEOREM 4.2.   *There is a unique stationary probability μ_j with $\mu_j(F_j) = 1$. The ergodic kernel F_j is the support of μ_j, and $\{\mu_1, \ldots, \mu_d\}$ is a basis for $\{\mu \in M(X) : T\mu = \mu\}$. For all $x \in X$ and $B \in \mathscr{B}$,*

$$K_1(x, B) = \sum_{j=1}^{d} g_j(x)\, \mu_j(B). \tag{4.1}$$

Proof. Let $\mu_1(B), \ldots, \mu_d(B)$ be the unique constants such that (4.1) holds for all $x \in X$. Taking $x \in F_j$, we obtain $K_1(x, B) = \mu_j(B)$ for all $B \in \mathscr{B}$. By Theorem 3.2, μ_j is a stationary probability, and, clearly, $\mu_j(F_i) = \delta_{ij}$, so the μ_j are linearly independent.

Suppose that $\mu \in M(X)$ and $T\mu = \mu$. Then $T_1^n\mu = \mu$. But, for $f \in L(X)$,

$$(T_1^n\mu, f) = (\mu, U_1^n f) \to (\mu, U_1 f) = (T_1\mu, f)$$

as $n \to \infty$. Thus $(\mu, f) = (T_1\mu, f)$ for all $f \in L(X)$ and

$$\mu = T_1\mu = \int \mu(dx) K_1(x, \cdot) = \sum_{j=1}^{d} \left[\int \mu(dx) g_j(x) \right] \mu_j.$$

Therefore the μ_j are a basis for $\{\mu \in M(X): T\mu = \mu\}$, and μ_j is the only stationary probability with $\mu_j(F_j) = 1$. Since, by Lemmas 2.2.3 and 4.3, the support S_j of μ_j is a stochastically as well as topologically closed subset of F_j, $S_j = F_j$. ∎

LEMMA 4.3. *Let K be a stochastic kernel in a separable metric space (X, d), such that $K(\cdot, B)$ is upper semicontinuous for B closed. Then the support S of any stationary probability μ on $\mathscr{B}$ is stochastically closed.*

Proof. Clearly $1 = \mu(S) = \int \mu(dx) K(x, S)$. Thus $\mu(S') = 1$, where

$$S' = \{x: K(x, S) = 1\} = X - \{x: K(x, S) < 1\}.$$

Since $K(\cdot, S)$ is upper semicontinuous, S' is topologically closed. Therefore $S' \supset S$; i.e., S is stochastically closed. ∎

The next theorem shows that a compact Markov process converges with probability 1 to a random ergodic kernel, and that $g_j(x)$ is the probability of convergence to F_j starting at x. Let

$$\Omega_j = \{\omega: d(X_n(\omega), F_j) \to 0 \quad \text{as} \quad n \to \infty\}.$$

THEOREM 4.3. *For any compact Markov process $\mathscr{X}$,*

$$P\left(\bigcup_{j=1}^{d} \Omega_j\right) = 1 \tag{4.2}$$

and

$$g_j(x) = P_x(\Omega_j). \tag{4.3}$$

If $f \in L(X)$ and f vanishes on F, then $U^n f = V^n f$, so that $\|U^n f\| \to 0$ geometrically as $n \to \infty$.

Proof. For $\lambda \in G$,

$$|U_\lambda^n f(x)| \leq U_1^n g(x),$$

where $g(x) = |f(x)| \in L(X)$ if $f \in L(X)$. As $n \to \infty$ the left side converges to $|U_\lambda f(x)|$ and the right to $U_1 g(x)$. The latter is 0 if f and thus g vanishes on F, since $K_1(x, \tilde{F}) = 0$ by Theorem 4.2. So $U_\lambda f = 0$, $U^n f = V^n f$, and

$$\|U^n f\| \leqslant \|V^n\| \|f\| .$$

Since $\|V^n\|$ converges geometrically to 0, the second statement of the theorem is proved.

Now $f = d(\cdot, F) \in L(X)$ and vanishes on F, so $|U^n f|$ converges geometrically to 0. And

$$E[f(X_n)] = E[E[f(X_n)|X_0]]$$
$$= E[U^n f(X_0)] \leqslant |U^n f| .$$

Therefore

$$E\left[\sum_{n=0}^{\infty} d(X_n, F)\right] = \sum_{n=0}^{\infty} E[f(X_n)] < \infty ,$$

so that $\sum_{n=0}^{\infty} d(X_n, F) < \infty$ and thus $d(X_n, F) \to 0$ a.s. In other words, $P(\Gamma) = 1$, where

$$\Gamma = \{\omega \in \Omega : \lim_{n \to \infty} d(X_n(\omega), F) = 0\} .$$

Since $Ug_j = g_j$,

$$E(g_j(X_{n+1})|X_n, \ldots, X_0) = g_j(X_n)$$

a.s. Thus $g_j(X_0), g_j(X_1), \ldots$ is a martingale. Since it is bounded (by $|g_j|$), it converges on a set Γ_j with $P(\Gamma_j) = 1$ [Neveu, 1965, (1), p. 137].

Suppose now that $\{x_n\}$ is any sequence in X such that $d(x_n, F) \to 0$, although there is no j for which $d(x_n, F_j) \to 0$. Then there are subsequences $x_{n'}$ and x_{n*}, and $j' \neq j^*$, such that

$$d(x_{n'}, F_{j'}) \to 0 \quad \text{and} \quad d(x_{n*}, F_{j*}) \to 0 .$$

Then $g_{j'}(x_{n'}) \to 1$ and $g_{j'}(x_{n*}) \to 0$, so that $g_{j'}(x_n)$ does not converge. From this we conclude that, if $d(x_n, F) \to 0$ and $g_j(x_n)$ converges for all j, there is some j such that $d(x_n, F_j) \to 0$ as $n \to \infty$.

If

$$\omega \in \Gamma \cap \bigcap_{j=1}^{d} \Gamma_j ,$$

then this result is applicable to $x_n = X_n(\omega)$. Thus there is a $j = j(\omega)$ such that $\omega \in \Omega_j$, and

$$\Gamma \cap \bigcap_{j=1}^{d} \Gamma_j \subset \bigcup_{j=1}^{d} \Omega_j .$$

Since the former has probability 1, the latter does too, and (4.2) is proved. For any $\omega \in \bigcup_{j=1}^{d} \Omega_j$ (thus a.s.),

$$g_j(X_n(\omega)) \to I_{\Omega_j}(\omega).$$

Therefore

$$g_j(x) = E_x(g_j(X_0)) = E_x(g_j(X_n))$$
$$\to E_x(I_{\Omega_j}) = P_x(\Omega_j)$$

as $n \to \infty$. This proves (4.3). ∎

In the remainder of this section we consider the asymptotic behavior of the proportion

$$\nu_n(A) = (1/n) \sum_{m=0}^{n-1} I_A(X_m)$$

of visits to the Borel set A among the first n steps. The random probability ν_n is the empirical distribution of $X_0, \dots, X_{n-1}$. We shall see that, with probability 1, ν_n converges weakly to $\mu_{j(\omega)}$, where $j(\omega)$ is the index of the ergodic kernel that X_n approaches. Let

$$y(f) = \int f d\mu_{j(\omega)},$$

and observe that

$$\int f d\nu_n = (1/n) \sum_{m=0}^{n-1} f(X_m) = (1/n) S_n(f)$$

for all $f \in B(X)$. Thus we wish to prove:

THEOREM 4.4. *For any compact Markov process $\mathscr{X}$, the probability is 1 that $(1/n) S_n(f) \to y(f)$ as $n \to \infty$ for all $f \in C(X)$.*

Proof. A theorem due to Jamison (1965, Theorem 3.2) shows that, under the sole assumption that the sequence $U_1^n f$ is equicontinuous for $f \in C(X)$ the probability is 1 that $(1/n) S_n(f)$ and $U_1 f(X_n)$ converge to the same limit for all $f \in C(X)$. But if $\omega \in \bigcup_{j=1}^{d} \Omega_j$, $U_1 f(X_j) \to y(f)$ for all $f \in B(X)$. In view of (4.2), the proof is complete. ∎

Chapter 5 gives additional information about the asymptotic behavior of the sums $S_n(f)$, when $f \in L'(X)$ and U is regular.

3.5. Subergodic Decomposition

In the last section we saw that the probabilities $g_j(x)$ of converging to the various ergodic kernels F_j are a basis for the set $D(1)$ of eigenfunctions for the eigenvalue 1 of U. Thus the structure of $D(1)$ depends on the behavior of corresponding compact Markov processes outside of $F = \bigcup_{j=1}^{d} F_j$. In this section we will see that compact Markov processes move cyclically with some period p_j within each F_j, and that the set G of eigenvalues of U of modulus 1 is just the collection of all p_jth roots of unity for all j. Thus G reflects the behavior of processes inside of F.

THEOREM 5.1. *For each $j = 1, \ldots, d$, there is a maximal $p_j \geqslant 1$ for which there are nonempty, pairwise disjoint, topologically closed sets F_j^m, $1 \leqslant m \leqslant p_j$, with union F_j, such that $K(x, F_j^{m+1}) = 1$ for $x \in F_j^m$ $(F_j^{n+p_j} = F_j^n)$. These sets are unique up to cyclic rearrangement. Furthermore*

$$G = \bigcup_{j=1}^{d} C_{p_j}, \tag{5.1}$$

where C_p is the set of pth roots of unity. Thus a compact Markov process is aperiodic if and only if $p_j = 1$ for all j.

The integer p_j is called the *period* of F_j, and the F_j^m are the *subergodic kernels* of F_j.

Suppose that X' is a stochastically and topologically closed subset of X, d' is the restriction of d to X', $\mathscr{B}'$ $(= \mathscr{B} \cap X')$ is the collection of Borel subsets of (X', d'), and K' is the restriction of K to X'; i.e., $K'(x, B) = K(x, B)$ if $x \in X'$ and $B \in \mathscr{B}'$. Since X' is stochastically closed, K' is a stochastic kernel, and, since X' is topologically closed, (X', d') is compact. The first step in the proof of Theorem 5.1 is to show that the corresponding transition operator U' is a Doeblin–Fortet operator, so that it corresponds to compact Markov processes according to Definition 3.1.

If $f' \in L(X')$, the same is true of its real and imaginary parts f_1' and f_2'. There is an extension f_i of f_i' to X, such that $\|f_i\| = \|f_i'\|'$ (Dudley, 1966, Lemma 5). Then $f = f_1 + if_2$ is an extension of f' with $|f| \leqslant \sqrt{2}|f'|'$ and $\mathrm{m}(f) \leqslant \sqrt{2}m(f')$, and consequently $\|f\| \leqslant \sqrt{2}\|f'\|'$. Next we observe that $U^n f | X' = U'^n f'$, where $g | X'$ denotes the restriction of g to X'. Therefore

$$\|U'f'\|' \leqslant \|Uf\| \leqslant \|U\| \|f\| \leqslant \sqrt{2}\|U\| \|f'\|,$$

so that U' is bounded on $L(X')$. And

$$\|U'^{mk}f'\|' \leqslant \|U^{mk}f\| \leqslant r^m \|f\| + R'|f|$$

for some $R' < \infty$ by Lemma 1.1, so that

$$\|U'^{mk}f'\|' \leqslant r^m \sqrt{2}\|f'\|' + R'\sqrt{2}|f'|'.$$

Thus U' satisfies (2.1.9) with $k' = mk$, if m is sufficiently large that $r^m \sqrt{2} < 1$.

Let K_j and U_j correspond in this way to $X' = F_j$, and let G_j be the eigenvalues of modulus 1 of U_j.

LEMMA 5.1. $G = \bigcup_{j=1}^{d} G_j$.

Proof.   If $f \in D(\lambda)$, then $f_j = f|F_j \in D_j(\lambda)$ for all j. If, in addition, $f \neq 0$, then $f_j \neq 0$ for some j by the Corollary to Lemma 4.2, so that $\lambda \in G_j$. Thus $G \subset \bigcup_{j=1}^{d} G_j$. Conversely, suppose that $\lambda \in' G$. For any $f_j \in L(F_j)$ let f be a Lipschitz extension of f_j to X. Then $U_{j,\lambda}^n f_j = U_\lambda^n f|F_j \to 0$ in $\|\cdot\|_j$; hence $\lambda \in' G_j$. Therefore $\bigcup_{j=1}^{d} G_j \subset G$.   ∎

It is easily seen that F_j is the only ergodic kernel of K_j. This fact is the basis for further analysis of U_j. Thus the next two lemmas deal with Doeblin–Fortet operators with compact state spaces (X, d), for which X is the only ergodic kernel.

LEMMA 5.2.   If X is the only ergodic kernel, then $G = C_p$ for some $p \geqslant 1$.

LEMMA 5.3.   There are nonempty, topologically closed sets $X^1, \ldots, X^p$, pairwise disjoint with union X, such that $K(x, X^{m+1}) = 1$ for all $x \in X^m$. If $Y^1, \ldots, Y^q$ is another such collection with $q \geqslant p$, then $q = p$ and there is an integer v such that $Y^m = X^{m+v}$ for all m.

Proof of Lemma 5.2.   First we show that G is a group under complex multiplication. If $\lambda_j \in G$, $j = 1, 2$, and f_j is a corresponding eigenfunction, then $|f_j(x)| \equiv |f_j| \neq 0$ by the Corollary to Lemma 4.2. The equation $Uf_j(x) = \lambda_j f_j(x)$ then implies

$$K(x, \{y : f_j(y) = \lambda_j f_j(x)\}) = 1, \qquad (5.2)$$

from which it follows that

$$Uf_1 f_2(x) = \lambda_1 \lambda_2 f_1(x) f_2(x)$$

and

$$Uf_1^{-1}(x) = \lambda_1^{-1} f_1^{-1}(x).$$

Since $f_1 f_2$ and $f_1^{-1} \in L(X)$, $\lambda_1 \lambda_2$ and $\lambda_1^{-1} \in G$, and G is a group, as claimed.

We now show that any finite subgroup G of $|\lambda| = 1$ is C_p for some p. For real t, let $e(t) = \exp(i2\pi t)$. If $\lambda \in G$, then, since G is finite, λ is a root of unity. Hence there are positive integers $o(\lambda)$ and $r(\lambda)$ such that $r(\lambda) \leqslant o(\lambda)$, $(r(\lambda), o(\lambda)) = 1$, and $\lambda = e(r(\lambda)/o(\lambda))$. Also $e(1/o(\lambda)) \in G$. For there are integers a and b such that $1 = ar(\lambda) + bo(\lambda)$; hence $1/o(\lambda) = ar(\lambda)/o(\lambda) + b$, so that $e(1/o(\lambda)) = \lambda^a \in G$. It follows that $C_{o(\lambda)} \subset G$.

Let $p = \max_{\lambda \in G} o(\lambda)$. Then for any $\lambda \in G$, $o(\lambda)|p$. For there are integers a and b such that $ao(\lambda) + bp = (o(\lambda), p)$, and $e(1/o(\lambda))$ and $e(1/p) \in G$. Thus $e(t) \in G$, where

$$t = \frac{a}{p} + \frac{b}{o(\lambda)} = \frac{(o(\lambda), p)}{o(\lambda)} \frac{1}{p}. \qquad (5.3)$$

Since $o(e(t)) \leqslant p$,

$$t = r(e(t))/o(e(t)) \geqslant 1/o(e(t)) \geqslant 1/p,$$

so, by (5.3), $o(\lambda) \leqslant (o(\lambda), p)$; i.e., $o(\lambda) = (o(\lambda), p)$. Thus $o(\lambda)|p$, as claimed. But then $\lambda \in C_p$, and $G \subset C_p$. Therefore $G = C_p$. ∎

Proof of Lemma 5.3. *Uniqueness.* Given $Y^1, \dots, Y^q$, let $\omega = \exp(i2\pi/q)$ and

$$g = \sum_{m=1}^{q} \omega^m I_{Y^m}.$$

Since the Y^j are compact, $d(Y^j, Y^k) > 0$ if $j \neq k$, so that $g \in L(X)$. Then $UI_{Y^m} = I_{Y^{m-1}}$, and

$$Ug = \sum_{m=1}^{q} \omega^m I_{Y^{m-1}} = \omega g.$$

Clearly $g \neq 0$, so $\omega \in G = C_p$. Since $q \geqslant p$, we must have $q = p$.

If $\lambda \in G$, $D(\lambda)$ is one dimensional. For let $f \in D(\lambda)$, $f \neq 0$, and let $x_0 \in X$. Then $f(x_0) \neq 0$, and, if $f' \in D(\lambda)$ and $c = f'(x_0)/f(x_0)$, $\Delta(x) = f'(x) - cf(x)$ belongs to $D(\lambda)$ and vanishes at x_0. Since $|\Delta(x)| \equiv |\Delta|$, $f' = cf$.

Let $\lambda = \exp(i2\pi/p)$ and

$$f = \sum_{n=1}^{p} \lambda^n I_{X^n}.$$

If g is as in the first paragraph of the proof, $f, g \in D(\lambda)$, so there is a complex constant c such that

$$g = cf. \tag{5.4}$$

For any $x_0 \in X$ there are $1 \leqslant m, n \leqslant p$ such that $x_0 \in Y^m \cap X^n$. Evaluating (5.4) at x_0 we obtain $\lambda^m = c\lambda^n$ or $c = \lambda^{-\nu}$ where $\nu = n - m$. Thus

$$\sum_{m=1}^{p} \lambda^m I_{Y^m} = \sum_{n=1}^{p} \lambda^{n-\nu} I_{X^n} = \sum_{m=1}^{p} \lambda^m I_{X^{m+\nu}}.$$

Equating powers of λ we obtain $Y^m = X^{m+\nu}$, for all m.

Existence. Let $\lambda = \exp(i2\pi/p)$, $f \in D(\lambda)$, $f \neq 0$, $x_0 \in X$, and

$$X^m = \{x : f(x) = \lambda^m f(x_0)\}$$

for $m \geqslant 0$. Note that $X^1, \dots, X^p$ are topologically closed and pairwise disjoint, and that $X^{m+p} = X^m$. By (5.2), $K(x, X^{m+1}) = 1$ for $x \in X^m$. Since $x_0 \in X^0$, it follows by induction that $X^m \neq \varnothing$. The set

$$X' = \bigcup_{m=1}^{p} X^m$$

is stochastically and topologically closed. Since X is an ergodic kernel, $X' = X$. ∎

Conclusion of proof of Theorem 5.1.   Let p_j be the integer p and F_j^m the set X^m obtained by applying Lemmas 5.2 and 5.3 to K_j and F_j. If $q_j \geqslant p_j$ and Y_j^m, $m = 1, \ldots, q_j$, are nonempty, topologically closed, and pairwise disjoint, with union F_j and $K(x, Y_j^{m+1}) = 1$ for $x \in Y_j^m$, then the Y_j^m are topologically closed in (F_j, d_j) and $K_j(x, Y_j^{m+1}) = 1$ for $x \in Y_j^m$. Thus the uniqueness assertion of Lemma 5.3 gives $q_j = p_j$ and $Y_j^m = F_j^{m+v}$. This is the uniqueness claimed by the theorem. Since $G_j = C_{p_j}$, (5.1) follows from Lemma 5.1. ∎

We now sketch some ramifications of the subergodic decomposition. Though these have their own interest, they play no role in subsequent developments.

For any $n \geqslant 1$, U^n is a Doeblin–Fortet operator. The subergodic kernel F_j^m is an ergodic kernel for $K^{(p_j)}$. Let g_j^m be the U^{p_j} invariant Lipschitz function that is one on F_j^m, and let μ_j^m be the T^{p_j} invariant probability with support F_j^m. If $\mathscr{X}$ is a compact Markov process with transition kernel K and initial distribution δ_x, then

$$g_j^m(x) = P(d(X_n, F_j^{n+m}) \to 0 \quad \text{as} \quad n \to \infty). \tag{5.5}$$

The set F_j^m is the unique ergodic kernel of $K^{(p_j)}|F_j^m$, $\mu_j^m|F_j^m$ is its only stationary probability, and the corresponding (Doeblin–Fortet) operator is regular. If $\lambda^{p_j} = 1$, let

$$h_{j,\lambda} = \sum_{m=1}^{p_j} \lambda^m g_j^m \quad \text{and} \quad v_{j,\lambda} = p_j^{-1} \sum_{m=1}^{p_j} \lambda^{-m} \mu_j^m.$$

We have $U g_j^m = g_j^{m-1}$ and $T \mu_j^m = \mu_j^{m+1}$, from which it follows that $U h_{j,\lambda} = \lambda h_{j,\lambda}$ and $T v_{j,\lambda} = \lambda v_{j,\lambda}$. The functions $h_{j,1}$ and g_j belong to $D(1)$ and agree on F, so, by the Corollary to Lemma 4.2,

$$h_{j,1} = g_j, \quad j = 1, \ldots, d. \tag{5.6}$$

Equations (5.5) and (5.6) amplify (4.3). Similarly $v_{j,1}$ is a stationary probability with $v_{j,1}(F_j) = 1$; so, according to Theorem 4.2,

$$v_{j,1} = \mu_j, \quad j = 1, \ldots, d.$$

The linear operator

$$W_{j,\lambda} f = \left(\int f \, dv_{j,\lambda} \right) h_{j,\lambda}$$

is bounded on $L(X)$. For $\lambda \in G$, let

$$U_\lambda' = \sum_{j:\lambda \in G_j} W_{j,\lambda}.$$

If $f \in L(X)$, a direct analysis of U^n for n large shows that

$$U_\lambda f(x) = U'_\lambda f(x)$$

for all $x \in F$. Since $U_\lambda f$ and $U'_\lambda f$ belong to $D(\lambda)$, the Corollary to Lemma 4.2 implies that $U_\lambda f = U'_\lambda f$. Thus $U_\lambda = U'_\lambda$, from which it follows that

$$U^n - V^n = \sum_{\lambda \in G} \lambda^n U_\lambda = \sum_{j=1}^{d} \sum_{\lambda \in G_j} \lambda^n W_{j,\lambda},$$

where $G_j = C_{p_j}$, for $n \geqslant 1$. The $W_{j,\lambda}$ satisfy

$$W_{j,\lambda} W_{j',\lambda'} = 0 \quad \text{if} \quad j \neq j' \quad \text{or} \quad \lambda \neq \lambda',$$

$$W_{j,\lambda}^2 = W_{j,\lambda}, \quad \text{and} \quad W_{j,\lambda} V = V W_{j,\lambda} = 0.$$

3.6. Regular and Absorbing Processes

Two types of aperiodic processes, regular and absorbing processes, are especially important in applications. According to Definition 2.2.1 and the paragraph that follows it, regularity means that $\|U^n - U_1\| \to 0$ as $n \to \infty$, and $U_1 f(x)$ does not depend on x. Theorems 4.1 and 5.1 show that a compact Markov process is regular if and only if it has but one ergodic kernel, and this kernel has period 1. Alternatively, there is a unique stationary probability μ, and the distribution μ_n of X_n converges to μ for any initial distribution μ_0.

DEFINITION 6.1. A Doeblin–Fortet operator for a compact state space (X, d) (or a corresponding compact Markov process X_n) is *absorbing* if all ergodic kernels are unit sets: $F_j = \{a_j\}$.

Aperiodicity is obvious, and, by Theorem 4.3, X_n converges with probability 1 to a random absorbing state a_j, $j = j(\omega)$. If there are two or more absorbing states, the probability of convergence to each of them depends on the initial distribution. In particular, such a process is not regular.

We now give useful criteria for a compact Markov process to be regular or absorbing. These criteria are expressed in terms of the support $\sigma_n(x)$ of $K^{(n)}(x, \cdot)$.

THEOREM 6.1. *A process is regular if and only if there is a $y \in X$ such that*

$$d(\sigma_n(x), y) \to 0 \quad as \quad n \to \infty \tag{6.1}$$

for all $x \in X$.

THEOREM 6.2. *A process is absorbing if and only if there are absorbing states $a_1, \ldots, a_i$ such that, for every x there is a $j = j(x)$ for which*

$$d(\sigma_n(x), a_j) \to 0 \quad as \quad n \to \infty. \tag{6.2}$$

Proof of Theorem 6.1. Suppose that (6.1) obtains. For any $x \in F_j^m$ and $n = kp_j$ we have $K^{(n)}(x, F_j^m) = 1$. Thus $\sigma_n(x) \subset F_j^m$, so that

$$d(F_j^m, y) \leqslant d(\sigma_n(x), y).$$

It then follows from (6.1), on letting $n \to \infty$, that $d(F_j^m, y) = 0$; i.e., $y \in F_j^m$. Therefore y belongs to all subergodic kernels. Since the subergodic kernels are disjoint, there must be only one, and U is regular.

Suppose, conversely, that U is regular with ergodic kernel F. Let $y \in F$ and, for any $\varepsilon > 0$, let O be the open sphere with radius ε and center y. Then

$$\liminf_{n \to \infty} K^{(n)}(x, O) \geqslant \mu(O) > 0,$$

the latter since the stationary probability μ has support F. Thus $K^{(n)}(x, O) > 0$, $\sigma_n(x) \cap O \neq \varnothing$, and $d(\sigma_n(x), y) < \varepsilon$ for all n sufficiently large. ∎

Proof of Theorem 6.2. Assume (6.2). If F' is an ergodic kernel, let $x \in F'$. Then $\sigma_n(x) \subset F'$, so that (6.2) implies that $a_j \in F'$. Since $\{a_j\}$ is stochastically and topologically closed, $\{a_j\} = F'$, and U is absorbing.

Suppose that U is absorbing. For any $x \in X$ there is a $j = j(x)$ such that $g_j(x) > 0$. If O is the open ε sphere about a_j, then

$$\liminf_{n \to \infty} K^{(n)}(x, O) \geqslant K_1(x, O) \geqslant g_j(x).$$

Therefore $K^{(n)}(x, O) > 0$ and $d(\sigma_n(x), a_j) < \varepsilon$ for n sufficiently large. ∎

Application of these criteria is facilitated by the following interrelationship among the sets $\sigma_n(x)$.

THEOREM 6.3. *For all $m, n \geqslant 0$ and $x \in X$,*

$$\sigma_{m+n}(x) = \overline{\bigcup_{y \in \sigma_m(x)} \sigma_n(y)}. \tag{6.3}$$

If $\sigma_1(x)$ is finite for each $x \in X$, the same is true of $\sigma_n(x)$, and

$$\sigma_{m+n}(x) = \bigcup_{y \in \sigma_m(x)} \sigma_n(y). \tag{6.4}$$

Proof. Let

$$\sigma = \bigcup_{y \in \sigma_m(x)} \sigma_n(y).$$

Clearly

$$K^{(m+n)}(x, \sigma) = \int_{\sigma_m(x)} K^{(m)}(x, dy) K^{(n)}(y, \sigma)$$

$$= K^{(m)}(x, \sigma_m(x)) = 1,$$

since $y \in \sigma_m(x)$ implies that $\sigma \supset \sigma_n(y)$ and thus $K^{(n)}(y, \sigma) = 1$. Therefore $\bar{\sigma} \supset \sigma_{m+n}(x)$.

To prove the reverse inclusion, we note first that

$$1 = K^{(m+n)}(x, \sigma_{m+n}(x))$$

$$= \int K^{(m)}(x, dy) K^{(n)}(y, \sigma_{m+n}(x)),$$

so that $K^{(m)}(x, \sigma^*) = 1$, where

$$\sigma^* = \{y : K^{(n)}(y, \sigma_{m+n}(x)) = 1\}.$$

Since $\sigma_{m+n}(x)$ is closed, $K^{(n)}(y, \sigma_{m+n}(x))$ is upper semicontinuous by Lemma 2.2.3, and σ^* is closed. Thus $\sigma^* \supset \sigma_m(x)$, so that $y \in \sigma_m(x)$ implies that $\sigma_{m+n}(x) \supset \sigma_n(y)$. In other words, $\sigma_{m+n}(x) \supset \sigma$; hence $\sigma_{m+n}(x) \supset \bar{\sigma}$. This completes the proof of (6.3).

If $\sigma_m(x)$ and $\sigma_n(y)$ are finite, σ is too. Hence $\bar{\sigma} = \sigma$, and (6.4) obtains. Using this equation and induction, we derive finiteness of $\sigma_n(x)$ from finiteness of $\sigma_1(x)$. ∎

3.7. Finite Markov Chains

When the state space X of a Markov process $\mathscr{X} = \{X_n\}_{n \geqslant 0}$ is a finite set, the process is a *finite Markov chain*. We noted in Section 3.3 that X is a compact space and $\mathscr{X}$ a compact process with respect to any metric d. In this section we collect various observations concerning specialization of the theory of compact Markov processes to this case. Though such specialization is an easy and instructive exercise, direct approaches to the theory of finite Markov chains (e.g. Kemeny and Snell, 1960; Feller, 1968; Chung, 1967) are much simpler.

The space $B(X) = L(X)$ of all complex valued functions or *vectors* on X is finite dimensional, so the norms $|\cdot|$ and $\|\cdot\|$ on this space are equivalent. The same is true of the corresponding norms on (bounded) linear operators on these spaces. Thus the same operators are orderly, ergodic, aperiodic, and regular with respect to the two norms. The fact that $\mathscr{X}$ is aperiodic or regular in $|\cdot|$ for certain finite state learning models is the basis for the treatment of their event sequences in Chapter 6.

One wants to have matrix interpretations of the various statements about operators in the preceding sections. For every operator W on $B(X)$, there is a unique complex valued function or *matrix* $w = \mathscr{M}(W)$ on $X \times X$ such that

$$Wf(x) = \sum_{y \in X} w(x, y) f(y)$$

or $Wf = w \cdot f$, where dot denotes matrix multiplication. Thus, if U and K are the transition operator and transition kernel of $\mathscr{X}$, the *transition matrix* $P = \mathscr{M}(U)$ has values or *elements* $P(x, y) = K(x, \{y\})$. The mapping $\mathscr{M}$ is an algebra isomorphism between operators and matrices:

$$\mathscr{M}(aV + bW) = a\mathscr{M}(V) + b\mathscr{M}(W),$$

and

$$\mathscr{M}(VW) = \mathscr{M}(V) \cdot \mathscr{M}(W).$$

In fact, it is not difficult to show that it is an isometry, $|w| = |W|$, with respect to the norm

$$|w| = \sup_x \sum_y |w(x, y)|$$

on matrices. These facts yield the desired matrix interpretations. For example, in the aperiodic case

$$U^n = U_1 + V^n,$$

where $|V^n| \to 0$ geometrically, so, if $P_1 = \mathscr{M}(U_1)$ and $v = \mathscr{M}(V)$,

$$P^n = P_1 + v^n,$$

where $|v^n| \to 0$ geometrically.

All subsets of X are topologically closed, so an ergodic kernel is a stochastically closed set with no stochastically closed proper subsets. The support of a measure on X is just the set of its atoms. Theorem 3.4.2 gives the following representation of the matrix $P_1 = \mathscr{M}(U_1)$:

$$P_1(x, y) = \sum_{j=1}^d g_j(x)\mu_j(\{y\}).$$

In the ergodic case $d = 1$, $P_1(x, y) = \mu_1(\{y\})$ for all x; i.e., all rows of P_1 are equal to the stationary distribution.

If $x_n, x \in X$, $d(x_n, x) \to 0$ as $n \to \infty$ if and only if $x_n = x$ for (all sufficiently) large n. Similarly, if $A \subset X$, $d(x_n, A) \to 0$ if and only if $x_n \in A$ for large n. Thus, for example, in Theorem 3.4.3

$$\Omega_j = \{\omega : X_n(\omega) \in F_j \quad \text{for large } n\}.$$

The fact that the empirical distribution v_n of $X_0, \ldots, X_{n-1}$ converges weakly to $\mu_{j(\omega)}$ (Theorem 3.4.4) with probability 1 is equivalent, in this context, to $v_n(\{x\}) \to \mu_{j(\omega)}(\{x\})$ with probability 1 for all $x \in X$.

The words "topologically closed" can be deleted from Theorem 3.5.1. In (3.5.5)

$$g_j^m(x) = P(X_n \in F_j^{n+m} \quad \text{for large } n).$$

If $P^n(x, y) > 0$ we say that y can be reached from x in n steps, and if this holds for some $n \geqslant 0$ we say that y can be reached from x. Theorems 3.6.1 and 3.6.2 can be rephrased in these terms as follows. A finite Markov chain is regular if and only if there is a $y \in X$ and, for every $x \in X$, an integer N_x, such that y can be reached from x in n steps if $n \geqslant N_x$. A finite Markov chain is absorbing if and only if, from any state x, some absorbing state a_j can be reached.

4 ○ Distance Diminishing Models with Noncompact State Spaces

In this chapter we consider a distance diminishing model $((X, d), (E, \mathscr{G}), p, u)$ whose state sequences have transition operator U. The state space is not assumed to be compact. Theorems 1.1 and 2.2 give conditions for regularity of U. The key assumptions in Theorem 1.1 are that (X, d) is bounded and $p(x, \cdot)$ has a lower bound that does not depend on x. Theorem 2.2 assumes "regularity in X'" for an "invariant" subset X' of X, such that $d(x, X')$ is bounded.

4.1. A Condition on p

Boundedness of (X, d) means, of course, that

$$b = \sup_{x, y \in X} d(x, y) < \infty. \tag{1.1}$$

Our condition on p is this:

(a)   There is a probability v on $\mathscr{G}$ and an $a > 0$ such that $p(x, A) \geqslant av(A)$ for all $A \in \mathscr{G}$.

66

If $p'(x, A) = v(A)$, then $p_j'(x, A) = v^j(A)$, where v^j on $\mathscr{G}^j$ is the jth Cartesian power of v on $\mathscr{G}$. Consequently, if r_j' is defined by (2.1.1) with p_j' in place of p_j,

$$r_j' = \sup_{x \neq y} \int v^j(de^j) \frac{d(u(x, e^j), u(y, e^j))}{d(x, y)}. \tag{1.2}$$

The following condition supplements the assumption $r_k < 1$ in the definition of a distance diminishing model (Definition 2.1.1).

(b)   There is a $k' \geqslant 1$ such that $r' = r_{k'}' < 1$.

If, in addition to (a) and (b),

$$d(u(x, e), u(y, e)) \leqslant d(x, y) \tag{1.3}$$

for all $e \in E$ and $x, y \in X$, we can take $k = k'$ in Definition 2.1.1. When $a = 1$ this is obvious, since $p = p'$, so that $r_j = r_j'$. In any case

$$p_j(x, A) \geqslant a^j v^j(A) \tag{1.4}$$

for all $j \geqslant 1$ and $A \in \mathscr{G}^j$. Thus, if $a < 1$, the equation

$$p_j(x, A) = a^j v^j(A) + (1 - a^j) p_j^*(x, A)$$

defines a stochastic kernel p_j^* on $X \times \mathscr{G}^j$, and

$$r_j \leqslant a^j r_j' + (1 - a^j) r_j^*, \tag{1.5}$$

where r_j^* is defined by (2.1.1) with p_j^* in place of p_j. However (1.3) implies that

$$d(u(x, e^j), u(y, e^j)) \leqslant d(x, y)$$

for all j, e^j, x, and y, so that $r_j^* \leqslant 1$ for any stochastic kernel p_j^*. Hence (1.5) and (b) yield $r_{k'} < 1$, as claimed.

The following result is a refinement due to Norman (1970a, Theorem 1) of Theorem 1 of Ionescu Tulcea (1959).

THEOREM 1.1.   *Under* (1.1), (a), *and* (b), *U is regular.*

The theorem is proved by combining several of our previous results with the following lemma.

LEMMA 1.1

$$s = \sup_{j \geqslant 1} s_j < 1, \tag{1.6}$$

where

$$s_j = \tfrac{1}{2} \sup_{x, y \in X} |\delta p_j(x, y, \cdot)|.$$

Proof of Lemma 1.1. First we define a family of stochastic kernels $v_{j,n}$ on $X \times \mathcal{G}^j$. For $1 \leqslant j \leqslant n$ let $v_{j,n}(x, \cdot) = v^j$, and for $j > n$ let

$$v_{j,n}(x, A) = \int v^n(de^n) \int p_{j-n}(x', de*^{j-n}) I_A(e^j),$$

where $x' = u(x, e^n)$ and $e*^{j-n} = (e_n, \ldots, e_{j-1})$. If $j \leqslant n$, then clearly $\delta v_{j,n}(x, y, A) = 0$ for all x, y, and A. If $j > n$, then

$$\delta v_{j,n}(x, y, A) = \int v^n(de^n) \int \delta p_{j-n}(x', y', de*^{j-n}) I_A(e^j).$$

Thus, by (1.1.4),

$$|\delta v_{j,n}(x, y, A)| \leqslant \int v^n(de^n) \tfrac{1}{2} |\delta p_{j-n}(x', y', \cdot)|$$

$$\leqslant R_{j-n} \int v^n(de^n) d(x', y')$$

$$\leqslant R_{j-n} r_n' d(x, y).$$

Theorem 2.1.1 and (1.1) then yield

$$|\delta v_{j,n}(x, y, A)| \leqslant R_\infty r_n' b$$

for all $j, n \geqslant 1$. Applying Lemma 2.1.2 to p' we obtain $r_{i+j}' \leqslant r_i' r_j'$, hence

$$|\delta v_{j,ik'}(x, y, A)| \leqslant R_\infty r'^i b = \gamma_i \tag{1.7}$$

for all $i, j \geqslant 1$, $x, y \in X$, and $A \in \mathcal{G}^j$.

It follows immediately from (1.4) and the definition of $v_{j,n}$ that

$$p_j(x, A) \geqslant a^n v_{j,n}(A)$$

for all $j, n \geqslant 1$, $x \in X$, and $A \in \mathcal{G}^j$. Thus there is a stochastic kernel $q_{j,n}$ on $X \times \mathcal{G}^j$ such that

$$p_j(x, A) = a^n v_{j,n}(x, A) + (1 - a^n) q_{j,n}(x, A).$$

Clearly

$$|\delta p_j(x, y, A)| \leqslant a^n |\delta v_{j,n}(x, y, A)| + (1 - a^n) |\delta q_{j,n}(x, y, A)|$$

$$\leqslant a^n \gamma_i + (1 - a^n) = \gamma_i'$$

by (1.7) if $n = ik'$. Taking the suprema over $A \in \mathcal{G}^j$, $x, y \in X$, and $j \geqslant 1$ we obtain $s \leqslant \gamma_i'$ for all $i \geqslant 1$. However γ_i and thus $\gamma_i' < 1$ for i sufficiently large. ■

Conclusion of proof of Theorem 1.1. By Lemma 2.1.3 and (1.1),

$$\mathrm{osc}(U^j f) \leqslant r_j bm(f) + s\, \mathrm{osc}(f)$$

for $f \in L(X)$, where $s < 1$ by the last lemma. Replacing f by $U^n f$ and noting that $m(U^n f) \leqslant J \|f\|$ as a consequence of Lemma 3.1.1, we get

$$\mathrm{osc}(U^{j+n}f) \leqslant r_j b J \|f\| + s \,\mathrm{osc}(U^n f).$$

Therefore

$$\varepsilon_{j+n} \leqslant s \varepsilon_n + t_j, \tag{1.8}$$

where

$$\varepsilon_n = \sup_{\|f\| \leqslant 1} \mathrm{osc}(U^n f), \tag{1.9}$$

and $t_j = r_j b J$. Now ε_n is a nonincreasing sequence. Letting $n \to \infty$ on both sides of (1.8) we obtain

$$\lim_{n \to \infty} \varepsilon_n \leqslant t_j / (1 - s)$$

for all $j \geqslant 1$. But, according to Theorem 2.1.1, $r_j \to 0$ and thus $t_j \to 0$ as $j \to \infty$. Therefore $\varepsilon_n \to 0$ as $n \to \infty$.

The closed convex hull $H(U^n f)$ of the range of $U^n f$ is compact, and, by (1.1.8),

$$H(U^{n+1}f) \subset H(U^n f);$$

hence

$$\bigcap_{n=1}^{\infty} H(U^n f) \neq \varnothing.$$

But, for $f \in L(X)$,

$$\mathrm{diam}\, H(U^n f) = \mathrm{osc}(U^n f) \to 0$$

as $n \to \infty$, so this intersection contains a single point $U^\infty f$. Since $U^n f(x)$ and $U^\infty f$ are both in $H(U^n f)$,

$$|U^n f(x) - U^\infty f| \leqslant \mathrm{osc}(U^n f)$$

for all $x \in X$. Thus

$$|U^n f - U^\infty f| \leqslant \mathrm{osc}(U^n f) \tag{1.10}$$

$$\leqslant \varepsilon_n \|f\|$$

for all $n \geqslant 1$. An application of Theorem 3.1.1 completes the proof. ∎

A NONMETRIC ANALOG OF THEOREM 1.1. The extreme case of a contractive operator is a constant operator: $u(x) \equiv u$. Theorem 1.2 (p. 70) is an analog of Theorem 1.1 for learning models in which the operators $u(\cdot, e^k)$ corresponding to certain combinations e^k of events are constant. Suppes' (1960) stimulus sampling model for a continuum of responses is of this sort, and Section 17.1 describes an application of Theorem 1.2 to this model.

THEOREM 1.2. *If a random system with complete connections satisfies* (a) (*p. 66*) *and* (b') *below, then U is regular on* $B(X)$.

(b') *There is a* $k \geqslant 1$ *and a* $G \in \mathscr{G}^k$ *such that* $v^k(G) > 0$ *and* $u(x, e^k) \equiv u(e^k)$ *if* $e^k \in G$.

The proof is much simpler than that of Theorem 1.1.

Proof. Clearly

$$p_k(x, A) \geqslant a^k v^k(A)$$

$$\geqslant a^k v^k(A \cap G) = cp'(A),$$

where $c = a^k v^k(G) > 0$, and

$$p'(A) = v^k(A \cap G)/v^k(G)$$

is a probability on $\mathscr{G}^k$ with $p'(G) = 1$. Thus, there is a stochastic kernel p^* such that

$$p_k(x, A) = cp'(A) + (1-c) p^*(x, A).$$

For $f \in B(X)$,

$$U^k f(x) = cU'f(x) + (1-c) U^* f(x),$$

where

$$U^* f(x) = \int p^*(x, de^k) f(u(x, e^k))$$

and

$$U'f(x) = \int p'(de^k) f(u(x, e^k))$$

$$= \int_G p'(de^k) f(u(e^k)).$$

Since $U'f$ is constant,

$$\mathrm{osc}(U^k f) = (1-c) \, \mathrm{osc}(U^* f)$$

$$\leqslant (1-c) \, \mathrm{osc}(f),$$

and

$$\mathrm{osc}(U^n f) \leqslant (1-c)^{[n/k]} \, \mathrm{osc}(f)$$

for all $n \geqslant 0$. On combination with (1.10) this yields

$$|U^n f - U^\infty f| \leqslant 2(1-c)^{[n/k]} |f|$$

or

$$|U^n - U^\infty| \leqslant 2(1-c)^{[n/k]}. \quad \blacksquare$$

4.2. Invariant Subsets

DEFINITION 2.1. A nonempty subset X' of X is *invariant* for a distance diminishing model if $u(X', e) \subset X'$ for all $e \in E$.

For any $j \geqslant 1$,

$$W_j = \bigcup_{e^j \in E^j} u(X, e^j) \tag{2.1}$$

is invariant. In multiresponse linear models,

$$u(x, e) = (1 - \theta_e) x + \theta_e \lambda_e,$$

and any convex set that includes $\{\lambda_e : \theta_e > 0\}$ is invariant.

An invariant Borel set is clearly stochastically closed for a state sequence $\mathscr{X}$. Furthermore, state sequences are attracted to invariant sets.

THEOREM 2.1. *If X' is invariant, $d(X_n, X') \to 0$ a.s. as $n \to \infty$.*

Proof. Let $d(x) = d(x, X')$. This function is Lipschitz, though it need not be bounded. If $x' \in X'$, then $u(x', e^n) \in X'$, so that

$$U^n d(x) = \int p_n(x, de^n) \, d(u(x, e^n), X')$$

$$\leqslant \int p_n(x, de^n) \, d(u(x, e^n), u(x', e^n)) \leqslant r_n d(x, x').$$

Taking the inf over $x' \in X'$, we obtain

$$U^n d(x) \leqslant r_n d(x).$$

Therefore, if $X_0 = x$ a.s.,

$$E \left(\sum_{n=0}^\infty d(X_n) \right) \leqslant d(x) \sum_{n=0}^\infty r_n < \infty$$

by Theorem 2.1.1, so that $\sum_{n=0}^\infty d(X_n) < \infty$ and $d(X_n) \to 0$ a.s. The same conclusion is obtained for an arbitrary initial distribution by conditioning on X_0. $\quad \blacksquare$

If X' is invariant and d', p', and u' are the restrictions of d, p, and u to X', then $R_j' \leqslant R_j$ and $r_j' \leqslant r_j$, and $((X', d'), (E, \mathscr{G}), p', u')$ is a distance diminishing model. This "submodel" sometimes satisfies the conditions for regularity given in Theorems 3.6.1 and 1.1, even when the "complete" model does not. Hence the importance of the following result of Norman (1970a, Theorem 2).

THEOREM 2.2. *If X' is invariant, $d(x, X')$ is bounded, and U' is regular, then U is regular.*

Clearly, if U is regular, then the quantity ε_n defined by (1.9) converges to 0 as $n \to \infty$. And the last paragraph of the proof of Theorem 1.1 establishes the converse. The corresponding equivalence is, of course, valid for U'. Thus our task reduces to showing that $\varepsilon_n' \to 0$ implies $\varepsilon_n \to 0$.

Proof. Let $f \in L(X)$ and let $f' = f|X'$. For any $x \in X$ and $x' \in X'$, we can write

$$U^n f(x) = g_n(x, x') + h_n(x, x'),$$

where

$$g_n(x, x') = \int p_n(x, de^n)\left(f(u(x, e^n)) - f(u(x', e^n))\right)$$

and

$$h_n(x, x') = \int p_n(x, de^n) f'(u(x', e^n)).$$

Consequently

$$|U^n f(x) - U^n f(y)| \leqslant |g_n(x, x')| + |g_n(y, y')| + |h_n(x, x') - h_n(y, y')|$$
$$\leqslant m(f) r_n d(x, x') + m(f) r_n d(y, y') + \mathrm{osc}(f'),$$

since $h_n(x, x')$ is in the closed convex hull of the range of f'. Take the infimum over x' and y' and then the supremum over x and y to get

$$\mathrm{osc}(U^n f) \leqslant 2m(f) r_n b' + \mathrm{osc}(f'),$$

where $b' < \infty$ is the supremum of $d(x, X')$. Then replace f by $U^n f$ and use Lemma 3.1.1 and $(U^n f)' = U'^n f'$ to obtain

$$\mathrm{osc}(U^{2n} f) \leqslant 2b' J r_n \|f\| + \varepsilon_n' \|f'\|'.$$

It follows that

$$\varepsilon_{2n} \leqslant 2b' J r_n + \varepsilon_n' \to 0$$

as $n \to \infty$. Since ε_n is nonincreasing, $\varepsilon_n \to 0$, as was to be shown. ∎

5 ○ Functions of Markov Processes

5.1. Introduction

This chapter is concerned with the time series analysis of processes of the form $Y_j = f(X_j)$, where X_j is a Markov process and f is a real valued function of its states. The theory includes bounded Lipschitz functions of a regular Doeblin–Fortet process, as well as other examples described later.

Here are our assumptions:

(a) $\mathscr{X} = \{X_j\}_{j \geqslant 0}$ is a Markov process with state space $(X, \mathscr{B})$, transition kernel K, and transition operator U.

(b)   The functions to which the theory applies form a subset L of $B^r(X)$, the set of bounded measurable real valued functions on X. The class L is a Banach space under a norm $\|\cdot\|$ and $1 \in L$. If $f, g \in L$ then $fg \in L$ and

$$\|fg\| \leqslant \|f\| \, \|g\|.$$

Thus L is a Banach algebra. The supremum norm is continuous at 0 in L, or, equivalently,

$$C = \sup_{\substack{f \in L \\ f \neq 0}} \frac{|f|}{\|f\|} < \infty.$$

(c) $U = U^\infty + V$ is a regular operator on L.

In addition to $L(X)$ functions of regular Doeblin–Fortet processes, the above assumptions are satisfied by a class of functions of a process $X_n' = (E_n, X_{n+1})$ from a distance diminishing model, assuming that the state sequence X_n is regular. This class includes all bounded measurable functions of E_n alone. Details of this important application of the theorems of this chapter are given in Section 6.1.

Another noteworthy special case is that in which $L = B^r(X)$ and $\|\cdot\| = |\cdot|$. Then U is regular if and only if Doeblin's condition is satisfied, there is only one ergodic set, and it is aperiodic ($r = 1$ and $d_1 = 1$ in the notation of Neveu, 1965, V.3). Functions of such processes have received much attention in the literature (see Iosifescu and Theodorescu, 1969, Section 1.2). If the state sequence of a random system with complete connections is of this type, the same is true of X_n' and $X_n'' = (X_n, E_n)$, as is noted in Section 6.1. This provides one approach to functions of event sequences in finite state models, and in Suppes' continuous-response stimulus sampling model.

Before beginning in earnest, let us briefly survey the chapter's contents. Let

$$y = U^\infty f,$$

$$\rho_u = \lim_{n\to\infty} \text{cov}(Y_n, Y_{n+u}), \tag{1.1}$$

$$\sigma^2 = \sum_{u=-\infty}^{\infty} \rho_u, \tag{1.2}$$

$$S_n = \sum_{j=0}^{n-1} Y_j,$$

and

$$Z_n = (S_n - ny)/\sqrt{n}.$$

It is shown in Section 5.2 that Z_n is asymptotically normally distributed with mean 0 and variance σ^2 [$Z_n \sim N(0, \sigma^2)$]. Estimation of ρ_u and σ^2 are considered, respectively, in Sections 5.3 and 5.4. Section 5.5 gives a representation of σ^2 in terms of U^∞ and K, and uses this representation to prove that $\sigma^2 > 0$ in an important special case. It is shown in Section 5.6 that the "shifted" process $\{Y_{N+j}\}_{j\geq 0}$ approaches stationarity as $N \to \infty$. Generalizations of these results to vector valued functions f and to spectral analysis are presented in Section 5.7.

5.2. Central Limit Theorem

This section is devoted to establishing the following theorems.

THEOREM 2.1. $S_n/n \to y$ a.s. *as* $n \to \infty$.

THEOREM 2.2. $E(Z_n^2) = \sigma^2 + O(1/n)$.

THEOREM 2.3. $Z_n \sim N(0, \sigma^2)$ *as* $n \to \infty$.

The proofs draw on many of the same estimates, so this background material is developed systematically, and the proof of each theorem is completed as its prerequisites become available. The proof of Theorem 2.3 is not finished until the end of the section.

We shall assume that $y = U^\infty f = 0$. The general case is obtained by applying this special case to $f' = f - y$. Let

$$\mathscr{F}_n = \mathscr{F}(X_0, \dots, X_n)$$

be the smallest Borel field with respect to which $X_0, \dots, X_n$ are measurable.

Moments of Y_n.   Note first that

$$E(Y_{m+j} | \mathscr{F}_m) = U^j f(X_m) = V^j f(X_m)$$

(a.s.), since $U^\infty f = 0$. Hence

$$|E(Y_{m+j} | \mathscr{F}_m)| \leqslant |V^j f| \leqslant C \|V^j f\|$$
$$\leqslant C D \alpha^j \|f\|,$$

where $\alpha < 1$, by (2.2.5). This is abbreviated

$$E(Y_{m+j} | \mathscr{F}_m) = O(\alpha^j). \tag{2.1}$$

In this chapter we use such notation only when the order of magnitude is uniform over all relevant variables that do not appear on the right ($m \geqslant 0$ and $\omega \in \Omega$ in this case). It follows that

$$E(Y_j) = E(E(Y_j | \mathscr{F}_0)) = O(\alpha^j). \tag{2.2}$$

Turning now to conditional second moments, we see that

$$E(Y_{m+j} Y_{m+k} | \mathscr{F}_m) = E\big(Y_{m+(j \wedge k)} E(Y_{m+(j \vee k)} | \mathscr{F}_{m+(j \wedge k)}) | \mathscr{F}_m\big), \tag{2.3}$$

where $j \wedge k$ and $j \vee k$, are, respectively, the smaller and larger of j and k;

$$E(Y_{m+j} Y_{m+k} | \mathscr{F}_m) = E\big(Y_{m+(j \wedge k)} O(\alpha^{|k-j|}) | \mathscr{F}_m\big),$$

by (2.1); and

$$E(Y_{m+j} Y_{m+k} | \mathscr{F}_m) = O(\alpha^{|k-j|}), \tag{2.4}$$

since $Y_n = O(1)$. It follows that

$$E(Y_j Y_k) = O(\alpha^{|k-j|}).\tag{2.5}$$

Returning to (2.3),

$$\begin{aligned}E(Y_{m+j}Y_{m+k}|\mathscr{F}_m) &= E(Y_{m+(j\wedge k)}V^{|k-j|}f(X_{m+(j\wedge k)})|\mathscr{F}_m)\\ &= U^{j\wedge k}(fV^{|k-j|}f)(X_m)\\ &= \rho_{k-j} + V^{j\wedge k}(fV^{|k-j|}f)(X_m),\end{aligned}$$

where

$$\rho_u = U^{\infty}(fV^{|u|}f).\tag{2.6}$$

But

$$|V^{j\wedge k}(fV^{|k-j|}f)| \leqslant CD^2\|f\|^2\alpha^{j\vee k},$$

thus

$$E(Y_{m+j}Y_{m+k}|\mathscr{F}_m) = \rho_{k-j} + O(\alpha^{j\vee k})\tag{2.7}$$

and

$$E(Y_j Y_k) = \rho_{k-j} + O(\alpha^{j\vee k}).\tag{2.8}$$

It follows from (2.8) and (2.2) that

$$\mathrm{cov}(Y_n, Y_{n+u}) = E(Y_n Y_{n+u}) - E(Y_n)E(Y_{n+u})$$

$$\to \rho_u$$

as $n \to \infty$. This reconciles (2.6) and (1.1). Clearly

$$|\rho_u| \leqslant |fV^{|u|}f| \leqslant |f||V^{|u|}f|,$$

so that

$$\rho_u = O(\alpha^{|u|}).\tag{2.9}$$

Thus the series in (1.2) converges absolutely.
    If $0 \leqslant i \leqslant j \leqslant k \leqslant l$,

$$\begin{aligned}E(Y_i Y_j Y_k Y_l) &= E(Y_i Y_j E(Y_k Y_l|\mathscr{F}_j))\\ &= E(Y_i Y_j)\rho_{l-k} + E(Y_i Y_j O(\alpha^{l-j}))\end{aligned}$$

by (2.7); hence

$$E(Y_i Y_j Y_k Y_l) = O(\alpha^{(j-i)+(l-k)} + \alpha^{l-j})\tag{2.10}$$

by (2.5) and (2.9).

Moments of sums. Let

$$S_{m,n} = \sum_{j=0}^{n-1} Y_{m+j}$$

and

$$s_n = \sum_{j,k=0}^{n-1} \rho_{j-k}.$$

From (2.1) we get

$$|E(S_{m,n}|\mathscr{F}_m)| \leqslant 1/(1-\alpha)$$

or

$$E(S_{m,n}|\mathscr{F}_m) = O(1). \tag{2.11}$$

Similarly, (2.7) yields

$$E(S_{m,n}^2|\mathscr{F}_m) = s_n + O(1), \tag{2.12}$$

since

$$\sum_{j,k=0}^{\infty} \alpha^{j \vee k} = \frac{1+\alpha}{(1-\alpha)^2} < \infty.$$

Now

$$s_n = \sum_{|u|<n} (n - |u|) \rho_u,$$

so that

$$s_n - n\sigma^2 = -\sum_{|u| \geqslant n} n\rho_u - \sum_{|u|<n} |u| \rho_u$$

and

$$|s_n - n\sigma^2| \leqslant \sum_{u=-\infty}^{\infty} |u| |\rho_u| < \infty.$$

On combination with (2.12) this gives

$$E(S_{m,n}^2|\mathscr{F}_m) = n\sigma^2 + O(1). \tag{2.13}$$

Since $S_{0,n} = S_n$,

$$E(S_n^2) = n\sigma^2 + O(1),$$

which yields Theorem 2.2 on division by n.

Turning to the fourth moment,

$$E(S_{m,n}^4) = \sum_{ijkl} E(Y_i Y_j Y_k Y_l),$$

where the summands vary independently between m and $m+n-1$;

$$E(S_{m,n}^4) \leqslant 4! \sum_{ijkl}' |E(Y_i Y_j Y_k Y_l)| ,$$

where the prime indicates that summation is restricted to $i \leqslant j \leqslant k \leqslant l$; and

$$E(S_{m,n}^4) \leqslant K \sum_{ijkl}' (\alpha^{j-i+l-k} + \alpha^{l-j}),$$

for some constant K, as a consequence of (2.10). Now

$$\sum_{ijkl}' \alpha^{j-i+l-k} \leqslant \frac{1}{1-\alpha} \sum_{ijk}' \alpha^{j-i}$$

$$\leqslant \frac{n}{1-\alpha} \sum_{ij}' \alpha^{j-i} \leqslant \frac{n^2}{(1-\alpha)^2},$$

and, similarly,

$$\sum_{ijkl}' \alpha^{l-j} = O(n^2),$$

so

$$E(S_{m,n}^4) = O(n^2). \tag{2.14}$$

It follows that

$$E((S_n/n)^4) = O(1/n^2); \tag{2.15}$$

hence

$$E\left(\sum_{n=0}^{\infty} (S_n/n)^4 \right) < \infty ,$$

$$\sum_{n=0}^{\infty} (S_n/n)^4 < \infty ,$$

and $S_n/n \to 0$ a.s. This completes the proof of Theorem 2.1.

Conclusion of proof of Theorem 2.3. As a consequence of Theorem 2.2, σ^2, which was defined by the series (1.2), is nonnegative. We need not distinguish below between the cases $\sigma^2 > 0$ and $\sigma^2 = 0$, but, in the latter case

$$Z_n \sim N(0, \sigma^2) = \delta_0$$

follows immediately from Theorem 2.2.

Of the various estimates obtained above, only (2.11), (2.13), and

$$E(|S_{m,n}|^3) = O(n^{3/2}), \tag{2.16}$$

which follows from (2.14), are needed henceforth. Our approach is drawn from a paper of Serfling (1968), to which the reader is referred for generalizations. At the end of Section 8.4 we show how, as an alternative to the following direct argument, Lemma 8.4.2 can be used to complete the proof.

Let $0 < \xi < 1$, $d = [n^{\xi}]$, and $q = [n/d]$, so that $d \sim n^{\xi}$ and $q \sim n^{1-\xi}$. Let

$$\zeta_j = \zeta_j^n = S_{jd}/\sqrt{n}$$

for $j \leqslant q$. Clearly

$$Z_n - \zeta_q = S_{qd,r}/\sqrt{n},$$

where $n = dq + r$, so

$$E(|Z_n - \zeta_q|^3) = O((r/n)^{3/2})$$

by (2.16). Since $0 \leqslant r < d = o(n)$, $Z_n - \zeta_q$ converges in probability to 0, so it suffices to show that $\zeta_q \sim N(0, \sigma^2)$.

Since

$$\Delta \zeta_j = \zeta_{j+1} - \zeta_j$$
$$= S_{jd,d}/\sqrt{n},$$

(2.11), (2.13), and (2.16) give

$$E(\Delta \zeta_j | \mathscr{F}_{jd}) = O(1/\sqrt{n}), \tag{2.17}$$

$$E((\Delta \zeta_j)^2 | \mathscr{F}_{jd}) = (d/n)\sigma^2 + O(1/n), \tag{2.18}$$

and

$$E(|\Delta \zeta_j|^3) = O((d/n)^{3/2}) \tag{2.19}$$

for $j < q$.

Let

$$h_j(\lambda) = h_j^n(\lambda) = E(\exp(i\lambda \zeta_j^n))$$

be the characteristic function of ζ_j. Then

$$h_{j+1}(\lambda) = E(\exp(i\lambda \zeta_j) \exp(i\lambda \Delta \zeta_j))$$
$$= E(\exp(i\lambda \zeta_j) E(\exp(i\lambda \Delta \zeta_j) | \mathscr{F}_{jd})). \tag{2.20}$$

Using the Taylor expansion

$$\exp(it) = 1 + it - t^2/2 + O(|t|^3)$$

in conjunction with (2.17) and (2.18), we obtain

$$E(\exp(i\lambda \Delta \zeta_j) | \mathscr{F}_{jd}) = 1 - (\lambda^2/2)(d/n)\sigma^2$$
$$+ O(1/\sqrt{n}) + O(E(|\Delta \zeta_j|^3 | \mathscr{F}_{jd})).$$

Substitution into (2.20) and application of (2.19) yield

$$h_{j+1}(\lambda) = (1 - (\lambda^2/2)(d/n)\sigma^2)h_j(\lambda) + O(1/\sqrt{n}) + O((d/n)^{3/2}).$$

Thus, by iteration,

$$h_q(\lambda) = (1 - (\lambda^2/2)(d/n)\sigma^2)^q + O(q/\sqrt{n}) + O(q(d/n)^{3/2}).$$

Since $dq/n \to 1$, the first term on the right converges to $\exp(-\lambda^2\sigma^2/2)$, and the third converges to zero. Clearly

$$q/\sqrt{n} \sim n^{1/2-\xi},$$

so the second term on the right converges to zero if $\xi > \frac{1}{2}$. Choosing ξ in this way we obtain

$$h_q(\lambda) \to \exp(-\lambda^2\sigma^2/2),$$

from which Theorem 2.3 follows via the continuity theorem (Breiman, 1968, Theorem 8.28). ∎

5.3. Estimation of ρ_u

The natural estimator of the asymptotic autocovariance ρ_u of Y_n and Y_{n+u} is the *sample autocovariance* given by

$$\hat{\rho}_u = \frac{1}{n-u} \sum_{i=0}^{n-1-u} (Y_i - Y_{\cdot})(Y_{i+u} - Y_{\cdot}) \tag{3.1}$$

and $\hat{\rho}_{-u} = \hat{\rho}_u$ for $u \geqslant 0$, where

$$Y_{\cdot} = S_n/n.$$

This estimator is consistent in both the quadratic mean (q.m.) and a.s. senses.

THEOREM 3.1. *As $n \to \infty$, $\hat{\rho}_u \to \rho_u$ in quadratic mean and almost surely.*

Proof. Since $\rho_{-u} = \rho_u$, we can assume that $u \geqslant 0$, and, since neither $\hat{\rho}_u$ nor ρ_u is affected if a constant is added to f, we can assume that $U^\infty f = 0$ without loss of generality.

Clearly

$$\hat{\rho}_u = \rho_u^* + \varepsilon_u, \tag{3.2}$$

where

$$\rho_u^* = \frac{1}{n-u} \sum_{i=0}^{n-1-u} Y_i Y_{i+u}, \tag{3.3}$$

$$\varepsilon_u = -Y'Y_. - Y_.Y'' + Y_.^2, \qquad (3.4)$$

$$Y' = S_{0,n-u}/(n-u),$$

and

$$Y'' = S_{u,n-u}/(n-u).$$

Consider ε_u first. By the Schwarz inequality,

$$E((Y'Y_.)^2) \leqslant E^{\frac{1}{2}}(Y'^4)E^{\frac{1}{2}}(Y_.^4)$$

$$= O(1/(n-u))O(1/n) = O(1/(n-u)n),$$

as a consequence of (2.14) and (2.15). The same estimate applies to the other two terms on the right in (3.4), so

$$E(\varepsilon_u^2) = O(1/(n-u)n). \qquad (3.5)$$

Thus $\varepsilon_u \to 0$ q.m. as $n \to \infty$. Theorem 2.2 implies that $\varepsilon_u \to 0$ a.s., so it remains only to show that $\rho_u^* \to \rho_u$ q.m. and a.s.

If

$$W_i = Y_i Y_{i+u} - \rho_u,$$

then

$$\rho_u^* - \rho_u = \frac{1}{n-u} \sum_{i=0}^{n-1-u} W_i. \qquad (3.6)$$

For $k \geqslant u$,

$$E(W_i W_{i+k}) = E(W_i E(W_{i+k}|\mathscr{F}_{i+u}))$$

$$= E(O(1)O(\alpha^k)) = O(\alpha^k)$$

by (2.7). While for $u \geqslant k \geqslant 0$,

$$E(W_i W_{i+k}) = O(1).$$

Therefore $\rho_u^* - \rho_u \to 0$ q.m. and a.s. as a consequence of Lemma 3.1. ∎

LEMMA 3.1. Let $\{W_i\}_{i \geqslant 0}$ be a real valued stochastic process such that

$$E(W_i W_{i+k}) \leqslant a_k$$

for $k \geqslant 0$, where $a_k \geqslant 0$ and

$$\sum_{k=0}^{\infty} a_k < \infty.$$

Then

$$E\left(\left(\sum_{i=0}^{n-1} W_i\right)^2\right) = O(n).$$ (3.7)

If $c_{n+1} \geqslant c_n > 0$ and

$$c = \sum_{n=2}^{\infty} \left(\frac{\ln n}{c_n}\right)^2 < \infty,$$

then

$$(1/c_n) \sum_{i=0}^{n-1} W_i \to 0$$ (3.8)

a.s., as $n \to \infty$.

Lemma 3.1 and (2.5) yield an alternative proof of Theorem 2.1. The lemma gives much stronger estimates of the magnitude of $\sum_i W_i$ than Theorems 2.1 and 3.1 require. For a fuller development of the method used to prove (3.8), see Serfling (1970a,b).

Proof. Note first that, for any real numbers $b_0, \ldots, b_{n-1}$,

$$\sum_{i,j=0}^{n-1} b_i b_j a_{|i-j|} \leqslant \tfrac{1}{2} \sum_{i,j=0}^{n-1} (b_i^2 + b_j^2) a_{|i-j|}$$

$$= \sum_{i=0}^{n-1} b_i^2 \sum_{j=0}^{n-1} a_{|i-j|}$$

$$\leqslant A \sum_{i=0}^{n-1} b_i^2,$$ (3.9)

where

$$A = \sum_{k=-\infty}^{\infty} a_{|k|}.$$

Thus

$$E\left(\left(\sum_{i=0}^{n-1} W_i\right)^2\right) = \sum_{i,j=0}^{n-1} E(W_i W_j)$$

$$\leqslant \sum_{i,j=0}^{n-1} a_{|i-j|} \leqslant An,$$

and (3.7) is proved.

Let

$$T_n = \sum_{i=0}^{n-1} W_i/c_i.$$

By (3.9),

$$E((T_m - T_n)^2) \leqslant A \sum_{i=m\wedge n}^{(m\vee n)-1} c_i^{-2}. \qquad (3.10)$$

Since $c < \infty$, $\sum_i c_i^{-2} < \infty$, and T_n is q.m. Cauchy. Let T be its q.m. limit. Letting $m \to \infty$ in (3.10) we see that

$$E((T - T_n)^2) \leqslant A \sum_{i \geqslant n} c_i^{-2}$$

$$\leqslant \frac{A}{\ln^2 n} \sum_{i \geqslant n} c_i^{-2} \ln^2 i \leqslant \frac{Ac}{\ln^2 n}$$

for $n \geqslant 2$. Thus the sequence

$$E((T - T_{2^j})^2) = O(j^{-2})$$

is summable, from which it follows that $T_{2^j} \to T$ a.s.

Once it is established that $T_n \to T$ a.s., (3.8) follows via Kronecker's lemma (Neveu, 1965, p.147). To complete the proof that $T_n \to T$ a.s., it remains only to show that

$$\Delta_j = \max_{2^j < n \leqslant 2^{j+1}} |T_n - T_{2^j}| \to 0$$

a.s. as $j \to \infty$. For any $0 \leqslant m \leqslant j$, the sum $T_{2^{j+1}} - T_{2^j}$ of 2^j terms can be partitioned into 2^{j-m} blocks of 2^m terms each. Let V_{mk} be the kth such block. Clearly

$$T_n - T_{2^j} = \sum_m{}' V_{mk_m},$$

where the prime indicates that the sum need not include all m, and k_m is chosen appropriately. Hence, by the Schwarz inequality,

$$|T_n - T_{2^j}|^2 \leqslant \left(\sum_m{}' 1 \right) \left(\sum_m{}' V_{mk_m}^2 \right)$$

$$\leqslant (j+1) \sum_{m,k} V_{mk}^2.$$

Thus

$$\Delta_j^2 \leqslant (j+1) \sum_{m,k} V_{mk}^2,$$

so that

$$E(\Delta_j^2) \leqslant (j+1) \sum_{m,k} E(V_{mk}^2)$$

$$\leqslant (j+1) \sum_m A \sum_i c_i^{-2},$$

by (3.10), where $2^j \leqslant i < 2^{j+1}$. It follows that

$$E(\Delta_j^2) \leqslant A(j+1)^2 \sum_i c_i^{-2} \leqslant \frac{4A}{\ln^2 2} \sum_i c_i^{-2} \ln^2 i$$

for $j \geqslant 1$. Therefore

$$\sum_{j=1}^{\infty} E(\Delta_j^2) \leqslant \frac{4A}{\ln^2 2} c < \infty,$$

and $\Delta_j \to 0$ a.s. as $j \to \infty$. ■

5.4. Estimation of σ^2

If $\sigma^2 > 0$ and s is a consistent estimator of σ^2, it follows from Theorem 2.3 that

$$(S_n - ny)/(ns)^{\frac{1}{2}} \sim N(0, 1). \tag{4.1}$$

This fact can serve as a basis for inference about y. Norman's (1971b) discussion of inference about the mean of a second order stationary time series extends easily to the case at hand. Although (4.1) does not presuppose stationarity of $\{Y_j\}_{j \geqslant 0}$, one expects the approximation to be better, for fixed n, when the process is nearly stationary than when it is not. Thus, in practice, it is advisable to disregard the initial, grossly transient, segment of the process. This amounts to considering a shifted process $\{Y_{N+j}\}_{j \geqslant 0}$, to which our assumptions are equally applicable, and which approaches stationarity as $N \to \infty$ according to Theorem 7.1.

The purpose of this section is to display a suitable estimator s and to estimate its mean square error. From among a number of closely related possibilities, we single out the truncated estimator

$$s = \sum_{|u| \leqslant t} \left(\frac{n - |u|}{n} \right) \hat{\rho}_u \tag{4.2}$$

[see (3.1) for $\hat{\rho}_u$] on the basis of its simplicity and small bias. The truncation point $t = t_n < n$ must be chosen judiciously. The danger of choosing t too large is amply illustrated by the fact that, if $t = n - 1$,

$$s = \frac{1}{n} \left(\sum_{j=0}^{n-1} (Y_j - Y.) \right)^2 = 0.$$

To achieve consistency, t should be small in comparison to n.

THEOREM 4.1. *$s \to \sigma^2$ in quadratic mean if $t \to \infty$ and $t/n \to 0$.*

THEOREM 4.2. *If*

$$0 < c < \ln(1/r(V)) \tag{4.3}$$

and

$$t - (1/2c)\ln n = O(1), \tag{4.4}$$

then

$$\frac{n}{\ln n} E((s-\sigma^2)^2) \to \frac{2\sigma^4}{c}. \tag{4.5}$$

For $r(V)$, see (2.2.4). Neither theorem requires $\sigma^2 > 0$, but, if this condition holds, (4.5) can be rewritten in the instructive form

$$E(((s/\sigma^2) - 1)^2) \sim 4t/n.$$

As we will see in Section 5.7, s is an example of a *spectral estimator*, and our proofs of the above theorems differ from arguments familiar in the theory of such estimators (Hannan, 1970, Chapter V) only in the simplifications attendant to this special case and the slight complications due to nonstationarity. A result concerning spectral estimators due to Parzen (1958, Eq. (5.6)) suggests that no estimator of σ^2 has mean square error of smaller order of magnitude than $(\ln n)/n$ under our assumptions.

Proofs. As usual, we can assume that $U^\infty f = 0$. Clearly

$$s - \sigma^2 = \varDelta + \varepsilon - \delta_1 - \delta_2, \tag{4.6}$$

where

$$\varDelta = \sum_{|u| \leqslant t} \frac{n - |u|}{n} (\rho_u{}^* - \rho_u),$$

$$\varepsilon = \sum_{|u| \leqslant t} \frac{n - |u|}{n} \varepsilon_u$$

[for $\rho_u{}^*$ and ε_u see (3.2), (3.3), and (3.4)]

$$\delta_1 = \sum_{|u| \leqslant t} (|u|/n)\rho_u,$$

and

$$\delta_2 = \sum_{|u| > t} \rho_u.$$

We postpone until later the proof that

$$(n/t) E(\varDelta^2) \to 4\sigma^4 \tag{4.7}$$

as $t \to \infty$ and $t/n \to 0$. As a consequence of (3.5),

$$E^{1/2}(\varepsilon^2) \leqslant \sum_{|u| \leqslant t} \frac{n - |u|}{n} E^{1/2}(\varepsilon_u^2)$$

$$\leqslant \frac{1}{n} \sum_{|u| \leqslant t} \left(\frac{n - |u|}{n} \right)^{1/2} \leqslant \frac{2t+1}{n}.$$

Thus

$$E(\varepsilon^2) = o(t/n) \tag{4.8}$$

if $t/n \to 0$. Clearly

$$|\delta_1| \leqslant (1/n) \sum_{u=-\infty}^{\infty} |u| \, |\rho_u|;$$

hence

$$\delta_1^2 = o(t/n) \tag{4.9}$$

as $n \to \infty$. Also

$$|\delta_2| \leqslant \sum_{|u| > t} |\rho_u| \leqslant 2D\alpha^{t+1}/(1 - \alpha),$$

so that

$$\delta_2^2 = O(\alpha^{2t}). \tag{4.10}$$

Theorem 4.1 follows immediately from (4.6) and (4.7)–(4.10). If t satisfies (4.4), where $\alpha = e^{-c}$, then (4.10) yields

$$\delta_2^2 = o(t/n). \tag{4.11}$$

Using this in conjunction with (4.7)–(4.9) and (4.6), we get

$$\lim (n/t) E((s - \sigma^2)^2) = \lim (n/t) E(\Delta^2) = 4\sigma^4,$$

and (4.5) follows on noting that

$$t \sim (1/2c) \ln n.$$

Inequalities (4.3) are equivalent to $1 > \alpha > r(V)$.   ■

   The remainder of the section is devoted to the proof of (4.7). Since

$$\rho_u^* - \rho_u = \frac{1}{n - |u|} \sum_{\substack{i,j=0 \\ j-i=u}}^{n-|u|} (Y_i Y_j - \rho_u),$$

$$\frac{n}{t} E(\Delta^2) = \frac{1}{nt} \sum \sum E((Y_i Y_j - \rho_u)(Y_k Y_l - \rho_v)), \tag{4.12}$$

where

$$\sum\sum = \sum_{\substack{|u|,|v| \leq t}} \sum_{\substack{ijkl=0 \\ j-i=u \\ l-k=v}}^{n-|u|} .$$

Also,

$$E((Y_i Y_j - \rho_u)(Y_k Y_l - \rho_v)) = Q + a, \tag{4.13}$$

where

$$Q = E(Y_i Y_j Y_k Y_l)$$
$$= \rho_u \rho_v + \rho_{k-i} \rho_{l-j} + \rho_{l-i} \rho_{k-j} + q, \tag{4.14}$$

and

$$a = \rho_u \rho_v - E(Y_i Y_j)\rho_v - E(Y_k Y_l)\rho_u$$
$$= -\rho_u \rho_v + O(\alpha^{(i \vee j) + |v|} + \alpha^{(k \vee l) + |u|})$$
$$= -\rho_u \rho_v + O^* \tag{4.15}$$

by (2.8). Combining (4.13), (4.14), and (4.15), we obtain

$$E((Y_i Y_j - \rho_u)(Y_k Y_l - \rho_v)) = \rho_{k-i} \rho_{l-j} + \rho_{l-i} \rho_{k-j} + q + O^*.$$

In view of (4.12) it suffices to establish the following points:

$$(1/nt)\sum\sum \rho_{k-i} \rho_{l-j} = (1/nt)\sum\sum \rho_{l-i} \rho_{k-j} \to 2\sigma^4, \tag{4.16}$$

$$(1/nt)\sum\sum q \to 0, \tag{4.17}$$

and

$$(1/nt)\sum\sum O^* \to 0$$

as $t \to \infty$ and $t/n \to 0$. The last of these presents no difficulty, since

$$\sum\sum \alpha^{(i \vee j) + |v|} \leq \left(\sum_{i,j=0}^{n-1} \alpha^{i \vee j}\right)\left(\sum_{k,l=0}^{n-1} \alpha^{|k-l|}\right)$$
$$= O(1)O(n) = O(n)$$

and the other component of O^* is similarly bounded.

Proof of (4.17). Clearly

$$\left|\sum\sum q\right| \leq \sum_{ijkl=0}^{n-1} |q|.$$

According to (4.14), q is the difference between two terms, each of which are invariant under permutations of i, j, k, and l, so q also has this property.

Thus

$$\left|\sum\sum q\right| \leqslant 4! \sum{}' |q|, \tag{4.18}$$

where $\sum'$ is the sum over $0 \leqslant i \leqslant j \leqslant k \leqslant l \leqslant n-1$.
Over this range,

$$\rho_{k-i}\rho_{l-j} = O(\alpha^{l-i}) \tag{4.19}$$

and

$$\rho_{l-i}\rho_{k-j} = O(\alpha^{l-i}) \tag{4.20}$$

by (2.9). The equation preceding (2.6) gives

$$Q = E(Y_i Y_j)\rho_v + E(Y_i g(X_j)), \tag{4.21}$$

where

$$g = fV^{k-j}(fV^{l-k}f).$$

The first term on the right in (4.21) is

$$\rho_u \rho_v + O(\alpha^{j+l-k}),$$

as a consequence of (2.8) and (2.9), while the second is

$$E(Y_i U^{j-i}g(X_i)) = E(Y_i) U^{\infty}g + E(Y_i V^{j-i}g(X_i))$$
$$= O(\alpha^{i+l-j} + \alpha^{l-i}).$$

Thus

$$Q - \rho_u \rho_v = O(\alpha^{j+l-k} + \alpha^{i+l-j} + \alpha^{l-i}).$$

Substituting this estimate, (4.19), and (4.20) into (4.14), we obtain

$$q = O(\alpha^{j+l-k} + \alpha^{i+l-j} + \alpha^{l-i}).$$

Now $\sum'$ of each of these powers of α is $O(n)$. Hence $\sum' |q|$ and, by (4.18), $\sum\sum q$ are $O(n)$, and (4.17) follows.

Proof of (4.16). The equality in (4.16) is obtained by interchanging k and l and replacing $-v$ by v in $\sum\sum$.
The inner sum of the term on the left is

$$\sum_{\substack{i,k: \\ 0 \leqslant i, i+u, k, k+v < n}} \rho_{k-i}\rho_{k-i+v-u}.$$

If k is replaced by $i+d$, this reduces to

$$\sum_{d=-\infty}^{\infty} M_n(u,v,d)\rho_d \rho_{d+v-u},$$

where $M_n(u,v,d)$ is the number of i (possibly 0) such that

$$0 \leqslant i, i+u, i+d, i+d+v < n.$$

It is not difficult to show that

$$M_n(u,v,d) = \max(0, n-\beta),\qquad(4.22)$$

where

$$\beta = \max(0, u, d, d+v) - \min(0, u, d, d+v).$$

Introducing

$$I(x) = \begin{cases} 1, & |x| \leqslant 1, \\ 0, & |x| > 1, \end{cases}$$

we can write

$$(1/nt)\sum\sum \rho_{k-i}\rho_{l-j} = (1/nt)\sum_{uvd=-\infty}^{\infty} M_n(u,v,d)\,\rho_d\rho_{d+v-u}I(u/t)\,I(v/t).$$

Under the further change of variables $v = u+w$, this becomes

$$(1/nt)\sum\sum \rho_{k-i}\rho_{l-j} = \sum_{d,\,w=-\infty}^{\infty} \rho_d\rho_{d+w}F_n(d,w),\qquad(4.23)$$

where

$$F_n(d,w) = \frac{1}{t}\sum_{u=-\infty}^{\infty}\frac{M_n(u,u+w,d)}{n}\,I\!\left(\frac{u}{t}\right)I\!\left(\frac{u+w}{t}\right)\qquad(4.24)$$

$$= \int_{-\infty}^{\infty} A_n(y)\,dy$$

and $A_n(y)$ is the summand evaluated at $u = [yt]$.

It follows easily from (4.22) that the factor M_n/n of $A_n(y)$ converges to 1 as $n\to\infty$ and $t/n\to 0$. If $|y|\neq 1$, the other factor converges to $I^2(y) = I(y)$ as $t\to\infty$. Thus

$$A_n(y) \to I(y),$$

except on a set of Lebesgue measure 0, as $t\to\infty$ and $t/n\to 0$. Furthermore, $0\leqslant A_n(y)\leqslant 1$ for all n and y, and $A_n(y)=0$ if $|y|>2$ (for then $|u/t|>1$). Thus, by the dominated convergence theorem,

$$F_n(d,w) \to \int_{-\infty}^{\infty} I(y)\,dy = 2$$

as $t\to\infty$ and $t/n\to 0$, for every d and w.

Since $0 \leqslant M_n \leqslant n$, it is clear from (4.24) that

$$|F_n(d, w)| \leqslant (2t+1)/t \leqslant 3.$$

Also

$$\sum_{d, w = -\infty}^{\infty} |\rho_d \rho_{d+w}| = \left(\sum_{d = -\infty}^{\infty} |\rho_d| \right)^2 < \infty.$$

Thus the dominated convergence theorem can be applied to the right-hand side of (4.23) to obtain the limit

$$2 \sum_{d, w = -\infty}^{\infty} \rho_d \rho_{d+w} = 2\sigma^4$$

given in (4.16).

This completes the proof of (4.7).

5.5. A Representation of σ^2

To obtain (4.1), it was assumed that $\sigma^2 > 0$, so it is useful to have simple criteria for positivity of this constant. Since

$$|\rho_u| \leqslant \rho_0$$

for all u, positivity of ρ_0 is certainly necessary for positivity of σ^2, but, in general, it is not sufficient. Theorem 4.1 gives a representation of σ^2 that permits us to show (Theorem 4.2) that $\rho_0 > 0$ implies $\sigma^2 > 0$ for the important special case of indicator functions $f = I_B$ of $B \in \mathscr{B}$, provided, of course, that $I_B \in L$. It is anticipated that Theorem 4.1 will be useful for establishing positivity of σ^2 for other functions $f \in L$.

For any $g \in L$, let

$$J(g)(x) = \int K(x, dy)(g(y) - Ug(x))^2$$

$$= Ug^2(x) - (Ug)^2(x).$$

Clearly $J(g) \in L$. If $f \in L$ with $U^\infty f = 0$, let

$$f^* = \sum_{j=0}^{\infty} U^j f = \sum_{j=0}^{\infty} V^j f.$$

The series converges absolutely in L, and L is complete, so $f^* \in L$. Clearly

$$(I - U)f^* = f. \tag{5.1}$$

THEOREM 5.1. $\sigma^2 = U^\infty J(f^*)$.

This theorem generalizes a formula of Fréchet (1952, p.84) for finite Markov chains.

Proof

$$\sigma^2 = \sum_{j=-\infty}^{\infty} U^\infty (fV^{|j|}f) = U^\infty \left(\sum_{j=-\infty}^{\infty} fV^{|j|}f \right),$$

since the second series converges in L and U^∞ is continuous on L. But

$$\sum_{j=-\infty}^{\infty} V^{|j|}f = 2f^* - f = f^* + Uf^*$$

by (5.1), so that

$$\sum_{j=-\infty}^{\infty} fV^{|j|}f = (f^* - Uf^*)(f^* + Uf^*)$$

$$= (f^*)^2 - (Uf^*)^2.$$

Thus

$$\sigma^2 = U^\infty (f^*)^2 - U^\infty (Uf^*)^2$$

$$= U^\infty U(f^*)^2 - U^\infty (Uf^*)^2 = U^\infty J(f^*). \quad \blacksquare$$

Let ρ_0 and σ^2 correspond to $I_B \in L$, or, equivalently, to $f = I_B - b$, where $b = U^\infty I_B$. Clearly $0 \leqslant b \leqslant 1$ and

$$\rho_0 = U^\infty f^2 = b(1-b),$$

so $\rho_0 > 0$ is equivalent to $0 < b < 1$.

THEOREM 5.2. *If $0 < b < 1$, then $\sigma^2 > 0$.*

Proof. Assume $\sigma^2 = 0$. We will show that $b \in' (0,1)$.
First,

$$E(|f^*(X_{j+1}) - Uf^*(X_j)|^2) = E(J(f^*)(X_j))$$

$$= E(U^j J(f^*)(X_0))$$

$$= E(V^j J(f^*)(X_0))$$

by Theorem 5.1, so

$$E(|f^*(X_{j+1}) - Uf^*(X_j)|^2) = O(\alpha^j).$$

Using (5.1) to eliminate Uf^* on the left, and taking square roots, we obtain

$$E(|Y_j - (Y_j^* - Y_{j+1}^*)|) = O(\alpha^{j/2}),$$

where $Y_j = f(X_j)$ and $Y_j^* = f^*(X_j)$. Thus

$$E(|S_{n,n} - (Y_n^* - Y_{2n}^*)|) = O(\alpha^{n/2}),$$

where

$$S_{n,n} = \sum_{j=n}^{2n-1} Y_j,$$

so that

$$S_{n,n} - (Y_n^* - Y_{2n}^*) \to 0 \qquad (5.2)$$

in probability as $n \to \infty$.

For any $k, m \geqslant 0$,

$$E(Y_n^{*k} Y_{2n}^{*m}) = E(U^n(f^{*k}U^n f^{*m})(X_0))$$

$$\to p_k p_m$$

as $n \to \infty$, where $p_k = U^\infty f^{*k}$. Since $Y_n^* = O(1)$, it follows easily that there is a unique probability μ on the set R of real numbers such that $\int_{-\infty}^\infty \xi^j \mu(d\xi) = p_j$, and the distribution of (Y_n^*, Y_{2n}^*) converges (weakly) to $\mu \times \mu$ as $n \to \infty$. Therefore the distribution of $Y_n^* - Y_{2n}^*$ converges to v, where v is the distribution of $\xi - \eta$ when (ξ, η) has distribution $\mu \times \mu$. By (5.2), the distribution of $S_{n,n}$ also converges to v.

It follows that, for any $\varepsilon > 0$,

$$\liminf_{n \to \infty} P(|S_{n,n}| < \varepsilon) \geqslant v\{\xi: |\xi| < \varepsilon\}$$

$$= \mu \times \mu\{(\xi, \eta): |\xi - \eta| < \varepsilon\}$$

$$= \int \mu(d\eta)\mu\{\xi: |\xi - \eta| < \varepsilon\} = \delta.$$

For any η in the support of μ, the integrand is positive. Thus $\delta > 0$, and

$$P(|S_{n,n}| < \varepsilon) > 0$$

for all $n \geqslant N = N_\varepsilon$. Hence

$$G_n = \{\omega: |S_{n,n}(\omega)| < \varepsilon\} \neq \varnothing$$

for $n \geqslant N$. Let $\omega_0 \in G_N$ and $\omega_1 \in G_{N+1}$, so that

$$|S_{N+1,N+1}(\omega_1) - S_{N,N}(\omega_0)| < 2\varepsilon. \qquad (5.3)$$

Since

$$S_{n,n} = T_n - nb,$$

where

$$T_n = \sum_{j=n}^{2n-1} I_B(X_j),$$

(5.3) can be rewritten

$$|(T_{N+1}(\omega_1) - T_N(\omega_0)) - b| < 2\varepsilon.$$

But $T_n(\omega_i)$ is an integer, so b is within 2ε of an integer. Since this holds for all $\varepsilon > 0$, b is an integer, and $b \in' (0, 1)$. ∎

5.6. Asymptotic Stationarity

If the distribution μ_0 of X_0 is stationary, then $\{X_n\}_{n \geqslant 0}$ is a (strictly) stationary process, so $\{Y_n\}_{n \geqslant 0}$ is too. If μ_0 is not stationary, we still expect $\{Y_n\}_{n \geqslant 0}$ to be nearly stationary if a sufficient number of observations at the beginning of the process are disregarded. In other words, we expect the shifted process $\mathscr{Y}^N = \{Y_{N+n}\}_{n \geqslant 0}$ to approach stationarity as $N \to \infty$. Theorem 6.1 gives a result of this type.

THEOREM 6.1.   *The finite-dimensional distributions of $\mathscr{Y}^N$ converge weakly to those of a stationary process $\mathscr{Y}^\infty$ as $N \to \infty$.*

The proof is based on the following lemma, special cases of which have been noted and used in preceding sections.

LEMMA 6.1.   For any $k \geqslant 1$ and $g_0, \ldots, g_{k-1} \in L$,

$$F(x; g_0, \ldots, g_{k-1}) = E_x \left(\prod_{i=0}^{k-1} g_i(X_i) \right) \in L.$$

Proof of Lemma 6.1.   For $k = 1$ we get $F(\cdot; g_0) = g_0 \in L$. Suppose, inductively, that the assertion of the lemma holds for some $k \geqslant 1$. Then

$$F(x; g_0, \ldots, g_k) = E_x \left(\prod_{i=0}^{k-1} g_i(X_i) \, U g_k(X_{k-1}) \right)$$

$$= F(x; g_0', \ldots, g_{k-1}'), \qquad (6.1)$$

where $g_i' = g_i$ for $0 \leqslant i < k-1$, and

$$g_{k-1}' = g_{k-1} U g_k \in L.$$

By hypothesis, the function on the right in (6.1) belongs to L, so the assertion of the lemma holds for $k+1$. ∎

Proof of Theorem 6.1.   It follows immediately from the lemma that

$$E\left(\prod_{i=0}^{k-1} g_i(X_{N+i})\right) = E(F(X_N; g_0, \ldots, g_{k-1}))$$

$$\to U^\infty F(\cdot\,; g_0, \ldots, g_{k-1})$$

as $N \to \infty$. For any nonnegative integers $m_1, \ldots, m_K$, and distinct non-negative integers $n_1, \ldots, n_K$, we can apply this to $k-1 = \max(n_1, \ldots, n_K)$ and

$$g_i = \begin{cases} f^{m_j}, & i = n_j, \\ 1, & i \neq n_j, \quad \text{all } j, \end{cases}$$

to obtain convergence of

$$E\left(\prod_{j=1}^{K} Y_{N+n_j}^{m_j}\right).$$

Since the variables Y_n are bounded (by $|f|$), such convergence of moments implies weak convergence of the joint distribution

$$D^N(n_1, \ldots, n_K)$$

of

$$Y_{N+n_1}, \ldots, Y_{N+n_K}.$$

But the distributions $D^N(n_1, \ldots, n_K)$, for fixed N, are consistent, so the asymptotic distributions

$$D^\infty(n_1, \ldots, n_K)$$

are too. Thus there is a distribution D^∞ on R^∞ with these finite-dimensional distributions (Neveu, 1965, p.82). Clearly

$$D^N(n_1+1, \ldots, n_K+1) = D^{N+1}(n_1, \ldots, n_K),$$

so

$$D^\infty(n_1+1, \ldots, n_K+1) = D^\infty(n_1, \ldots, n_K),$$

and any process $\mathcal{Y}^\infty$ with distribution D^∞ is stationary.   ∎

5.7. Vector Valued Functions and Spectra

This section sketches some generalizations of the results of previous sections. Proofs are omitted, since they are slight extensions of arguments given earlier.

If I is a positive integer and $f_i \in L$ for $1 \leqslant i \leqslant I$, let

$$f = \begin{pmatrix} f_1 \\ \vdots \\ f_I \end{pmatrix}, \qquad y = \begin{pmatrix} U^\infty f_1 \\ \vdots \\ U^\infty f_I \end{pmatrix},$$

$$Y_n = f(X_n), \qquad Z_n = (1/\sqrt{n}) \sum_{j=0}^{n-1} (Y_j - y),$$

and

$$\mathrm{cov}(Y_n, Y_{n+u}) = E\big((Y_n - E(Y_n))(Y_{n+u} - E(Y_{n+u}))^*\big),$$

where $*$ indicates transposition. Then the limit

$$P_u = \lim_{n \to \infty} \mathrm{cov}(Y_n, Y_{n+u}) \tag{7.1}$$

exists, $P_u = O(\alpha^{|u|})$, the matrix

$$\Sigma = \sum_{u=-\infty}^{\infty} P_u \tag{7.2}$$

is positive semidefinite, and the distribution of Z_n converges to the multivariate normal distribution with mean 0 and covariance matrix Σ:

$$Z_n \sim N(0, \Sigma). \tag{7.3}$$

This multivariate central limit theorem can be proved by applying Theorem 2.3, the univariate case, to $\lambda^* f$, for each I-vector λ.

Just as in Theorem 6.1, the finite dimensional distributions of $\{Y_{N+n}\}_{n \geqslant 0}$ converge to those of a stationary process as $N \to \infty$.

In the remainder of the section, it is assumed that $L \subset B^c(X)$, rather than $B^r(X)$, and that L is closed under complex conjugation (denoted $\bar{f}$). If W and Y are complex valued random variables, let

$$\mathrm{cov}(W, Y) = E\big((W - E(W))(\overline{Y - E(Y)})\big).$$

For any $f, g \in L$, the limit

$$\rho_u(f, g) = \lim_{n \to \infty} \mathrm{cov}(f(X_n), g(X_{n+u}))$$

exists, and $\rho_u(f, g) = O(\alpha^{|u|})$. The j, kth element of the matrix P_u in (7.1) is $\rho_u(f_j, f_k)$. For real λ,

$$\sigma(f, g; \lambda) = (1/2\pi) \sum_{u=-\infty}^{\infty} \rho_u(f, g) e^{-iu\lambda}$$

is the *cross spectral density function of f and g*, and $\sigma(f, f; \lambda)$ is the *spectral density function of f*. See Hannan (1970) for a full discussion of spectra and their estimation. Note that

$$2\pi\sigma(f, f; 0) = \sigma^2$$

is the asymptotic variance in the univariate central limit theorem, while

$$2\pi\sigma(f_j, f_k; 0) = \Sigma_{jk}$$

is the j,kth element of the asymptotic covariance matrix of the multivariate central limit theorem (7.3). The quantity

$$w(f; \lambda) = \frac{1}{(2\pi n)^{1/2}} \sum_{j=0}^{n-1} f(X_j) e^{ij\lambda}$$

is the *finite Fourier transform* of $f(X_0), \ldots, f(X_{n-1})$. The following relation between the cross spectral density function and finite Fourier transform generalizes Theorem 2.2:

$$\operatorname{cov}(w(f; \lambda), w(g; \lambda)) = \sigma(f, g; \lambda) + O(1/n).$$

The natural estimator

$$\hat{\rho}_u(f, g) = \frac{1}{n - |u|} \sum_{\substack{j,k=0 \\ k-j=u}}^{n-1} (f(X_j) - f.)(\overline{g(X_k) - g.}),$$

where

$$f. = \frac{1}{n} \sum_{j=0}^{n-1} f(X_j),$$

converges to $\rho_u(f, g)$ in quadratic mean and almost surely as $n \to \infty$. The estimator

$$s(f, g; \lambda) = \frac{1}{2\pi} \sum_{|u| \leqslant t} \left(\frac{n - |u|}{n} \right) \hat{\rho}_u(f, g) e^{-iu\lambda},$$

which generalizes s in (4.2), converges to $\sigma(f, g; \lambda)$ in quadratic mean as $t \to \infty$ and $t/n \to 0$. If t is chosen in accordance with (4.3) and (4.4), and $-\pi < \lambda \leqslant \pi$,

$$\frac{n}{2t} E(|s(f, g; \lambda) - \sigma(f, g; \lambda)|^2)$$

$$\to \begin{cases} \sigma(f, f; \lambda)\sigma(g, g; \lambda) & \text{if } \lambda \neq 0, \pi, \\ \sigma(f, f; \lambda)\sigma(g, g; \lambda) + |\sigma(\bar{f}, g; \lambda)|^2 & \text{if } \lambda = 0, \pi, \end{cases}$$

as $n \to \infty$.

Let

$$J(f, g)(x) = \int K(x, dy)(f(y) - Uf(x))(\overline{g(y) - Ug(x)})$$

$$= Uf\bar{g}(x) - Uf(x)U\bar{g}(x),$$

and, if $U^\infty f = 0$,

$$f^\lambda = (2\pi)^{-\frac{1}{2}} \sum_{j=0}^{\infty} e^{ij\lambda} U^j f.$$

The representation

$$\sigma(f, g; \lambda) = U^\infty J(f^\lambda, g^\lambda)$$

generalizes Theorem 5.1.

6 ○ Functions of Events

Throughout this chapter $((X, \mathcal{B}), (E, \mathcal{G}), p, u)$ is a random system with complete connections and $\mathcal{S} = X_0, E_0, X_1, E_1, \ldots$ is an associated stochastic process. We are often interested in functions $g(E_n)$ of the event E_n, or, more generally, in functions $g(E_n, \ldots, E_{n+k-1})$ of the events on k successive trials. In the learning context, $g(E_n)$ might describe a subject's response on trial n, while $g(E_n, \ldots, E_{n+k-1})$ describes his responses on trials n through $n+k-1$. This chapter analyzes such processes.

6.1. The Process $X_n' = (E_n, X_{n+1})$

Any function of E_n can be regarded as a function of $X_n' = (E_n, X_{n+1})$ and $X_n'' = (X_n, E_n)$. In this section we obtain information about bounded functions of E_n by applying the theory of Chapter 5 to functions of the processes $\mathcal{X}' = \{X_n'\}_{n \geqslant 0}$ and $\mathcal{X}'' = \{X_n''\}_{n \geqslant 0}$, which are Markovian according to Theorems 1.2.2 and 1.2.3. We first consider $\mathcal{X}'$ for distance diminishing models whose state sequences are regular with respect to $L(X)$. Then we give comparable results for $\mathcal{X}'$ and $\mathcal{X}''$ for learning models in which $\mathcal{X}$ is regular with respect to $B(X)$.

98

Let U be the transition operator for a state sequence $\mathscr{X}$ of a distance diminishing model, let U' be the transition operator for $\mathscr{X}'$, and let $X' = E \times X$. For $f \in B(X')$ (real or complex) let

$$m'(f) = \sup_{e \in E} m(f(e, \cdot)),$$

$$\|f\|' = m'(f) + |f|,$$

and

$$L' = \{f \in B(X'): \|f\|' < \infty\}.$$

THEOREM 1.1. *If U is regular with respect to the norm $\|\cdot\|$ on $L(X)$, then $\mathscr{X}'$, U', L', and $\|\cdot\|'$ satisfy the assumptions of Chapter 5 [i.e., (a), (b), and (c) of Section 5.1 or the corresponding assumptions in the complex case considered in Section 5.7].*

It follows that all of the theorems of Chapter 5 are applicable to $f(X_n')$ if $f \in L'$. We now call attention to some interesting subclasses of L'. If $f(e, x) = g(e)h(x)$, where $g \in B(E)$ and $h \in L(X)$, then $f \in L'$. In fact, $|f| = |g| \, |h|$ and $m'(f) = |g| \, m(h)$, so $\|f\|' = |g| \, \|h\| < \infty$. If $f = h$ [i.e., $g(e) \equiv 1$], then $m'(f) = m(h)$ and $\|f\|' = \|h\|$. If $f = g$ [i.e., $h(x) \equiv 1$], then $m'(f) = 0$ and $\|f\|' = |g|$. Thus $B(E)$ and $L(X)$ are naturally isometrically embedded in L', and all theorems of Chapter 5 are applicable to $g(E_n)$, $g \in B(E)$, and to $h(X_n)$, $h \in L(X)$. In the latter case, these results can be obtained more simply by applying the same theorems to $\mathscr{X}$, U, $L(X)$, and $\|\cdot\|$. So the primary interest in Theorem 1.1 is that it gives asymptotic properties of $g(E_n)$.

COROLLARY. *All of the results of Chapter 5 are applicable to $g(E_n)$ for $g \in B(E)$.*

Proof of Theorem 1.1. By Theorem 1.2.2, assumption (a) of Section 5.1 is satisfied. We omit the elementary verification of (b) (and its complex analog).

If $f \in L'$,

$$f'(x) - f'(y) = \int p(x, de) \left(f(e, u(x, e)) - f(e, u(y, e)) \right)$$

$$+ \int (p(x, de) - p(y, de)) f(e, u(y, e)),$$

so that (1.2.10) yields

$$m'(U'f) = m(f') \leqslant m'(f) r_1 + 2|f| R_1.$$

Thus U' is a bounded linear operator on L'.

If U is aperiodic with limit U^∞, let

$$U'^\infty f(e, x) = U^\infty f'(x). \tag{1.1}$$

Then

$$\|U'''f - U'^\infty f\|' = \|U^{n-1}f' - U^\infty f'\|$$

by (1.2.11), so that

$$\|U'''f - U'^\infty f\|' \leqslant \|U^{n-1} - U^\infty\| \|f'\|$$

$$\leqslant \|U^{n-1} - U^\infty\| \|U'\|' \|f\|'.$$

Thus $\|U'''^n - U'^\infty\| \to 0$ as $n \to \infty$.

It follows immediately from (1.1) that, if $U^\infty h$ is constant for each $h \in L(X)$, $U'^\infty f$ is constant for each $f \in L'$. This completes the verification of (c).

Finally, it is clear that, when $L' \subset B^c(X')$, L' is closed under conjugation (with $\|\bar f\|' = \|f\|'$). ∎

There are interesting learning models whose transition operators U are regular with respect to the norm $|\cdot|$ on $B(X)$. Finite state models furnish many examples, and Suppes' stimulus sampling model for a continuum of responses is another. Criteria for regularity in this sense are given in the last paragraph of Section 3.7 and in Theorem 4.1.2. According to Theorem 1.2 below, such regularity is inherited by both U' and U''.

THEOREM 1.2. *If U is regular on $B(X)$, then the assumptions of Chapter 5 are satisfied by $\mathscr{X}'$, U', $L' = B(X')$, and $\|\cdot\|' = |\cdot|$, and by $\mathscr{X}''$, U'', $L'' = B(X'')$, and $\|\cdot\|'' = |\cdot|$. As a consequence, all results of Chapter 5 are applicable to $g(E_n)$ for $g \in B(E)$.*

Proof. Only (c) need be checked. If U'^∞ is defined by (1.1),

$$\|U'''f - U'^\infty f\|' = |U^{n-1}f' - U^\infty f'|$$

by (1.2.11). Thus

$$\|U'''f - U'^\infty f\|' \leqslant |U^{n-1} - U^\infty| |f'|$$

$$\leqslant |U^{n-1} - U^\infty| \|f\|',$$

so $\|U'''^n - U'^\infty\|' \to 0$. Clearly $U'^\infty f$ is constant. The case of U'' can be treated similarly, using (1.2.12) instead of (1.2.11). ∎

6.2. Unbounded Functions of Several Events

The approach of the last section to limit theorems for functions of the event sequence $\mathscr{E} = \{E_n\}_{n \geqslant 0}$ was limited to bounded functions of a single event. In this section we obtain a strong law of large numbers and a central limit theorem for functions of several events satisfying suitable integrability conditions. Our approach leans heavily on that of Iosifescu and Theodorescu

(1969, proofs of Theorems 2.2.12 and 2.2.22), though their terminology differs slightly from ours.

DEFINITION 2.1.   A random system with complete connections is *uniformly aperiodic* if there is a function r on $X \times \mathscr{G}^\infty$ such that

$$\phi_N = \sup_{\substack{x \in X \\ A \in \mathscr{G}^\infty}} |p_\infty(x, S^{-N}A) - r(x, A)| \to 0$$

as $N \to \infty$. If $r(x, A) = r(A)$ does not depend on x, it is *uniformly regular*.

The probability $p_\infty(x, S^{-N} \cdot)$ is the distribution of $\mathscr{E}^N = \{E_{n+N}\}_{n \geq 0}$ when $X_0 = x$ a.s. The Vitali–Hahn–Saks theorem (Neveu, 1965, Corollary IV.2.1) ensures that $r(x, \cdot)$ is a probability on $\mathscr{G}^\infty$, and, clearly, $r(x, S^{-1}A) = r(x, A)$. Thus the sequence $\mathscr{E}^\infty = \{F_n\}_{n \geq 0}$ of coordinate functions on E^∞ is a stationary process with respect to $r(x, \cdot)$. This probability is understood whenever $\mathscr{E}^\infty$ appears below.

Theorem 2.1 links uniform aperiodicity and uniform regularity of learning models to aperiodicity and regularity of their transition operators.

THEOREM 2.1.   *A learning model is uniformly aperiodic (uniformly regular) if U is aperiodic (regular) on $B(X)$. Then $r(x, A) = U^\infty p_\infty(x, A)$ and $\phi_N = O(\alpha^N)$, where $\alpha < 1$. The same conclusions obtain if U is aperiodic or regular on $L(X)$ in a distance diminishing model.*

Proof.   Let $r(x, A)$ be defined as above. Then

$$|p_\infty(x, S^{-N}A) - r(x, A)| = |U^N p_\infty(x, A) - U^\infty p_\infty(x, A)|,$$

by (1.2.9); hence

$$|p_\infty(x, S^{-N}A) - r(x, A)| \leq \begin{cases} |V^N| \, |p_\infty(\cdot, A)| & \text{if } U \text{ is aperiodic on } B(X), \\ \|V^N\| \, \|p_\infty(\cdot, A)\| & \text{if } U \text{ is aperiodic on } L(X), \end{cases}$$

$$\leq D\alpha^N \begin{cases} 1, \\ R_\infty + 1, \end{cases}$$

by (2.2.5). Theorem 2.1.1 says that $R_\infty < \infty$ for a distance diminishing model.

The definition of r ensures that it does not depend on its first variable when U is regular.   ∎

The strong law of large numbers and central limit theorem given in Theorems 2.3 and 2.4 apply to uniformly regular models. Theorem 2.2 is of a rather different kind and applies to uniformly aperiodic models. Under the hypotheses of Theorem 2.1, ϕ_N converges to 0 geometrically, so the hypotheses $\sum \phi_N < \infty$ and $\sum \phi_N^{1/2} < \infty$ of Theorems 2.2 and 2.4, respectively, are certainly satisfied.

For $A \in \mathscr{G}^\infty$, let T be the total number of trials N for which $\mathscr{E}^N \in A$, i.e.,

$$T = \sum_{N=0}^{\infty} I_A(\mathscr{E}^N),$$

and let

$$h(x) = E_x(T).$$

THEOREM 2.2.   *If a model is uniformly aperiodic with $\sum_{N=0}^{\infty} \phi_N < \infty$, and if $r(\cdot, A) = 0$, then h is the unique bounded measurable function such that*

$$U^n h(x) \to 0 \qquad (2.1)$$

as $n \to \infty$ for all x, and

$$h = p_\infty(\cdot, A) + Uh. \qquad (2.2)$$

If the model is distance diminishing, $h \in L(X)$.

If U is aperiodic on $B(X)$ or $L(X)$, (2.1) is equivalent to $U^\infty h = 0$. Thus, for a distance diminishing model, h is the unique bounded Lipschitz function such that $U^\infty h = 0$ and (2.2) holds. If (X, d) is compact and U is absorbing according to Definition 3.6.1, the conditions $r(\cdot, A) = 0$ and $U^\infty g = 0$ are equivalent to $p_\infty(a_i, A) = 0$ and $g(a_i) = 0$ for all absorbing states a_i.

Proof

$$h(x) = \sum_{N=0}^{\infty} p_\infty(x, S^{-N}A) \leqslant \sum_{N=0}^{\infty} \phi_N < \infty,$$

so $h \in B(X)$. [In the distance diminishing case,

$$\|p_\infty(\cdot, S^{-N}A)\| = O(\alpha^N),$$

so $h \in L(X)$.] The series converges uniformly, so

$$U^n h(x) = \sum_{N=0}^{\infty} U^n p_\infty(x, S^{-N}A)$$

$$= \sum_{N=0}^{\infty} p_\infty(x, S^{-(N+n)}A).$$

Thus $Uh = h - p_\infty(\cdot, A)$, which is (2.2), and

$$|U^n h| \leqslant \sum_{N=n}^{\infty} \phi_N \to 0$$

as $n \to \infty$.

If, on the other hand, $h' \in B(X)$ and satisfies (2.1) and (2.2), let $\Delta = h - h'$.

Then $\Delta \in B(X)$ and $\Delta = U\Delta$ by (2.2), so that

$$\Delta(x) = U^n \Delta(x) = U^n h(x) - U^n h'(x) \to 0$$

as $n \to \infty$ for all x. Thus $\Delta = 0$; i.e., $h = h'$. ∎

THEOREM 2.3. *If a model is uniformly regular, and if g is $\mathscr{G}^k$ measurable with $\int |g| \, dr < \infty$, then*

$$(1/n) S_n = (1/n) \sum_{j=0}^{n-1} g_j \to y = \int g \, dr$$

a.s. as $n \to \infty$, where $g_j = g(E_j, \ldots, E_{j+k-1})$.

THEOREM 2.4. *If a model is uniformly regular with $\sum \phi_N^{1/2} < \infty$, and if $\int g^2 \, dr < \infty$, then the series*

$$\sigma^2 = \sum_{j=-\infty}^{\infty} \rho_j,$$

where

$$\rho_j = \int g \cdot g \circ S^{|j|} dr - y^2,$$

converges absolutely, $\sigma^2 \geqslant 0$, and

$$(S_n - ny)/\sqrt{n} \sim N(0, \sigma^2)$$

as $n \to \infty$.

In both theorems the distribution of X_0 is arbitrary. Note that

$$\int |g|^\beta dr \leqslant \liminf_{j \to \infty} E(|g_j|^\beta)$$

for any $\beta > 0$ [see Loève, 1963, (i) of 11.4A], since the distribution of $|g_j|^\beta$ converges to that of $|g(F_0, \ldots, F_{k-1})|^\beta$ as $n \to \infty$. Thus, for $\int |g|^\beta dr$ to be finite, it suffices that, for some initial distribution, $E(|g_j|^\beta)$ have a bounded subsequence.

The proofs of these theorems are based on the lemmas that follow. Lemma 2.1, which requires only uniform aperiodicity, permits us to transpose results from $\mathscr{E}^\infty$ to $\mathscr{E}$. Part (A) is relevant to Theorem 2.3, part (B) to Theorem 2.4.

LEMMA 2.1. (A) If A is a tail event ($A \in \mathscr{T} = \bigcap_{n=0}^{\infty} \mathscr{G}_n$, where $\mathscr{G}_n = \{S^{-n}A : A \in \mathscr{G}^\infty\}$), then $p_\infty(x, A) = r(x, A)$ for all $x \in X$.

(B) If $\{a_n\}_{n \geqslant 0}$ is a sequence of real numbers, $\{b_n\}_{n \geqslant 0}$ is a sequence of positive numbers with $b_n \to \infty$ as $n \to \infty$,

$$T_n = \sum_{j=0}^{n-1} g_j^*, \qquad g_j^* = g(F_j, \ldots, F_{j+k-1}),$$

and

$$\Delta_n(t) = E_x(\exp it(S_n b_n^{-1} - a_n)) - E(\exp it(T_n b_n^{-1} - a_n)),$$

then $\Delta_n(t) \to 0$ as $n \to \infty$ for all real t.

Proof. (A) Since $A \in \mathcal{G}_n$, $A = S^{-n}B$ for some $B \in \mathcal{G}^\infty$. But $r(x, A) = r(x, B)$, so

$$|p_\infty(x, A) - r(x, A)| = |p_\infty(x, S^{-n}B) - r(x, B)| \leqslant \phi_n.$$

Since $\phi_n \to 0$ as $n \to \infty$, (A) is proved.

(B) Let $0 \leqslant m \leqslant n$. Then

$$|\Delta_n(t)| \leqslant E_x(|\exp it(S_m b_n^{-1}) - 1|) + E(|\exp it(T_m b_n^{-1}) - 1|)$$
$$+ |E_x(\exp it((S_n - S_m) b_n^{-1} - a_n)) - E(\exp it((T_n - T_m) b_n^{-1} - a_n))|$$
$$\leqslant c_x(m, n) + d(m, n) + 2\phi_m$$

by (1.1.4), where $c_x(m, n)$ and $d(m, n) \to 0$ as $n \to \infty$. Thus

$$\limsup_{n \to \infty} |\Delta_n(t)| \leqslant 2\phi_m$$

for all $m \geqslant 0$. This implies (B). ∎

Subsequent lemmas assume uniform regularity.

LEMMA 2.2. The process $\mathscr{E}^\infty$ is mixing, in the sense that, for any $j \geqslant 1$, $B \in \mathcal{G}^j$, and $A \in \mathcal{G}_{j+N}$,

$$|r(B \cap A) - r(B)r(A)| \leqslant \phi_N r(B).$$

Proof. For any $C \in \mathcal{G}^\infty$,

$$P_x(\mathscr{E}^{n+N+1} \in C | E_n, \ldots, E_0)$$
$$= E_x(P(\mathscr{E}^{n+N+1} \in C | X_{n+1}, E_n, \ldots) | E_n, \ldots, E_0)$$
$$= E_x(p_\infty(X_{n+1}, S^{-N}C) | E_n, \ldots, E_0)$$
$$= p_\infty(u(x, E_0, \ldots, E_n), S^{-N}C) \quad \text{a.s.}$$

Thus

$$|P_x(\mathscr{E}^{n+N+1} \in C | E_n, \ldots, E_0) - r(C)| \leqslant \phi_N \quad \text{a.s.}$$

If $A = S^{-(j+N)}C$, $B \in \mathcal{G}^j$, and $m = n - j + 1 \geqslant 0$, it follows that

$$|P_x(\mathscr{E}^m \in B \cap A) - P_x(\mathscr{E}^m \in B)r(A)|$$
$$= |P_x(\mathscr{E}^m \in B, \mathscr{E}^{n+N+1} \in C) - P_x(\mathscr{E}^m \in B)r(C)|$$
$$= |E_x(I_{\mathscr{E}^m \in B}[P_x(\mathscr{E}^{n+N+1} \in C | E_n, \ldots, E_0) - r(C)])|$$
$$\leqslant P_x(\mathscr{E}^m \in B)\phi_N.$$

The desired inequality is then obtained by letting n (and hence m) approach infinity on the extreme right and left. ∎

LEMMA 2.3. The tail field $\mathcal{T}$ is trivial according to r.

Proof. Suppose that $A \in \mathcal{T}$, $B \in \mathcal{G}^j$. Then $A \in \mathcal{G}_{j+N}$, so, by Lemma 2.2,

$$|r(B \cap A) - r(B)r(A)| \leqslant \phi_N \to 0$$

as $N \to \infty$. Thus

$$r(B \cap A) = r(B)r(A). \tag{2.3}$$

But there is a sequence $B_i \in \mathcal{G}^{n_i}$ such that $r(A \Delta B_i) \to 0$ as $i \to \infty$; hence $r(B_i) \to r(A)$ and $r(B_i \cap A) \to r(A)$. Thus, applying (2.3) to B_i and letting $i \to \infty$, we obtain $r(A) = r^2(A)$; i.e. $r(A) = 0$ or 1. ∎

Conclusion of proof of Theorem 2.3. The process $\{g_n^*\}_{n \geqslant 0}$ is strictly stationary, and $E(|g_n^*|) < \infty$. If A is an invariant event for this process, it is a tail event for this process (Breiman, 1968, Proposition 6.32), hence for $\mathcal{E}^\infty$. Thus, by Lemma 2.3, $r(A) = 0$ or 1, and $\{g_n^*\}_{n \geqslant 0}$ is ergodic. Therefore, the ergodic theorem for stationary processes (Breiman, 1968, Theorem 6.28) implies that $T_n/n \to y$ with r probability 1. But the event $\lim_{n \to \infty} T_n/n = y$ (call it A) is a tail event for $\mathcal{E}^\infty$, so, by (A) of Lemma 2.1,

$$P_x(S_n/n \to y) = p_\infty(x, A) = r(A) = 1,$$

for all $x \in X$. The same result for an arbitrary initial distribution is obtained by conditioning on X_0. ∎

Conclusion of proof of Theorem 2.4. There is a stationary process $\{g_n'\}_{n=-\infty}^\infty$ such that $\{g_n'\}_{n=0}^\infty$ and $\{g_n^*\}_{n=0}^\infty$ have the same distribution. It follows easily from Lemma 2.2 that g_n' satisfies the similar condition (I) of Ibragimov (1962), with

$$\phi(n) = \begin{cases} \phi_{n-k} & \text{for } n \geqslant k, \\ 1 & \text{for } n < k. \end{cases}$$

Since $\sum \phi(n)^{1/2} < \infty$, $E(g_n') = y$, and

$$E(g_n'^2) = \int g^2 \, dr < \infty,$$

Ibragimov's Theorem 1.5 (see also the first paragraph of its proof) is applicable to $x_j = g_j' - y$, and yields all conclusions of Theorem 2.4, but with T_n in place of S_n. The latter difference is unessential according to (B) of Lemma 2.1. ∎

Part II ○ SLOW LEARNING

7 ○ Introduction to Slow Learning

7.1. Two Kinds of Slow Learning

Consider a learning model $((X, \mathscr{B}), (E, \mathscr{G}), p, u)$ with state sequence X_n. There are at least two different types of slow learning. If the probability

$$P(X_{n+1} \neq X_n | X_n = x) = p(x, \{e : u(x, e) \neq x\})$$

of any change in x is small, we say that learning occurs *with small probability*. If, on the other hand, $|\Delta X_n|$ is small, or, alternatively, $|u(x, e) - x|$ is small, then we say that learning occurs *by small steps*. Note that the formulation of the latter notion requires that X be a subset of a normed linear space. In fact, all of our results on learning by small steps pertain to subsets of finite-dimensional Euclidean spaces.

In order to study X_n when $P(X_{n+1} \neq X_n | X_n)$ or ΔX_n is "small," we consider families of processes X_n^ρ, indexed by a "learning rate" parameter ρ, such that these quantities are of the order of magnitude of ρ. The limiting behavior of X_n^ρ, suitably normalized, as $\rho \to 0$ is then sought. The alternative notations c, θ, and τ are used for ρ, the first in connection with small probability and the last two for small steps.

109

Learning with small probability is normally attributable to large probability of events with identity operators [$u(x,e) = x$ for all x]. In the five-operator models introduced in Section 0.1, the last coordinate of e can be taken to be a variable k whose value (1 or 0) indicates whether conditioning is effective or ineffective (C_1 or C_0). An identity operator applies whenever conditioning is ineffective. The possibility of ineffective conditioning can be introduced into any model $((X, \mathcal{B}), (E, \mathcal{G}), p, u)$ as follows. Let $X' = X$, $E' = E \times \{0, 1\}$, $u'(x, (e, 1)) = u(x, e)$, $u'(x, (e, 0)) \equiv x$, and

$$p'(x, G \times \{k\}) = \begin{cases} \displaystyle\int\!\!\int_G p(x, de)\, c_e & \text{if } k = 1, \\[2ex] \displaystyle\int_G p(x, de)\,(1 - c_e) & \text{if } k = 0, \end{cases}$$

where c_e is a measurable mapping of E into $[0, 1]$, which represents the probability of effective conditioning given e. To study small values of c_e, we assume that $c_e = cd_e$, where $0 \leqslant c$, $d_e \leqslant 1$. The function $d.$ is regarded as fixed, and limits are taken as $c \to 0$.

If K_c is the transition kernel for state sequences in the model described above, then

$$K_c(x, B) = (1 - c)\,\delta_x(B) + cK_1(x, B). \tag{1.1}$$

[*Proof.* By definition $K_c(x, B) = p'(x, B^*)$, where

$$B^* = \{e' : u'(x, e') \in B\}.$$

But

$$B^* \cap \{e' : k = 1\} = \{e : u(x, e) \in B\} \times \{1\}$$

and

$$B^* \cap \{e' : k = 0\} = \begin{cases} \varnothing & \text{if } x \in' B, \\[1ex] E \times \{0\} & \text{if } x \in B. \end{cases}$$

Thus

$$K_c(x, B) = \int_{u(x, e) \in B} p(x, de)\,c_e + \delta_x(B)\left(1 - \int_E p(x, de)\,c_e\right),$$

from which linear dependence on c is apparent. ∎]

Equation (1.1) is the starting point for the theory of learning with small probability presented in the next section.

Learning by small steps usually involves step size parameters θ_e that are analogous to the step probability parameters c_e. Such parameters may be introduced into a learning model $((X, \mathscr{B}), (E, \mathscr{G}), p, u)$ by defining new event operators $u'(\cdot, e)$ as follows:

$$u'(x, e) - x = \theta_e(u(x, e) - x)$$

or, equivalently,

$$u'(x, e) = (1 - \theta_e)x + \theta_e u(x, e).$$

This operator maps into X if X is a full linear space, or if X is convex and $0 \leqslant \theta_e \leqslant 1$.

For examples, we turn to five-operator models, where the event e is of the form $A_i O_j C_k$ or, more compactly, (i, j, k). The state space $[0, 1]$ for the linear model is convex, and we may take $\theta_e = k\theta_{ij}$, and $u(x, e) = j$ for all x if $k = 1$. The state space $(-\infty, \infty)$ of the additive model is linear, and we may take $\theta_e = kb_{ij}$, and $u(x, e) - x = 1$ for all x if $k = 1$.

To study small values of θ_e, it is assumed that $\theta_e = \theta\eta_e$, where $\theta > 0$ (and $\eta_e \geqslant 0$ if X is only convex). The function $\eta_.$ is fixed, and small values of θ are considered. If X_n^θ is a state sequence in such a model, it follows that the conditional distribution, given $X_n^\theta = x$, of the normalized increment $H_n^\theta = \Delta X_n^\theta/\theta$ does not depend on θ:

$$\mathscr{L}(H_n^\theta | X_n^\theta = x) = \mathscr{L}(x). \tag{1.2}$$

For

$$P(H_n^\theta \in A | X_n^\theta = x) = p(x, \{e : (u'(x, e) - x)/\theta \in A\})$$

$$= p(x, \{e : \eta_e(u(x, e) - x) \in A\}).$$

The theory of learning by small steps presented below encompasses slightly more general dependence on θ than the prototypical case (1.2). The need for greater generality is seen by noting that not only u but also X and p depend on $\theta = s/N$ in the fixed sample size model. Furthermore, it is often convenient to reformulate a model in terms of a transformed state variable $h = h(x)$ [e.g., $p = p(x)$ in additive models] and the dependence of the transformed state sequence on θ may be slightly more complex than (1.2).

Conditions (1.1) and (1.2) refer only to state sequences, and this is characteristic of other conditions to be given later. Thus it is natural to frame the theory of slow learning as a collection of limit theorems for certain families of Markov processes. Applications to various special models then appear as implications of rather general results.

7.2. Small Probability

Let K be any transition kernel in a measurable space $(X, \mathscr{B})$, and, for any $0 < c \leqslant 1$, let $K_c = (1 - c)\delta_x + cK$. We are interested in the limiting behavior of $K_c^{(n)}$ as $c \to 0$. The following construction shows us what to expect.

If $\{X_j\}_{j \geqslant 0}$ is a Markov process with kernel K, $\{Y_k\}_{k \geqslant 1}$ is a sequence of random variables with $P(Y_k = 1) = c$ and $P(Y_k = 0) = 1 - c$ that are independent of each other and of $\{X_j\}$, and $S(n) = \sum_{k=1}^{n} Y_k$, then $X_n^c = X_{S(n)}$ is Markovian with kernel K_c. Let $N(t)$, $t \geqslant 0$, be a Poisson process with mean interevent time 1 that is independent of $\{X_j\}$. As $c \to 0$ and $nc \to t$ the binomial distribution $B(n, c)$ of $S(n)$ converges to the Poisson distribution $P(t)$ of $N(t)$. Thus it is to be expected that the distribution $K_c^{(n)}(x, \cdot)$ of X_n^c converges to the distribution $L_t(x, \cdot)$ of $X_{N(t)}$. Theorem 2.1 shows somewhat more than this. Clearly

$$K_c^{(n)}(x, B) = \sum_{j=0}^{n} b_j K^{(j)}(x, B) \tag{2.1}$$

and

$$L_t(x, B) = \sum_{j=0}^{\infty} p_j K^{(j)}(x, B), \tag{2.2}$$

where

$$b_j = \binom{n}{j} c^j (1 - c)^{n-j} \quad \text{and} \quad p_j = e^{-t}(t^j/j!).$$

The limiting Markov process $X_{N(t)}$ is of pseudo-Poisson type (Feller, 1971, p. 322).

THEOREM 2.1. *For all $x \in X$, $B \in \mathcal{B}$, $0 < c \leqslant 1$, and $n \geqslant 0$,*

$$|K_c^{(n)}(x, B) - L_{nc}(x, B)| \leqslant nc(1 - e^{-c}). \tag{2.3}$$

Proof. By (2.1) and (2.2),

$$K_c^{(n)}(x, B) - L_{nc}(x, B) = \sum_{j=0}^{\infty} (b_j - p_j) K^{(j)}(x, B)$$

($b_j = 0$ for $j > n$), thus

$$K_c^{(n)}(x, B) - L_{nc}(x, B) \leqslant \sum_{j : b_j > p_j} (b_j - p_j)$$

$$= |B(n, c) - P(nc)|/2.$$

Replacing B by $\tilde{B}$ we obtain

$$|K_c^{(n)}(x, B) - L_{nc}(x, B)| \leqslant |B(n, c) - P(nc)|/2. \tag{2.4}$$

So (2.3) follows from the form of the Poisson theorem given by Lemma 2.1. ∎

LEMMA 2.1. $|B(n,c) - P(nc)|/2 \leqslant nc(1-e^{-c})$.   (2.5)

Proof. If P_i and Q_i are any Borel probabilities on the line,

$$|P_1 * P_2 - Q_1 * Q_2| \leqslant |P_1 - Q_1| + |P_2 - Q_2|,$$ (2.6)

where $*$ denotes convolution. For

$$P_1 * P_2 - Q_1 * Q_2 = P_1 * (P_2 - Q_2) + (P_1 - Q_1) * Q_2$$

and

$$\begin{aligned}
|P_1 * (P_2 - Q_2)(B)| &= \left| \int P_1(dx)(P_2 - Q_2)(B-x) \right| \\
&\leqslant \sup_x |(P_2 - Q_2)(B-x)| \\
&\leqslant |P_2 - Q_2|/2,
\end{aligned}$$

so that

$$|P_1 * (P_2 - Q_2)| \leqslant |P_2 - Q_2|.$$

Using (2.6) inductively we obtain

$$|P^{*n} - Q^{*n}| \leqslant n|P-Q|.$$

Since $B(1,c)^{*n} = B(n,c)$ and $P(c)^{*n} = P(nc)$, this yields

$$|B(n,c) - P(nc)| \leqslant n|B(1,c) - P(c)|.$$

But

$$|B(1,c) - P(c)|/2 = \sum_{j:b_j > p_j} (b_j - p_j),$$

where $b_j = B(1,c)(\{j\})$ and $p_j = P(c)(\{j\})$, and

$$b_0 = 1 - c < e^{-c} = p_0,$$

so

$$|B(1,c) - P(c)|/2 = b_1 - p_1 = c(1-e^{-c}). \quad \blacksquare$$

The bounds in (2.3) and (2.5) are useful only when n is not too large relative to $1/c$, as, for example, when nc is bounded or converges to $t < \infty$. Using the fact that the distribution functions of $B(n,c)$ and $P(nc)$ both approximate the normal distribution function with mean and variance nc when nc is large and c is small, it can be shown that

$$\sup_{n \geqslant 0} |B(n,c) - P(nc)| \to 0$$

as $c \to 0$. Thus, according to (2.4),

$$\sup_{n,x,B} |K_c^{(n)}(x,B) - L_{nc}(x,B)| \to 0$$

as $c \to 0$. For explicit bounds, see Vervaat (1969).

7.3. Small Steps: Heuristics

The assumptions of the theory of learning by small steps will be spelled out in detail in subsequent chapters, but enough was said in Section 7.1 to support an informal discussion of the kinds of results to be obtained in Chapters 8 and 9. Let $\{X_n^\theta\}_{n \geqslant 0}$ be a state sequence corresponding to the value θ of the learning rate parameter. In general, X_n^θ is an N-dimensional random (column) vector. We do not work directly with X_n^θ in Chapter 8, but, rather, with a linear normalization

$$Z_n^\theta = (X_n^\theta - f(n\theta))/\sqrt{\theta},$$

where the function f is defined in (B) of Theorem 8.1.1. In Chapter 9, no spatial normalization is necessary. The time scales in Chapters 8 and 9 must also be handled differently. Let $\tau = \theta$ and $Y_n^\tau = Z_n^\theta$ in the former case, and let $\tau = \theta^2$ and $Y_n^\tau = X_n^\theta$ in the latter. Just as in the case of learning with small probability, we will obtain approximations to $\mathscr{L}(Y_n^\tau)$ (the distribution of Y_n^τ) by distributions of the form $\mathscr{L}(Y(n\tau))$, where $Y(t)$, $t \geqslant 0$, is a Markov process with continuous time parameter. However, unlike the pseudo-Poisson limit $X_{N(t)}$ in the previous case, the process $Y(t)$ is a *diffusion*; i.e., it has continuous sample paths. This reflects the basic assumption that ΔX_n^θ is small when θ is small.

We will see in subsequent chapters that the variables Y_n^τ satisfy the fundamental equations

$$E(\Delta Y_n^\tau | Y_n^\tau = y) = \tau a(y,n,\tau) + o(\tau),$$

$$E((\Delta Y_n^\tau)^2 | Y_n^\tau = y) = \tau b(y,n,\tau) + o(\tau), \tag{3.1}$$

and

$$E(|\Delta Y_n^\tau|^3 | Y_n^\tau = y) = o(\tau),$$

where $y^2 = yy^*$, $|y|^2 = y^*y$ (* indicates transposition),

$$a(y,n,\tau) \rightarrow a(y,t), \quad \text{and} \quad b(y,n,\tau) \rightarrow b(y,t) \tag{3.2}$$

as $\tau \rightarrow 0$ and $n\tau \rightarrow t$. For any t and τ, let $n = [t/\tau]$ and $Y^\tau(t) = Y_n^\tau$. Then $Y^\tau(t+\tau) = Y_{n+1}^\tau$, so (3.1) can be rewritten

$$\tau^{-1}E(Y^\tau(t+\tau) - Y^\tau(t)|Y^\tau(t) = y) = a(y,n,\tau) + o(1),$$

$$\tau^{-1}E((Y^\tau(t+\tau) - Y^\tau(t))^2|Y^\tau(t) = y) = b(y,n,\tau) + o(1), \tag{3.3}$$

and

$$\tau^{-1}E(|Y^\tau(t+\tau) - Y^\tau(t)|^3 | Y^\tau(t) = y) = o(1).$$

Now $n\tau \to t$ as $\tau \to 0$, so (3.2) applies and (3.3) suggests that

$$\mathscr{L}(Y^\tau(t)) \to \mathscr{L}(Y(t)) \tag{3.4}$$

as $\tau \to 0$, where $Y(t)$ is a diffusion such that

$$\lim_{\tau \to 0} \tau^{-1} E(Y(t+\tau) - Y(t)|Y(t) = y) = a(y,t),$$

$$\lim_{\tau \to 0} \tau^{-1} E((Y(t+\tau) - Y(t))^2|Y(t) = y) = b(y,t), \tag{3.5}$$

and

$$\lim_{\tau \to 0} \tau^{-1} E(|Y(t+\tau) - Y(t)|^3 |Y(t) = y) = 0.$$

More generally, we might expect convergence of the higher-dimensional distributions,

$$\mathscr{L}(\{Y^\tau(t_j)\}_{j=1}^k) \to \mathscr{L}(\{Y(t_j)\}_{j=1}^k),$$

where $0 < t_1 < t_2 < \cdots < t_k$, or even convergence of the distribution, over a suitable function space, of entire trajectories of the process,

$$\mathscr{L}(Y^\tau(t), t \leqslant T) \to \mathscr{L}(Y(t), t \leqslant T)$$

as $\tau \to 0$. If, instead of $Y^\tau(t)$, we consider the *random polygonal curve* $\tilde{Y}^\tau(t)$ with vertices $\tilde{Y}^\tau(n\tau) = Y_n^\tau$, i.e.,

$$\tilde{Y}^\tau(t) = \left(\frac{(n+1)\tau - t}{\tau}\right) Y_n^\tau + \left(\frac{t - n\tau}{\tau}\right) Y_{n+1}^\tau$$

for $n\tau \leqslant t \leqslant (n+1)\tau$, the natural path space is the set $C([0,T])$ of continuous (vector valued) functions on $[0,T]$.

For the sake of simplicity, we will focus our attention on the distribution at a single value of t in the chapters that follow. The importance of this circle of ideas for us is that we shall now not be surprised to find that $\mathscr{L}(Y^\tau(t))$ converges when (3.1) and certain auxiliary conditions obtain. The characterization of the limit as $\mathscr{L}(Y(t))$, while intuitively satisfying, is not always convenient for proving convergence, so alternative descriptions of the limit will be used later. Furthermore, plausible though the transition from (3.1) to (3.4) may be, the theorems currently available to justify it (e.g., Theorem 1 on p. 460 of Gikhman and Skorokhod, 1969) do not cover the cases considered in subsequent chapters. Thus we will have to provide our own theorems of this type.

8 ○ Transient Behavior in the Case of Large Drift

8.1. A General Central Limit Theorem

We now introduce the notation and state precisely the assumptions of Theorem 1.1, which is a general central limit theorem for learning by small steps. Let J be a bounded set of positive real numbers with $\inf J = 0$. Let N be a positive integer, and let R^N be the set of N-tuples of real numbers, regarded as column vectors. For every $\theta \in J$, $\{X_n^\theta\}_{n \geqslant 0}$ is a Markov process with stationary transition probabilities and state space a subset I_θ of R^N. Let I be the smallest closed convex set including all I_θ, $\theta \in J$. Let H_n^θ be the normalized increment of X_n^θ,

$$H_n^\theta = \Delta X_n^\theta / \theta,$$

and let $w(x,\theta)$, $S(x,\theta)$, $s(x,\theta)$, and $r(x,\theta)$ be, respectively, its conditional mean vector, cross moment matrix, covariance matrix, and absolute third moment, given $X_n^\theta = x$:

$$w(x,\theta) = E(H_n^\theta | X_n^\theta = x),$$

$$S(x,\theta) = E((H_n^\theta)^2 | X_n^\theta = x),$$

$$s(x,\theta) = E((H_n^\theta - w(x,\theta))^2 | X_n^\theta = x)$$

$$= S(x,\theta) - w^2(x,\theta),$$

and

$$r(x,\theta) = E(|H_n^\theta|^3 | X_n^\theta = x).$$

116

Here $x^2 = xx^*$ and $|x|^2 = x^*x$ for $x \in R^N$, where * indicates transposition. For any $N \times N$ matrix A, let

$$|A|^2 = \sum_{i,j=1}^{N} a_{ij}^2.$$

We assume that I_θ approximates I as $\theta \to 0$ in the sense that, for any $x \in I$,

(a.1) $\lim_{\substack{\theta \to 0 \\ y \in I_\theta}} \inf |x - y| = 0.$

Next we suppose that there are functions $w(x)$ and $s(x)$ on I that approximate $w(x, \theta)$ and $s(x, \theta)$ when θ is small, and that, in the former case, the error is $O(\theta)$:

(a.2) $\sup_{x \in I_\theta} |w(x, \theta) - w(x)| = O(\theta)$

and

(a.3) $\varepsilon = \sup_{x \in I_\theta} |s(x, \theta) - s(x)| \to 0$

as $\theta \to 0$. Let

$$S(x) = s(x) + w^2(x).$$

The function w is assumed to be differentiable, in the sense that there is an $N \times N$ matrix valued function on I such that

(b.1) $\lim_{\substack{y \to x \\ y \in I}} \dfrac{|w(y) - w(x) - w'(x)\,(y - x)|}{|y - x|} = 0$

for all $x \in I$. We assume that $w'(x)$ is bounded,

(b.2) $\alpha = \sup_{x \in I} |w'(x)| < \infty,$

and that $w'(x)$ and $s(x)$ satisfy Lipschitz conditions,

(b.3) $\beta = \sup_{\substack{x, y \in I \\ x \neq y}} \dfrac{|w'(x) - w'(y)|}{|x - y|} < \infty$

and

(b.4) $\sup_{\substack{x, y \in I \\ x \neq y}} \dfrac{|s(x) - s(y)|}{|x - y|} < \infty.$

Finally, we suppose that $r(x, \theta)$ is bounded:

(c) $r = \sup_{\substack{\theta \in J \\ x \in I_\theta}} r(x, \theta) < \infty.$

As a consequence of (c), $|w(x, \theta)|$ is bounded, so that the *drift* $E(\Delta X_n^\theta | X_n^\theta = x)$ is of the order of magnitude of θ. The possibility

$$E(\Delta X_n^\theta | X_n^\theta = x) = O(\theta^2)$$

is not precluded. We refer to this as the case of *small drift*, while the general case is called the case of *large drift*. Note that $w(x, \theta) = O(\theta)$, so, by (a.2), $w(x) \equiv 0$, when the drift is small.

We can now survey briefly the main results of this and the next three chapters. Theorem 1.1 below describes the behavior of $\mathscr{L}(X_n^\theta)$ under the above assumptions, when θ is small and n is not too large, specifically, $n = O(1/\theta)$. Such a restriction on the size of n means that the theorem pertains to the transient behavior of the process $\{X_n^\theta\}_{n \geqslant 0}$. Theorem 9.1.1 gives an approximation to $\mathscr{L}(X_n^\theta)$ that is valid for larger values of n, $n = O(1/\theta^2)$, in certain families of processes with small drift. The final chapters of Part II provide small step approximations to the asymptotic behavior of real valued processes. Chapter 10 treats stationary probabilities, and Chapter 11 considers absorption probabilities.

For $\theta \in J$ and $x \in I_\theta$, let

$$\mu_n(\theta, x) = E_x(X_n^\theta)$$

and

$$\omega_n(\theta, x) = E_x(|X_n^\theta - \mu_n(\theta, x)|^2).$$

THEOREM 1.1. (A) $\omega_n(\theta, x) = O(\theta)$ *uniformly in* $x \in I_\theta$ *and* $n\theta \leqslant T$, *for any* $T < \infty$.

(B) *For any* $x \in I$, *the differential equation*

$$f'(t) = w(f(t)) \tag{1.1}$$

has a unique solution $f(t) = f(t, x)$ *with* $f(0) = x$. *For all* $t \geqslant 0$, $f(t) \in I$, *and*

$$\mu_n(\theta, x) - f(n\theta, x) = O(\theta) \tag{1.2}$$

uniformly in $x \in I_\theta$ *and* $n\theta \leqslant T$.

(C) *If* $x \in I$, *the matrix differential equation*

$$A'(t) = -w'(f(t, x))^* A(t) \tag{1.3}$$

has a unique solution $A(t) = A(t, x)$ *with* $A(0)$ *the identity matrix, and* $A(t)$ *is nonsingular. For any* $\theta \in J$, *let* $\{X_n^\theta\}_{n \geqslant 0}$ *have initial state* $x_\theta \in I_\theta$. *If* $x \in I$, *and* $x_\theta \to x$ *as* $\theta \to 0$, *then the distribution* $\mathscr{L}_n^\theta$ *of*

$$Z_n^\theta = (X_n^\theta - f(n\theta, x_\theta))/\sqrt{\theta}$$

converges to the normal distribution $\mathscr{L}(t, x)$ *with mean* 0 *and covariance matrix*

$$g(t, x) = \int_0^t [A(u) A(t)^{-1}]^* s(f(u)) [A(u) A(t)^{-1}] \, du \tag{1.4}$$

as $\theta \to 0$ *and* $n\theta \to t$.

The function $g(t) = g(t, x)$ can be characterized, like $f(t)$, as the unique solution of a differential equation with a given initial value. In this case, the equation is

$$g'(t) = w'(f(t))g(t) + g(t)w'(f(t))^* + s(f(t)),$$

and the initial value is 0.

Part (A) means that there is a constant C_T such that $\omega_n(\theta, x) \leqslant C_T \theta$ for all $\theta \in J$, $x \in I_\theta$, and $n \leqslant T/\theta$. In (B), (1.2) has an analogous interpretation. If d is any metric on probabilities over R^N such that $P_n \to P$ weakly implies $d(P_n, P) \to 0$ (e.g., Dudley's metric described in Section 2.2), it follows from (C) that

$$\sup_{\substack{n \leqslant T/\theta \\ |x_\theta| \leqslant T}} d(\mathcal{L}_n^\theta, \mathcal{L}(n\theta, x_\theta)) \to 0$$

as $\theta \to 0$. The routine argument, which we omit, is based on the compactness of the interval $0 \leqslant t \leqslant T$ and the ball $|x| \leqslant T$, and the joint weak continuity of $\mathcal{L}(t, x)$.

Another corollary of Theorem 1.1 is convergence of finite dimensional distributions

$$\mathcal{L}(Z_{n_1}^\theta, \ldots, Z_{n_k}^\theta)$$

as $\theta \to 0$ and $n_j \theta \to t_j$. If (c) is replaced by the stronger assumption

$$\sup_{\substack{\theta \in J \\ x \in I_\theta}} E(|H_n^\theta|^4 \,|\, X_n^\theta = x) < \infty,$$

it can also be shown that the distribution over $C([0, T])$ of the random polygonal curve $Z^\theta(t)$ with vertices $Z^\theta(n\theta) = Z_n^\theta$ converges weakly to the distribution of a diffusion as $\theta \to 0$.

If $I_\theta = I$ for all θ, (a.1) is certainly satisfied. And if, in addition, (7.1.2) holds, $w(x, \theta)$, $s(x, \theta)$, and $r(x, \theta)$ do not depend on θ, so (a.2) and (a.3) are satisfied, and the supremum over θ in (c) can be omitted. A simple and important example of this sort is the five-operator linear model with $\theta_{ij} = \theta \eta_{ij}$, where $\eta_{ij} \geqslant 0$ and $0 < \theta \leqslant \max^{-1} \eta_{ij}$. In this case, $w(x)$ and $s(x)$ are polynomials, so that (b) holds, and $|H_n| \leqslant \max \eta_{ij}$ a.s., so (c) does too. Thus Theorem 1.1 is applicable.

Another example satisfying $I_\theta = I$ and (7.1.2) is the standard multidimensional central limit theorem. Let $W_1, W_2, \ldots$ be a sequence of independent and identically distributed random vectors, and let

$$X_n^\theta = \theta \sum_{j=1}^n W_j$$

($X_0^\theta = 0$). Then $\{X_n^\theta\}_{n \geqslant 0}$ is a Markov process in $I = R^N$. Since $H_n^\theta = W_{n+1}$, we have

$$w(x, \theta) = E(W_j) = w,$$

$$s(x, \theta) = \text{covariance matrix of } W_j = s,$$

and

$$r(x, \theta) = E(|W_j|^3) = r.$$

Thus, assuming $r < \infty$, the remaining assumption (b) is trivially satisfied. Clearly $f(t, 0) = tw$ and $g(t, x) = ts$, so (C) with $x_\theta = x = 0$ and $\theta = 1/n$ gives

$$\left(\sum_{j=1}^n W_j - nw \right) \Big/ \sqrt{n} = Z_n^\theta \sim N(0, s)$$

as $n \to \infty$. This result falls short of the standard central limit theorem only because the assumption $r < \infty$ is stronger than necessary. In fact, the Lyapounov condition (c) can be replaced by the Lindeberg condition

$$\lim_{\substack{H \to \infty}} \sup_{\substack{\theta \in J \\ x \in I_\theta}} E(|H_n^\theta|^2 I_{|H_n^\theta| > H} | X_n^\theta = x) = 0\dagger$$

without altering the conclusions of Theorem 1.1, and this more general condition is equivalent to $E(|W_j|^2) < \infty$ in the case considered above.

Theorem 1.1 was stated by Norman (1968c, Theorem 3.1), and proved in the special case $N = 1$, $I_\theta = I$, and $\mathscr{L}(H_n^\theta | X_n^\theta = x) = \mathscr{L}(x)$. Proofs of (A) and (B) are given in Section 8.3, the proof of (C) in Section 8.4. The latter is rather different from the comparable proof (that of Theorem 2.3) in the paper mentioned above.

8.2. Properties of $f(t)$

A number of arguments in the proofs of (B) and (C) of Theorem 1.1 hinge on properties of $f(t)$ that follow from its characterization as the solution of (1.1). To avoid repeated interruptions of the main development, these properties are collected in this section. The simple proofs given are quite standard.

We consider first $w(x)$. For $x, y \in I$, and $0 \leqslant p \leqslant 1$, let $h(p) = w(x + p(y - x))$. It follows from (b.1) that

$$h'(p) = w'(x + p(y - x)) (y - x);$$

hence, by (b.3), h' is continuous. Thus the fundamental theorem of calculus gives

$$w(y) - w(x) = h(1) - h(0) = \int_0^1 w'(x + p(y - x)) \, dp \, (y - x), \quad (2.1)$$

$\dagger$ If $F \subset \Omega$, $I_F = I_F(\omega)$ is 1 or 0, depending on whether or not $\omega \in F$.

and (b.2) then implies that w is Lipschitz,

$$|w(y) - w(x)| \leqslant \alpha|y-x|. \tag{2.2}$$

Also,

$$w(y) - w(x) - w'(x)(y-x) = \int_0^1 \left(w'(x+p(y-x)) - w'(x)\right) dp\,(y-x),$$

so that

$$|w(y) - w(x) - w'(x)(y-x)| \leqslant (\beta/2)|y-x|^2 \tag{2.3}$$

as a consequence of (b.3). Now

$$|w(x,\theta)| \leqslant r(x,\theta)^{1/3} \leqslant r^{1/3} \tag{2.4}$$

[see (c)], from which it follows, via (a.1) and (a.2), that

$$|w(x)| \leqslant r^{1/3}. \tag{2.5}$$

If $I = R^N$, the method of successive approximations (see, for example, the proof of Theorem 6 in Chapter 6 of Birkhoff and Rota, 1969) can be used in conjunction with (2.2) to construct a solution $f(t) = f(t,x)$ to (1.1) with $f(0) = x$. The more devious existence proof for general I is given in the next section. Whether or not $I = R^N$, there is at most one solution. For if $f(t)$ and $\tilde{f}(t)$ both satisfy (1.1) and start at x, then

$$f(t) - \tilde{f}(t) = \int_0^t \left(w(f(u)) - w(\tilde{f}(u))\right) du,$$

so that

$$|f(t) - \tilde{f}(t)| \leqslant \alpha \int_0^t |f(u) - \tilde{f}(u)|\, du$$

by (2.2). Thus $f(t) = \tilde{f}(t)$ follows from this form of Gronwall's lemma (Hille, 1969, Corollary 2 of Theorem 1.5.7).

GRONWALL'S LEMMA. If $c, k \geqslant 0$, and $h(t) \geqslant 0$ is continuous, then

$$h(t) \leqslant c + k \int_0^t h(u)\, du$$

for $0 \leqslant t \leqslant T$ implies

$$h(t) \leqslant ce^{kt}$$

for $0 \leqslant t \leqslant T$.

Throughout the rest of the section we suppose that, for every $x \in I$, $f(t) = f(t, x)$ is a solution of (1.1) with $f(0) = x$. For $\delta > 0$

$$f(t+\delta) - f(t) = \delta \int_0^1 w(f(t+p\delta)) \, dp,$$

so

$$|f(t+\delta) - f(t)| \leqslant \delta r^{\frac{1}{3}} \tag{2.6}$$

by (2.5). Also,

$$f(t+\delta) - f(t) - \delta w(f(t)) = \delta \int_0^1 \big(w(f(t+p\delta)) - w(f(t)) \big) \, dp;$$

thus

$$|f(t+\delta) - f(t) - \delta w(f(t))| \leqslant \delta \alpha \int_0^1 |f(t+p\delta) - f(t)| \, dp$$

$$\leqslant (r^{\frac{1}{3}} \alpha / 2) \delta^2 \tag{2.7}$$

by (2.6).

Next, note that

$$f(t, y) - f(t, x) = (y - x) + \int_0^t \big(w(f(u, y)) - w(f(u, x)) \big) \, du. \tag{2.8}$$

Therefore,

$$|f(t, y) - f(t, x)| \leqslant |y - x| + \alpha \int_0^t |f(u, y) - f(u, x)| \, du,$$

so that

$$|f(t, y) - f(t, x)| \leqslant |y - x| e^{\alpha t} \tag{2.9}$$

by Gronwall's lemma. Returning to (2.8) we get

$$|(f(t, y) - f(t, x)) - (y - x)| \leqslant \alpha \int_0^t |f(u, y) - f(u, x)| \, du$$

$$\leqslant (e^{\alpha t} - 1)|y - x|. \tag{2.10}$$

Note that $(e^{\alpha t} - 1)/t$ is an increasing function of t; hence $e^{\alpha t} - 1 \leqslant Ct$, where $C = (e^{\alpha T} - 1)/T$, for $t \leqslant T$.

From (2.6) and (2.9) we get

$$|f(t, y) - f(u, x)| \leqslant |f(t, y) - f(u, y)| + |f(u, y) - f(u, x)|$$

$$\leqslant r^{\frac{1}{3}}|t - u| + e^{\alpha u}|y - x|,$$

which converges to 0 as $t \to u$ and $y \to x$. Thus $f(\cdot, \cdot)$ is jointly continuous.

The existence of solutions $A(t) = A(t, x)$ and $B(t) = B(t, x)$ of the linear differential equations (1.3) and

$$B'(t) = w'(f(t)) B(t) \tag{2.11}$$

with $A(0)$ and $B(0)$ the identity matrix can be proved by successive approximations, and, in view of (b.2), the uniqueness proof given above for (1.1) applies here also. Both $A(t)$ and $B(t)$ are invertible; in fact,

$$B(t)^* = A(t)^{-1}, \tag{2.12}$$

since

$$\frac{d}{dt} B(t)^* A(t) = \left(\frac{d}{dt} B(t)\right)^* A(t) + B(t)^* \frac{d}{dt} A(t) = 0$$

and $B(0)^* A(0)$ is the identity matrix. The matrix $B(t, x)$ is the differential at x of $f(t, \cdot)$, as we will see below. This fact is needed in Section 8.5.

Clearly,

$$F(t) = f(t, y) - f(t, x) - B(t, x)\,(y - x)$$

$$= \int_0^t \left[w(f(u, y)) - w(f(u, x)) - w'(f(u, x)) B(u, x)\,(y - x) \right] du$$

$$= \int_0^t \left[w(f(u, y)) - w(f(u, x)) - w'(f(u, x))\,(f(u, y) - f(u, x)) \right] du$$

$$+ \int_0^t w'(f(u, x)) F(u)\, du.$$

Thus

$$|F(t)| \leqslant (\beta/2) \int_0^t |f(u, y) - f(u, x)|^2\, du + \alpha \int_0^t |F(u)|\, du$$

by (2.3), so that

$$|F(t)| \leqslant (\beta/4\alpha)\,(e^{2\alpha T} - 1)\,|y - x|^2 + \alpha \int_0^t |F(u)|\, du$$

for $t \leqslant T$ by (2.9). Thus Gronwall's lemma gives

$$|F(t)| \leqslant (\beta/4\alpha)\,(e^{2\alpha T} - 1)\,|y - x|^2\, e^{\alpha t}$$

for $t \leqslant T$. Taking $T = t$ we obtain

$$|f(t, y) - f(t, x) - B(t, x)\,(y - x)| \leqslant (\beta/4\alpha)\, e^{\alpha t} (e^{2\alpha t} - 1)\,|y - x|^2. \tag{2.13}$$

8.3. Proofs of (A) and (B)

In the rest of this chapter, we use the notation K for bounds that do not depend on θ, n, and x (e.g., α, β, and r), and C for bounds that are valid for all x and $n\theta \leqslant T$. In this section the process $X_n = X_n^\theta$ has initial state $x \in I_\theta$, $H_n = \Delta X_n/\theta$, $\mu_n = \mu_n(\theta, x)$, $\omega_n = \omega_n(\theta, x)$, and $Y_n = X_n - \mu_n$.

Proof of (A).   Clearly

$$\omega_{n+1} = \omega_n + 2E(Y_n^* \Delta Y_n) + E(|\Delta Y_n|^2). \tag{3.1}$$

Since $X_n \in I$, and I is closed and convex, $\mu_n \in I$, and $w(\mu_n)$ is defined. We have

$$E(Y_n^* \Delta Y_n)/\theta = E\big(Y_n^*(H_n - w(\mu_n))\big)$$

since $E(Y_n^*) = 0$,

$$E(Y_n^* \Delta Y_n)/\theta = E\big(Y_n^*(w(X_n, \theta) - w(\mu_n))\big)$$

because $E(H_n | X_n) = w(X_n, \theta)$,

$$E(Y_n^* \Delta Y_n)/\theta = E\big(Y_n^*(w(X_n, \theta) - w(X_n))\big) + E\big(Y_n^*(w(X_n) - w(\mu_n))\big)$$

$$\leqslant E(|Y_n|\,|w(X_n, \theta) - w(X_n)|) + E(|Y_n|\,|w(X_n) - w(\mu_n)|)$$

$$\leqslant K\theta E(|Y_n|) + KE(|Y_n|^2)$$

by (a.2) and (2.2), and

$$E(Y_n^* \Delta Y_n)/\theta \leqslant K\theta + K\omega_n \tag{3.2}$$

since $E(|Y_n|) \leqslant (1 + \omega_n)/2$.

Finally,

$$E(|\Delta Y_n|^2)/\theta^2 \leqslant E(|H_n|^2)$$

$$= E(E(|H_n|^2 | X_n)) \leqslant K \tag{3.3}$$

as a consequence of (c). Using (3.2) and (3.3) in (3.1) we obtain

$$\omega_{n+1} \leqslant (1 + K\theta)\omega_n + K\theta^2,$$

which, on iteration, yields

$$\omega_n \leqslant K\theta^2 \sum_{j=0}^{n-1} (1 + K\theta)^j,$$

since $\omega_0 = 0$. Thus

$$\omega_n \leqslant \theta((1 + K\theta)^n - 1)$$

$$\leqslant \theta(e^{Kn\theta} - 1) \tag{3.4}$$

$$\leqslant \theta(e^{KT} - 1)$$

for $n\theta \leqslant T$. ∎

Proof of (B).   To begin with,

$$\Delta\mu_n/\theta = E(w(X_n, \theta)),$$

so that

$$|\Delta\mu_n/\theta - w(\mu_n)| \leqslant |E(w(X_n, \theta) - w(X_n))| + |E(w(X_n) - w(\mu_n))|.$$

As a consequence of (2.3),

$$\begin{aligned}
|E(w(X_n) - w(\mu_n))| &= |E(w(X_n) - w(\mu_n) - w'(\mu_n)(X_n - \mu_n))| \\
&\leqslant K\omega_n \\
&\leqslant C\theta,
\end{aligned}$$

by (A). Therefore,

$$|\Delta\mu_n - \theta w(\mu_n)| \leqslant C\theta^2. \tag{3.5}$$

If $f(t) = f(t, x)$ satisfies (1.1) with $f(0) = x$, then, according to (2.7) with $\delta = \theta$ and $t = n\theta$, $v_n = f(n\theta)$ also satisfies (3.5). Since $v_0 = x = \mu_0$, we expect to find $v_n \doteq \mu_n$. However, at this point the existence of $f(t, x)$ can only be guaranteed when $I = R^N$. Thus we shall extend $w(x)$ to all of R^N, define f in terms of the extended function, prove (1.2), and then show that $f(t) \in I$, so that f satisfies (1.1).

According to (2.2) and (2.5), $w(x)$ is bounded and Lipschitz. Thus all of the coordinate functions $w_j(x)$ of $w(x)$ are bounded Lipschitz real valued functions; hence they possess bounded Lipschitz extensions $W_j(x)$ to R^N (Dudley, 1966, Lemma 5). The function $W(x)$ with coordinates $W_j(x)$ maps R^N into R^N and satisfies (2.2) and (2.5) for suitable constants α and r. It follows that, for every $x \in I$ (in fact, for every $x \in R^N$), there is a unique function $f(t) = f(t, x)$ such that

$$f'(t) = W(f(t))$$

and $f(0) = x$, and that (2.7) holds with W in place of w. Thus, if $v_n = v_n(\theta, x) = f(n\theta, x)$,

$$v_{n+1} = v_n + \theta W(v_n) + k_n \theta^2, \tag{3.6}$$

where $|k_n| \leqslant K$.

Since $\mu_n \in I$, (3.5) can be rewritten in the form

$$\mu_{n+1} = \mu_n + \theta W(\mu_n) + c_n \theta^2, \tag{3.7}$$

$|c_n| \leqslant C$. Subtracting (3.6) from (3.7) and letting $d_n = \mu_n - v_n$, we obtain

$$d_{n+1} = d_n + \theta(W(\mu_n) - W(v_n)) + c_n \theta^2,$$

so that

$$|d_{n+1}| \leqslant (1 + K\theta)|d_n| + C\theta^2.$$

If $v_0 = \mu_0 = x \in I_\theta$, then $d_0 = 0$, so iteration yields

$$|d_n| \leqslant \theta C(e^{Kn\theta} - 1) \leqslant \theta C(e^{KT} - 1)$$

for $n\theta \leqslant T$, and (1.2) is proved.

Suppose now that $x \in I$ and $t > 0$. We wish to show that $f(t, x) \in I$, so that $f(\cdot, x)$ satisfies (1.1). As a consequence of (a.1), there is a function x on J such that $x_\theta \in I_\theta$ and $x_\theta \to x$ as $\theta \to 0$. If $n = [t/\theta]$ then $f(n\theta, x_\theta) \to f(t, x)$ as $\theta \to 0$. But

$$\mu_n(\theta, x_\theta) - f(n\theta, x_\theta) \to 0$$

by (1.2), so $\mu_n(\theta, x_\theta) \to f(t, x)$ as $\theta \to 0$. Since $\mu_n(\theta, x_\theta) \in I$ and I is closed, $f(t, x) \in I$, as claimed. ∎

8.4. Proof of (C)

In this section, $o(\theta)$ denotes a random variable such that

$$\max_{n \leqslant T/\theta} E(|o(\theta)|)/\theta \to 0$$

as $\theta \to 0$. The properties of $Z_n = Z_n^\theta$ that are crucial for (C) are given in the following lemma.

LEMMA 4.1.   For any $T > 0$,

$$E(\Delta Z_n | Z_n) = \theta a_n Z_n + o(\theta), \tag{4.1}$$

$$E((\Delta Z_n)^2 | Z_n) = \theta b_n + o(\theta), \tag{4.2}$$

and

$$E(|\Delta Z_n|^3 | Z_n) = o(\theta) \tag{4.3}$$

a.s. for $n\theta \leqslant T$, where $a_n = a_n^\theta = w'(v_n)$, $b_n = b_n^\theta = s(v_n)$, and $v_n = f(n\theta, x_\theta)$. Furthermore,

$$E(|Z_{n+m} - Z_n|^2) \leqslant \chi(m\theta) \tag{4.4}$$

if $(n+m)\theta \leqslant T$, where $\chi(t) = Ct$.

Proof

$$\zeta = E(\Delta Z_n | Z_n)/\sqrt{\theta} = w(X_n, \theta) - \Delta v_n/\theta$$
$$= (w(X_n, \theta) - w(X_n)) + (w(X_n) - w(v_n)) - (\Delta v_n/\theta - w(v_n)). \tag{4.5}$$

Therefore,

$$|\zeta| \leqslant K\theta + K|X_n - v_n| + K\theta \leqslant K(\theta + |X_n - v_n|)$$

by (a.2), (2.2), and (2.7), so that

$$|\zeta^2| = |\zeta|^2 \leqslant K(\theta^2 + |X_n - v_n|^2). \tag{4.6}$$

Now

$$\eta = E((\Delta Z_n)^2 | Z_n)/\theta = s(X_n, \theta) + \zeta^2;$$

thus

$$\eta - s(v_n) = (s(X_n, \theta) - s(X_n)) + (s(X_n) - s(v_n)) + \zeta^2,$$

and

$$|\eta - s(v_n)| \leqslant \varepsilon + K|X_n - v_n| + K(\theta^2 + |X_n - v_n|^2)$$

by (a.3), (b.4), and (4.6). Therefore,

$$E(|\eta - s(v_n)|) \leqslant \varepsilon + KE(|X_n - v_n|) + K(\theta^2 + E(|X_n - v_n|^2)).$$

But

$$E(|X_n - v_n|^2) = \omega_n(\theta, x_\theta) + |\mu_n(\theta, x_\theta) - v_n|^2 \leqslant C\theta \tag{4.7}$$

as a consequence of (A) and (1.2), so

$$\max_{n\theta \leqslant T} E(|\eta - s(v_n)|) \to 0$$

as $\theta \to 0$. This is (4.2).

From (4.5) and (2.3) we obtain

$$|\zeta - w'(v_n)(X_n - v_n)| \leqslant K\theta + K|X_n - v_n|^2;$$

thus

$$E(|\zeta/\sqrt{\theta} - w'(v_n)Z_n|) \leqslant C\sqrt{\theta}$$

as a consequence of (4.7). This implies (4.1).

Finally,

$$E(|Z_n|^3 | Z_n)/\theta^{3/2} \leqslant 4(r(x, \theta) + |\Delta v_n/\theta|^3) \leqslant K$$

by (c) and (2.6), and (4.3) follows.

Now $f(t, f(s, x)) = f(t + s, x)$, so

$$\sqrt{\theta}(Z_{n+m} - Z_n) = X_{n+m} - f(m\theta, X_n) + [(f(m\theta, X_n) - f(m\theta, v_n)) - (X_n - v_n)].$$

Thus

$$\sqrt{\theta}|Z_{n+m} - Z_n| \leqslant |X_{n+m} - f(m\theta, X_n)| + Cm\theta|X_n - v_n|$$

by (2.10), so that

$$\theta E(|Z_{n+m} - Z_n|^2 | X_n)/2 \leqslant \Gamma + C(m\theta)^2 |X_n - v_n|^2,$$

where

$$\Gamma = E(|X_{n+m} - f(m\theta, X_n)|^2 | X_n).$$

But

$$\Gamma = \omega_m(\theta, X_n) + |\mu_m(\theta, X_n) - \nu_m(\theta, X_n)|^2$$

$$\leqslant Cm\theta^2$$

by (3.4) and (1.2). Thus

$$E(|Z_{n+m} - Z_n|^2) \leqslant Cm\theta + C(m\theta)^2 E(|X_n - \nu_n|^2)/\theta \leqslant Cm\theta$$

if $(n+m)\theta \leqslant T$, by (4.7). ∎

Note that a_n^θ and b_n^θ are bounded and that

$$a_n^\theta \to a(t) \qquad \text{and} \qquad b_n^\theta \to b(t) \tag{4.8}$$

as $\theta \to 0$ and $n\theta \to t$, where $a(t) = w'(f(t, x))$ and $b(t) = s(f(t, x))$ are continuous. Thus (C) of Theorem 1.1 follows from Lemma 4.2.

LEMMA 4.2.   Suppose that $Z_n = Z_n^\theta$, $\theta \in J$, $n\theta \leqslant T$, is any family of stochastic processes in R^N, with $Z_0 = 0$, that satisfies (4.1)–(4.4). Suppose further that $a_n = a_n^\theta$ and $b_n = b_n^\theta$ are bounded, and that (4.8) obtains as $\theta \to 0$ and $n\theta \to t$, where $a(t)$ and $b(t)$ are continuous. Suppose, finally, that $\chi(t)$ is continuous with $\chi(0) = 0$. Then

$$Z_n \sim N(0, g(t))$$

as $\theta \to 0$ and $n\theta \to t$, where

$$g(t) = \int_0^t [A(u)A(t)^{-1}]^* b(u)[A(u)A(t)^{-1}] \, du,$$

and $A(t)$ is the solution of

$$A'(t) = -a(t)^* A(t)$$

with $A(0)$ the identity matrix.

Note that Lemma 4.2 does not assume that Z_n is Markovian. The lemma is proved below by a variant of the method of Rosén (1967a,b).

Proof.   Using the third-order expansion of $\exp(iu)$ for real u we obtain, for any $\lambda \in R^N$,

$$E(\exp(i\lambda^* \Delta Z_n)|Z_n) = 1 + i\lambda^* E(\Delta Z_n|Z_n)$$

$$- \lambda^* E((\Delta Z_n)^2 | Z_n)\lambda/2 + k|\lambda|^3 E(|\Delta Z_n|^3 | Z_n),$$

where $|k| \leqslant \frac{1}{6}$; hence

$$E(\exp(i\lambda^* \varDelta Z_n) | Z_n) = 1 + i\theta\lambda^* a_n Z_n - \theta\lambda^* b_n \lambda/2 + o(\theta)$$

by (4.1)–(4.3). Substituting this into

$$E(\exp(i\lambda^* Z_{n+1})) = E(\exp(i\lambda^* Z_n) E(\exp(i\lambda^* \varDelta Z_n) | Z_n)),$$

we obtain

$$E(\exp(i\lambda^* Z_{n+1})) = E(\exp(i\lambda^* Z_n)) + E(o(\theta))$$
$$+ \theta\lambda^* a_n E(\exp(i\lambda^* Z_n) i Z_n) - \theta\lambda^* b_n \lambda E(\exp(i\lambda^* Z_n))/2.$$

Summation over n then yields

$$E(\exp(i\lambda^* Z_n)) - 1 = \varepsilon + \sum_{j=0}^{n-1} \theta\lambda^* a_j E(\exp(i\lambda^* Z_j) i Z_j)$$
$$- \sum_{j=0}^{n-1} \theta\lambda^* b_j \lambda E(\exp(i\lambda^* Z_j))/2, \qquad (4.9)$$

where

$$\varepsilon = \sum_{j=0}^{n-1} E(o(\theta)). \qquad (4.10)$$

Let

$$h^\theta(\lambda, t) = E(\exp(i\lambda^* Z_n)), \qquad a^\theta(t) = a_n^\theta, \qquad \text{and} \qquad b^\theta(t) = b_n^\theta,$$

where $n = [t/\theta]$. Note that

$$\nabla h^\theta(\lambda, t) = \begin{pmatrix} \partial h^\theta(\lambda, t)/\partial\lambda_1 \\ \vdots \\ \partial h^\theta(\lambda, t)/\partial\lambda_N \end{pmatrix} = E(\exp(i\lambda^* Z_n) i Z_n).$$

In these notations, (4.9) becomes

$$h^\theta(\lambda, t) - 1 = \varepsilon + \int_0^{n\theta} \lambda^* a^\theta(u) \nabla h^\theta(\lambda, u) \, du$$
$$- \frac{1}{2} \int_0^{n\theta} \lambda^* b^\theta(u) \lambda h^\theta(\lambda, u) \, du. \qquad (4.11)$$

Let θ_k be a sequence in J that converges to 0. Suppose that, for all $t \leqslant T$, $\mathscr{L}(Z_n^\theta)$ converges weakly to a probability distribution $\mathscr{L}(t)$, when $\theta \to 0$ along this sequence. *We will show that $\mathscr{L}(t) = N(0, g(t))$.* This requires a somewhat lengthy argument.

Let $h(\lambda, t)$ be the characteristic function of $\mathscr{L}(t)$. Then $h^\theta(\lambda, t) \to h(\lambda, t)$. Furthermore, (4.4) yields

$$E(|Z_n|^2) \leqslant \max_{0 \leqslant u \leqslant T} \chi(u) = |\chi|, \qquad (4.12)$$

from which it follows that

$$\int |z|^2 \mathscr{L}(t)\,(dz) \leqslant |\chi|, \tag{4.13}$$

$$\nabla h(\lambda, t) = \int \exp(i\lambda^* z)\, iz \mathscr{L}(t)\,(dz), \tag{4.14}$$

and

$$\nabla h^\theta(\lambda, t) \to \nabla h(\lambda, t)$$

(see Loève, 1963, Theorem A, p. 183).

Next we show that $h(\lambda, \cdot)$ and $\nabla h(\lambda, \cdot)$ are continuous. Let $u > t$ and let $m = [u/\theta] - [t/\theta]$, so that $[u/\theta] = m + n$. Then

$$h^\theta(\lambda, u) - h^\theta(\lambda, t)$$
$$= E\big(\exp(i\lambda^* Z_n)\,(\exp(i\lambda^*(Z_{n+m} - Z_n)) - 1)\big),$$

so that

$$|h^\theta(\lambda, u) - h^\theta(\lambda, t)| \leqslant |\lambda|\, E(|Z_{n+m} - Z_n|)$$
$$\leqslant |\lambda|\, \chi(m\theta)^{\frac{1}{2}} \tag{4.15}$$

by (4.4). Letting $\theta \to 0$ along θ_k we obtain

$$|h(\lambda, u) - h(\lambda, t)| \leqslant |\lambda|\, \chi(u - t)^{\frac{1}{2}}. \tag{4.16}$$

Since $\chi(0) = 0$, $h(\lambda, \cdot)$ is continuous. Similarly,

$$(\nabla h^\theta(\lambda, u) - \nabla h^\theta(\lambda, t))/i = E\big[(\exp(i\lambda^* Z_{n+m}) - \exp(i\lambda^* Z_n))\, Z_n\big]$$
$$+ E\big[\exp(i\lambda^* Z_{n+m})\,(Z_{n+m} - Z_n)\big],$$

thus

$$|\nabla h^\theta(\lambda, u) - \nabla h^\theta(\lambda, t)| \leqslant |\lambda|\, E(|Z_{n+m} - Z_n|\,|Z_n|) + E(|Z_{n+m} - Z_n|)$$
$$\leqslant (|\lambda|\, \chi(n\theta)^{\frac{1}{2}} + 1)\, \chi(m\theta)^{\frac{1}{2}}$$

by the Schwarz inequality, and

$$|\nabla h(\lambda, u) - \nabla h(\lambda, t)| \leqslant (|\lambda|\,|\chi|^{\frac{1}{2}} + 1)\, \chi(u - t)^{\frac{1}{2}}.$$

As a consequence of (4.12)

$$|\nabla h^\theta(\lambda, t)| \leqslant E(|Z_n|) \leqslant |\chi|^{\frac{1}{2}},$$

so the integrands in (4.11) are bounded over u and θ. And, referring to (4.10),

$$|\varepsilon| \leqslant \sum_{j=0}^{n-1} E(|o(\theta)|)$$
$$\leqslant n\theta \max_{j \leqslant T/\theta} E(|o(\theta)|)/\theta \to 0$$

as $\theta \to 0$. Thus we can let $\theta \to 0$ along θ_k in (4.11) to obtain

$$h(\lambda, t) - 1 = \int_0^t \lambda^* a(u) \nabla h(\lambda, u) \, du - \tfrac{1}{2} \int_0^t \lambda^* b(u) \lambda h(\lambda, u) \, du.$$

Since the integrands are continuous in u, differentiation yields

$$\frac{\partial h}{\partial t}(\lambda, t) = \lambda^* a(t) \nabla h(\lambda, t) - \tfrac{1}{2} \lambda^* b(t) \lambda h(\lambda, t). \qquad (4.17)$$

To solve (4.17), let $\xi \in R^N$, $\lambda(t) = A(t) \xi$, and $F(t) = h(\lambda(t), t)$. Then

$$\lambda'(t) = -a(t)^* \lambda(t).$$

From this and (4.17) we obtain

$$F'(t) = \lambda'(t)^* \nabla h(\lambda, t) + \frac{\partial h}{\partial t}(\lambda, t)$$

$$= -\tfrac{1}{2} \lambda(t)^* b(t) \lambda(t) F(t).$$

The unique solution of this ordinary differential equation with $F(0) = h(\xi, 0) = 1$ is

$$h(\lambda(t), t) = \exp\left(-\tfrac{1}{2} \int_0^t \lambda(u)^* b(u) \lambda(u) \, du\right).$$

For $\xi = A(t)^{-1} \lambda$, $\lambda(t) = \lambda$, and $\lambda(u) = A(u) A(t)^{-1} \lambda$, so

$$h(\lambda, t) = \exp(-\tfrac{1}{2} \lambda^* g(t) \lambda),$$

the characteristic function of $N(0, g(t))$. Thus $\mathscr{L}(t) = N(0, g(t))$, *as claimed.*

Suppose now that there is some $t' \leqslant T$ such that $\mathscr{L}(Z_{n'}^\theta)$, where $n' = [t'/\theta]$, does not converge to $N(0, g(t'))$ as $\theta \to 0$. We will show that this leads to a contradiction.

There is a bounded continuous function G on R^N such that

$$E(G(Z_{n'}^\theta)) \nrightarrow \int G(z) \, N(0, g(t')) \, (dz) = l.$$

Hence, there is a $\delta > 0$ and, for every j, a $\theta_j' < 1/j$ such that

$$|E(G(Z_{n'}^\theta)) - l| \geqslant \delta \qquad (4.18)$$

if $\theta = \theta_j'$. Let $n = [t/\theta]$. Using (4.12) and the diagonal method, we can construct a subsequence θ_k of θ_j' such that $\mathscr{L}(Z_n^\theta)$ converges weakly to a probability $\mathscr{L}(t)$ as $\theta \to 0$ for all rational $t \leqslant T$. If $h(\lambda, t)$ is the characteristic function of $\mathscr{L}(t)$, (4.16) applies to rational t and u. Since $h(\lambda, \cdot)$ is uniformly continuous on the rationals, it has a unique continuous extension to all of

$[0, T]$, for which the same notation will be used. The extension satisfies (4.16); hence $h(\lambda, u) \to h(\lambda, t)$ uniformly in $|\lambda| \leqslant K$ as $u \to t$. Taking t irrational and u rational, the continuity theorem implies that $h(\lambda, t)$ is the characteristic function of a probability $\mathscr{L}(t)$ for all $0 \leqslant t \leqslant T$.

For any $0 \leqslant t, u \leqslant T$,

$$|h(\lambda, t) - h^\theta(\lambda, t)| \leqslant |h(\lambda, t) - h(\lambda, u)|$$
$$+ |h(\lambda, u) - h^\theta(\lambda, u)| + |h^\theta(\lambda, u) - h^\theta(\lambda, t)|.$$

Estimating the third term on the right by (4.15), taking u rational, and letting $\theta \to 0$ along θ_k we obtain

$$\limsup |h(\lambda, t) - h^\theta(\lambda, t)| \leqslant |h(\lambda, t) - h(\lambda, u)| + |\lambda| \chi(|u - t|)^{1/2}.$$

Since the right side converges to 0 as $u \to t$, $h^\theta(\lambda, t) \to h(\lambda, t)$ and thus $\mathscr{L}(Z_n^\theta) \to \mathscr{L}(t)$ for all $t \leqslant T$, as $\theta \to 0$ along θ_k. It follows that $\mathscr{L}(t) = N(0, g(t))$ for all $t \leqslant T$; in particular, for $t = t'$. Hence $\mathscr{L}(Z_{n'}^\theta) \to N(0, g(t'))$, and

$$E(G(Z_{n'}^\theta)) \to l$$

as $\theta \to 0$ along θ_k. Since θ_k is a subsequence of θ_j', this contradicts (4.18). Our conclusion is that $\mathscr{L}(Z_n^\theta) \to N(0, g(t))$ for all $t \leqslant T$ as $\theta \to 0$.

It remains only to relax the strict dependence of n on θ ($n = [t/\theta]$). Let n' be any integer between 0 and T/θ. As in (4.15),

$$|E(\exp(i\lambda^* Z_n)) - E(\exp(i\lambda^* Z_{n'}))| \leqslant |\lambda| \chi(|n\theta - n'\theta|)^{1/2},$$

which converges to 0 if $\theta \to 0$ and $n'\theta \to t$. Thus $\mathscr{L}(Z_{n'}) \to N(0, g(t))$. ∎

Alternative proof of Theorem 5.2.3. Lemma 4.2 can be used in place of the final two paragraphs of Section 5.2, which complete the proof of Theorem 5.2.3. This simple exercise throws additional light on that theorem, and provides an example of an application of Lemma 4.2 to a non-Markovian process.

In the notation of the final paragraphs of Section 5.2, we have a family $\{\zeta_j^n\}_{j=1}^q$ of normalized partial sums indexed by n, and we wish to show that $\zeta_q^n \sim N(0, \sigma^2)$ as $n \to \infty$. Taking the conditional expectation given ζ_j in (5.2.18) and letting $\theta = d/n$ we obtain

$$E((\Delta\zeta_j)^2 | \zeta_j) = \theta\sigma^2 + o(\theta).$$

It follows from (5.2.19) that

$$E(|\Delta\zeta_j|^3 | \zeta_j) = o(\theta),$$

and, if $\xi > \frac{1}{2}$, (5.2.17) yields

$$E(\Delta\zeta_j | \zeta_j) = o(\theta).$$

These equations are instances of (4.2), (4.3), and (4.1), where $a_j = 0$ and

$b_j = \sigma^2$. Thus (4.8) holds, with $a(t) = 0$ and $b(t) = \sigma^2$. From (5.2.16) we get

$$E(|\zeta_{j+k} - \zeta_j|^2) \leqslant Kk\theta,$$

which is (4.4) with $\chi(t) = Kt$. Thus Lemma 4.2 is applicable, and $g(t) = t\sigma^2$. Since $q\theta \to 1$ as $n \to \infty$, $\zeta_q \sim N(0, \sigma^2)$, as claimed. $\blacksquare$

8.5. Near a Critical Point

Instead of subtracting $f(n\theta, x_\theta)$, where $X_0^\theta = x_\theta$, from X_n^θ, as in (C) of Theorem 1.1, it is natural to consider the alternative normalization

$$z_n^\theta = (X_n^\theta - f(n\theta, x))/\sqrt{\theta},$$

where $x = \lim_{\theta \to 0} x_\theta$. Clearly

$$z_n^\theta = (X_n - f(n\theta, x_\theta))/\sqrt{\theta} + (f(n\theta, x_\theta) - f(n\theta, x))/\sqrt{\theta}.$$

The first term is asymptotically $N(0, g(t))$ by Theorem 1.1, and, since $z_0^\theta = (x_\theta - x)/\sqrt{\theta}$,

$$|(f(n\theta, x_\theta) - f(n\theta, x))/\sqrt{\theta} - B(n\theta) z_0^\theta| \leqslant C\sqrt{\theta}|z_0^\theta|^2$$

by (2.13). Since $B(\cdot)$ (see (2.11)) is continuous,

$$(f(n\theta, x_\theta) - f(n\theta, x))/\sqrt{\theta} \to B(t)z$$

as $\theta \to 0$, $n\theta \to t$, and $z_0^\theta \to z$. Thus Theorem 1.1 has the corollary

$$z_n^\theta \sim N(B(t)z, g(t)) = \mathscr{L}(t) \tag{5.1}$$

as $\theta \to 0$, $n\theta \to t$, and $z_0^\theta \to z$.

This result has special interest when x is a *critical point*, that is, a point such that $w(x) = 0$. In this case $f(t) \equiv x$, so that

$$z_n^\theta = (X_n^\theta - x)/\sqrt{\theta}. \tag{5.2}$$

Furthermore,

$$B(t) = e^{tw'(x)}, \tag{5.3}$$

$$A(t) = e^{-tw'(x)^*},$$

and

$$g(t) = \int_0^t e^{uw'(x)} s(x) e^{uw'(x)^*} du.$$

Note that $s(x) = S(x) - w^2(x) = S(x)$. In the case $N = 1$, $g(t) = ts(x)$ if

$w'(x) = 0$, and

$$g(t) = s(x)\,(e^{2tw'(x)} - 1)/2w'(x) \qquad (5.4)$$

if $w'(x) \neq 0$.

The result (5.1) suggests the possibility that, if $z_0^\theta \to z$,

$$\mathscr{L}_\infty^\theta = \lim_{n \to \infty} \mathscr{L}(z_n^\theta) \sim \lim_{t \to \infty} \mathscr{L}(t) = \mathscr{L}(\infty) \qquad (5.5)$$

as $\theta \to 0$. Elaborations of this statement assume rather different forms depending on the sign of $w'(x)$, so we examine the cases $w'(x) < 0$ and $w'(x) > 0$ separately.

If $w'(x) < 0$, then, according to (5.3) and (5.4), $B(t) \to 0$ and

$$g(t) \to \sigma^2 = s(x)/2|w'(x)|, \qquad (5.6)$$

so $\mathscr{L}(\infty) = N(0, \sigma^2)$. If x is the only critical point [hence $w(y) > 0$ for $y < x$ and $w(y) < 0$ for $y > x$], and if the asymptotic distribution $\mathscr{L}_\infty^\theta$ exists (perhaps in the sense of Cesaro convergence), then we expect it to be the unique stationary probability of the Markov process $\{z_n^\theta\}_{n \geqslant 0}$. A generalization of (5.5) that does not presuppose the existence of $\mathscr{L}_\infty^\theta$ or uniqueness of the stationary probability is

$$\mu_\theta \to N(0, \sigma^2) \qquad (5.7)$$

as $\theta \to 0$, where μ_θ is any stationary probability of z_n^θ, or, equivalently, the normalization (5.2) of any stationary probability of X_n^θ. We do not require $z_0^\theta \to z$ for (5.7), since μ_θ does not depend on z_0^θ and σ^2 does not depend on z. A theorem of this type is given in Section 10.1.

For any $y \in R^1$,

$$\mathscr{L}(t)\,(y, \infty) = \Phi\big((B(t)z - y)/(g(t))^{1/2}\big),$$

where Φ is the standard normal distribution function. If $w'(x) > 0$ and $s(x) > 0$, $g(t) \to \infty$ and

$$B(t)/(g(t))^{1/2} \to 1/\sigma;$$

thus

$$\lim_{t \to \infty} \mathscr{L}(t)\,(y, \infty) = \Phi(z/\sigma)$$

for all y. If $X_n^\theta \to \pm \infty$ a.s. as $n \to \infty$, then

$$\lim_{n \to \infty} \mathscr{L}(z_n^\theta)\,(y, \infty) = P(X_n^\theta \to \infty),$$

so (5.5) suggests

$$P(X_n^\theta \to \infty) \to \Phi(z/\sigma) \qquad (5.8)$$

as $\theta \to 0$ and $(x_\theta - x)/\sqrt{\theta} \to z$. A theorem of this type for additive models is proved in Section 14.5 with the aid of Theorem 11.2.1 and Lemma 5.1 below.

For proofs of (5.7) and (5.8), we need the following lemma about the moments of $\Delta z_n^\theta = \Delta X_n^\theta / \sqrt{\theta}$. The lemma is applicable to any N. Unlike Lemma 4.1, nothing is assumed about the distribution of z_0^θ; thus we are free to consider a stationary initial distribution later. Furthermore, $o(\theta)$ is a function of z_n and θ such that

$$\delta = \sup_{z_n} |o(\theta)|/\theta \to 0 \qquad (5.9)$$

as $\theta \to 0$.

LEMMA 5.1. If x is a critical point, then a.s.,

$$E(\Delta z_n | z_n) = \theta w'(x) z_n + o(\theta)(1 + |z_n|^2), \qquad (5.10)$$

$$E((\Delta z_n)^2 | z_n) = \theta s(x) + o(\theta)(1 + |z_n|^2), \qquad (5.11)$$

and

$$E(|\Delta z_n|^3 | z_n) = o(\theta). \qquad (5.12)$$

Proof. The proof is very similar to that of Lemma 4.1, but simpler. First,

$$\zeta = E(\Delta z_n | z_n)/\sqrt{\theta} = w(X_n, \theta)$$
$$= (w(X_n, \theta) - w(X_n)) + (w(X_n) - w(x)), \qquad (5.13)$$

so that

$$|\zeta| \leqslant K\theta + K\sqrt{\theta}|z_n|$$

by (a.2) of Section 8.1 and (2.2), and

$$|\zeta^2| \leqslant K\theta^2 + K\theta |z_n|^2. \qquad (5.14)$$

But

$$\eta = E((\Delta z_n)^2 | z_n)/\theta = s(X_n, \theta) + \zeta^2;$$

thus

$$\eta - s(x) = (s(X_n, \theta) - s(X_n)) + (s(X_n) - s(x)) + \zeta^2,$$

and

$$|\eta - s(x)| \leqslant \varepsilon + K\sqrt{\theta}|z_n| + K\theta^2 + K\theta |z_n|^2$$

by (a.3), (b.4), and (5.14), so that

$$|\eta - s(x)| \leqslant (\varepsilon + K\sqrt{\theta})(1 + |z_n|^2).$$

Thus $o(\theta)$ in (5.11) satisfies

$$|o(\theta)|/\theta \leqslant \varepsilon + K\sqrt{\theta}.$$

From (5.13) we get

$$|\zeta - w'(x)(X_n - x)| \leqslant K\theta + K\theta|z_n|^2$$

by (a.2) and (2.3). Thus

$$|\zeta/\sqrt{\theta} - w'(x)z_n| \leqslant K\sqrt{\theta}(1 + |z_n|^2),$$

which implies (5.10). Finally, (5.12) follows directly from (c) of Section 8.1. ∎

9 ○ Transient Behavior in the Case of Small Drift

9.1. Diffusion Approximation in a Bounded Interval

The corollary (8.5.1) of Theorem 8.1.1 gives an approximation to the distribution of X_n^θ when θ is small, $X_0^\theta = x_\theta$ is near a critical point x [i.e., a point such that $w(x) = 0$], and $n\theta$ is bounded. Some one-dimensional cases where $w'(x) \neq 0$ and where this approximation continues to be useful when $n\theta$ is unbounded are described roughly in Section 8.5, and will be discussed further in subsequent chapters. In the case of small drift [i.e., $w(x) \equiv 0$], all points of I are critical, and $w'(x) \equiv 0$. For a critical point x with $w'(x) = 0$, (8.5.1) gives

$$(X_n^\theta - x)/\sqrt{\theta} \sim N((x_\theta - x)/\sqrt{\theta}, \, n\theta s(x))$$

or

$$X_n^\theta \sim N(x_\theta, \, n\theta^2 s(x)),$$

which suggests that

$$\mathcal{L}(X_n^\theta) \to N(x, ts(x))$$

as $\theta \to 0$, $x_\theta \to x$, and $n\theta \to \infty$ in such a way that $n\theta^2 \to t$. If $s(x) > 0$ and I

137

is bounded, this conjecture is definitely wrong, since $\mathscr{L}(X_n^\theta)$ is confined to I and the normal distribution $N(x, ts(x))$ is not. However, we shall show in this chapter that $\mathscr{L}(X_n^\theta)$ does converge as $\theta \to 0$, $x_\theta \to x$, and $n\theta^2 \to t$, in many cases of slow learning with small drift in bounded intervals. The limiting distribution is $\mathscr{L}(X(t))$, where $X(t)$, $t \geqslant 0$, is a certain diffusion in I with $X(0) = x$.

Under hypotheses (a)–(c) of Section 8.1, with $w(x) \equiv 0$, the conditional moments of ΔX_n^θ are of the form

$$E(\Delta X_n | X_n = x) = O(\tau),$$
$$E((\Delta X_n)^2 | X_n = x) = \tau S(x) + o(\tau),$$

and

$$E(|\Delta X_n|^3 | X_n = x) = O(\tau^{3/2}),$$

where $\tau = \theta^2$. In order to describe the asymptotic behavior of X_n^θ as $n\tau \to t$, we must specify $E(\Delta X_n | X_n = x)$ more precisely as $\tau a(x) + o(\tau)$, and we must impose various conditions on $a(x)$ and $S(x)$ [which corresponds to $b(x)$ below]. These remarks serve to place the assumptions that follow within the framework of the preceding chapter. However, these assumptions are self-contained, and it is not necessary to refer to Chapter 8 in order to apply the theory in this chapter.

Let J be a bounded set of positive real numbers with infimum 0, and let $I = [d_0, d_1]$ be a closed bounded interval. For every $\tau \in J$, let K_τ be a transition kernel in a Borel subset I_τ of I. Corresponding Markov processes are denoted X_n^τ. Suppose that

$$E(\Delta X_n^\tau | X_n^\tau = x) = \tau a(x) + o(\tau),$$
$$E((\Delta X_n^\tau)^2 | X_n^\tau = x) = \tau b(x) + o(\tau), \tag{1.1}$$

and

$$E(|\Delta X_n^\tau|^3 | X_n^\tau = x) = o(\tau),$$

where $o(\tau)$ is uniform over I_τ; i.e.,

$$\sup_{x \in I_\tau} |o(\tau)| / \tau \to 0$$

as $\tau \to 0$. It is assumed that a has three (bounded) continuous derivatives throughout I ($a \in C^3$). We emphasize that $a^{(j)}(x)$, $j = 1, 2, 3$, exists and is continuous even at the boundaries $x = d_i$. Furthermore, $a(d_0) \geqslant 0$ and $a(d_1) \leqslant 0$.

Our conditions on b are rather unusual but, nonetheless, quite general, as we will see. It is assumed that b admits a factorization

$$b(x) = \sigma_0(x)\sigma_1(x), \tag{1.2}$$

where $\sigma_i \in C^3$, $\sigma_i(d_i) = 0$, $\sigma_i(x) > 0$ for $d_0 < x < d_1$,

$$p(x) = \sigma_0(x)/(\sigma_0(x) + \sigma_1(x))$$

is nondecreasing over this interval, and, letting

$$p(d_i) = \lim_{x \to d_i} p(x),$$

$p \in C^3$. These conditions imply that $b \in C^3$, $b(d_i) = 0$, and $b(x) > 0$ for $d_0 < x < d_1$.

A very broad class of functions b having suitable factorizations are those of the form

$$b(x) = (x - d_0)^j (d_1 - x)^k h(x), \tag{1.3}$$

where j and k are positive integers, $h \in C^3$, and $h(x) > 0$ for all $x \in I$. Let

$$\sigma_0(x) = (x - d_0)^j (h(x))^{1/2}$$

and

$$\sigma_1(x) = (d_1 - x)^k (h(x))^{1/2}.$$

Since $\sqrt{h}$ is in C^3, σ_i is too; since σ_0/σ_1 is increasing, p is also increasing; and since $\sigma_0 + \sigma_1$ is positive throughout I, $p \in C^3$. Another interesting class of examples are those with $b(d_i) = 0$, $b(x) > 0$ on (d_0, d_1), and $\sqrt{b} \in C^3$. Here we can take $\sigma_i = \sqrt{b}$ to obtain $p(x) \equiv \frac{1}{2}$.

Let $\mathscr{B}$ be the collection of Borel subsets of I. A *transition probability* is a function P on $[0, \infty) \times I \times \mathscr{B}$ such that $P(t) = P(t; \cdot, \cdot)$ is a stochastic kernel, $P(0; x, \cdot) = \delta_x$, and the *Chapman–Kolmogorov equation*

$$\int P(s; x, dy) P(t; y, A) = P(s + t; x, A) \tag{1.4}$$

holds for all s, t, x, and A.

Theorem 1.1 is our main result on transient behavior for slow learning with small drift.

THEOREM 1.1. *If a and b satisfy the conditions given above, there is one and only one transition probability P such that*

$$\int (y - x) P(\tau; x, dy) = \tau a(x) + o(\tau),$$

$$\int (y - x)^2 P(\tau; x, dy) = \tau b(x) + o(\tau), \tag{1.5}$$

and

$$\int |y - x|^3 P(\tau; x, dy) = o(\tau),$$

where $o(\tau)$ is uniform over $x \in I$. If (1.1) holds,

$$K_\tau^{(n)}(x_\tau, \cdot) = \mathscr{L}(X_n^\tau | X_0^\tau = x_\tau) \to P(t; x, \cdot) \qquad (1.6)$$

weakly, as $\tau \to 0$, $x_\tau \to x$, and $n\tau \to t$.

The uniqueness of P follows immediately from (1.6). For if Q is a transition probability that satisfies (1.5), $K_\tau = Q(\tau)$ is a family of transition kernels in I that satisfy (1.1), and $K_\tau^{(n)} = Q(n\tau)$ by (1.4). Taking $\tau = t/n$ and $x_\tau = x$ in (1.6) we obtain $Q(t; x, \cdot) \to P(t; x, \cdot)$ as $n \to \infty$; i.e., $Q(t; x, \cdot) = P(t; x, \cdot)$.

As a consequence of the last equation in (1.5), there is a diffusion $X(t)$, $t \geq 0$, with $X(0) = x$ and

$$P(X(s+t) \in A | X(s)) = P(t; X(s), A)$$

a.s. (Lamperti, 1966, Theorem 24.1). In particular,

$$\mathscr{L}(X(t)) = P(t; x, \cdot).$$

Under the same hypotheses as in Theorem 1.1, it can be shown that

$$\mathscr{L}(X_{n_1}^\tau, \dots, X_{n_k}^\tau) \to \mathscr{L}(X(t_1), \dots, X(t_k))$$

as $\tau \to 0$, $x_\tau \to x$, and $n_j \tau \to t_j$, $j = 1, \dots, k$. If $o(\tau)$ in (1.1) is replaced by $O(\tau^{1+v})$ for some $v > 0$, then

$$\mathscr{L}(X^\tau(t), t \leq T) \to \mathscr{L}(X(t), t \leq T),$$

where $X^\tau(t)$ is the random polygonal line with vertices $X^\tau(n\tau) = X_n^\tau$.

The family of linear models discussed in the last three paragraphs of Chapter 0 provides a simple illustration of Theorem 1.1. Since failure is ineffective ($\theta^* c^* = 0$), (0.3.1) specializes to

$$\Delta X_n = \begin{cases} \theta(1 - X_n) & \text{with probability } X_n \pi_{11} c, \\ -\theta X_n & \text{with probability } (1 - X_n) \pi_{00} c, \\ 0 & \text{otherwise.} \end{cases} \qquad (1.7)$$

It is assumed that $c > 0$ and $\pi_{11} > 0$ are fixed, and that π_{00} approaches π_{11} as $\theta \to 0$ along the line

$$\pi_{00}/\pi_{11} = 1 + \theta k, \qquad (1.8)$$

where, for our present purposes, k can be any real constant. Taking $\tau = \theta^2$ and $d_i = i$, (1.1) holds with

$$a(x) = Ax(1-x) \qquad \text{and} \qquad b(x) = Bx(1-x), \qquad (1.9)$$

where $B = \pi_{11} c$ and $A = -k\pi_{11} c$. The special case of Theorem 1.1 corresponding to such functions a and b is contained in an earlier result (Norman, 1971a, Theorem 4.3).

9.2. Invariance

In this section we introduce a special family of transition kernels L_τ satisfying (1.1), and show that, if K_τ is any other such family, then $K_\tau^{(n)}(x, \cdot) - L_\tau^{(n)}(x, \cdot)$ converges to zero, uniformly over $x \in I_\tau$ and $n\tau \leqslant v$, as $\tau \to 0$. Thus the behavior of $K_\tau^{(n)}$ when τ is small is invariant over all families of kernels satisfying (1.1). Such invariance is at once an important implication of Theorem 1.1 and a basic component of its proof. The remainder of the proof of Theorem 1.1 is given in the next section. The family L_τ is distinguished by its exceptional simplicity, which permits us to establish a crucial property (Lemma 2.2) by a rather direct computation.

Let $v_1 = \sigma_1$, $v_0 = -\sigma_0$, $\theta = \sqrt{\tau}$,

$$u_i(x) = u_i(x, \tau) = x + \tau a(x) + \theta v_i(x),$$

$p_1 = p$, and $p_0 = 1 - p$. Then

$$u_i'(x) = 1 + \tau a'(x) + \theta v_i'(x)$$
$$\geqslant 1 - \tau|a'| - \theta|v_i'| > 0$$

if $\tau \leqslant \tau_0$, for some $\tau_0 > 0$ sufficiently small. The condition $\tau \leqslant \tau_0$ is assumed in all that follows. Now $u_i(d_0) \geqslant d_0$, since $a(d_0) \geqslant 0$ and $v_i(d_0) \geqslant 0$; and $u_i(d_1) \leqslant d_1$, since $a(d_1) \leqslant 0$ and $v_i(d_1) \leqslant 0$. Since u_i is increasing, u_i maps I into I. Thus the requirement that a transition from x to $u_i(x)$ occurs with probability $p_i(x)$ defines a transition kernel $L = L_\tau$ in I. The corresponding transition operator $V = V_\tau$ is

$$Vf(x) = \sum f(u_i(x)) p_i(x),$$

where the summation is over $i = 0$ and 1. Since $u_i \in C^3$ and $p_i \in C^3$, V maps $C = C(I)$ into C and C^3 into C^3.

LEMMA 2.1. L_τ satisfies (1.1).

Proof.   First,

$$\sum (u_i(x) - x) p_i(x) = \tau a(x) + \theta \sum v_i(x) p_i(x),$$

and

$$\sum v_i(x) p_i(x) = \sigma_1(x) p(x) - \sigma_0(x) q(x) = 0 \qquad (2.1)$$

as a consequence of the definition of p $(q = 1 - p)$. Next,

$$\sum (u_i(x) - x)^2 p_i(x) = \tau \sum v_i^2(x) p_i(x) + \tau^2 a^2(x),$$

while $|a| < \infty$, and

$$\sum v_i^2(x) p_i(x) = \sigma_1^2(x) p(x) + \sigma_0^2(x) q(x)$$
$$= \sigma_1(x) \sigma_0(x) q(x) + \sigma_0(x) \sigma_1(x) p(x)$$

by (2.1), so that

$$\sum v_i^2(x) p_i(x) = \sigma_1(x)\sigma_0(x) = b(x)$$

by (1.2). The last equation in (1.1), with $O(\tau^{3/2})$ in place of $o(\tau)$, is a consequence of the boundedness of a and v_i. ∎

For $f \in C^3$, let

$$\|f\| = |f'| + |f''| + |f'''|.$$

LEMMA 2.2. There is a $\gamma > 0$ such that

$$\|V_\tau^n f\| \leq e^{\gamma n\tau} \|f\| \tag{2.2}$$

for all $n \geq 0$, $\tau \leq \tau_0$, and $f \in C^3$.

Proof. We often suppress the argument x in the following derivation, writing, for example, p_i instead of $p_i(x)$. This renders the notation $|g|$ ambiguous, so we denote the supremum norm $|g|_\infty$.

Clearly,

$$(Vf)'(x) = \sum f'(u_i) u_i' p_i + \sum f(u_i) p_i'.$$

Since $u_i' \geq 0$,

$$\left|\sum f'(u_i) u_i' p_i\right| \leq |f'|_\infty \sum u_i' p_i$$
$$\leq |f'|_\infty \left(1 + \theta \sum v_i' p_i + \tau |a'|_\infty\right). \tag{2.3}$$

Also, $p_0' = -p_1'$, so

$$\sum f(u_i) p_i' = (f(u_1) - f(u_0)) p_1'.$$

However, $p_1' = p' \geq 0$, and

$$u_1 - u_0 = \theta(v_1 - v_0) \geq 0;$$

hence

$$\left|\sum f(u_i) p_i'\right| \leq |f'|_\infty (u_1 - u_0) p_1'$$
$$= |f'|_\infty \theta \sum v_i p_i'. \tag{2.4}$$

Differentiating (2.1) we obtain

$$\sum v_i' p_i + \sum v_i p_i' = 0, \tag{2.5}$$

so addition of (2.3) and (2.4) yields

$$|(Vf)'(x)| \leq |f'|_\infty (1 + \tau |a'|_\infty)$$

and thus

$$|(Vf)'|_\infty \leq |f'|_\infty (1 + \tau |a'|_\infty). \tag{2.6}$$

We next show that there is a constant $c < \infty$ such that

$$|(Vf)''|_\infty \leqslant |f''|_\infty(1+c\tau) + c\tau|f'|_\infty \qquad (2.7)$$

for all $\tau \leqslant \tau_0$ and $f \in C^3$. We use the notation c below for a number of different bounds that do not depend on x, τ, or f.

By the chain and product rules for differentiation,

$$(Vf)''(x) = \sum f''(u_i) u_i'^2 p_i + \sum f'(u_i) u_i'' p_i$$
$$+ 2\sum f'(u_i) u_i' p_i' + \sum f(x_i) p_i''.$$

Since $u_i' = 1 + \theta v_i' + O(\tau)$ and $u_i'' = \theta v_i'' + O(\tau)$, this can be written

$$(Vf)''(x) = A_1 + A_2 + B_1 + B_2 + C, \qquad (2.8)$$

where

$$A_1 = \sum f''(u_i) u_i'^2 p_i,$$
$$A_2 = 2\sum f'(u_i) p_i',$$
$$B_1 = \sum f'(u_i) \theta(2v_i' p_i' + v_i'' p_i),$$
$$B_2 = \sum f(x_i) p_i'',$$

and

$$|C| \leqslant c|f'|_\infty \tau. \qquad (2.9)$$

We shall examine each of these components in turn.

First,

$$|A_1| \leqslant |f''|_\infty \sum u_i'^2 p_i$$

and

$$u_i'^2 = 1 + 2\theta v_i' + O(\tau),$$

so

$$|A_1| \leqslant |f''|_\infty (1 + 2\theta \sum v_i' p_i + c\tau). \qquad (2.10)$$

Also,

$$A_2 = 2(f'(u_1) - f'(u_0)) p_1',$$

so that

$$|A_2| \leqslant 2|f''|_\infty \theta \sum v_i p_i'. \qquad (2.11)$$

Adding (2.10) and (2.11) and using (2.5) we get

$$|A_1| + |A_2| \leqslant |f''|_\infty(1 + c\tau). \qquad (2.12)$$

Turning next to B_2, we see that

$$B_2 = (f(u_1) - f(u_0)) p_1''$$
$$= \Delta(u_1 - u_0) p_1'' = \Delta\theta \sum v_i p_i'',$$

where

$$\Delta = (f(u_1) - f(u_0))/(u_1 - u_0)$$

[or $f'(u_0)$ if $u_1 = u_0$]. Making use of the equality obtained by differentiating (2.5) we obtain

$$B_2 = -\Delta\theta \sum (2v_i' p_i' + v_i'' p_i).$$

Therefore

$$B_1 + B_2 = \theta \sum (f'(u_i) - \Delta)(2v_i' p_i' + v_i'' p_i).$$

But

$$|f'(u_i) - \Delta| \leqslant c|f''|_\infty \theta,$$

so

$$|B_1 + B_2| \leqslant c|f''|_\infty \tau. \tag{2.13}$$

Inequality (2.7) follows directly from (2.8), (2.9), (2.12), and (2.13). A similar computation yields

$$|(Vf)'''|_\infty \leqslant |f'''|_\infty (1 + c\tau) + c\tau(|f'|_\infty + |f''|_\infty).$$

When this is added to (2.6) and (2.7),

$$\|Vf\| \leqslant (1 + c\tau)\|f\| \leqslant e^{c\tau}\|f\|$$

results, and (2.2) with $\gamma = c$ follows by induction. ∎

The next lemma is our main result in this section.

LEMMA 2.3. Let U_τ, $\tau \in J$, be a family of transition operators whose kernels K_τ satisfy (1.1). For any $v < \infty$ and $f \in C$,

$$\sup_{n\tau \leqslant v} |U_\tau^n f - V_\tau^n f| \to 0 \tag{2.14}$$

as $\tau \to 0$.

In (2.14) and its proof, $|g|$ is understood to be the supremum of g over the largest set on which g is defined. This is I_τ in (2.14).

Proof. We first establish the basic inequality

$$|U^n f - V^n f| \leqslant \sum_{j=0}^{n-1} |UV^j f - VV^j f|, \tag{2.15}$$

for f bounded and measurable. If $x \in I_\tau$ and $n \geqslant 1$,

$$U^n f(x) - V^n f(x) = U(U^{n-1} f - V^{n-1} f)(x)$$
$$+ UV^{n-1} f(x) - VV^{n-1} f(x).$$

Since U is a contraction,

$$|U^n f - V^n f| \leqslant |U^{n-1} f - V^{n-1} f| + |UV^{n-1} f - VV^{n-1} f|,$$

and (2.15) follows by induction.

If $g \in C^3$, then

$$g(y) = g(x) + (y-x)g'(x) + \frac{(y-x)^2}{2} g''(x) + \omega |y-x|^3 |g'''|,$$

where $|\omega| \leqslant \frac{1}{6}$. Integrating this equality with respect to $K_\tau(x, dy)$ and using (1.1) we obtain

$$U_\tau g(x) = g(x) + \tau \Gamma g(x) + o(\tau) \|g\|, \tag{2.16}$$

where

$$\Gamma g(x) = a(x)g'(x) + 2^{-1}b(x)g''(x), \tag{2.17}$$

and $o(\tau)$ is uniform over $x \in I_\tau$ and $g \in C^3$.

Similarly,

$$V_\tau g(x) = g(x) + \tau \Gamma g(x) + o(\tau) \|g\|.$$

Subtracting this from (2.16), we get

$$|U_\tau g - V_\tau g| \leqslant \tau \varepsilon \|g\|, \tag{2.18}$$

for some function $\varepsilon = \varepsilon(\tau)$ of τ alone such that $\varepsilon \to 0$ as $\tau \to 0$.

If $f \in C^3$, $g = V_\tau^j f$ does too, so we can apply (2.18) to $V_\tau^j f$. By (2.2)

$$\|V_\tau^j f\| \leqslant e^{\gamma v} \|f\| = k$$

if $j\tau \leqslant v$, so

$$|U_\tau V_\tau^j f - V_\tau V_\tau^j f| \leqslant \tau \varepsilon k.$$

This estimate, in conjunction with (2.15), yields

$$|U_\tau^n f - V_\tau^n f| \leqslant v k \varepsilon$$

for $n\tau \leqslant v$. This implies (2.14) for $f \in C^3$. Since C^3 is dense in C, and U^n and V^n are contractions, (2.14) holds for all $f \in C$. ∎

9.3. Semigroups

It is shown in this section that there is a transition probability P satisfying (1.5), and that

$$T_t f(x) = \int P(t; x, dy) f(y), \tag{3.1}$$

where $f \in C$, has the following continuity properties: $T_t f \in C$, and

$$\lim_{u \to t} |T_u f - T_t f| = 0. \tag{3.2}$$

Granting this, it is easy to complete the proof of (1.6). By Lemma 3.1,

$$|U_\tau^n f - V_\tau^n f| \to 0 \tag{3.3}$$

as $\tau \to 0$, if n varies in such a way that $n\tau \leqslant v$. According to (1.5), $K_\tau = P(\tau)$ satisfies (1.1), and according to (1.4), T_t has the semigroup property $T_s T_t = T_{s+t}$, so that $T_\tau^n = T_{n\tau}$. Thus, as a special case of (3.3),

$$|T_{n\tau} f - V_\tau^n f| \to 0,$$

and this can be combined with (3.3) to yield

$$|U_\tau^n f - T_{n\tau} f| \to 0$$

as $\tau \to 0$ and $n\tau \leqslant v$. But

$$|T_{n\tau} f - T_t f| \to 0$$

as $n\tau \to t$, by (3.2); and

$$T_t f(x_\tau) \to T_t f(x)$$

as $x_\tau \to x$, since $T_t f \in C$. Therefore, for all $f \in C$,

$$U_\tau^n f(x_\tau) \to T_t f(x)$$

as $\tau \to 0$, $n\tau \to t$, and $x_\tau \to x$, and this differs from (1.6) only notationally.

Before proceeding further, it is useful to summarize some of the terminology and basic results of semigroup theory. A family T_t, $t \geqslant 0$, of bounded linear operators on a Banach space B is a *semigroup* if $T_0 = E$, the identity operator, and $T_s T_t = T_{s+t}$ for all $s, t \geqslant 0$. The semigroup is strongly continuous if, for each $f \in B$, $T_t f$ is continuous with respect to the norm of B. The *generator* Γ of such a semigroup is the linear operator defined by

$$\Gamma f = \lim_{t \to 0} t^{-1}(T_t f - f)$$

for f in the *domain* $\mathscr{D}(\Gamma)$ of Γ, the set of f for which this limit exists in the norm of B. The semigroup is uniquely determined by Γ [and $\mathscr{D}(\Gamma)$]. If

$f \in \mathscr{D}(\Gamma)$, then $T_t f \in \mathscr{D}(\Gamma)$, and

$$\frac{d}{dt} T_t f = \Gamma T_t f = T_t \Gamma f. \tag{3.4}$$

A strongly continuous semigroup on $C = C(I)$ is *contractive* if $|T_t f| \leqslant |f|$ for all $f \in C$, and T_t maps nonnegative functions into nonnegative functions. A contractive semigroup is *conservative* if $T_t 1 = 1$.

Let C^2 be the set of functions with two continuous derivatives throughout I.

LEMMA 3.1. There is a conservative semigroup T_t on C whose generator Γ has the following properties:

(A) $\mathscr{D}(\Gamma) \supset C^2$, and
(B) for $f \in C^2$ and $x \in I$,

$$\Gamma f(x) = a(x) f'(x) + 2^{-1} b(x) f''(x). \tag{3.5}$$

Proof. Let $d_0 < d < d_1$,

$$B(x) = 2 \int_d^x \frac{a(y)}{b(y)} \, dy,$$

$$p(x) = \int_d^x e^{-B(y)} \, dy,\dagger$$

and

$$m(x) = \int_d^x 2b(y)^{-1} e^{B(y)} \, dy.$$

Let $\mathscr{D}$ be the set of $f \in C$ satisfying these two conditions:

(i) f has two continuous (but not necessarily bounded) derivatives on (d_0, d_1). For $d_0 < x < d_1$, put

$$\Gamma^* f(x) = a(x) f'(x) + 2^{-1} b(x) f''(x) = \frac{d}{dm} \frac{d}{dp} f(x). \tag{3.6}$$

(ii) $\Gamma^* f(x)$ has finite limits [denoted $\Gamma^* f(d_i)$] at d_0 and d_1. Thus $\Gamma^* f \in C$.

The generator Γ of T_t is the restriction of Γ^* to a subset of $\mathscr{D}$ determined by the type of boundary at d_0 and d_1. Let

$$\alpha_i = \int_d^{d_i} m(x) \, dp(x) \quad \text{and} \quad \beta_i = \int_d^{d_i} p(x) \, dm(x),$$

† This function should not be confused with $\sigma_0/(\sigma_0 + \sigma_1)$ in the preceding sections.

where the range of integration excludes d_i. The boundary d_i is

regular if $\alpha_i < \infty$ and $\beta_i < \infty$,

exit if $\alpha_i < \infty$ and $\beta_i = \infty$,

entrance if $\alpha_i = \infty$ and $\beta_i < \infty$,

natural if $\alpha_i = \infty$ and $\beta_i = \infty$.

Regular and exit boundaries are termed *accessible*; others are *inaccessible*. If d_i is inaccessible, let $\mathscr{D}_i = \mathscr{D}$. If d_i is exit, let

$$\mathscr{D}_i = \{f \in \mathscr{D}: \Gamma^* f(d_i) = 0\}.$$

Finally, if d_i is regular, let

$$\mathscr{D}_i = \{f \in \mathscr{D}: \lim_{x \to d_i} e^{B(x)} f'(x) = 0\}$$

or, equivalently,

$$\mathscr{D}_i = \left\{f \in \mathscr{D}: \frac{d}{dp} f(d_i) = 0\right\}.$$

Let $\mathscr{D}(\Gamma) = \mathscr{D}_0 \cap \mathscr{D}_1$ and $\Gamma = \Gamma^* | \mathscr{D}(\Gamma)$. The fact that Γ generates a contractive semigroup T_t is a consequence of Feller's semigroup theory. The results needed here are all presented in Section 5 of Chapter II of Mandl (1968).

Note that $\mathscr{D} \supset C^2$, and (3.6) holds for all $x \in I$ if $f \in C^2$. If $\mathscr{D}(\Gamma) \supset C^2$, then $\Gamma f = \Gamma^* f$ for $f \in C^2$, and (3.5) follows. Thus (B) follows from (A). Granted (A) and (B), $1 \in \mathscr{D}(\Gamma)$ and $\Gamma 1 = 0$; hence, by the outer equality in (3.4), $dT_t 1/dt = 0$. Since $T_0 1 = 1$, T_t is conservative. Therefore it remains only to establish (A).

It suffices to show that $\mathscr{D}_i \supset C^2$ for each i. If d_i is inaccessible this is certainly the case. If d_i is an exit boundary, we shall see below that $a(d_i) = 0$; hence $\Gamma^* f(d_i) = 0$ for all $f \in C^2$. If d_i is a regular boundary, we shall see that $(-1)^i a(d_i) > 0$. But

$$b(y) \leqslant |b'| \, |d_i - y|,$$

so

$$(-1)^{i+1} \int_d^x \frac{1}{b(y)} \, dy \to \infty \tag{3.7}$$

as $x \to d_i$. Therefore $B(x) \to -\infty$, and $e^{B(x)} f'(x) \to 0$ for all $f \in C^2$, as $x \to d_i$.

We now establish the facts cited above about $a(d_i)$ when d_i is accessible. If d_1 is regular, then $p(d_1) < \infty$ and $m(d_1) < \infty$, so, by the Schwarz inequality,

$$(p'(x) m'(x)/2)^{1/2} = 1/(b(x))^{1/2}$$

is integrable over (d, d_1). If $b'(d_1) = 0$, $b(y) = O((d_1 - y)^2)$, and this would not be the case, so $b'(d_1) < 0$. But then $a(d_1) = 0$ would imply boundedness of $a(y)/b(y)$, hence of $B(x)$, and, in view of (3.7), $m(d_1) = \infty$ would follow. Therefore we must have $a(d_1) < 0$ if d_1 is regular. Similarly, $a(d_0) > 0$ if d_0 is regular.

Now $m(d_1) = \infty$ if d_1 is an exit boundary. Thus, to show that $a(d_1) = 0$ for such a boundary, it suffices to show that $a(d_1) < 0$ implies $m(d_1) < \infty$. If $a(d_1) < 0$ there is a $\xi < d_1$ and an $\alpha < 0$ such that $a(x) \leqslant \alpha$ if $x \geqslant \xi$. In particular, $B'(x) < 0$, so that $e^{B(x)}$ is decreasing for $x \geqslant \xi$. Thus $de^{B(x)}/dx$ is integrable over $[\xi, d_1)$, and

$$m'(x) = a(x)^{-1} de^{B(x)}/dx$$

is too. The proof that $a(d_0) = 0$ if d_0 is an exit boundary is similar. ∎

Since T_t, $t \geqslant 0$, is a conservative semigroup, there is a transition probability P that satisfies (3.1) for all $f \in C$ and $x \in I$.

LEMMA 3.2. *P satisfies (1.5).*

Proof. Let

$$\Omega_\tau = \tau^{-1}(T_\tau - E) - \Gamma,$$

and let $f(y) = (y - x)^2$. Since $f(x) = 0$, and $\Gamma f(x) = b(x)$ by (B) of Lemma 3.1,

$$\delta_\tau(x) = \tau^{-1} \int (y - x)^2 P(\tau; x, dy) - b(x) = \Omega_\tau f(x),$$

so that $|\delta_\tau(x)| \leqslant |\Omega_\tau f|$. But

$$f = \mathscr{I}^2 - 2x\mathscr{I} + 1,$$

where $\mathscr{I}(y) \equiv y$ and $1(y) \equiv 1$, and Ω_τ is linear with $\Omega_\tau 1 = 0$, so

$$|\delta_\tau(x)| \leqslant |\Omega_\tau \mathscr{I}^2| + 2|x| |\Omega_\tau \mathscr{I}|$$

and, letting c be the maximum of $2|x|$ for $x \in I$,

$$|\delta_\tau| \leqslant |\Omega_\tau \mathscr{I}^2| + c|\Omega_\tau \mathscr{I}|.$$

By (A) of Lemma 3.1, $\mathscr{I}^j \in \mathscr{D}(\Gamma)$ for all $j \geqslant 0$; thus $|\Omega_\tau \mathscr{I}^j| \to 0$ and $|\delta_\tau| \to 0$ as $\tau \to 0$. This establishes the second equation in (1.5).

Applying the same argument to $f(y) = y - x$ and $f(y) = (y - x)^4$, we obtain the first equation in (1.5) and $|\varepsilon_\tau^4| \to 0$, where

$$\varepsilon_\tau^j(x) = \tau^{-1} \int |y - x|^j P(\tau; x, dy).$$

But

$$|\varepsilon_\tau^3| \leqslant (|\varepsilon_\tau^2| \, |\varepsilon_\tau^4|)^{1/2},$$

by the Schwarz inequality, and

$$|\varepsilon_\tau^2| \leqslant |\delta_\tau| + |b|,$$

so that $|\varepsilon_\tau^2|$ is bounded as $\tau \to 0$. Hence $|\varepsilon_\tau^3| \to 0$, which is the last equation in (1.5). ∎

This completes the proof of Theorem 1.1.

The proof of Lemma 3.2 uses only the properties of T_t given in Lemma 3.1. Since, according to Theorem 1.1, there is only one transition probability P satisfying (1.5), we conclude that there is only one semigroup T_t with these properties.

Let D be the set of all $f \in C^2$ for which f'' is Lipschitz; i.e.,

$$D = \{ f \in C^2 : m(f'') < \infty \},$$

where

$$m(g) = \sup_{x \neq y} \frac{|g(x) - g(y)|}{|x - y|}.$$

For $f \in D$, let

$$\|f\| = |f'| + |f''| + m(f'').$$

Clearly $C^3 \subset D$ and $m(f'') = |f'''|$ on C^3, so this seminorm is an extension of $\|\cdot\|$ defined previously on C^3. It can be shown that, if $f_k \in D$, $\{\|f_k\|\}_{k \geqslant 0}$ is bounded, and $|f_k - f| \to 0$ as $k \to \infty$, then $f \in D$, and

$$\|f\| \leqslant \liminf_{k \to \infty} \|f_k\|.$$

Thus, taking $n = [t/\tau]$ in (2.2) and letting $\tau \to 0$, we see that, for any $f \in C^3$ and $t \geqslant 0$, $T_t f \in D$ and

$$\|T_t f\| \leqslant e^{\gamma t} \|f\|. \tag{3.8}$$

This bound is very interesting in its own right. Furthermore, were it available from another source, T_τ could be used in place of V_τ in Section 9.2. This approach would be reminiscent of that of Khintchine (1948, Section 1 of Chapter 3), who postulated properties analogous to (3.8).

DENSITIES. For $d_0 < x < d_1$, the restriction of the distribution $P(t; x, \cdot)$ to (d_0, d_1) has a density $\zeta(t; x, \cdot)$ with respect to Lebesgue measure. To describe this density, we need the boundary terminology and the notations $\mathscr{D}$, $\mathscr{D}_i$, Γ^*, $m(x)$, and $p(x)$ from the proof of Lemma 3.1.

Let $\mathscr{E}_i = \mathscr{D}_i$ unless d_i is an exit boundary, in which case

$$\mathscr{E}_i = \{f \in \mathscr{D} : f(d_i) = 0\}.$$

Let $\bar{\Gamma}$ be the restriction of Γ^* to $\mathscr{E}_0 \cap \mathscr{E}_1$. If neither d_0 nor d_1 is a natural boundary,

$$\zeta(t; x, y) = m'(y) \sum_{n=1}^{\infty} e^{\lambda_n t} \phi_n(x) \phi_n(y), \qquad (3.9)$$

where $0 \geqslant \lambda_1 > \lambda_2 > \cdots$ are the eigenvalues of $\bar{\Gamma}$, and $\phi_1, \phi_2, \ldots$ are the corresponding eigenfunctions, normalized so that $\int \phi_n^2 \, dm = 1$ (Elliott, 1955). The series converges uniformly over $t \geqslant \delta$ and $e_0 \leqslant x, y \leqslant e_1$, for any $\delta > 0$ and $d_0 < e_0 < e_1 < d_1$. A counterpart of (3.9) for natural boundaries is given by McKean (1956).

If d_i is not an exit boundary,

$$h_i(t; x) = P(t; x, \{d_i\}) = 0.$$

For an exit boundary d_i, the following formulas relate h_i to ζ:

$$h_i(t; x) = 1 - \int \zeta(t; x, y) \, dy \qquad (3.10)$$

if the other boundary is not exit, and

$$h_i(t; x) = p_i(x) - \int \zeta(t; x, y) p_i(y) \, dy \qquad (3.11)$$

if both boundaries are exit, where

$$p_1(x) = \frac{p(x) - p(d_0)}{p(d_1) - p(d_0)},$$

$p_0 = 1 - p_1$, and the integrals are over (d_0, d_1). We omit the proofs of these equalities.

10 ○ Steady-State Behavior

10.1. A Limit Theorem for Stationary Probabilities

Assumptions (a), (b), and (c) of Section 8.1 are in force throughout this chapter, and $N = 1$. We are concerned here with the limit as $\theta \to 0$ of stationary probabilities of nonabsorbing or recurrent processes. Typically, the distribution of X_n^θ converges as $n \to \infty$ to a stationary probability that does not depend on the distribution of X_0^θ, but, whether or not this is the case, stationary probabilities represent the possible modes of steady-state behavior of $\{X_n^\theta\}_{n \geqslant 0}$. Let $\mathscr{S}_\theta$ be the set of stationary probabilities (with finite fourth moments if I is unbounded) of the transition kernel K_θ of this process. Naturally, we assume $\mathscr{S}_\theta \neq \varnothing$.

The processes considered in this chapter are distinguished by the existence of a (critical) point λ in the interior of I, such that $E(\Delta X_n^\theta | X_n^\theta = x)$ is positive when $x < \lambda$ and negative when $x > \lambda$ if θ is small. More precisely:

(d) There is an interior point λ of I, such that

$$w(x) > 0 \qquad \text{if} \quad x < \lambda,$$

$$w(x) = 0 \qquad \text{if} \quad x = \lambda,$$

$$w(x) < 0 \qquad \text{if} \quad x > \lambda,$$

and

$$w'(\lambda) < 0.$$

Theorem 1.1 requires additional assumptions when I is unbounded, as in additive learning models.

Henceforth, we assume that, for any $\theta \in J$, $p_\theta = \mathscr{L}(X_0^\theta) \in \mathscr{S}_\theta$. Then $\mathscr{L}(X_n^\theta) = p_\theta$ for all n; in fact, X_n^θ and

$$z_n^\theta = (X_n^\theta - \lambda)/\sqrt{\theta}$$

are strictly stationary processes.

THEOREM 1.1. *If*

(i) $I = [c, d]$ *is bounded, or*
(ii.1) $Q(x, \theta) = E((H_n^\theta)^4 | X_n^\theta = x)$ *is bounded, and*
(ii.2)   *there are $A > 0$ and $B > 0$ such that*

$$(\lambda - x) w(x, \theta) \geqslant B$$

for all $\theta \in J$ and $x \in I_\theta$ with $|x - \lambda| > A$, then

(A) $E((X_n^\theta - \lambda)^2) = O(\theta)$, *and*
(B) $z_n^\theta \sim N(0, \sigma^2)$ *as $\theta \to 0$, where*

$$\sigma^2 = s(\lambda)/2|w'(\lambda)| = S(\lambda)/2|w'(\lambda)|.$$

Theorem 1.1 under condition (i) is similar to the central limit theorem of Norman and Graham (1968), while (ii) generalizes Theorem 6 of Norman (1970b).

Note that (A) implies

$$E(X_n^\theta) - \lambda = O(\sqrt{\theta}). \tag{1.1}$$

An improved estimate, valid under (i), (ii.1), and additional conditions, is obtained in Section 10.3. Note also that (B) differs only notationally from (8.5.7).

The five-operator linear model with $\theta_{ij} = \theta \eta_{ij}$ and with π_{ij} and c_{ij} fixed provides the simplest example of a family X_n^θ of processes to which Theorem 1.1 can be applied. We have already noted that it satisfies (a), (b), and (c) of Section 8.1. For this model

$$E(\Delta X_n | X_n = x) = \theta w(x)$$

$$= (\theta_{11} \Pi_{11} - \theta_{00} \Pi_{00}) x(1-x) + \theta_{01} \Pi_{01} (1-x)^2 - \theta_{10} \Pi_{10} x^2,$$

where $\Pi_{ij} = \pi_{ij} c_{ij}$, so the quadratic polynomial w has $w(0) = \eta_{01} \Pi_{01}$ and $-w(1) = \eta_{10} \Pi_{10}$. If both of these quantities are positive, (d) is satisfied. Furthermore, neither 0 nor 1 is absorbing, and it will be shown in Section

12.1 that there is a unique stationary probability p_θ, to which $\mathscr{L}(X_n^\theta)$ converges as $n \to \infty$, regardless of $\mathscr{L}(X_0^\theta)$. Since $I = [0, 1]$, all of the conditions of (i) of Theorem 1.1 are met.

10.2. Proof of the Theorem

As in Chapter 8, we denote a variety of bounds by K.

Proof of (A) *under* (i).   Clearly

$$(X_{n+1} - \lambda)^2 = (X_n - \lambda)^2 + 2(X_n - \lambda)\,\Delta X_n + (\Delta X_n)^2,$$

so, taking expectations on both sides, canceling $E((X_n - \lambda)^2)$ on the left and right, and dividing by 2θ we obtain

$$0 = E((X_n - \lambda)\,w(X_n, \theta)) + \theta E(S(X_n, \theta))/2.$$

Since $S(x, \theta) \leqslant K$ by (c) of Section 8.1,

$$0 \leqslant E((X_n - \lambda)\,w(X_n, \theta)) + K\theta. \tag{2.1}$$

Thus

$$E((\lambda - X_n)\,w(X_n)) \leqslant E((X_n - \lambda)\,(w(X_n, \theta) - w(X_n))) + K\theta$$
$$\leqslant K\theta, \tag{2.2}$$

by (a.2) and the boundedness of I.

Let

$$\rho(x) = \begin{cases} w(x)/(\lambda - x), & x \neq \lambda, \\ -w'(\lambda), & x = \lambda. \end{cases}$$

Since ρ is positive and continuous by (d), and I is compact, there is a $k > 0$ such that $\rho(x) \geqslant k$ for all $x \in I$. Thus

$$(\lambda - X_n)\,w(X_n) = (\lambda - X_n)^2 \rho(X_n) \geqslant k(X_n - \lambda)^2, \tag{2.3}$$

which yields (A) on substitution into (2.2).   ∎

Proof of (A) *under* (ii).   Since, by (ii.2),

$$(X_n - \lambda)\,w(X_n, \theta) < 0$$

a.s. for $|X_n - \lambda| > A$, (2.1) yields

$$0 \leqslant E((X_n - \lambda)\,w(X_n, \theta)\,G) + K\theta,$$

where

$$G = I_{|X_n - \lambda| \leqslant A}.$$

Thus

$$E((\lambda - X_n) w(X_n) G) \leqslant E((X_n - \lambda) (w(X_n, \theta) - w(X_n)) G) + K\theta$$
$$\leqslant K\theta.$$

But (2.3) is valid for $|X_n - \lambda| \leqslant A$, so

$$\alpha = E((\lambda - X_n)^2 G) \leqslant K\theta. \tag{2.4}$$

The binomial expansion of $((X_n - \lambda) + \Delta X_n)^4$ is

$$(X_{n+1} - \lambda)^4 = (X_n - \lambda)^4 + 4(X_n - \lambda)^3 \Delta X_n$$
$$+ 6(X_n - \lambda)^2 (\Delta X_n)^2 + 4(X_n - \lambda)(\Delta X_n)^3 + (\Delta X_n)^4. \tag{2.5}$$

We have assumed that

$$E((X_{n+1} - \lambda)^4) = E((X_n - \lambda)^4) < \infty,$$

and

$$E((\Delta X_n)^4) = \theta^4 E(Q(X_n, \theta)) < \infty$$

by (ii.1). Furthermore, if $j, k > 0$ and $j + k = 4$, then $j/4 + k/4 = 1$; so, by Hölder's inequality,

$$E(|X_n - \lambda|^j |\Delta X_n|^k) \leqslant E(|X_n - \lambda|^4)^{j/4} E(|\Delta X_n|^4)^{k/4} < \infty.$$

Thus we can take the expectation on both sides of (2.5), cancel $E((X_n - \lambda)^4)$, and divide by 4θ to obtain

$$0 = E((X_n - \lambda)^3 w(X_n, \theta)) + \tfrac{3}{2}\theta E((X_n - \lambda)^2 S(X_n, \theta))$$
$$+ \theta^2 E((X_n - \lambda) T(X_n, \theta)) + \tfrac{1}{4}\theta^3 E(Q(X_n, \theta)), \tag{2.6}$$

where

$$T(x, \theta) = E((H_n^\theta)^3 | X_n^\theta = x).$$

But $T(X_n, \theta)$ is bounded as a consequence of (ii.1), so

$$0 \leqslant E((X_n - \lambda)^3 w(X_n, \theta)) + K\theta E((X_n - \lambda)^2)$$
$$+ K\theta^2 E(|X_n - \lambda|) + K\theta^3.$$

And

$$E(|X_n - \lambda|) \leqslant (E((X_n - \lambda)^2)/\theta + \theta)/2;$$

thus

$$0 \leqslant E((X_n - \lambda)^3 w(X_n, \theta)) + K\theta E((X_n - \lambda)^2) + K\theta^3. \tag{2.7}$$

Now

$$(X_n - \lambda)^3 w(X_n, \theta) = (X_n - \lambda)^3 w(X_n, \theta) ((1 - G) + G)$$
$$\leqslant -B(X_n - \lambda)^2 (1 - G) + (X_n - \lambda)^3 (w(X_n, \theta) - w(X_n)) G$$

by (ii.2) and (d), so that

$$(X_n - \lambda)^3 w(X_n, \theta) \leqslant -B(X_n - \lambda)^2 (1 - G) + K\theta(X_n - \lambda)^2$$

by (a.2) of Section 8.1. This inequality and (2.7) yield

$$B\beta = BE((X_n - \lambda)^2 (1 - G)) \leqslant K\theta E((X_n - \lambda)^2) + K\theta^3.$$

Thus

$$B\beta \leqslant K\theta(\alpha + \beta) + K\theta^3$$
$$\leqslant K\theta\beta + K\theta^2$$

by (2.4), and

$$B\beta \leqslant B\beta/2 + K\theta^2$$

for $\theta \leqslant \delta = B/2K$. Thus $\beta \leqslant K\theta^2$. Adding this to (2.4), we obtain (A). ∎

Part (B) of Theorem 1.1 is proved by noting that, as a consequence of (A) and Lemma 8.5.1, Lemma 2.1 below applies to z_n^θ.

LEMMA 2.1. For every $\theta \in J$, let $\{z_n^\theta\}_{n \geqslant 0}$ be a real valued stationary process. Suppose that

$$E(\Delta z_n^\theta | z_n^\theta) = \theta a z_n^\theta + o(\theta),$$
$$E((\Delta z_n^\theta)^2 | z_n^\theta) = \theta b + o(\theta), \tag{2.8}$$

and

$$E(|\Delta z_n^\theta|^3 | z_n^\theta) = o(\theta)$$

a.s., where $a < 0$ and

$$E(|o(\theta)|)/\theta \to 0$$

as $\theta \to 0$. Then

$$z_n^\theta \sim N(0, \sigma^2)$$

as $\theta \to 0$, where $\sigma^2 = b/2|a|$.

This lemma is a steady-state analog of Lemma 8.4.2. Both results apply to non-Markovian processes. The proof of Lemma 2.1 is much simpler than that of Lemma 8.4.2.

Proof. As in the proof of Lemma 8.4.2,

$$E(e^{i\omega \Delta z_n}|z_n) = 1 + i\omega E(\Delta z_n|z_n)$$
$$-\omega^2 E((\Delta z_n)^2|z_n)/2 + k|\omega|^3 E(|\Delta z_n|^3|z_n),$$

where $|k| \leqslant \frac{1}{6}$; thus

$$h^\theta(\omega) = E(e^{i\omega z_{n+1}}) = E(e^{i\omega z_n}E(e^{i\omega \Delta z_n}|z_n))$$
$$= h^\theta(\omega) + i\omega E(e^{i\omega z_n}E(\Delta z_n|z_n))$$
$$-\omega^2 E(e^{i\omega z_n}E((\Delta z_n)^2|z_n))/2 + |\omega|^3 E(e^{i\omega z_n}kE(|\Delta z_n|^3|z_n)).$$

Canceling $h^\theta(\omega)$ and dividing by ω we obtain

$$0 = iE(e^{i\omega z_n}E(\Delta z_n|z_n)) - \omega E(e^{i\omega z_n}E((\Delta z_n)^2|z_n))/2$$
$$+\omega^2 E(e^{i\omega z_n}kE(|\Delta z_n|^3|z_n)).$$

Thus, by (2.8),

$$0 = i\theta a E(e^{i\omega z_n}z_n) - \omega\theta b E(e^{i\omega z_n})/2$$
$$+ E(o(\theta)) + \omega E(o(\theta)) + \omega^2 E(o(\theta))$$

[the first and last equations in (2.8) imply that $E(|z_n|) < \infty$ when θ is small], or

$$0 = (d/d\omega)h^\theta(\omega) + \omega\sigma^2 h^\theta(\omega) + \varepsilon(\omega),$$

where

$$\delta = \sup_\omega |\varepsilon(\omega)|/(1+\omega^2) \to 0$$

as $\theta \to 0$. Since $h^\theta(0) = 1$, it follows that

$$h^\theta(\omega) = \exp(-\sigma^2\omega^2/2)\left(1 - \int_0^\omega \exp(\sigma^2 x^2/2)\varepsilon(x)\,dx\right).$$

But

$$\left|\int_0^\omega \exp(\sigma^2 x^2/2)\varepsilon(x)\,dx\right| \leqslant \delta \int_0^{|\omega|} \exp(\sigma^2 x^2/2)(1+x^2)\,dx \to 0$$

as $\theta \to 0$; thus $h^\theta(\omega) \to \exp(-\sigma^2\omega^2/2)$, and $z_n^\theta \sim N(0, \sigma^2)$. ∎

10.3. A More Precise Approximation to $E(X_n^\theta)$

THEOREM 3.1. *If the assumptions of Theorem 1.1(i) are augmented by* (ii.1), *then*

$$E((X_n^\theta - \lambda)^4) = O(\theta^2). \tag{3.1}$$

If, in addition,

$$w(x, \theta) = w(x) + \theta v(x) + o(\theta) \tag{3.2}$$

uniformly over $x \in I_\theta$, where v and w'' are Lipschitz, then

$$E(X_n^\theta) = \lambda + \theta \gamma + o(\theta), \tag{3.3}$$

where

$$\gamma = (\sigma^2 w''(\lambda)/2 + v(\lambda))/|w'(\lambda)|.$$

Proof. The derivation of (2.7) is valid under our present assumptions (integrability is not a problem here). Thus

$$E((\lambda - X_n)^3 w(X_n)) \leqslant E((X_n - \lambda)^3 (w(X_n, \theta) - w(X_n)))$$
$$+ K\theta E((X_n - \lambda)^2) + K\theta^3.$$

Using (2.3) on the left, and (a.2) and $|X_n - \lambda| \leqslant K$ on the right, we obtain

$$E((X_n - \lambda)^4) \leqslant K\theta E((X_n - \lambda)^2) + K\theta^3$$
$$\leqslant K\theta^2$$

by (A) of Theorem 1.1.

To prove (3.3), we note first that

$$0 = E(\Delta X_n)/\theta = E(w(X_n, \theta))$$
$$= E(w(X_n)) + \theta E(v(X_n)) + o(\theta). \tag{3.4}$$

Also

$$|E(v(X_n)) - v(\lambda)| \leqslant E(|v(X_n) - v(\lambda)|)$$
$$\leqslant KE(|X_n - \lambda|) \leqslant K\sqrt{\theta}$$

by (A) of Theorem 1.1(i), and

$$|E(w(X_n)) - w(\lambda) - w'(\lambda) E(X_n - \lambda) - w''(\lambda) E((X_n - \lambda)^2)/2|$$
$$\leqslant E(|w(X_n) - w(\lambda) - w'(\lambda)(X_n - \lambda) - w''(\lambda)(X_n - \lambda)^2/2|)$$
$$\leqslant KE(|X_n - \lambda|^3)$$

since w'' is Lipschitz, so that

$$|E(w(X_n)) - w(\lambda) - w'(\lambda) E(X_n - \lambda) - w''(\lambda) E((X_n - \lambda)^2)/2| \leqslant K\theta^{3/2}$$

by (3.1). When combined with (3.4) these estimates yield

$$|w'(\lambda)|(E(X_n) - \lambda) = w''(\lambda) E((X_n - \lambda)^2)/2 + \theta v(\lambda) + o(\theta)$$
$$= \theta w''(\lambda) E(z_n^2)/2 + \theta v(\lambda) + o(\theta).$$

Since $E(z_n^4) \leqslant K$ for all θ by (3.1), (B) of Theorem 1.1(i) implies that $E(z_n^2) \to \sigma^2$ as $\theta \to 0$ (Loève, 1963, Corollary to B, p. 184). Thus

$$|w'(\lambda)|(E(X_n) - \lambda) = \theta[w''(\lambda)\sigma^2/2 + v(\lambda)] + o(\theta). \quad \blacksquare$$

Let $h^\theta(\omega) = E(e^{i\omega z_n})$. Then

$$(d/d\omega)h^\theta(0) = iE(z_n) = i\sqrt{\theta}\gamma + o(\sqrt{\theta})$$

by (3.3). A heuristic derivation of asymptotic expansions of $h^\theta(\omega)$ and its ω derivatives in powers of $\sqrt{\theta}$ has been given by Norman (1968b, Section III.A), under hypotheses somewhat more restrictive than those of Theorem 3.1.

It is easy to see that Theorem 3.1 is applicable to the family of linear models considered in the last paragraph of Section 10.1. Since $w(x, \theta) \equiv w(x)$ for these models, $v(x) \equiv 0$. The application of Theorem 3.1 that follows is of a rather different kind.

Consider a model for simple learning with two responses (see Subsection A of Section 0.1), whose state variable x represents A_1 response probability. Assuming only that all response–outcome pairs $A_i O_j$ are equally effective for learning (see the paragraphs on "Symmetry"), and incorporating a step-size parameter $\theta > 0$, we obtain the equations

$$\Delta X_n = \begin{cases} \theta F(X_n) & \text{if } O_{1n}C_{1n}, \\ -\theta F(1-X_n) & \text{if } O_{0n}C_{1n}, \\ 0 & \text{if } C_{0n}, \end{cases} \quad (3.5)$$

where $F(x) \geqslant 0$ for all $0 \leqslant x \leqslant 1$, and

$$c_{ij} = P(C_{1n}|A_{in}O_{jn}) = c > 0$$

for all i and j. Suppose that outcomes are noncontingent; that is, $\pi_{11} = \pi_{01} = \pi$, where $0 < \pi < 1$. Thus the three rows in (3.5) have probabilities πc, $(1-\pi)c$, and $1-c$, respectively.

Five-operator linear models with $\theta_{ij} = \theta\eta$ and $\eta > 0$ satisfy (3.5), with

$$F(x) = \eta(1-x). \quad (3.6)$$

In this case,

$$E(\Delta X_n|X_n) = \theta\eta c(\pi - X_n),$$

so that

$$\Delta E(X_n) = \theta\eta c(\pi - E(X_n))$$

and

$$E(X_n) - \pi = (1 - \theta\eta c)^n(E(X_0) - \pi).$$

Thus probability matching,

$$x_\infty(\pi, \theta) = \lim_{n \to \infty} E(X_n) = \pi, \tag{3.7}$$

is predicted for all θ and π. The question arises whether there are functions besides (3.6) that predict (3.7), or various generalizations such as

$$x_\infty(\pi, \theta) = \pi + o(1) \tag{3.8}$$

or

$$x_\infty(\pi, \theta) = \pi + o(\theta) \tag{3.9}$$

for all $0 < \pi < 1$. We will show that, within a wide class of functions to be described shortly, only those of the form (3.6) predict (3.9) [or (3.7), which is a special case]. There are, however, other functions that predict (3.8).

In order to keep X_n within $[0, 1]$, it is certainly necessary to assume $F(1) = 0$, and, to meet the smoothness conditions of Theorem 3.1, we assume that F has a bounded third derivative. The final and most important condition concerning F is that $F'(x) < 0$ for all $0 \leqslant x \leqslant 1$. If $0 \leqslant x < 1$, let

$$G(x) = F(x)/(1-x).$$

COROLLARY.   *Under these conditions,* (3.8) *holds for some* $0 < \pi < 1$ *if and only if*

$$G(\pi) = G(1-\pi), \tag{3.10}$$

and (3.9) *is satisfied for all* $0 < \pi < 1$ *if and only if* F *is given by* (3.6).

The result concerning (3.8) is similar to Theorem 4 of Norman and Yellott (1966).

Proof.   We first show that, if $\theta \leqslant K = |F'|^{-1}$, then the model with events $O_1 C_1$, $O_0 C_1$, and C_0 is distance diminishing, and its state sequences $\{X_n\}_{n \geqslant 0}$ are regular compact Markov processes. Let

$$u_1(x) = x + \theta F(x) \qquad \text{and} \qquad u_0(x) = x - \theta F(1-x)$$

be the operators for the events $O_1 C_1$ and $O_0 C_1$. Then, for all $0 \leqslant x \leqslant 1$,

$$0 \leqslant u_1(x) \leqslant x + \theta |F'|(1-x) \leqslant 1,$$

and similarly, $0 \leqslant u_0(x) \leqslant 1$, so the model is at least well defined. Furthermore,

$$1 > u_1'(x) = 1 + \theta F'(x) \geqslant 1 - \theta |F'| \geqslant 0,$$

so, since u_1' is continuous, $|u_1'| < 1$. The same is true of u_0; thus, in the notation of Proposition 1 of Section 2.1, $\iota(u_i) < 1$. Since $p(x, O_1 C_1) = \pi c > 0$ for all x, this proposition shows that the model is distance diminishing. Moreover, if $u_1^{(n)}$ is the nth iterate of u_1, $u_1^{(n)}(x) \in \sigma_n(x)$ for all $n \geqslant 0$, and $u_1^{(n)}(x) \to 1$ as $n \to \infty$ for all $0 \leqslant x \leqslant 1$, so X_n is regular by Theorem 3.6.1.

Thus there is a unique stationary probability p_θ, and $\mathscr{L}(X_n) \to p_\theta$ as $n \to \infty$, so that

$$x_\infty(\pi, \theta) = \int x p_\theta(dx).$$

It is easy to see that all of the hypotheses of Theorem 3.1 are satisfied. To check (d) of Section 10.1, for example, we note that

$$w(x) = w_\pi(x) = F(x)\pi c - F(1-x)(1-\pi)c; \tag{3.11}$$

thus $w(0) = F(0)\pi c > 0$, $w(1) = -F(0)(1-\pi)c < 0$, and

$$w'(x) = F'(x)\pi c + F'(1-x)(1-\pi)c < 0 \tag{3.12}$$

for all $0 \leqslant x \leqslant 1$.

By (3.3) [or (1.1)], $x_\infty(\pi, \theta) \to \lambda = \lambda(\pi)$ as $\theta \to 0$, so (3.8) is equivalent to $\lambda(\pi) = \pi$ or $w_\pi(\pi) = 0$. In view of (3.11), this means that

$$F(\pi)\pi = F(1-\pi)(1-\pi),$$

which is equivalent to (3.10).

We have already seen that (3.6) implies (3.7), hence (3.9). Suppose now that (3.9) is satisfied for all $0 < \pi < 1$. Then $G(x) \equiv G(1-x)$, so (3.11) yields

$$w(x) = G(x)(\pi - x)c. \tag{3.13}$$

Furthermore, $\gamma = \gamma(\pi) = 0$, by (3.3). Since $v(x) \equiv 0$, and

$$S(\pi) = F^2(\pi)\pi c + F^2(1-\pi)(1-\pi)c > 0$$

so that $\sigma^2 > 0$, this implies $w''(\pi) = 0$. But $w''(\pi) = -2G'(\pi)c$, by (3.13); therefore $G'(\pi) \equiv 0$. It follows that there is a positive constant η such that $G(x) = \eta$ or $F(x) = \eta(1-x)$ on $(0, 1)$. Since both $F(x)$ and $\eta(1-x)$ are continuous at 0 and 1, (3.6) holds throughout $[0, 1]$. ∎

It is not difficult to display functions F, other than those in (3.6), that satisfy (3.10) and thus (3.8) for all $0 < \pi < 1$. Let $F(x) = G(x)(1-x)$, where

$$G(x) = k + H(x(1-x)),$$

$k > 0$, $H(y) \geqslant 0$, H has three bounded derivatives in $[0, \frac{1}{4}]$, and $0 < |H'| < k$.

Any such function is of the type considered in the corollary, for

$$|G'(x)| \leqslant |H'| < k \leqslant G(x),$$

and thus

$$F'(x) = G'(x)(1-x) - G(x) < 0.$$

Since H is not constant, neither is G, but $G(x) \equiv G(1-x)$.

11 ○ Absorption Probabilities

11.1. Bounded State Spaces

In this chapter we study real Markov processes that are attracted to the upper and lower boundaries of their state spaces, and attempt to approximate the asymptotic mass at the upper boundary.

Let $I = [c, d]$ be a closed bounded interval. For every $\tau \in J$, K_τ is a transition kernel in a Borel set I_τ such that

$$I_\tau^+ = I_\tau \cap [d, \infty) \neq \varnothing,$$
$$I_\tau^- = I_\tau \cap (-\infty, c] \neq \varnothing, \tag{1.1}$$

and

$$I_\tau^* = I_\tau \cap (c, d) \neq \varnothing.$$

Corresponding Markov processes are denoted X_n^τ. All states of $I_\tau^+ \cup I_\tau^-$ are absorbing, and, for any $x \in I_\tau^*$, the asymptotic distribution of X_n^τ when $X_0^\tau = x$ is concentrated on these absorbing states:

$$K_\tau^{(n)}(x, \cdot) \to K_\tau^\infty(x, \cdot) \tag{1.2}$$

163

weakly as $n \to \infty$, where

$$K_\tau^\infty(x, I_\tau^+ \cup I_\tau^-) = 1. \tag{1.3}$$

[Of course $K_\tau^{(n)}(x, \cdot) = \delta_x(\cdot) = K_\tau^\infty(x, \cdot)$ for $x \in I_\tau^+ \cup I_\tau^-$.] Let

$$\phi_\tau(x) = K_\tau^\infty(x, I_\tau^+)$$

be the asymptotic probability of I_τ^+.

Suppose further that there are functions $a(x)$ and $b(x) > 0$ on (c, d) such that

$$E(\Delta X_n^\tau | X_n^\tau = x) = \tau a(x) + o(\tau),$$

$$E((\Delta X_n^\tau)^2 | X_n^\tau = x) = \tau b(x) + o(\tau), \tag{1.4}$$

and

$$E(|\Delta X_n^\tau|^3 | X_n^\tau = x) = o(\tau),$$

where the quantities $o(\tau)$ satisfy

$$\delta = \sup_{x \in I_\tau^*} |o(\tau)/\tau b(x)| \to 0 \tag{1.5}$$

as $\tau \to 0$. Suppose finally that the function

$$r(x) = 2a(x)/b(x)$$

on (c, d) can be extended to a continuously differentiable function on I. Note that, although (1.4) has the same form as (9.1.1), our conditions on $o(\tau)$, a, and b differ from those in Section 9.1.

Let ψ be the solution of

$$\psi''(x) + r(x)\psi'(x) = 0, \tag{1.6}$$

such that $\psi(c) = 0$ and $\psi(d) = 1$. The following theorem combines results of Khintchine (1948, Section 2 of Chapter 3) and Norman (1971a, Theorem 6.1).

THEOREM 1.1.   *Under these conditions,*

$$|\phi_\tau - \psi| = \sup_{x \in I_\tau^*} |\phi_\tau(x) - \psi(x)| \to 0$$

as $\tau \to 0$.

Let $U = U_\tau$ and $U^\infty = U_\tau^\infty$ be the transition operators corresponding to K_τ and K_τ^∞. If $\gamma(x)$ is a bounded continuous function on I_τ,

$$\lim_{n \to \infty} U_\tau^n \gamma(x) = U_\tau^\infty \gamma(x)$$

for all $x \in I_\tau$ by (1.2). Since $|U_\tau^n \gamma(x)|$ is bounded by the supremum of $|\gamma(x)|$

over I_τ,

$$\lim_{n \to \infty} U_\tau^n \gamma(x) = \lim_{n \to \infty} U_\tau U_\tau^n \gamma(x) = U_\tau U_\tau^\infty \gamma(x)$$

by the bounded convergence theorem, so that

$$U_\tau^\infty \gamma(x) = U_\tau U_\tau^\infty \gamma(x).$$

If $\gamma(x)$ is 1 on I_τ^+ and 0 on I_τ^-, $U_\tau^\infty \gamma(x) = \phi_\tau(x)$; thus

$$U_\tau \phi_\tau(x) = \phi_\tau(x).$$

This equation is closely related to (1.6). Expanding $\phi = \phi_\tau$ formally about $x \in I_\tau^*$ and using (1.4) we obtain

$$0 = E(\phi(X_{n+1}) - \phi(x)|X_n = x)$$

$$= \tau a(x) \phi'(x) + \tau \frac{b(x)}{2} \phi''(x) + o(\tau),$$

or, dividing by $\tau b(x)/2$,

$$\phi''(x) + r(x) \phi'(x) = o(1).$$

Since $\phi(x)$ is 1 on I_τ^+ and 0 on I_τ^-, the conclusion of Theorem 1.1 appears reasonable. We present some applications before giving a proof.

Theorem 1.1 applies to the family of linear models with small drift considered at the end of Section 9.1. In that case, $I_\tau = I = [0,1]$, so $I_\tau^+ = \{1\}$ and $I_\tau^- = \{0\}$. As we shall see in Section 12.1,

$$P_x(X_n^\tau \to 0 \text{ or } X_n^\tau \to 1) = 1$$

for all $0 < x < 1$, which implies (1.2) and (1.3). The functions a and b for (1.4) are given in (9.1.9), and $r(x) \equiv -2k$ is certainly continuously differentiable on I, even though $b(i) = 0$. The remaining assumption (1.5) is easily verified. As was noted at the end of Chapter 0,

$$\psi(x) = (e^{2kx} - 1)/(e^{2k} - 1)$$

for $k \neq 0$.

The following application is of the type considered by Khintchine in the section of his monograph cited above. Suppose that, for every $\tau \in J$, K_τ is a transition kernel in a Borel set I_τ satisfying (1.1). It is not assumed that states of $I_\tau^+ \cup I_\tau^-$ are absorbing, but, rather, that X_n^τ eventually enters this set wherever it starts:

$$P_x(X_n^\tau \in I_\tau^+ \cup I_\tau^- \text{ for some } n \geqslant 0) = 1. \tag{1.7}$$

Let $N = N^\tau$ be the first index n such that $X_n^\tau \in I_\tau^+ \cup I_\tau^-$. Thus X_N^τ is the first point of $I_\tau^+ \cup I_\tau^-$ to be reached, and

$$\psi_\tau(x) = P_x(X_N^\tau \geqslant d)$$

is the probability that X_n^τ goes above d before it goes below c. Suppose that K_τ satisfies (1.4), where a and b are continuously differentiable and $b(x) > 0$ throughout $[c, d]$, and the terms $o(\tau)$ satisfy

$$\sup_{x \in I_\tau^*} |o(\tau)/\tau| \to 0. \tag{1.8}$$

[It follows that $r(x) = 2a(x)/b(x)$ is continuously differentiable throughout I, and (1.5) holds.]

COROLLARY. *Under these conditions,* $|\psi_\tau - \psi| \to 0$, *where* ψ *is the solution of* (1.6) *with* $\psi(c) = 0$ *and* $\psi(d) = 1$.

This is proved by modifying K_τ to make states of $I_\tau^+ \cup I_\tau^-$ absorbing, and applying Theorem 1.1. Clearly, $Y_n^\tau = X_{n \wedge N}^\tau$ $(n \wedge N = \min\{n, N\})$ is a Markov process in I_τ, with kernel

$$L_\tau(x, \cdot) = \begin{cases} K_\tau(x, \cdot) & \text{if } x \in I_\tau^*, \\ \delta_x(\cdot) & \text{if } x \in I_\tau^+ \cup I_\tau^-. \end{cases}$$

For $n \geqslant N$, $Y_n^\tau = X_N^\tau$; thus, for all Borel subsets A of I_τ,

$$L_\tau^{(n)}(x, A) = P_x(Y_n^\tau \in A) \to P_x(X_N^\tau \in A) = L_\tau^\infty(x, A).$$

It follows that L_τ satisfies (1.2) and (1.3), and

$$\psi_\tau(x) = L_\tau^\infty(x, I_\tau^+).$$

Since $K_\tau(x, \cdot) = L_\tau(x, \cdot)$ on I_τ^*, L_τ satisfies (1.4), where, as was noted above, (1.5) holds. Thus L_τ satisfies all of the assumptions of Theorem 1.1.

Proof of Theorem 1.1. Let $f = f_\varepsilon$ be the solution of

$$f''(x) + r(x) f'(x) = \varepsilon$$

in I, such that $f'(c) = 1$ and $f(c) = 0$; i.e.,

$$f(x) = \int_c^x f'(y) \, dy,$$

where

$$f'(x) = e^{-B(x)} \left(1 + \varepsilon \int_c^x e^{B(y)} \, dy\right)$$

and

$$B(x) = \int_c^x r(y) \, dy.$$

Let $|\varepsilon|$ be sufficiently small that $f'(x) > 0$ for all $x \in I$. Then $f(d) > 0$, so $g(x) = g_\varepsilon(x) = f(x)/f(d)$ is the solution of

$$g''(x) + r(x)g'(x) = \varepsilon/f(d) = \tilde{\varepsilon} \qquad (1.9)$$

in I, such that $g(c) = 0$ and $g(d) = 1$. Since g' and r are differentiable on I, g'' is too, as a consequence of (1.9). Differentiating (1.9) we get

$$g^{(3)}(x) + r'(x)g'(x) + r(x)g''(x) = 0,$$

from which we see that $g^{(3)}$ is continuous throughout I. It is easily shown that, for any $\alpha > 0$, there is an extension $h = h_{\varepsilon,\alpha}$ of g_ε to R^1 such that

$$d_3 = \sup_{x \in R^1} |h^{(3)}(x)| < \infty,$$

$$|h(x) - 1| \leqslant \alpha \qquad (1.10)$$

for $x \geqslant d$, and

$$|h(x)| \leqslant \alpha \qquad (1.11)$$

for $x \leqslant c$. (If $I_\tau \subset I$, this extension is unnecessary, and the proof can be simplified slightly.) For $j = 1, 2$, let

$$d_j = \sup_{x \in I} |h^{(j)}(x)|.$$

Let $U = U_\tau$ be the transition operator with kernel K_τ. From (1.4) we get

$$Uh(x) - h(x) = \tau\left(a(x)h'(x) + \frac{b(x)}{2}\, h''(x) \right)$$

$$+ o(\tau)h'(x) + \frac{o(\tau)}{2}\, h''(x) + \frac{o(\tau)}{6}\, \omega d_3,$$

where $|\omega| \leqslant 1$, for $x \in I_\tau^*$. Division by $\tau b(x)/2$ yields

$$\left| \frac{Uh(x) - h(x)}{\tau b(x)/2} - \tilde{\varepsilon} \right| \leqslant \delta_1 d_1 + \delta_2 d_2 + \delta_3 d_3,$$

where δ_i is a function only of τ, such that $\delta_i \to 0$ as $\tau \to 0$. Suppose now that $\varepsilon \neq 0$, so that $\tilde{\varepsilon} \neq 0$. If τ is sufficiently small that the quantity on the right is less than $|\tilde{\varepsilon}|$ [we write $\tau \leqslant \tau(\varepsilon, \alpha)$], then $Uh(x) - h(x)$ has the same sign as $\tilde{\varepsilon}$ on I_τ^*. Since $Uh(x) = h(x)$ on $I_\tau^+ \cup I_\tau^-$, we conclude that

$$Uh(x) \geqslant h(x) \qquad \text{if} \quad \varepsilon > 0,$$

$$Uh(x) \leqslant h(x) \qquad \text{if} \quad \varepsilon < 0,$$

for all $x \in I_\tau$ and $\tau \leqslant \tau(\varepsilon, \alpha)$.

Applying the positive operator U^n to both sides, we see that $U^n h(x)$ is a monotonic sequence; hence

$$U^n h(x) \geqslant h(x) \quad \text{if} \quad \varepsilon > 0,$$

$$U^n h(x) \leqslant h(x) \quad \text{if} \quad \varepsilon < 0.$$

Since h is continuous, (1.2) implies that

$$U^\infty h(x) \geqslant h(x) \quad \text{if} \quad \varepsilon > 0,$$

$$U^\infty h(x) \leqslant h(x) \quad \text{if} \quad \varepsilon < 0, \tag{1.12}$$

where $U^\infty = U_\tau^\infty$ is the transition operator with kernel K_τ^∞.

As a consequence of (1.3),

$$U^\infty h(x) - \phi_\tau(x) = \int_{I_\tau^+ \cup I_\tau^-} K^\infty(x, dy) h(y) - K^\infty(x, I_\tau^+)$$

$$= \int_{I_\tau^+} K^\infty(x, dy)\,(h(y) - 1) + \int_{I_\tau^-} K^\infty(x, dy) h(y);$$

thus

$$|U^\infty h(x) - \phi_\tau(x)| \leqslant \alpha K^\infty(x, I_\tau^+ \cup I_\tau^-) = \alpha$$

by (1.10) and (1.11). Henceforth, we assume $x \in I_\tau^*$, so that $h(x) = g_\varepsilon(x)$. By (1.12),

$$\phi_\tau(x) = U^\infty h(x) + (\phi_\tau(x) - U^\infty h(x))$$

$$\geqslant g_\varepsilon(x) - \alpha \quad \text{if} \quad \varepsilon > 0,$$

and

$$\phi_\tau(x) \leqslant g_\varepsilon(x) + \alpha \quad \text{if} \quad \varepsilon < 0,$$

for $\tau \leqslant \tau(\varepsilon, \alpha)$. Finally,

$$\phi_\tau(x) - \psi(x) \geqslant -|g_\varepsilon(x) - \psi(x)| - \alpha \quad \text{if} \quad \varepsilon > 0,$$

$$\phi_\tau(x) - \psi(x) \leqslant |g_\varepsilon(x) - \psi(x)| + \alpha \quad \text{if} \quad \varepsilon < 0;$$

hence, taking $\varepsilon > 0$,

$$|\phi_\tau - \psi| \leqslant |g_\varepsilon - \psi| \vee |g_{-\varepsilon} - \psi| + \alpha$$

for all $\tau \leqslant \tau(\varepsilon, \alpha) \wedge \tau(-\varepsilon, \alpha)$. But $\psi = g_0$ and $|g_\delta - g_0| \to 0$ as $\delta \to 0$, so the right-hand side can be made arbitrarily small by choosing ε and α sufficiently small. Therefore, $|\phi_\tau - \psi| \to 0$ as $\tau \to 0$. ∎

11.2. Unbounded State Spaces

In this section, we treat processes in unbounded state spaces. For every $\tau \in J$, K_τ is a transition kernel in a Borel subset I_τ of R^1 with

$$\sup I_\tau = \infty \quad \text{and} \quad \inf I_\tau = -\infty.$$

As usual, X_n^τ is a corresponding Markov process. In place of (1.2) and (1.3), it is assumed that

$$P_x(X_n^\tau \to \infty \text{ or } X_n^\tau \to -\infty \text{ as } n \to \infty) = 1$$

for all $x \in R^1$. Let

$$\phi_\tau(x) = P_x(X_n^\tau \to \infty),$$

and suppose that

$$\lim_{\substack{x \to -\infty \\ \tau \to 0}} \phi_\tau(x) = \lim_{\substack{x \to \infty \\ \tau \to 0}} 1 - \phi_\tau(x) = 0. \tag{2.1}$$

We assume that (1.4) holds, where a and b are continuously differentiable and $b(x) > 0$ throughout R^1, and, in place of (1.5),

$$\sup_{\substack{x \in I_\tau \\ |x| < k}} |o(\tau)|/\tau \to 0 \tag{2.2}$$

as $\tau \to 0$ for each $k < \infty$. Finally, we assume that

$$v = \int_{-\infty}^{\infty} e^{-B(x)} dx < \infty, \tag{2.3}$$

where

$$B(x) = \int_0^x r(y) \, dy.$$

Let ψ be the solution of (1.6) with $\psi(-\infty) = 0$ and $\psi(\infty) = 1$; i.e.,

$$\psi(x) = \int_{-\infty}^x e^{-B(y)} dy / v.$$

Theorem 2.1 is completely analogous to Theorem 1.1.

THEOREM 2.1. *Under these conditions,*

$$|\phi_\tau - \psi| = \sup_{x \in I_\tau} |\phi_\tau(x) - \psi(x)| \to 0$$

as $\tau \to 0$.

This result will be applied to additive learning models in Chapter 14.

Proof. For any positive constant k, let N be the first index n for which $|X_n| \geq k$, and let

$$\psi_{\tau k}(x) = P_x(X_N \geq k).$$

Also, let $\psi_k(x)$ be the solution of (1.6) on $|x| \leq k$ for which $\psi_k(k) = 1$ and $\psi_k(-k) = 0$; i.e.,

$$\psi_k(x) = \frac{\psi(x) - \psi(-k)}{\psi(k) - \psi(-k)}.$$

Take $\psi_k(x) = 1$ for $x \geq k$ and $\psi_k(x) = 0$ for $x \leq -k$. It follows from the corollary to Theorem 1.1 that

$$\alpha_{\tau k} = |\psi_{\tau k} - \psi_k| \to 0 \qquad \text{as} \quad \tau \to 0. \tag{2.4}$$

And it is easily shown that

$$\beta_k = |\psi_k - \psi| \to 0 \qquad \text{as} \quad k \to \infty. \tag{2.5}$$

Suppose now that

$$\gamma_k = \limsup_{\tau \to 0} |\phi_\tau - \psi_{\tau k}| \to 0 \qquad \text{as} \quad k \to \infty. \tag{2.6}$$

Clearly

$$|\phi_\tau - \psi| \leq |\phi_\tau - \psi_{\tau k}| + \alpha_{\tau k} + \beta_k,$$

so that

$$\limsup_{\tau \to 0} |\phi_\tau - \psi| \leq \gamma_k + \beta_k$$

by (2.4), and the theorem would follow from (2.5) and (2.6). Thus it remains only to demonstrate (2.6).

Clearly

$$|\phi_\tau(x) - \psi_{\tau k}(x)| \leq P_x(G_\infty - G_k) \vee P_x(G_k - G_\infty), \tag{2.7}$$

where G_∞ and G_k are the events

$$G_\infty = (\lim_{n \to \infty} X_n = \infty) = (\lim_{n \to \infty} X_{n+N} = \infty)$$

and

$$G_k = (X_N \geq k).$$

Using the same notation for indicator variables, we obtain

$$P_x(G_k - G_\infty) = E_x(G_k \tilde{G}_\infty)$$
$$= E_x(G_k P(\tilde{G}_\infty | X_n, n \leqslant N))$$
$$= E_x(G_k(1 - \phi_\tau(X_N)))$$
$$\leqslant \sup_{y \geqslant k} 1 - \phi_\tau(y).$$

Similarly,

$$P_x(G_\infty - G_k) \leqslant \sup_{y \geqslant k} \phi_\tau(-y).$$

Hence, by (2.7),

$$|\phi_\tau - \psi_{\tau k}| \leqslant \sup_{y \geqslant k} (1 - \phi_\tau(y)) \vee \phi_\tau(-y),$$

so that

$$\gamma_k \leqslant \limsup_{\tau \to 0} \sup_{y \geqslant k} (1 - \phi_\tau(y)) \vee \phi_\tau(-y).$$

But (2.1) implies that the right-hand side converges to 0 as $k \to \infty$, so (2.6) is proved. ∎

Part III ○ SPECIAL MODELS

12 ○ The Five-Operator Linear Model

Let us first recall the notation of Section 0.1 for two-choice simple learning experiments. There are two responses, A_1 and A_0, each of which can be followed by an outcome O_j that reinforces A_j, and conditioning is effective (C_1) or ineffective (C_0). Occurrences on trial n are indicated by adding a subscript n. The reinforcement schedule and effectiveness of conditioning parameters are

$$\pi_{ij} = P(O_{jn}|A_{in})$$

and

$$c_{ij} = P(C_{1n}|A_{in}O_{jn}).$$

Let

$$\Pi_{ij} = \pi_{ij}c_{ij} = P(O_{jn}C_{1n}|A_{in}).$$

Technically, occurrences like A_{in} are subsets of an underlying sample space. It is convenient to use the same notation for their indicator random variables. Thus

$$A_{1n} = \begin{cases} 1 & \text{if } A_{1n}, \\ 0 & \text{if } A_{0n}. \end{cases}$$

175

It will always be clear from the context whether a set or its indicator is meant.

For the five-operator linear model, the state random variable X_n can be interpreted as a subject's probability of A_{1n}, and the event random variable is

$$E_n = (A_{1n}, O_{1n}, C_{1n}).$$

The model is defined within the framework of Section 0.2 by the following specifications.

State space: $X = [0, 1]$

Event space: $E = \{0, 1\} \times \{0, 1\} \times \{0, 1\}$.

Transformation of x effected by $e = (i, j, k)$:

$$u(x, e) = x + k\theta_{ij}(j - x).$$

Probability of e given x:

$$p(x, e) = \begin{cases} x\pi_{1j}c_{1j} & \text{if } i = 1, \quad k = 1, \\ x\pi_{1j}c'_{1j} & \text{if } i = 1, \quad k = 0, \\ x'\pi_{0j}c_{0j} & \text{if } i = 0, \quad k = 1, \\ x'\pi_{0j}c'_{0j} & \text{if } i = 0, \quad k = 0, \end{cases}$$

where

$$x' = 1 - x.$$

More precisely, these relations define a family of models indexed by parameters θ_{ij}, π_{ij}, and c_{ij}, subject to

$$0 \leqslant \theta_{ij}, \pi_{ij}, c_{ij} \leqslant 1$$

and

$$\sum_j \pi_{ij} = 1.$$

Two useful auxiliary notations are

$$\theta_i = \sum_j \theta_{ij} \Pi_{ij}$$

and

$$\omega_i = \theta_{ii'} \Pi_{ii'}.$$

Note that $\omega_1 > 0$ if and only if θ_{10}, π_{10}, and c_{10} are all positive, while $\theta_1 > 0$ if and only if there is some j such that θ_{1j}, π_{1j}, and c_{1j} are positive.

12.1. Criteria for Regularity and Absorption

The quantities θ_i determine whether or not the model is distance diminishing with respect to the natural metric $d(x, y) = |x - y|$ on X.

THEOREM 1.1. *The model is distance diminishing if and only if $\theta_1 > 0$ and $\theta_0 > 0$.*

Proof. If $\theta_i > 0$, there is a j such that $\theta_{ij} > 0$, $\pi_{ij} > 0$, and $c_{ij} > 0$. Hence, in the notation of Proposition 1 of Section 2.1,

$$\iota(u(\cdot, e)) = 1 - \theta_{ij} < 1$$

for $e = (i, j, 1)$, and $p(x, e) > 0$ if $x \neq i'$. Thus, if $\theta_0 > 0$ and $\theta_1 > 0$, it follows from this proposition that the model is distance diminishing.

If, conversely, $\theta_1 = 0$ or $\theta_0 = 0$, it is not difficult to show that $r_k = 1$ for all $k \geq 1$, so that the model is not distance diminishing. ∎

The qualitative asymptotic behavior of state and event sequences depends on which states, if any, are absorbing. This is determined by the quantities ω_i.

LEMMA 1.1. *The state i is absorbing if and only if $\omega_i = 0$. A state $x \in (0, 1)$ is absorbing if and only if $\theta_1 = \theta_0 = 0$, in which case all states are absorbing and the model is said to be trivial.*

In view of Theorem 1.1, a distance diminishing model is not subject to this form of degeneracy.

Proof. If $e = (i, i', 1)$, $\omega_i > 0$ is equivalent to

$$|u(i, e) - i| = \theta_{ii'} > 0$$

and

$$p(i, e) = \Pi_{ii'} > 0,$$

which conditions are necessary and sufficient for i not to be absorbing.

A state $x \in (0, 1)$ is absorbing if and only if $\theta_{ij} \Pi_{ij} = 0$ for all i and j; i.e., $\theta_1 = \theta_0 = 0$. ∎

Since X is compact, a state sequence X_n of a distance diminishing five-operator linear model is a compact Markov process (Proposition 1 of Section 3.3). Except for one degenerate case, such state sequences are either regular or absorbing processes. We recall that, for a regular process, the distribution $\mathscr{L}(X_n)$ of X_n converges to a limit μ that does not depend on $\mathscr{L}(X_0)$, while, for an absorbing process, X_n converges almost surely (a.s.) to a random absorbing state. For further discussion of regular and absorbing compact Markov processes, see Section 3.6.

THEOREM 1.2. *If either 0 or 1 is an absorbing state for a distance diminishing linear model, then X_n is an absorbing process.*

THEOREM 1.3. *If neither 0 nor 1 is absorbing, then the model is distance diminishing. Either (a) $\omega_0 = \omega_1 = 1$, or (b) X_n is regular.*

The proof of Theorem 1.2 is based on the following lemma. The set of possible values of X_n when $X_0 = x$ is denoted $\sigma_n(x)$.

LEMMA 1.2. If $\theta_i > 0$ and i is absorbing, then $d(\sigma_n(x), i) \to 0$ as $n \to \infty$, for all $x \neq i'$.

Proof. Since $\theta_i > 0$ and $\omega_i = 0$, $\theta_{ii} > 0$ and $\Pi_{ii} > 0$. Let $x^0 = x$ and

$$x^n = u(x^{n-1}, (i, i, 1)).$$

Assuming, inductively, that $x^{n-1} \in \sigma_{n-1}(x)$, and noting that $x^{n-1} \neq i'$, we see that

$$x^n \in \sigma_1(x^{n-1}) \subset \sigma_n(x).$$

Thus $x^n \in \sigma_n(x)$ for all $n \geqslant 0$, and

$$d(\sigma_n(x), i) \leqslant |x^n - i|$$
$$= (1 - \theta_{ii})^n |x - i| \to 0. \quad \blacksquare$$

Proof of Theorem 1.2. Suppose that i is absorbing. (1) If i' is absorbing too, then $d(\sigma_n(i'), i') = 0$ for all n. In conjunction with Lemma 1.2, this implies that X_n is absorbing, according to Theorem 3.6.2. (2) If i' is not absorbing, then there is an $x \neq i'$ such that $x \in \sigma_1(i')$. So $\sigma_{n-1}(x) \subset \sigma_n(i')$, and

$$d(\sigma_n(i'), i) \leqslant d(\sigma_{n-1}(x), i) \to 0$$

by Lemma 1.2. Thus, again, Theorem 3.6.2 is applicable. $\quad \blacksquare$

Proof of Theorem 1.3. If neither endpoint is absorbing, then $\theta_i \geqslant \omega_i > 0$ for $i = 0, 1$, so that the model is distance diminishing by Theorem 1.1. Suppose now that $\omega_i < 1$. We will show that $d(\sigma_n(x), i') \to 0$ as $n \to \infty$ for all $x \in X$, so that regularity follows from Theorem 3.6.1.

Consider first the case $x \neq i'$.

(1) If $\theta_{ii'} < 1$, let $x^0 = x$ and

$$x^n = u(x^{n-1}, (i, i', 1)).$$

Since $x^{n-1} \neq i'$, $x^n \in \sigma_1(x^{n-1})$. By induction, $x^n \in \sigma_n(x)$. But $\theta_{ii'} > 0$, so

$$d(\sigma_n(x), i') \leqslant d(x^n, i')$$
$$= (1 - \theta_{ii'})^n |x - i'| \to 0.$$

(2) If $\Pi_{ii'} < 1$, there is an event e such that

$$|u(x, e) - i'| \geqslant |x - i'|$$

and $p(x, e) > 0$, so that $u(x, e) \in \sigma_1(x)$. Therefore $x^n = u(x^{n-1}, e) \neq i'$ and

$x^n \in \sigma_n(x)$. Thus if $\theta_{ii'} = 1$, so that $i' \in \sigma_1(x^{n-1})$, we have $i' \in \sigma_n(x)$ for all $n \geqslant 1$.

Since i' is not absorbing, there is a $y \neq i'$ in $\sigma_1(i')$. Thus $\sigma_n(i') \supset \sigma_{n-1}(y)$, and

$$d(\sigma_n(i'), i') \leqslant d(\sigma_{n-1}(y), i') \to 0$$

as $n \to \infty$ by the previous case. ∎

When $\omega_0 = \omega_1 = 1$, the process X_n moves to 0 or 1 on its first step and thereafter alternates between these two states. Clearly the process is ergodic, with ergodic kernel $\{0, 1\}$ and period 2. Such *cyclic* models are of no interest psychologically.

12.2. The Mean Learning Curve

The mean learning curve

$$x_n = P(A_{1n}) = E(X_n)$$

is the traditional starting point for both mathematical and empirical studies of models for learning in two-choice experiments. The standard tactic for obtaining information about x_n is to use the equation

$$\Delta x_n = E(W(X_n)), \tag{2.1}$$

where

$$W(X_n) = E(\Delta X_n | X_n),$$

to obtain a relation between x_n and x_{n+1}. Clearly

$$E(A_{1n} \Delta X_n | X_n = x) = \theta_{11} x'x\Pi_{11} - \theta_{10} xx\Pi_{10} = \theta_1 x'x - \omega_1 x,$$
$$\tag{2.2}$$

$$E(A_{0n} \Delta X_n | X_n = x) = -\theta_{00} xx'\Pi_{00} + \theta_{01} x'x'\Pi_{01} = \omega_0 x' - \theta_0 xx'.$$

These equations are at the root of most of the computations in this chapter. Adding them, we obtain

$$W(x) = (\theta_1 - \theta_0) xx' - \omega_1 x + \omega_0 x'.$$

Let

$$\delta = \theta_1 - \theta_0, \qquad \omega = \omega_1 + \omega_0,$$

and, if $\omega > 0$ (i.e., 0 and 1 are not both absorbing),

$$l = \omega_0 / \omega.$$

In terms of these quantities,

$$W(x) - \delta xx' = \omega_0 x' - \omega_1 x = \begin{cases} 0 & \text{if } \omega = 0, \\ \omega(l - x) & \text{if } \omega > 0. \end{cases} \qquad (2.3)$$

Substitution into (2.1) then yields

$$\Delta x_n - \delta E(X_n X_n') = \omega_0 x_n' - \omega_1 x_n = \begin{cases} 0 & \text{if } \omega = 0, \\ \omega(l - x_n) & \text{if } \omega > 0, \end{cases} \qquad (2.4)$$

which is the relation sought.

We first consider the asymptotic A_1 response probability

$$x_\infty = \lim_{n \to \infty} x_n.$$

Later in the section we return to the problem of computing or approximating x_n. It is assumed that the model is distance diminishing and (in the case of no absorbing states) noncyclic, so that the limit x_∞ exists. If both 0 and 1 are absorbing states, the process X_n is absorbing. Thus the probability is 1 that X_n converges to either 0 or 1, and

$$x_\infty = P(X_n \to 1)$$

depends on the distribution of X_0. The only case in which x_∞ is known exactly is $\delta = 0$. Then (2.4) gives $\Delta x_n = 0$, so that $x_\infty = x_0$. An approximation to x_∞ when δ, θ_{11}, and θ_{00} are small is given in Section 12.4. If i is the only absorbing state, $X_n \to i$ a.s., and $x_\infty = i$.

The quantity x_∞ is of particular interest when there are no absorbing states. Let

$$\bar{A}_{1n} = (1/n) \sum_{m=0}^{n-1} A_{1m}$$

be the proportion of A_1 responses in the first n trials. The corollary to Theorem 6.1.1 implies that $\bar{A}_{1n} \to x_\infty$ a.s., and

$$\sqrt{n}(\bar{A}_{1n} - x_\infty) \sim N(0, \sigma^2),$$

where

$$\sigma^2 = x_\infty x_\infty' + 2 \sum_{j=1}^{\infty} \rho_j \qquad (2.5)$$

and

$$\rho_j = \lim_{n \to \infty} P(A_{1n} A_{1\,n+j}) - x_\infty^2.$$

Once σ^2 has been estimated, this result can be used to construct confidence intervals for or test hypotheses about x_∞, on the basis of a single subject's proportion $\bar{A}_{1n}$ of A_1 responses. When a formula for σ^2 like (3.23) is available, the problem of estimating σ^2 reduces to that of estimating the parameters that appear therein. A model-free approach to the estimation of σ^2 is described in Section 5.4. It is worth noting that the quantities x_∞, ρ_j, and σ^2 do not depend on the distribution of X_0.

Since W is quadratic with $W(0) = \omega_0 > 0$ and $W(1) = -\omega_1 < 0$, this function has a unique root λ in $(0, 1)$.

THEOREM 2.1.   *If there are no absorbing states, and $\theta_{01} < 1$ or $\theta_{10} < 1$, then*

$$l < x_\infty < \lambda \quad \text{if} \quad \delta > 0,$$

$$l = x_\infty = \lambda \quad \text{if} \quad \delta = 0, \qquad (2.6)$$

$$l > x_\infty > \lambda \quad \text{if} \quad \delta < 0.$$

In the symmetric case, $\theta_{ii} = \theta$, $\theta_{ii'} = \theta^*$, $c_{ii} = c$, $c_{ii'} = c^*$, and the quantities δ and l reduce to

$$\delta = (\theta c - \theta^* c^*)\,(\pi_{01} - \pi_{10}) \qquad (2.7)$$

and

$$l = \pi_{01}/(\pi_{01} + \pi_{10}).$$

We noted in Section 0.1 that, for any two-choice simple learning model, this ratio is the value of $P(A_{1\infty})$ associated with probability matching: $P(A_{1\infty}) = P(O_{1\infty})$.

The quantity λ is the *expected operator approximation* to x_∞ (see p.183). It is especially useful in the case of learning by small steps, as we shall see in Section 12.4.

Proof of Theorem 2.1.   Letting $n \to \infty$ in (2.4), we obtain

$$0 = \delta\alpha + \omega(l - x_\infty); \qquad (2.8)$$

hence

$$x_\infty - l = \delta\alpha/\omega,$$

where

$$\alpha = \int xx'\mu(dx)$$

and μ is the stationary probability of X_n. Clearly, $\alpha \geqslant 0$. To obtain the relations between x_∞ and l listed in (2.6), it remains only to show that $\alpha > 0$.

If $\alpha = 0$, then $\mu(\{0, 1\}) = 1$. If $\mu(\{i\}) = 1$, then, by Lemma 3.4.3, i is absorbing, contrary to assumption. Hence, $\mu(\{i\}) < 1$ for both i, and $\{0, 1\}$

is the support of μ. Therefore, $\{0, 1\}$ is stochastically closed, according to Lemma 3.4.3. If $e = (i, i', 1)$, $\omega_i > 0$ implies $u(i, e) \in \sigma_1(i)$, and $u(i, e) \neq i$. Thus $u(i, e) = i'$; that is, $\theta_{ii'} = 1$, for both i. Since we are assuming that this is not the case, we must have $\alpha > 0$.

Note that

$$\alpha - x_\infty x_\infty' = -\int x^2 \mu(dx) + x_\infty^2 = -v_\infty,$$

where

$$v_\infty = \int (x - x_\infty)^2 \mu(dx) \tag{2.9}$$

is the variance of μ. Thus (2.8) yields

$$0 = \delta(x_\infty x_\infty' - v_\infty) + \omega(l - x_\infty),$$

or $W(x_\infty) = \delta v_\infty$. If $v_\infty = 0$, x_∞ would support μ, hence would be absorbing, contrary to assumption. Thus $v_\infty > 0$, and the right-hand relations in (2.6) follow immediately. ∎

We now give some results for x_n analogous to those in Theorem 2.1. There are no restrictions on the parameters of the model other than those specifically mentioned below. Note first that, when $\delta = 0$ and $\omega > 0$, (2.4) gives

$$x_{n+1} - l = (1 - \omega)(x_n - l),$$

so that

$$x_n = l + (1 - \omega)^n (x_0 - l). \tag{2.10}$$

Consider now the case $\delta > 0$ ($\delta < 0$ is similar). Rewriting (2.4)

$$x_{n+1} = \delta E(X_n X_n') + (1 - \omega) x_n + \omega_0,$$

and noting that $E(X_n X_n') \leqslant x_n x_n'$, we obtain

$$t(x_n) \leqslant x_{n+1} \leqslant u(x_n), \tag{2.11}$$

where

$$t(x) = (1 - \omega)x + \omega_0$$

and

$$u(x) = \delta x x' + (1 - \omega)x + \omega_0.$$

Let $l_0 = \lambda_0 = x_0$,

$$l_{n+1} = t(l_n), \qquad \text{and} \qquad \lambda_{n+1} = u(\lambda_n).$$

When $\omega = 0$, $l_n = x_0$, and, when $\omega > 0$, l_n is the quantity on the right in (2.10). If $0 < \omega < 2$, $l_n \to l$ as $n \to \infty$. The function u is just the *expected operator*

$$E(X_{n+1}|X_n = x) = x + W(x) = u(x),$$

so λ_n is the expected operator approximation to x_n (Sternberg, 1963, Section 3.2). If λ_n converges to a limit λ as $n \to \infty$, then $\lambda = u(\lambda)$; i.e., $W(\lambda) = 0$.

THEOREM 2.2. *Suppose* $\delta > 0$. *If* $\omega \leqslant 1$, *then* $l_n \leqslant x_n$. *Under the stronger condition* $\omega + \delta \leqslant 1$, $x_n \leqslant \lambda_n$.

Proof. If $\omega \leqslant 1$, $dt(x)/dx \geqslant 0$. Thus $l_n \leqslant x_n$ implies

$$l_{n+1} = t(l_n) \leqslant t(x_n)$$

$$\leqslant x_{n+1}$$

by (2.11). Also

$$\frac{du}{dx}(x) = \delta(1-2x) + (1-\omega) \geqslant 1 - (\omega+\delta)$$

for $x \leqslant 1$. Thus $\omega + \delta \leqslant 1$ implies $du(x)/dx \geqslant 0$ for $0 \leqslant x \leqslant 1$. Noting that $0 \leqslant \lambda_n \leqslant 1$, the above argument yields $x_n \leqslant \lambda_n$. ∎

An approximation to x_n, valid when the parameters θ_{ij} are small, is described in Section 12.4. This approximation is closely related to λ_n.

12.3. Interresponse Dependencies

This section treats the relationship between responses on two different trials. Successive trials are considered first. Let a_n denote response alternation between trials n and $n+1$, i.e.,

$$a_n = A_{0n}A_{1\,n+1} \cup A_{1n}A_{0\,n+1},$$

and let

$$\xi = 2 - \theta_1 - \theta_0.$$

THEOREM 3.1

$$P(a_n) = \xi E(X_n X_n') + \omega_0 x_n' + \omega_1 x_n. \tag{3.1}$$

Proof. Clearly,

$$P(A_{0n}A_{1\,n+1}) = E(A_{0n}A_{1\,n+1})$$

$$= E(A_{0n}E(A_{1\,n+1}|X_{n+1}E_n))$$

$$= E(A_{0n}X_{n+1})$$

$$= E(E(A_{0n}X_{n+1}|X_n)). \tag{3.2}$$

But, by (2.2),

$$E(A_{0n} X_{n+1}|X_n) = X_n E(A_{0n}|X_n) + E(A_{0n} \Delta X_n|X_n)$$

$$= X_n X_n' + \omega_0 X_n' - \theta_0 X_n X_n'$$

$$= (1-\theta_0) X_n X_n' + \omega_0 X_n'. \tag{3.3}$$

Substitution of this into (3.2) yields

$$P(A_{0n} A_{1\ n+1}) = (1-\theta_0) E(X_n X_n') + \omega_0 x_n'.$$

By symmetry,

$$P(A_{1n} A_{0\ n+1}) = (1-\theta_1) E(X_n X_n') + \omega_1 x_n.$$

Equation (3.1) is obtained by adding these equations. ∎

To use (3.1) as it stands, we must know x_n and $E(X_n X_n')$. The only case in which a simple exact formula for x_n is available is $\delta = 0$. If, in addition,

$$\delta_2 = s_1 - s_0 = 0,$$

where

$$s_i = \sum_j \theta_{ij}^2 \Pi_{ij}, \tag{3.4}$$

$E(X_n X_n')$ can be calculated from (3.15). Equations (3.9)–(3.11) and Theorem 3.2 give expressions for some derivatives of $P(a_n)$ under these rather restrictive conditions. Our immediate objective is to treat the "difficult" case $\delta \neq 0$ by an altogether different method. Some slow learning approximations to quantities involving alternations are given in Section 12.4.

When $\delta \neq 0$, comparison of (2.4) and (3.1) suggests that the troublesome term $E(X_n X_n')$ be eliminated between them to obtain the relation

$$\delta P(a_n) - \xi \Delta x_n = \delta(\omega_0 x_n' + \omega_1 x_n) - \xi(\omega_0 x_n' - \omega_1 x_n)$$

$$= -2(1-\theta_1)\omega_0 x_n' + 2(1-\theta_0)\omega_1 x_n \tag{3.5}$$

between the mean learning and alternation curves. Even though (3.5) relates the "observable" quantities $P(a_n)$, x_n, and x_{n+1}, it is not easy to test directly. We now note some immediate consequences that are more amenable to comparison with data. It is assumed that the model is distance diminishing and noncyclic. Then the limit

$$P(a_\infty) = \lim_{n \to \infty} P(a_n)$$

exists, and (3.5) yields

$$\delta P(a_\infty) = -2(1-\theta_1)\omega_0 x_\infty' + 2(1-\theta_0)\omega_1 x_\infty. \tag{3.6}$$

This result is interesting only in the case of no absorbing states. If there are absorbing states, $P(a_\infty) = 0$. In fact, $E(\#a_n) < \infty$, by Theorem 6.2.2, where $\#a_n$ is the total number of trials on which a_n occurs. If 0 is the only absorbing state, $E(\#A_{1n}) < \infty$ too. Summation of (3.5) over $0 \leqslant n \leqslant N$ yields

$$\delta \sum_{n=0}^{N} P(a_n) - \zeta(x_{N+1}-x_0)$$

$$= -2(1-\theta_1)\omega_0 \sum_{n=0}^{N} x_n' + 2(1-\theta_0)\omega_1 \sum_{n=0}^{N} x_n.$$

When $N \to \infty$ this becomes

$$\delta E(\#a_n) = 2(1-\theta_0)\omega_1 E(\#A_{1n}) - \zeta x_0 \tag{3.7}$$

if 0 is the only absorbing state, and

$$\delta E(\#a_n) = \zeta(x_\infty - x_0) \tag{3.8}$$

if both 0 and 1 are absorbing. For a derivation of (3.8) via the functional equation (6.2.2), see Norman (1968d, Theorem 2).

We now turn our attention to the case $\delta = 0$. If there are no absorbing states, (3.1) yields

$$P(a_\infty) = 2(1-\theta_i) E(X_\infty X_\infty') + 2\omega ll', \tag{3.9}$$

where $E(X_\infty X_\infty') = \lim_{n \to \infty} E(X_n X_n')$. Summation of (3.1) over all n gives

$$E(\#a_n) = 2(1-\theta_i) \sum_{n=0}^{\infty} E(X_n X_n') + x_0 \tag{3.10}$$

as a consequence of (2.10), if 0 is the only absorbing state, and

$$E(\#a_n) = 2(1-\theta_i) \sum_{n=0}^{\infty} E(X_n X_n') \tag{3.11}$$

in the case of two absorbing states. The quadratic means in these equations can be calculated explicitly when $\delta_2 = 0$. Let

$$g = s_i + 2(\omega - t_0 - t_1),$$

where

$$t_i = \theta_{ii'}^2 \Pi_{ii'}.$$

THEOREM 3.2. *Suppose that* $\delta = 0$ *and* $\delta_2 = 0$. *If there are no absorbing states,*

$$gE(X_\infty X_\infty') = ll'\omega(2 - \theta_{01} - \theta_{10}). \tag{3.12}$$

If 0 is the only absorbing state,

$$g \sum_{n=0}^{\infty} E(X_n X_n') = E(X_0 X_0') + (1 - \theta_{10}) x_0. \tag{3.13}$$

Finally, if both endpoints are absorbing,

$$g \sum_{n=0}^{\infty} E(X_n X_n') = E(X_0 X_0'). \tag{3.14}$$

Proof. Clearly,

$$X_{n+1} X_{n+1}' = X_n X_n' + (X_n' - X_n) \Delta X_n - (\Delta X_n)^2 ;$$

thus

$$E(X_{n+1} X_{n+1}' | X_n = x) = xx' + (x' - x) W(x) - Z(x),$$

where $Z(x) = E((\Delta X_n)^2 | X_n = x)$. Since $\delta = 0$, (2.3) yields

$$(x' - x) W(x) = \omega_0 x' + \omega_1 x - 2\omega xx'.$$

And

$$
\begin{aligned}
Z(x) &= x(\theta_{11}^2 x'^2 \Pi_{11} + \theta_{10}^2 x^2 \Pi_{10}) + x'(\theta_{01}^2 x'^2 \Pi_{01} + \theta_{00}^2 x^2 \Pi_{00}) \\
&= x(s_1 x'^2 - 2t_1 x' + t_1) + x'(s_0 x^2 - 2t_0 x + t_0) \\
&= s_i xx' - 2(t_1 + t_0) xx' + t_0 x' + t_1 x,
\end{aligned}
$$

since $s_1 = s_0$. Therefore, since $t_i = \theta_{ii'} \omega_i$,

$$E(X_{n+1} X_{n+1}' | X_n = x) = xx' - gxx' + (1 - \theta_{01}) \omega_0 x' + (1 - \theta_{10}) \omega_1 x, \tag{3.15}$$

so that

$$\Delta E(X_n X_n') = -gE(X_n X_n') + (1 - \theta_{01}) \omega_0 x_n' + (1 - \theta_{10}) \omega_1 x_n. \tag{3.16}$$

Letting $n \to \infty$ in (3.16), we obtain (3.12). Summation of (3.16) over $n \geq 0$ yields (3.13) and (3.14). ∎

Some light is shed on the meaning of the condition $\delta = \delta_2 = 0$ by considering the symmetric case. The analog of (2.7) is

$$\delta_2 = (\theta^2 c - \theta^{*2} c^*)(\pi_{01} - \pi_{10}). \tag{3.17}$$

From this it follows that $\delta = \delta_2 = 0$ if and only if $\pi_{01} = \pi_{10}$, or $\theta = \theta^*$ and $c = c^*$. For the latter condition clearly implies the former, and, under the former, $\pi_{01} \neq \pi_{10}$ implies

$$\theta c = \theta^* c^* \qquad \text{and} \qquad \theta^2 c = \theta^{*2} c^*.$$

Since the model is distance diminishing, either θc or $\theta^* c^*$ is positive; thus both are positive. Dividing the second equation by the first yields $\theta = \theta^*$, from which $c = c^*$ follows. The condition $\pi_{10} = \pi_{01}$ means that the probability π_{ii} that A_i is "successful" does not depend on i. Yellott (1969) showed that such *noncontingent success* schedules are especially useful in assessing the relative merits of the linear model with $\theta = \theta^*$ and $c = c^*$ and the pattern model with $c = c^*$.

Either $\pi_{10} = \pi_{01}$, or $\theta = \theta^*$ and $c = c^*$ is compatible with no absorbing states. In the second case, (3.12) reduces to

$$E(X_\infty X_\infty{}') = ll' \frac{2(\pi_{01} + \pi_{10})(1 - \theta)}{\theta + 2(\pi_{01} + \pi_{10})(1 - \theta)}. \tag{3.18}$$

Generally speaking, explicit computation in symmetric models with $\delta = \delta_2 = 0$ is limited mainly by one's stamina. When $\theta = \theta^*$ and $c = c^*$, such computations often simplify somewhat if outcomes are noncontingent ($\pi_{01} = \pi_{11}$).

AUTOCOVARIANCES. We now obtain expressions for the asymptotic response autocovariance function ρ_j and the important quantity σ^2 [see (2.5)] when $\delta = 0$. Like (3.9), these expressions involve $E(X_\infty X_\infty{}')$, our formulas [(3.12) and (3.18)] for which require $\delta_2 = 0$.

THEOREM 3.3. *If $\delta = 0$ and X_n has no absorbing states and is noncyclic, then*

$$\rho_j = (1 - \omega)^{j-1}((1 - \omega) ll' - (1 - \theta_i) E(X_\infty X_\infty{}')) \tag{3.19}$$

for $j \geqslant 1$, and

$$\sigma^2 = 2((1 - \omega/2) ll' - (1 - \theta_i) E(X_\infty X_\infty{}'))/\omega. \tag{3.20}$$

Proof. For $j \geqslant 1$,

$$\begin{aligned}
P(A_{1n} A_{1\,n+j}) &= E(E(A_{1n} A_{1\,n+j} | E_n X_{n+1})) \\
&= E(A_{1n} E(A_{1\,n+j} | X_{n+1})) \\
&= E(A_{1n}(l + (1 - \omega)^{j-1}(X_{n+1} - l)))
\end{aligned}$$

by (2.10), so that

$$P(A_{1n} A_{1\,n+j}) = lP(A_{1n}) + (1 - \omega)^{j-1}(E(A_{1n} X_{n+1}) - lP(A_{1n})). \tag{3.21}$$

And, by a computation like that in (3.3),

$$E(A_{1n} X_{n+1}) = (1-\theta_1) E(X_n^2) + (\theta_1 - \omega_1) x_n. \tag{3.22}$$

Substituting this expression into (3.21) and taking the limit, we obtain

$$\rho_j = (1-\omega)^{j-1} ((1-\theta_1) E(X_\infty^2) + (\theta_1 - \omega_1) l - l^2),$$

from which (3.19) follows. Consequently,

$$\sigma^2 = ll' + (2/\omega) ((1-\omega) ll' - (1-\theta_i) E(X_\infty X_\infty')),$$

which reduces to (3.20). ∎

When $\theta_{ij} = \theta$ and $c_{ij} = c$ for all i and j, (3.18) and (3.20) can be combined to yield

$$\sigma^2 = \frac{ll'}{\pi_{01} + \pi_{10}} \left(\pi_{11} + \pi_{00} + \frac{2(1-c\theta) c^{-1}}{\theta + 2(\pi_{01} + \pi_{10})(1-\theta)} \right). \tag{3.23}$$

We conclude this section by considering two special topics very briefly.

CONTINUOUS REINFORCEMENT.   There is one class of models for which a great many analytic results are known even when $\delta \neq 0$. These are the continuous reinforcement models (i.e., $\pi_{00} = \pi_{10} = 1$) with $c_{00} = c_{10} = 1$. The reader is referred to Bush (1959), Tatsuoka and Mosteller (1959), and Sternberg [1963, Eq. (80)] for this interesting development. A number of predictions for continuous reinforcement models with $c_{00} = c_{10}$ and $\theta_{00} = \theta_{10}$ (and thus $\delta = \delta_2 = 0$) are given by Norman (1964).

CONTINUA OF OPERATORS.   It may happen that one or both responses in a two-response experiment have more than two experimenter-defined outcomes, or, alternatively, one such outcome can produce several effects. Say response A_i can be followed by outcomes $O_{i\alpha}$, where α belongs to a discrete index set $\mathscr{A}$, with probability $\Pi_i(\alpha) [\sum_\alpha \Pi_i(\alpha) = 1]$, in which case the operator

$$u(x, (i, \alpha)) = (1 - \theta_{i\alpha}) x + \gamma_{i\alpha},$$

with $\gamma_{i\alpha} = \theta_{i\alpha}$ or 0, is applied. In fact, we can even consider an arbitrary (measurable) index space $\mathscr{A}$, in which case Π_i is a probability on the index space. Most of the results of this and the preceding sections carry over to this generalized linear model if we take

$$\theta_i = \int \theta_{i\alpha} \Pi_i(d\alpha), \qquad s_i = \int \theta_{i\alpha}^2 \Pi_i(d\alpha),$$

$$\omega_i = \int \omega_{i\alpha} \Pi_i(d\alpha), \qquad t_i = \int \omega_{i\alpha}^2 \Pi_i(d\alpha),$$

where

$$\omega_{i\alpha} = |u(i, (i, \alpha)) - i| = \begin{cases} \gamma_{0\alpha} & \text{if } i = 0, \\ \theta_{i\alpha} - \gamma_{i\alpha} & \text{if } i = 1. \end{cases}$$

Since the behavior of state and response sequences depends only on the distribution of $(\theta_{i\alpha}, \omega_{i\alpha})$ induced by Π_i, specification of this distribution, rather than Π_i itself, would suffice for the study of these processes.

12.4. Slow Learning

This section presents various approximations that apply when the step-size parameters θ_{ij} are small. Two different types of variation of the model's parameters are considered. The first of these produces large drift while the second leads to small drift.

LARGE DRIFT.   Here we assume that $\theta_{ij} = \theta \eta_{ij}$, where θ varies and $\eta_{ij} \geqslant 0$ is fixed, as are c_{ij} and π_{ij}. Under these conditions, the following quantities do not depend on θ:

$$\bar{\theta}_i = \theta_i / \theta = \sum_j \eta_{ij} \Pi_{ij},$$

$$\bar{\delta} = \delta / \theta = \bar{\theta}_1 - \bar{\theta}_0,$$

$$\bar{\omega}_i = \omega_i / \theta = \eta_{ii'} \Pi_{ii'},$$

$$w(x) = W(x) / \theta = \bar{\delta} x x' + \bar{\omega}_0 x' - \bar{\omega}_1 x, \tag{4.1}$$

and

$$S(x) = E((\Delta X_n / \theta)^2 | X_n = x)$$
$$= \eta_{11}^2 \Pi_{11} x'^2 x + \eta_{10}^2 \Pi_{10} x^3 + \eta_{01}^2 \Pi_{01} x'^3 + \eta_{00}^2 \Pi_{00} x^2 x'.$$

Let $s(x) = S(x) - w^2(x)$.

According to Theorem 8.1.1, if $X_0 = x$ a.s., and if $n\theta$ is bounded,

$$(X_n - f(n\theta)) / \sqrt{\theta} \sim N(0, g(\theta n)) \tag{4.2}$$

as $\theta \to 0$, where f and g satisfy the differential equations

$$\frac{df}{dt}(t) = w(f(t)) \tag{4.3}$$

and

$$\frac{dg}{dt}(t) = 2w'(f(t))g(t) + s(f(t)), \dagger \tag{4.4}$$

---

† In this section, prime is used to denote reflection about $\frac{1}{2}$ ($x' = 1 - x$) and d/dt to denote differentiation, with one exception: w' is the derivative of w.

and the initial conditions $f(0) = x$ and $g(0) = 0$. The normality assertion of (4.2) and the precise value of $g(n\theta)$ are of less importance than the fact that *the distribution of X_n is tightly clustered about $f(n\theta)$ when θ is small.*

We now make some observations about f and g. Except where indicated, these do not depend on the special form of w and s. First, if $w(x) = 0$, then $f(t) \equiv x$ and

$$g(t) = s(x) \cdot (e^{2w'(x)t} - 1)/2w'(x),$$

assuming $w'(x) \neq 0$. When $w'(x) = 0$, $g(t) = ts(x)$. If $w(x) \neq 0$, then the quantity in (4.3) never vanishes (Norman, 1968c, Lemma 5.1). Thus we can integrate

$$\frac{1}{w(f(t))} \frac{df}{dt}(t) = 1$$

to obtain $H(f(t)) = t$, where

$$H(f) = \int_x^f \frac{1}{w(u)} \, du. \tag{4.5}$$

For the linear model, w is at worst a quadratic polynomial, so H is easily computed and then inverted to give f. The most difficult case is that in which

$$w(x) = \bar{\delta}(x - \lambda)(x - \zeta)$$

has distinct roots λ and ζ. Let λ be the root such that

$$w'(\lambda) = \bar{\delta}(\lambda - \zeta) < 0. \tag{4.6}$$

Using the partial fraction representation

$$\frac{1}{w(u)} = \frac{1}{\bar{\delta}(\lambda - \zeta)} \left(\frac{1}{u - \lambda} - \frac{1}{u - \zeta} \right)$$

in (4.5), we obtain

$$\frac{f(t) - \lambda}{f(t) - \zeta} = \frac{x - \lambda}{x - \zeta} \exp(t\bar{\delta}(\lambda - \zeta)) = \frac{1}{z(t)}$$

or

$$f(t) - \lambda = \frac{\lambda - \zeta}{z(t) - 1}. \tag{4.7}$$

As a consequence of (4.6), $f(t) \to \lambda$ as $t \to \infty$. Of course, $0 \leqslant \lambda \leqslant 1$, but it is possible that $0 \leqslant \zeta \leqslant 1$ also. For example, in the two-absorbing-barrier case $\bar{\omega}_1 = \bar{\omega}_0 = 0$, $\lambda = 1$ and $\zeta = 0$ if $\bar{\delta} > 0$, while $\lambda = 0$ and $\zeta = 1$ if $\bar{\delta} < 0$.

When $w(x) \neq 0$, f is strictly monotonic, so we can write $g(t) = G(f(t))$. As a consequence of (4.4) and (4.3),

$$w(f)\frac{dG}{df}(f) = 2w'(f)G(f) + s(f).$$

The solution with $G(x) = 0$ is

$$G(f) = w^2(f)\int_x^f \frac{s(u)}{w(u)^3}\,du. \tag{4.8}$$

No absorbing states. The models considered above have no absorbing states if and only if $\bar{\omega}_1 > 0$ and $\bar{\omega}_0 > 0$. In this case, w has a unique root λ in $[0, 1]$, and, in fact, $0 < \lambda < 1$. Since $W = \theta w$, λ is also the unique root of W, referred to in Theorem 2.1, for any $\theta > 0$. Assuming that $\theta\eta_{ii'} < 1$,

$$\mathscr{L}((X_n - \lambda)/\sqrt{\theta}) \to \mathscr{L}_\infty^\theta$$

as $n \to \infty$, where $\mathscr{L}_\infty^\theta$ does not depend on $\mathscr{L}(X_0)$. By Theorem 10.1.1,

$$\mathscr{L}_\infty^\theta \to N(0, \sigma^2)$$

as $\theta \to 0$, where

$$\sigma^2 = S(\lambda)/2|w'(\lambda)|.$$

Clearly $\sigma^2 > 0$. As in the transient case, asymptotic normality is not as significant as the clustering of $\lim_{n \to \infty} \mathscr{L}(X_n)$ about λ when θ is small.

Let

$$x_\infty = \lim_{n \to \infty} E(X_n)$$

and

$$E((X_\infty - \lambda)^2) = \lim_{n \to \infty} E((X_n - \lambda)^2).$$

As a consequence of (10.3.1),

$$E((X_\infty - \lambda)^2) = \theta\sigma^2 + o(\theta), \tag{4.9}$$

while (10.3.3) gives

$$x_\infty = \lambda + \theta\gamma + o(\theta), \tag{4.10}$$

where

$$\gamma = \sigma^2 \bar{\delta}/w'(\lambda). \tag{4.11}$$

Thus $\lambda + \theta\gamma$ is a better approximation to x_∞ than λ is, when θ is small. Note that γ has the same sign as $-\bar{\delta}$ (or $-\delta$), as Theorem 2.1 requires.

It is fairly obvious that $P(a_\infty) \to 2\lambda\lambda'$ as $\theta \to 0$. A more precise approximation to $P(a_\infty)$ can be derived from (4.9) and (4.10). Letting $n \to \infty$ in (3.1),
we obtain

$$P(a_\infty) = \xi E(X_\infty X_\infty') + \omega_0 x_\infty' + \omega_1 x_\infty.$$

Since

$$xx' = \lambda\lambda' + (1-2\lambda)(x-\lambda) - (x-\lambda)^2,$$

$$E(X_\infty X_\infty') = \lambda\lambda' + (1-2\lambda)(x_\infty - \lambda) - E((X_\infty - \lambda)^2).$$

Thus, by (4.9) and (4.10),

$$E(X_\infty X_\infty') = \lambda\lambda' + \theta p + o(\theta),$$

where

$$p = (1-2\lambda)\gamma - \sigma^2 = \sigma^2 \overline{\omega}/w'(\lambda).$$

But $\xi = 2 - \theta(\overline{\theta}_1 + \overline{\theta}_0)$, and

$$\omega_0 x_\infty' + \omega_1 x_\infty = \theta(\overline{\omega}_0 \lambda' + \overline{\omega}_1 \lambda) + o(\theta),$$

so

$$P(a_\infty) = 2\lambda\lambda' + [2p - (\overline{\theta}_1 + \overline{\theta}_0)\lambda\lambda' + \overline{\omega}_0 \lambda' + \overline{\omega}_1 \lambda]\theta + o(\theta). \quad (4.12)$$

SMALL DRIFT.   Except in special cases to be identified below, it is necessary
to let both Π_{ij} and θ_{ij} depend on an auxiliary parameter θ in order to obtain
slow learning with small drift in linear models. Let $\tau = \theta^2$, and suppose that
Π_{ij} and θ_{ij} vary with θ in such a way that the following conditions are met:

$$\theta_{ii} = O(\theta), \quad (4.13)$$

$$\theta_{ii}^2 \Pi_{ii} = \tau\beta_i + o(\tau), \quad (4.14)$$

$$\theta_{11}\Pi_{11} - \theta_{00}\Pi_{00} = \tau\alpha + o(\tau), \quad (4.15)$$

$$\omega_i = \theta_{ii'}\Pi_{ii'} = \tau\alpha_i + o(\tau), \quad (4.16)$$

$$\theta_{ii'}^2 \Pi_{ii'} = o(\tau). \quad (4.17)$$

In these equations, $i = 1$ and 0, α is any real constant, $\alpha_i \geqslant 0$, $\beta_i \geqslant 0$, and
$\beta_0 > 0$ or $\beta_1 > 0$.
      The quantity $\theta_{ij}\Pi_{ij}$ takes into account the two learning-rate parameters
θ_{ij} and c_{ij} associated with $A_i O_j$, as well as the probability π_{ij} that O_j follows
A_i. Thus it is natural to refer to it as the *weight* of O_j given A_i. According
to (4.15), the difference between the weights of success given A_1 and A_0 is
very small $(O(\tau))$. And (4.16) implies that the weight of failure given either
response is very small. This might mean that $\theta_{ii'} = O(\tau)$, $\theta_{ii'} = O(\theta)$ and

$\Pi_{ii'} = O(\theta)$, or $\Pi_{ii'} = O(\tau)$. If $\theta_{ii'} = o(1)$ or $\alpha_i = 0$, then (4.16) implies (4.17). Finally, we note that, when $\beta_i > 0$, (4.13) and (4.14) imply

$$\liminf_{\theta \to 0} \Pi_{ii} > 0.$$

It is interesting to inquire as to the conditions under which our "large drift" scheme satisfies (4.13)–(4.17). Substituting $\theta_{ij} = \theta \eta_{ij}$ into (4.15) and (4.16), we obtain the equations

$$\eta_{11} \Pi_{11} = \eta_{00} \Pi_{00}$$

and

$$\eta_{01} \Pi_{01} = \eta_{10} \Pi_{10} = 0,$$

which are sufficient as well as necessary.

We now show that, under (4.13)–(4.17), all of the hypotheses of Theorem 9.1.1 are satisfied. Note first that $\delta = \alpha^*\tau + o(\tau)$, where $\alpha^* = \alpha + \alpha_1 - \alpha_0$. Therefore, letting

$$a(x) = \alpha^* x x' + \alpha_0 x' - \alpha_1 x,$$

$$E(\Delta X_n | X_n = x) = W(x) = \tau a(x) + o(\tau). \tag{4.18}$$

Similarly, (4.14) and (4.17) imply that

$$E((\Delta X_n)^2 | X_n = x) = \tau b(x) + o(\tau), \tag{4.19}$$

where

$$b(x) = (\beta_1 x' + \beta_0 x) x x'.$$

Finally, $\theta_{ii}^3 \Pi_{ii} = o(\tau)$ by (4.13) and (4.14), and $\theta_{ii'}^3 \Pi_{ii'} = o(\tau)$ by (4.17), so

$$E(|\Delta X_n|^3 | X_n = x) = o(\tau). \tag{4.20}$$

All $o(\tau)$'s are uniform over x, and the functions a and b satisfy the requirements of the theorem.

It follows that, if $X_0 = x$ a.s. and $n\tau$ is bounded, then $X_n \sim P(n\tau; x, \cdot)$ as $\theta \to 0$, where P is the transition probability that satisfies (9.1.5).

Two absorbing states. Suppose that (4.13), (4.14), and (4.15) hold, and that $\omega_0 = \omega_1 = 0$ for all θ, so that 0 and 1 are absorbing. Then (4.16) and (4.17) are satisfied, and $a(x)$ in (4.18) reduces to $a(x) = \alpha x x'$. If, in addition, $\beta_0 > 0$ and $\beta_1 > 0$, let

$$r(x) = 2a(x)/b(x) = 2\alpha/(\beta_1 x' + \beta_0 x),$$

and let ψ be the solution of

$$\frac{d^2\psi}{dx^2}(x) + r(x)\frac{d\psi}{dx}(x) = 0, \tag{4.21}$$

with $\psi(0) = 0$ and $\psi(1) = 1$. According to Theorem 11.1.1,

$$\phi(x) = P_x(X_n \to 1 \quad \text{as} \quad n \to \infty) \to \psi(x)$$

as $\theta \to 0$. Combining this with (3.8) we obtain

$$E_x(\#a_n) \sim 2(\psi(x) - x)/\tau\alpha \tag{4.22}$$

as $\theta \to 0$, if $\alpha \neq 0$.

To justify application of Theorem 11.1.1, it is necessary to verify that the $o(\tau)$'s in (4.18)–(4.20) satisfy

$$\sup_{0 < x < 1} |o(\tau)/\tau b(x)| \to 0 \tag{4.23}$$

as $\tau \to 0$. In the case of (4.18),

$$o(\tau) = (\delta - \tau\alpha) xx' ;$$

hence

$$|o(\tau)/\tau b(x)| \leqslant |\delta/\tau - \alpha|/\min_i \beta_i,$$

and (4.23) follows. The other two equations can be handled similarly, using

$$E(|\Delta X_n|^j | X_n = x) = (\theta_{11}^j \Pi_{11} x'^{j-1} + \theta_{00}^j \Pi_{00} x^{j-1}) xx'.$$

It is not difficult to solve (4.21). Clearly,

$$\frac{d\psi}{dx}(x) = C \exp - \int r,$$

where $C > 0$. If $\beta_1 \neq \beta_0$, and $\rho = 2\alpha/(\beta_1 - \beta_0)$, this yields

$$\frac{d\psi}{dx}(x) = C(\beta_1 x' + \beta_0 x)^\rho.$$

Thus, if $\rho \neq -1$,

$$\psi(x) = \frac{h(x) - h(0)}{h(1) - h(0)}, \tag{4.24}$$

where

$$h(x) = (\beta_1 x' + \beta_0 x)^{\rho+1}.$$

When $\beta_1 = \beta_0$ and $\alpha \neq 0$, as in the example at the end of Chapter 0, (4.24) holds with

$$h(x) = \exp - 2\alpha x/\beta_1.$$

13 ○ The Fixed Sample Size Model

In the first three sections of this chapter we will give an account of the fixed sample size model that closely parallels the treatment of the linear model in the last chapter. In fact, most of our results for the linear model apply without change to this stimulus sampling model. The close relationship between these models is further emphasized in Section 13.4, where it is shown that the distributions of the state and event sequences of certain linear models are limits of the corresponding distributions for sequences of fixed sample size models.

We recall that, in the fixed sample size model, the state variable x represents the proportion of elements in the total stimulus population conditioned to A_1. The event variable $e = (m, i, j, k)$ gives the number of elements in the sample conditioned to A_1, and the response, outcome, and effectiveness of reinforcement indices. It is a finite state model defined formally as follows.

State space: $X = \{v/N : 0 \leqslant v \leqslant N\}$.
Event space: $E = \{(m, i, j, k) : 0 \leqslant m \leqslant s, 0 \leqslant i, j, k \leqslant 1\}$.
Transformation of x corresponding to $e = (m, i, j, k)$:

$$u(x, e) = x + k\theta(j - m/s), \qquad \theta = s/N.$$

Probability of e given x: $p(x, e) = H(m, x) L(m/s; i, j, k)$,

where $H(m, x)$ is the hypergeometric distribution

$$H(m, x) = \binom{Nx}{m} \binom{Nx'}{s-m} \bigg/ \binom{N}{s}, \qquad x' = 1 - x,$$

and L is the event probability function for the linear model:

$$L(y; i, j, k) = \begin{cases} y\pi_{1j}c_{1j} & \text{if } i = 1, \quad k = 1, \\ y\pi_{1j}c'_{1j} & \text{if } i = 1, \quad k = 0, \\ y'\pi_{0j}c_{0j} & \text{if } i = 0, \quad k = 1, \\ y'\pi_{0j}c'_{0j} & \text{if } i = 0, \quad k = 0. \end{cases}$$

The restrictions on the model's parameters are

$$1 \leqslant s \leqslant N, \qquad 0 \leqslant \pi_{ij}, c_{ij} \leqslant 1, \qquad \sum_j \pi_{ij} = 1.$$

The formula given above for $u(x, e)$ applies only if $p(x, e) > 0$. The definition in other cases is arbitrary. For example, if $m > Nx$, $j = 0$, and $k = 1$, the formula gives

$$u(x, e) = x - m/N < 0.$$

However, in this case

$$\binom{Nx}{m} = 0,$$

so $p(x, e) = 0$.

With the following notations, many of the formulas of the last chapter become applicable to the fixed sample size model:

$$\theta_i = \zeta(\Pi_{i0} + \Pi_{i1}), \qquad \omega_i = \theta\Pi_{ii'},$$

where

$$\zeta = (s-1)/(N-1), \qquad \Pi_{ij} = \pi_{ij}c_{ij}.$$

It is understood that $\zeta = 0$ if $N = 1$. Then $\zeta = 0$ if and only if $s = 1$ (the pattern model), in which case $\theta_i = 0$ too.

13.1. Criteria for Regularity and Absorption

A state sequence X_n for a fixed sample size model is a finite Markov chain. The theory of such chains is discussed in Section 3.7, and in standard sources (e.g., Kemeny and Snell, 1960).

The following simple properties of the transition kernel K of X_n are used repeatedly below.

LEMMA 1.1. If $\Pi_{ii'} > 0$ and $x \neq i'$, then, starting at x, the process can move closer to i':

$$K(x, \{y: |y-i'| < |x-i'|\}) > 0.$$

LEMMA 1.2. If $(s-1)\Pi_{ii} > 0$ and $0 < x < 1$, then the process can move closer to i:

$$K(x, \{y: |y-i| < |x-i|\}) > 0.$$

Proofs. In the first case, some event of the following sort has positive probability: The sample contains elements conditioned to A_i, response A_i is made, and $A_{i'}$ is effectively reinforced. Any such event moves the process toward i'. In the second case, since $0 < x < 1$ and $s \geqslant 2$, a sample can be drawn containing elements conditioned to each response. Then A_i can be made and effectively reinforced. ∎

As for the linear model, the presence of absorbing states exerts a decisive influence on X_n. The criterion for i to be absorbing is the same as in the linear model.

LEMMA 1.3. The state i is absorbing if and only if $\omega_i = 0$. A state $0 < x < 1$ is absorbing if and only if $\Pi_{ii'} = 0$ and $(s-1)\Pi_{ii} = 0$ for $i = 0$ and 1. Then all states are absorbing and the model is said to be trivial.

Proof. If $\Pi_{ii'} = 0$, i is certainly absorbing, while if $\Pi_{ii'} > 0$, it is not, according to Lemma 1.1. But $\omega_i > 0$ if and only if $\Pi_{ii'} > 0$.

If $0 < x < 1$ is absorbing, $\Pi_{ii'} = 0$ and $(s-1)\Pi_{ii} = 0$ follow from Lemmas 1.1 and 1.2. Suppose, conversely, that the latter conditions hold. If $s = 1$, then the response made is the one to which the sampled element is conditioned, and a change of state occurs only if the other response is effectively reinforced, which has probability 0. If $s \neq 1$, then $\Pi_{ii} = 0$, $i = 0, 1$, and no response is effectively reinforced with positive probability. Thus, again, all states are absorbing. ∎

Theorems 1.1 and 1.2 differ only slightly from the comparable theorems (12.1.2 and 12.1.3) for the linear model. All states can be absorbing in Theorem 1.1, but the distance diminishing assumption of Theorem 12.1.2 rules this out. And there is a cyclic case in addition to the one ($\omega_1 = \omega_0 = 1$) given by Theorem 12.1.3.

THEOREM 1.1. *If there is an absorbing state, then X_n is an absorbing process.*

THEOREM 1.2. *If there are no absorbing states, then either* (a) $\Pi_{01} = \Pi_{10} = 1$ *and* $s = 1$ *or* N, *in which case* X_n *is ergodic with period 2, or* (b) X_n *is regular.*

Proof of Theorem 1.1. Suppose i' is absorbing and i is not. The latter implies $\Pi_{ii'} > 0$, according to Lemma 1.3. Thus, if $x \neq i'$, $K^{(n)}(x, i') = K^{(n)}(x, \{i'\}) > 0$ for some $n \leq N$ by Lemma 1.1. Hence the criterion for absorption given at the end of Section 3.7 is met.

If some $0 < x < 1$ is absorbing, Lemma 1.3 shows that all states are absorbing. Suppose now that this is not the case. By the same lemma, $\Pi_{j'j} > 0$ or $(s-1)\Pi_{jj} > 0$ for some j. Lemmas 1.1 and 1.2 then imply that, if $0 < x < 1$, $K^{(n)}(x, j) > 0$ for some $n \leq N - 1$. Thus the process is absorbing if both 0 and 1 are absorbing states. ∎

Proof of Theorem 1.2. By Lemma 1.1, both 0 and 1 can be reached from any state, so X_n is ergodic, and both 0 and 1 belong to the single ergodic kernel F. Clearly $K(0, s/N) > 0$ and $K(s/N, 0) > 0$, so $K^{(2)}(0, 0) > 0$. Since the period p of F divides all return times, $p \leq 2$.

If $\Pi_{ii'} < 1$ for some i, then

$$K(i, i) = 1 - \Pi_{ii'} > 0,$$

so $p = 1$ and the process is regular. If $1 < s < N$, then $K^{(3)}(0, 0) > 0$, so, again, $p = 1$. For $\Pi_{01} > 0$ and $\Pi_{10} > 0$ imply $K(0, s/N) > 0$ and $K(1/N, 0) > 0$. If, in addition, $1 < s < N$, then starting at $x = s/N$, a sample with $s-1$ elements conditioned to A_1 can be drawn, A_1 made, and A_0 effectively reinforced, leading to state $1/N$. Thus $K(s/N, 1/N) > 0$, and

$$K^{(3)}(0, 0) \geq K(0, s/N) K(s/N, 1/N) K(1/N, 0) > 0,$$

as claimed.

Suppose now that $\Pi_{01} = \Pi_{10} = 1$. If $s = N$, then $K(0, 1) = K(1, 0) = 1$, so that $p = 2$. If $s = 1$, then

$$K(x, \{y : |y - x| = 1/N\}) = 1,$$

so, again, $p = 2$. ∎

Part I of this volume showed that the theories of finite state models and distance diminishing models with compact state spaces are completely parallel. Thus the remarks in Sections 12.2 and 12.3 about the asymptotic behavior of distance diminishing linear models are applicable to nontrivial fixed sample size models with the same absorbing states. For example, the proportion $\bar{A}_{1n}$ of A_1 responses in the first n trials is asymptotically normal with mean $P(A_{1\infty})$ and variance σ^2/n, where σ^2 is given by (12.2.5), if the model has no absorbing states and is noncyclic.

13.2. Mean Learning Curve and Interresponse Dependencies

Our first order of business in this section is to find suitable expressions for

$$P(A_{in} O_{jn} C_{kn}|X_n), \qquad E((\varDelta X_n) A_{in} O_{jn} C_{kn}|X_n),$$

and various quantities that derive from them. These formulas are compared with analogous expressions for the linear model. Some differences are noted, but there are important similarities that are exploited in the remainder of the section.

If f is any complex valued function on $[-1,1]$,

$$E(f(\varDelta X_n) A_{in} O_{jn} C_{kn}|X_n = x) = M[f(k\theta(j-m/s))L(m/s; i,j,k)], \quad (2.1)$$

where M denotes expectation with respect to the distribution $H(m,x)$. If $f(y) \equiv 1$, (2.1) and $M(m/s) = x$ yield

$$P(A_{in} O_{jn} C_{kn}|X_n = x) = L(x; i,j,k), \qquad (2.2)$$

just as in the linear model. Summing over j and k for $i = 1$, we obtain

$$P(A_{1n}|X_n = x) = x,$$

so that

$$P(A_{1n}) = E(X_n) = x_n.$$

If $f(y) \equiv y$, (2.1) reduces to

$$E((\varDelta X_n) A_{in} O_{jn} C_{kn}|X_n = x) = k\theta M[(j-m/s) L(m/s; i,j,k)].$$

From

$$M((m/s-x)^2) = \frac{1}{s} \frac{N-s}{N-1} xx' \qquad (2.3)$$

[Wilks, 1962, Eq. (6.1.5)], it follows that

$$M((1-m/s)m/s) = rxx', \qquad (2.4)$$

$$M((m/s)^2) = x - rxx',$$

$$M((1-m/s)^2) = x' - rxx',$$

where

$$r = \zeta/\theta.$$

Thus

$$E((\Delta X_n)\,A_{in}\,O_{jn}\,C_{kn}|X_n = x) = \begin{cases} \zeta x'x\Pi_{11} & \begin{array}{ccc} i & j & k \\ \hline 1 & 1 & 1 \end{array} \\[4pt] -\theta(1-rx')\,x\Pi_{10} & \begin{array}{ccc} 1 & 0 & 1 \end{array} \\[4pt] \theta(1-rx)\,x'\Pi_{01} & \begin{array}{ccc} 0 & 1 & 1 \end{array} \quad (2.5) \\[4pt] -\zeta xx'\Pi_{00} & \begin{array}{ccc} 0 & 0 & 1 \end{array} \\[4pt] 0 & \begin{array}{c} 0. \end{array} \end{cases}$$

When (2.2) is not 0, we divide it into (2.5) to obtain the interesting formula

$$E(\Delta X_n|X_n = x, A_{in}\,O_{jn}\,C_{kn}) = \begin{cases} \zeta x' & \begin{array}{ccc} i & j & k \\ \hline 1 & 1 & 1 \end{array} \\[4pt] -\theta(1-rx') & \begin{array}{ccc} 1 & 0 & 1 \end{array} \\[4pt] \theta(1-rx) & \begin{array}{ccc} 0 & 1 & 1 \end{array} \\[4pt] -\zeta x & \begin{array}{ccc} 0 & 0 & 1 \end{array} \\[4pt] 0 & \begin{array}{c} 0. \end{array} \end{cases}$$

Though all rows are linear functions of x, the second and third differ essentially from the corresponding expressions for any five-operator linear model. This is most striking for the pattern model where they are, respectively, $-1/N$ and $1/N$ for all x.

Returning to (2.5), and adding the first and second and the third and fourth rows, we get

$$E(A_{in}\,\Delta X_n|X_n = x) = \begin{cases} (\theta_1 x' - \omega_1)x & \text{if} \quad i = 1, \\ (\omega_0 - \theta_0 x)x' & \text{if} \quad i = 0, \end{cases} \quad (2.6)$$

which is identical to the corresponding linear model expression (12.2.2). Most of the formulas in Sections 12.2 and 12.3 follow directly from (12.2.2), and thus apply to the fixed sample size model. We now discuss these results in more detail.

Considering Section 12.2 first, the expressions (12.2.3) for $W(x) = E(\Delta X_n|X_n=x)$ and (12.2.4) for Δx_n apply here. As in the linear model, $\delta = \theta_1 - \theta_0$, $\omega = \omega_1 + \omega_0$, and

$$l = \omega_0/\omega = \Pi_{01}/(\Pi_{01} + \Pi_{10}).$$

If the condition $\theta_{ii'} < 1$ in Theorem 12.2.1 is replaced by $s < N$, the system

(12.2.6) of bounds for x_∞ is valid in the present context. Clearly,

$$\delta = \zeta[(\Pi_{11}+\Pi_{10}) - (\Pi_{00}+\Pi_{01})],$$

so that $\delta = 0$ if and only if $s = 1$ or

$$\Pi_{11} + \Pi_{10} = \Pi_{00} + \Pi_{01}. \tag{2.7}$$

In the symmetric case, $c_{ii} = c$, $c_{ii'} = c^*$, we have

$$\delta = \zeta(c-c^*)(\pi_{01}-\pi_{10}),$$

which is analogous to (12.2.7). Finally, the formula (12.2.10) for x_n when $\delta = 0$ and the bounds for x_n when $\delta > 0$ given by Theorem 12.2.2 apply here.

Turning to Section 12.3, the expression (12.3.1) for $P(a_n)$ is valid for the fixed sample size model, as is the relation (12.3.5) between $P(a_n)$ and x_n when $\delta \neq 0$ and its corollaries (12.3.6)–(12.3.8). When $\delta = 0$, $P(a_\infty)$ and $E(\#a_n)$ are related to $E(X_n X_n')$ according to (12.3.9)–(12.3.11). Under the same assumption (no analog of "$\delta_2 = 0$" is needed), the expression (12.3.15) for $E(X_{n+1} X_{n+1}'|X_n=x)$ applies, with

$$g = \theta\theta_i + 2(1-\zeta)\omega$$

and $\theta_{ii'}$ replaced by θ, as is shown in the next paragraph. The formulas for $E(X_\infty X_\infty')$ and $\sum_n E(X_n X_n')$ in Theorem 12.3.2 follow. In the symmetric case with $c = c^*$, we have this analog to (12.3.18):

$$E(X_\infty X_\infty') = \frac{ll'2(\pi_{01}+\pi_{10})(1-\theta)}{\zeta + 2(\pi_{01}+\pi_{10})(1-\zeta)}.$$

Finally, Theorem 12.3.3 on response autocovariance when $\delta = 0$ holds here.

Proof of (12.3.15). We will obtain an expression for

$$Z(x) = E((\Delta X_n)^2|X_n = x)$$

from which (12.3.15) follows just as in the proof of Theorem 12.3.2. Letting $y = m/s$,

$$\begin{aligned}
E((\Delta X_n)^2 A_{1n}|X_n = x) \\
= \theta^2[M(y'^2 y)\Pi_{11} + M((1-y')^2 y)\Pi_{10}] \\
= \theta^2[M(y'^2 y)(\Pi_{11}+\Pi_{10}) - 2M(y'y)\Pi_{10} + M(y)\Pi_{10}] \\
= \theta^2(\Pi_{11}+\Pi_{10})M(y'^2 y) - 2\zeta\omega_1 xx' + \theta\omega_1 x. \tag{2.8}
\end{aligned}$$

Similarly,

$$E((\Delta X_n)^2 A_{0n}|X_n = x) = \theta^2(\Pi_{00}+\Pi_{01})M(y^2 y') - 2\zeta\omega_0 xx' + \theta\omega_0 x'. \tag{2.9}$$

As was noted earlier, if $\delta = 0$ and $s \neq 1$, (2.7) holds. Thus

$$\theta^2(\Pi_{11} + \Pi_{10})\,M(y'^2 y) + \theta^2(\Pi_{00} + \Pi_{01})\,M(y^2 y')$$
$$= \theta^2(\Pi_{i1} + \Pi_{io})\,M(yy') = \theta\theta_i xx',$$

and this is valid even when $s = 1$, since both sides vanish in that case. Therefore, addition of (2.8) and (2.9) yields

$$Z(x) = (\theta\theta_i - 2\zeta\omega)\,xx' + \theta\omega_1 x + \theta\omega_0 x',$$

the desired equation. ∎

In the fixed sample size model with $\delta = 0$, just as in certain linear models satisfying this condition, one can obtain complicated formulas for practically any quantity of interest by rather straightforward computation. Some ingenious work has led to elegant expressions for the distribution of NX_n in the pattern model. This development was begun by Estes (1959) and carried forward by Chia (1970). Estes also showed that the asymptotic distribution of NX_n is binomial, with parameters N and l. The assumption that $c_{01} = c_{10}$ in these papers is unessential.

13.3. Slow Learning

The implications of Part II for the fixed sample size model are essentially the same as for the linear model (see Section 12.4), but slight additional effort is required to verify the hypotheses of the relevant theorems. This section is mainly devoted to checking these hypotheses. We assume throughout that s is fixed, so $\theta \to 0$ if and only if $N \to \infty$.

LARGE DRIFT. For easy reference we quote (12.2.3):

$$E(\varDelta X_n | X_n = x) = W(x) = \delta xx' + \omega_0 x' - \omega_1 x. \qquad (3.1)$$

Division by θ yields

$$w(x,\theta) = (\delta/\theta)\,xx' + \Pi_{01} x' - \Pi_{10} x, \qquad (3.2)$$

for x in

$$I_\theta = \{v/N : 0 \leqslant v \leqslant N\}.$$

Now

$$\frac{\zeta}{\theta} = \frac{s-1}{s}\frac{N}{N-1} = \frac{s-1}{s}\frac{1}{1-1/N}$$
$$= \frac{s-1}{s}\left(1 + \frac{\theta}{s} + O(\theta^2)\right);$$

hence

$$\delta/\theta = \bar{\delta}(1+\theta/s+O(\theta^2)),\qquad(3.3)$$

where

$$\bar{\delta} = \frac{s-1}{s}\,(\Pi_{11}+\Pi_{10}-\Pi_{01}-\Pi_{00}).$$

Combining (3.2) and (3.3), we obtain

$$w(x,\theta) = w(x) + \theta v(x) + O(\theta^2),\qquad(3.4)$$

where

$$w(x) = \bar{\delta}xx' + \Pi_{01} x' - \Pi_{10} x$$

and

$$v(x) = \bar{\delta}xx'/s.$$

This takes care of assumption (a.2) of Theorem 8.1.1 and also (10.3.2) of Theorem 10.3.1.

As a consequence of (2.1),

$$S(x,\theta) = E((\Delta X_n/\theta)^2 | X_n = x)$$

$$= \sum_{ij} M[(j-m/s)^2 L(m/s; i,j,1)].\qquad(3.5)$$

It is easy to see that

$$H(m,x) = \binom{s}{m}\frac{x(x-1/N)\cdots(x-(m-1)/N)x'\cdots(x'-(s-m-1)/N)}{(1-1/N)\cdots(1-(s-1)/N)}$$

$$\to b_m(x)= \binom{s}{m} x^m x'^{s-m}$$

as $N \to \infty$, uniformly over $0 \leqslant x \leqslant 1$. It follows that

$$S(x,\theta) = S(x) + o(1)\qquad(3.6)$$

uniformly over $x \in I_\theta$, where

$$S(x) = \sum_{ij} M^*[(j-m/s)^2 L(m/s; i,j,1)],$$

and M^* is the expectation with respect to the binomial distribution $b_{\cdot}(x)$. Condition (a.3) of Theorem 8.1.1 follows from (3.4) and (3.6).

The smoothness conditions (b) on $w(x)$ and $s(x) = S(x) - w(x)^2$ are trivially satisfied, and (c) follows from $|\Delta X_n| \leqslant \theta$. Thus all of the assumptions of Theorem 8.1.1 hold.

When $\Pi_{01} > 0$ and $\Pi_{10} > 0$, so that there are no absorbing states, w has a unique root λ in $[0, 1]$. Thus Theorems 10.1.1 and 10.3.1 apply to the stationary distribution p_θ of X_n. Since $W(x)$ is not quite proportional to $w(x)$, the root $\lambda = \lambda_\theta$ of $W(x)$ [or of $w(x, \theta)$], which figures in (12.2.6), need not equal the root λ of $w(x)$; however, $\lambda_\theta \to \lambda$ as $\theta \to 0$. The formula (12.4.11) for γ is no longer valid, since $v(x)$ need not vanish, but (12.4.12) holds if we take $p = (1 - 2\lambda)\gamma - \sigma^2$ and replace $\bar{\theta}_1 + \bar{\theta}_0$ and $\bar{\omega}_i$ by

$$\frac{s-1}{s} \sum_{ij} \Pi_{ij}$$

and $\Pi_{ii'}$, respectively.

SMALL DRIFT.   Under the conditions

$$\Pi_{ii} = \beta + O(\theta), \qquad \beta > 0, \tag{3.7}$$

$$\Pi_{11} - \Pi_{00} = \alpha\theta + o(\theta), \tag{3.8}$$

$$\Pi_{ii'} = \theta\alpha_i + o(\theta), \tag{3.9}$$

and $s > 1$, which are analogous to (12.4.13)–(12.4.17), Theorem 9.1.1 is applicable, with $\tau = \theta^2$,

$$a(x) = \frac{s-1}{s} (\alpha + \alpha_1 - \alpha_0) xx' + \alpha_0 x' - \alpha_1 x,$$

and

$$b(x) = \beta \frac{s-1}{s} xx'.$$

In the case $\Pi_{01} = \Pi_{10} = 0$ of two absorbing barriers, $a(x)$ reduces to

$$a(x) = \frac{s-1}{s} \alpha xx',$$

and Theorem 11.1.1 applies also. We will verify the hypotheses of the latter theorem only.

Since

$$\zeta = \theta \frac{s-1}{s} + o(\theta), \tag{3.10}$$

(3.8) gives

$$\delta = \tau \frac{s-1}{s} \alpha + o(\tau)$$

and

$$E(\Delta X_n | X_n = x) = \tau a(x) + o(\tau).$$

Note that $o(\tau)$ in the last equation has a factor xx', so

$$\max_{\substack{0 < x < 1 \\ x \in I_\theta}} |o(\tau)/\tau b(x)| \to 0 \tag{3.11}$$

as $\tau \to 0$. Next, by (3.5),

$$E((\Delta X_n)^2 | X_n = x)/\tau = M(y'^2 y) \Pi_{11} + M(y^2 y') \Pi_{00}$$
$$= \beta M(yy') + M(y'^2 y) \xi_1 + M(y^2 y') \xi_0,$$

where $y = m/s$ and $\xi_i = \Pi_{ii} - \beta$. But (2.4) and (3.10) imply that

$$M(yy') = \frac{s-1}{s} xx' + o(1) xx',$$

and (3.7) yields

$$M(y'^2 y)|\xi_1| + M(y^2 y')|\xi_0| \leqslant K\theta M(yy') \leqslant K\theta xx'.$$

Therefore

$$E((\Delta X_n)^2 | X_n = x) = \tau b(x) + o(\tau), \tag{3.12}$$

and (3.11) holds. Finally,

$$E(|\Delta X_n|^3 | X_n = x) \leqslant \theta E((\Delta X_n)^2 | X_n = x) = o(\tau)$$

by (3.12). Thus (11.1.4) and (11.1.5) hold, and the other conditions of Theorem 11.1.1 are easy to check.

13.4. Convergence to the Linear Model

We begin by noting that, according to (2.3), the variance of m/s is small when s and N are large:

$$M((m/s - x)^2) \leqslant 1/4s. \tag{4.1}$$

Thus m/s tends to approximate x under these conditions, so that, referring to the definition of u at the beginning of the chapter, $u(x, (m, i, j, k))$ approximates $x + k\theta(j-x)$, the corresponding event operator for the linear model with $\theta_{ij} = \theta$. Furthermore, the probability of $A_{in} O_{jn} C_{kn}$ given $X_n = x$ is $L(x; i, j, k)$ in either model. This suggests that, if s and N approach infinity in such a way that $\theta \to \theta^*$, while the distribution μ of X_0 converges to a distribution μ^*, then the joint distribution $\mathcal{D}(n; s, N, \mu)$ of $X_0, E_0, X_1, \ldots,$ E_{n-1}, X_n for the fixed sample size model should converge, in some sense, to the comparable distribution $\mathcal{D}(n; \theta^*, \mu^*)$ for the linear model with $\theta_{ij} = \theta^*$ and initial distribution μ^*. In this section, it is shown that this convergence does indeed occur. Of course, E_n above refers to (A_{1n}, O_{1n}, C_{1n}), that part of the event for the fixed sample size model that has a counterpart in the linear model. This notation is used throughout the section.

The intuitive notion that the linear model is a stimulus sampling model with an infinity of stimulus elements is deeply ingrained in this subject. On the mathematical side, a technical report by Estes and Suppes (1959b) presents a general but arduous approach to convergence of event probabilities. Theorem 4.1, the proof of which is not difficult, is the first result of this kind to be published.

THEOREM 4.1.   *For any $n \geqslant 0$, $0 \leqslant \theta^* \leqslant 1$, and distribution μ^* on $[0, 1]$, $\mathcal{D}(n; s, N, \mu)$ converges to $\mathcal{D}(n; \theta^*, \mu^*)$ as $s \to \infty$, $\theta \to \theta^*$, and $\mu \to \mu^*$.*

The convergence to which the theorem refers is weak sequential convergence in the following sense. Let $s = s_j$, $N = N_j$, and $\mu = \mu_j$ be any sequences such that $s_j \to \infty$, $s_j/N_j \to \theta^*$, and μ_j converges weakly to μ^* (see Section 2.2) as $j \to \infty$. Let $\mathcal{E}_0^{n-1} = (E_0, ..., E_{n-1})$, and let $[\mathcal{E}_0^{n-1} \in A]$ be the random variable that is one if $\mathcal{E}_0^{n-1} \in A$ and zero otherwise. Then

$$E_{sN\mu}([\mathcal{E}_0^{n-1} \in A] h(\mathcal{X}_0^n)) \to E_{\theta^*\mu^*}([\mathcal{E}_0^{n-1} \in A] h(\mathcal{X}_0^n)) \qquad (4.2)$$

as $j \to \infty$, for any

$$A \subset \Gamma_n = \{0, 1\} \times \{0, 1\} \times \cdots (3n \text{ times})$$

and bounded continuous real valued function h. The cases $A = \Gamma_n$ and $h(x_0, ..., x_n) \equiv 1$ are, of course, of particular interest.

Proof.   Let us denote

$$E(f(\Delta X_n) A_{in} O_{jn} C_{kn} | X_n = x)$$

by $J(x)$ in the fixed sample size model and by $J^*(x)$ in the linear model. An expression for $J(x)$ is given by (2.1), and

$$J^*(x) = f(k\theta^*(j - x)) L(x; i, j, k).$$

We first show that, if f has a bounded second derivative,

$$J(x) = J^*(x) + \varepsilon(x), \qquad (4.3)$$

where $\varepsilon(x) \to 0$ uniformly in x as $s \to \infty$ and $\theta \to \theta^*$.

If g has a bounded second derivative on $[0, 1]$, the second-order Taylor expansion

$$g(y) = g(x) + (y - x)g'(x) + \gamma |g''| (y - x)^2,$$

where $|\gamma| \leqslant \frac{1}{2}$ and $|g''| = \sup_x |g''(x)|$, yields

$$|M(g(m/s)) - g(x)| \leqslant |g''| M((m/s-x)^2)/2$$
$$\leqslant |g''|/8s$$

by (4.1). If f has a bounded second derivative on $[-1,1]$ and

$$g(y) = f(k\theta(j-y)) L(y),$$

where $L(y) = L(y; i,j,k)$, it is easy to see that

$$|g''| \leqslant |f''| + 2|f'|,$$

so that

$$|M[f(k\theta(j-m/s))L(m/s)] - f(k\theta(j-x))L(x)| \leqslant (|f''| + 2|f'|)/8s.$$

But

$$|f(k\theta(j-x))L(x) - f(k\theta^*(j-x))L(x)| \leqslant |\theta - \theta^*| |f'|.$$

Thus

$$|J(x) - J^*(x)| \leqslant (|f''| + 2|f'|)/8s + |\theta - \theta^*| |f'|,$$

as required.

The proof of the theorem now proceeds by induction. All limits below are taken along an arbitrary but fixed sequence $(s, N, \mu) = (s_j, N_j, \mu_j)$ with the required asymptotic behavior. Since $\mathscr{D}(0; s, N, \mu) = \mu$ and $\mathscr{D}(0; \theta^*, \mu^*) = \mu^*$, there is nothing to prove when $n = 0$. Suppose that (4.2) holds for some $n \geqslant 0$ and all A and h. We must show that n can be replaced by $n+1$.

It clearly suffices to consider unit sets $A = \{(e_0, \ldots, e_n)\}$. Furthermore, it follows from the continuity theorem for multidimensional distributions (Breiman, 1968, Theorem 11.6) that only functions of the form

$$h(x_0, \ldots, x_{n+1}) = \exp\left(i \sum_{m=0}^{n+1} t_m x_m\right)$$

need be considered. Now

$$E_{sN\mu}\left([\mathscr{E}_0^n = e_0^n] \exp\left(i \sum_{m=0}^{n+1} t_m X_m\right)\right)$$
$$= q = E_{sN\mu}\left([\mathscr{E}_0^{n-1} = e_0^{n-1}] \exp\left(i \sum_{m=0}^{n} t_m X_m\right) \exp(it_{n+1} X_n) J(X_n)\right),$$

where (i,j,k) and $f(y)$ in the definition of $J(x)$ are e_n and $\exp((-1)^{1/2} t_{n+1} y)$;

$$q = E_{sN\mu}\left([\mathscr{E}_0^{n-1} = e_0^{n-1}] \exp\left(i \sum_{m=0}^{n} t_m X_m\right) \exp(it_{n+1} X_n) J^*(X_n)\right) + \delta$$

by (4.3), where $|\delta| \leqslant \max_x |\varepsilon(x)| \to 0$; and

$$q \to E_{\theta^* \mu^*}\left([\mathscr{E}_0^{n-1} = e_0^{n-1}] \exp\left(i \sum_{m=0}^{n} t_m X_m\right) \exp(it_{n+1} X_n) J^*(X_n)\right)$$

by the induction hypothesis (4.2), since $J^*(x)$ is bounded and continuous. The quantity on the right reduces to

$$E_{\theta^* \mu^*}\left([\mathscr{E}_0^n = e_0^n] \exp\left(i \sum_{m=0}^{n+1} t_m X_m\right)\right). \quad \blacksquare$$

14 ○ Additive Models

In additive models for simple two-choice experiments, A_1 response probability is a Borel measurable function $p(x)$ on the state space $X = R^1$, and state transformations are translations:

$$u(x, e) = x + b_e.$$

An event $e = (i, z)$ is determined by a response A_i and a consequence z, which is drawn from a measurable space $(Z, \mathcal{Z})$ in accordance with a specified distribution

$$\Pi_i(D) = P(z \in D | A_i).$$

Thus the distribution $p(x, \cdot)$ of e given x satisfies

$$p(x, \{(1, z): z \in D\}) = p(x) \Pi_1(D)$$

and

$$p(x, \{(0, z): z \in D\}) = q(x) \Pi_0(D),$$

where $q(x) = 1 - p(x)$. It is easy to see that Π_i and b_e affect the distribution of the (Markovian) sequence (X_n, A_{1n}) of states and responses only through the conditional distribution

$$Q_i(B) = P(b_e \in B | A_i) = \Pi_i(\{z: b_{iz} \in B\})$$

of b_e given A_i.

Though it is natural to require that p meet various criteria of smoothness, it is unnecessary to do so for Sections 14.1 and 14.2. Of course, $0 \leqslant p(x) \leqslant 1$. The interpretation of x or $v = e^x$ as an "A_1 response strength" variable suggests that p be strictly increasing, with $p(\infty) = 1$ and $p(-\infty) = 0$. The latter conditions are assumed, but, in place of monotonicity, it suffices for the time being to suppose that $p(x)$ is bounded away from 0 and 1 on finite intervals. Equivalently, $p(x_n) \to 1$ if and only if $x_n \to \infty$, and $p(x_n) \to 0$ if and only if $x_n \to -\infty$. All of these conditions are satisfied in beta models, which are additive models with $p(x) = v/(v+1)$.

Our final assumption is that the moment generating functions

$$M_i(\lambda) = E(\exp \lambda b_e | A_i) = \int_{-\infty}^{\infty} e^{\lambda y} Q_i(dy)$$

exist, for λ in some open interval Λ containing 0. The significance of these quantities is suggested by the equation

$$E((v_{n+1}/v_n)^\lambda | v_n) = M_1(\lambda) p_n + M_0(\lambda) q_n$$

a.s., where $v_n = e^{X_n}$, $p_n = p(X_n)$, and $q_n = q(X_n)$, which shows that they determine the tendency of v_n^λ to increase or decrease. If $k \geqslant 0$ and $\lambda \in \Lambda$, $\int y^k e^{\lambda y} Q_i(dy)$ and $M_i^{(k)}(\lambda)$ exist and are equal. In particular, if

$$m_i = E(b_e | A_i) = \int y Q_i(dy),$$

then $m_i = M_i'(0)$, so that m_i determines the departure of $M_i(\lambda)$ from $M_i(0) = 1$, when $|\lambda|$ is small. If $m_i < 0$, then $M_i(\lambda) < 1$ for $\lambda > 0$ sufficiently small, while if $m_i > 0$, then $M_i(\lambda) < 1$ for $\lambda < 0$ sufficiently large. Actually, since $M_i''(x) = \int y^2 e^{\lambda y} Q_i(dy) \geqslant 0$, M_i is convex, so that $M_i(\lambda) < 1$ implies that $M_i(\omega) < 1$ whenever ω is between λ and 0. Henceforth it is understood that an argument of M_i is an element of Λ.

Analogous to five-operator linear models, five-operator additive models are defined by $z = (j,k)$, where A_j is the response reinforced and $k = 1$ or 0 depending on whether or not conditioning is effective. Thus, $b_{ij0} = 0$, and, letting $b_{ij} = b_{ij1}$, $b_{i1} \geqslant 0$ and $b_{i0} \leqslant 0$. Also,

$$\Pi_i(j,k) = \pi_{ij} \begin{cases} c_{ij} & \text{if } k = 1, \\ 1 - c_{ij} & \text{if } k = 0, \end{cases}$$

where π_{ij} is the probability of reinforcing A_j after A_i, and c_{ij} is the attendant probability of effective conditioning. In this case, $m_i = \sum_j b_{ij} \pi_{ij} c_{ij}$. As for the linear model, the symmetric case, defined here by

$$c_{11} = c_{00} = c, \qquad c_{01} = c_{10} = c^*,$$

$$b_{11} = -b_{00} = b, \qquad b_{01} = -b_{10} = b^*,$$

is of particular interest.

Much of this chapter follows Norman (1970b).

14.1. Criteria for Recurrence and Absorption

In this section we establish Theorem 1.1, which shows that the qualitative asymptotic behavior of p_n (or X_n or v_n) is determined by the signs of the mean increments m_i.

THEOREM 1.1.(A)   *If $m_0 > 0$ and $m_1 > 0$, $\lim p_n = 1$ a.s.*

(B)   *If $m_0 < 0$ and $m_1 < 0$, $\lim p_n = 0$ a.s.*

(C)   *If $m_0 < 0$ and $m_1 > 0$, $g_0(x) + g_1(x) = 1$, where $g_i(x) = P_x(\lim p_n = i)$. In addition, $g_0(x) > 0$, $g_1(x) > 0$, $g_0(x) \to 1$ as $x \to -\infty$, and $g_1(x) \to 1$ as $x \to \infty$.*

(D)   *If $m_0 > 0$ and $m_1 < 0$, then $\limsup p_n = 1$ and $\liminf p_n = 0$ a.s.*

The proof is based on a number of lemmas, some of which will find other uses later.

Let

$$F_\lambda(v) = M_1(\lambda) p(x) + M_0(\lambda) q(x),$$

so that

$$E((v_{n+1}/v_n)^\lambda | v_n) = F_\lambda(v_n). \tag{1.1}$$

Note that $F_\lambda(v) \to M_1(\lambda)$ as $v \to \infty$.

LEMMA 1.1.   If $m_1 < 0$, $\liminf X_n < \infty$ a.s. If $\lambda > 0$ and $M_1(\lambda) < 1$, there are constants $B(\lambda)$ and $C(\lambda) < 1$ such that

$$E_x(v_n^\lambda) \leqslant v^\lambda C^n(\lambda) + B(\lambda). \tag{1.2}$$

Similarly $\limsup X_n > -\infty$ if $m_0 > 0$, and (1.2) holds if $\lambda < 0$ and $M_0(\lambda) < 1$.

Proof.   For V sufficiently large,

$$C(\lambda) = \sup_{v \geqslant V} F_\lambda(v) < 1.$$

Thus, by (1.1),

$$E(v_{n+1}^\lambda | v_n) \leqslant C(\lambda) v_n^\lambda$$

for $v_n \geqslant V$. But for $v_n < V$,

$$E(v_{n+1}^\lambda | v_n) \leqslant \max(M_i(\lambda)) V^\lambda = D(\lambda).$$

Therefore

$$E(v_{n+1}^\lambda | v_n) \leqslant C(\lambda) v_n^\lambda + D(\lambda)$$

a.s., so that

$$E_x(v_{n+1}^\lambda) \leqslant C(\lambda) E_x(v_n^\lambda) + D(\lambda).$$

Taking $B(\lambda) = D(\lambda)/(1 - C(\lambda))$, (1.2) follows by induction.

Letting $n \to \infty$ in (1.2), we obtain

$$B(\lambda) \geqslant \liminf E_x(v_n^\lambda)$$

$$\geqslant E_x(\liminf v_n^\lambda)$$

by Fatou's lemma. Thus $\liminf v_n^\lambda < \infty$ and $\liminf X_n < \infty$ a.s. if $P(X_0 = x) = 1$. It follows immediately that $\liminf X_n < \infty$ a.s. for any initial distribution. ∎

For two events A and A^*, we say that A implies A^* a.s. if $P(A - A^*) = 0$. Similarly, A and A^* are a.s. equivalent if $P(A \Delta A^*) = 0$.

LEMMA 1.2. If $m_1 > 0$, then $\limsup X_n = \infty$ implies $\lim X_n = \infty$ a.s. If $\lambda < 0$, $M_1(\lambda) < 1$, and V is sufficiently large that $F_\lambda(v) \leqslant 1$ for all $v \geqslant V$, then

$$g_0(x) \leqslant (v/V)^\lambda \tag{1.3}$$

for all $v > 0$.

An analogous result holds if $m_0 < 0$.

Proof. Let $H_n = \min(v_n^\lambda, V^\lambda)$. This process is a supermartingale. For

$$E(H_{n+1} | v_n, \ldots, v_0) \leqslant E(v_{n+1}^\lambda | v_n)$$

$$\leqslant v_n^\lambda = H_n$$

a.s. if $v_n \geqslant V$, while

$$E(H_{n+1} | v_n, \ldots, v_0) \leqslant V^\lambda = H_n$$

a.s. if $v_n < V$. Thus

$$E(H_{n+1} | v_n, \ldots, v_0) \leqslant H_n,$$

a.s., as claimed.

Since $H_n \geqslant 0$, $\lim H_n$ exists a.s. [Neveu, 1965, (1), p. 137]. If $\limsup X_n = \infty$, $\liminf H_n = 0$. But the latter implies $\lim H_n = 0$ a.s., which in turn implies $\lim X_n = \infty$. Thus $\limsup X_n = \infty$ implies $\lim X_n = \infty$ a.s.

To obtain the last assertion of the lemma, note that

$$E_x(H_n) \leqslant \min(v^\lambda, V^\lambda) \leqslant v^\lambda. \qquad (1.4)$$

But $\lim H_n \geqslant V^\lambda I_A$, where A is the event $\lim X_n = -\infty$. Thus letting $n \to \infty$ in (1.4) yields (1.3). ∎

The last lemma is of a rather different kind.

LEMMA 1.3. If $m_0 > 0$ or $m_1 > 0$, $P(\limsup X_n \in X) = 0$.

Similarly if $m_0 < 0$ or $m_1 < 0$, the probability that $\liminf X_n$ is real is 0.

Proof. If $m_i > 0$, then $Q_i([2\varepsilon, \infty)) > 0$ for some $\varepsilon > 0$. For any x,

$$P(X_{n+1} \geqslant x + \varepsilon | X_n, \dots, X_0)$$

$$= Q_1([x - X_n + \varepsilon, \infty)) p_n + Q_0([x - X_n + \varepsilon, \infty)) q_n$$

$$\geqslant Q_1([2\varepsilon, \infty)) \alpha_x + Q_0([2\varepsilon, \infty)) \beta_x = \gamma_x$$

a.s. if $|X_n - x| < \varepsilon$, where $\alpha_x = \inf_{|y-x|<\varepsilon} p(y)$ and $\beta_x = \inf_{|y-x|<\varepsilon} q(y)$. Since p is bounded away from 0 and 1 over finite intervals, $\alpha_x > 0$ and $\beta_x > 0$, thus $\gamma_x > 0$.

It follows that $|X_n - x| < \varepsilon$ infinitely often (i.o.) implies

$$\sum_{n=0}^{\infty} P(X_{n+1} \geqslant x+\varepsilon | X_n, \dots, X_0) = \infty$$

a.s. The latter event is a.s. equivalent to $X_n \geqslant x+\varepsilon$ i.o. (Neveu, 1965, Corollary to Proposition IV.6.3). Thus the probability that $|X_n - x| < \varepsilon$ i.o. but not $X_n \geqslant x+\varepsilon$ i.o. is 0. However, $|\limsup X_n - x| < \varepsilon$ implies the latter event, so

$$P(|\limsup X_n - x| < \varepsilon) = 0.$$

Since X is a denumerable union of intervals of the form $(x-\varepsilon, x+\varepsilon)$, the lemma follows. ∎

Proof of Theorem 1.1. Suppose $m_1 > 0$. By Lemma 1.3, $\limsup X_n = -\infty$ or $\limsup X_n = \infty$ a.s. By Lemma 1.2, $\limsup X_n = \infty$ implies $\lim X_n = \infty$ a.s.; hence $\limsup X_n = -\infty$ or $\lim X_n = \infty$ a.s. When $m_0 > 0$, $\limsup X_n > -\infty$ a.s. by (an analog of) Lemma 1.1, so that, when $m_1 > 0$ and $m_0 > 0$, $\lim X_n = \infty$ a.s. This proves (A), and (B) is similar.

Returning to the case where our only assumption is $m_1 > 0$, we have $\lim X_n = -\infty$ or $\lim X_n = \infty$ a.s. Thus $g_0(x) + g_1(x) = 1$. It follows from (1.3) that $g_0(x) \to 0$; hence $g_1(x) \to 1$ as $x \to \infty$. In particular, there is a constant d such that $g_1(x) > 0$ for $x \geqslant d$. It is easily shown that, for any $n \geqslant 1$

and $x \in X$,

$$P_x(\Delta X_j \geqslant \varepsilon, j = 0, \ldots, n-1) \geqslant (\delta c)^n,$$

where $c = \inf_{y \geqslant x} p(y) > 0$ and $\delta = Q_1([\varepsilon, \infty)) > 0$ for ε sufficiently small. Hence $P_x(X_n \geqslant d) > 0$ if n is sufficiently large that $x + n\varepsilon \geqslant d$. But $g_1(x) = E_x(g_1(X_n))$, so $g_1(x) > 0$ for all $x \in X$. The other assertions in (C) follow similarly from $m_0 < 0$.

Suppose $m_1 < 0$. Then $\liminf X_n = \pm \infty$ a.s. (Lemma 1.3) and $\liminf X_n < \infty$ a.s. (Lemma 1.1), so $\liminf X_n = -\infty$ a.s. Thus $\liminf p_n = 0$ a.s. Similarly, $m_0 > 0$ implies $\limsup p_n = 1$ a.s., and (D) is proved. ∎

If $p(x) = O(e^{\alpha x})$ as $x \to -\infty$ for some $\alpha > 0$, as in the beta model, the conclusion in (B) of Theorem 1.1 can be strengthened to $\sum_{n=0}^{\infty} p_n < \infty$ a.s. In fact

$$E_x \left(\sum_{n=0}^{\infty} p_n \right) = E_x(\#A_{1n}) < \infty$$

for all $x \in X$ (Norman, 1970b, Theorem 2).

The recurrent case $m_1 < 0$, $m_0 > 0$ is the subject of the next three sections.

14.2. Asymptotic A_1 Response Frequency

As in zero-absorbing-barrier linear and stimulus sampling models, A_1 response frequency

$$\bar{A}_{1n} = (1/n) \sum_{j=0}^{n-1} A_{1j}$$

and average A_1 response probability

$$\bar{p}_n = (1/n) \sum_{j=0}^{n-1} p_j$$

admit strong laws of large numbers in recurrent additive models. Furthermore, there is a simple expression

$$\zeta = m_0/(m_0 - m_1) \tag{2.1}$$

for the a.s. limit of these sequences in the additive case. Theorem 2.1 also shows that the expectations of $\sqrt{n}(\bar{A}_{1n} - \zeta)$ and $\sqrt{n}(\bar{p}_n - \zeta)$ converge to 0, and their second moments are bounded. Presumably their distributions are asymptotically normal under suitable additional conditions yet to be found. It would also be of interest to have laws of large numbers and central limit theorems for other functions $g(E_n)$ and $f(X_n)$ of events and states.

THEOREM 2.1. *Suppose that $m_0 > 0$ and $m_1 < 0$.*
(A) $\bar{A}_{1n} \to \zeta$ *and* $\bar{p}_n \to \zeta$ *a.s.*
(B) *For any $K < \infty$,*

$$E_x((\bar{A}_{1n} - \zeta)^2) = O(1/n), \tag{2.2}$$

$$E_x((\bar{p}_n - \zeta)^2) = O(1/n), \tag{2.3}$$

$$E_x(\bar{p}_n) - \zeta = O(1/n), \tag{2.4}$$

uniformly over $|x| \leqslant K$.

Proof. Let $V_n = \Delta X_n - (m_1 p_n + m_0 q_n)$ and $W_n = A_{1n} - p_n$. Then

$$E(V_n | X_n, E_{n-1}, X_{n-1}, \ldots) = 0$$

and

$$E(W_n | X_n, E_{n-1}, X_{n-1}, \ldots) = 0,$$

from which it follows that $E(V_m V_n) = 0$ and $E(W_m W_n) = 0$ if $m \neq n$. Furthermore, if $s_i = \int x^2 Q_i(dx)$ and $\max s_i = s$,

$$E(V_n^2 | X_n) \leqslant E((\Delta X_n)^2 | X_n)$$

$$= s_1 p_n + s_0 q_n \leqslant s$$

a.s., so $E(V_n^2) \leqslant s$. Also $E(W_n^2) \leqslant 1$. Therefore

$$E(\bar{V}_n^2) \leqslant s/n \tag{2.5}$$

and

$$E(\bar{W}_n^2) \leqslant 1/n, \tag{2.6}$$

and, by Lemma 5.3.1,

$$\bar{V}_n \to 0 \quad \text{a.s.}, \tag{2.7}$$

and

$$\bar{A}_{1n} - \bar{p}_n = \bar{W}_n \to 0 \quad \text{a.s.} \tag{2.8}$$

Note that

$$\bar{V}_n = X_n/n - X_0/n + \delta(\bar{p}_n - \zeta), \tag{2.9}$$

where $\delta = m_0 - m_1$.

Now if $\lambda > 0$ is sufficiently small,

$$E_x(v_n^{\pm \lambda}) \leqslant v^{\pm \lambda} + B(\pm \lambda)$$

by (1.2). Adding these equations, and observing that $e^y + e^{-y} \geqslant y^2$, we obtain

$$\lambda^2 E_x(X_n^2) \leqslant 2\cosh \lambda x + B,$$

where $B = B(\lambda) + B(-\lambda)$. Thus

$$E_x(X_n^2) \leqslant (2\cosh \lambda K + B)/\lambda^2 = J \tag{2.10}$$

for all $n \geqslant 0$ and $|x| \leqslant K$. Clearly

$$E_x\left(\sum_{n=1}^{\infty} X_n^2/n^2\right) = \sum_{n=1}^{\infty} E_x(X_n^2)/n^2 < \infty,$$

so $X_n/n \to 0$ a.s. This, in conjunction with (2.7) and (2.9), yields $\bar{p}_n \to \zeta$ a.s. But then (2.8) implies $\bar{A}_{1n} \to \zeta$ a.s., and (A) is proved.

The expectation of (2.9) is

$$0 = E_x(\bar{V}_n) = E_x(X_n)/n - x/n + \delta(E(\bar{p}_n) - \zeta);$$

therefore

$$\delta|E_x(\bar{p}_n) - \zeta| \leqslant (|x| + |E_x(X_n)|)/n$$
$$\leqslant (K + J^{1/2})/n$$

for $|x| \leqslant K$, as a consequence of (2.10). Thus (2.4) is established. Equation (2.9) and Minkowski's inequality yield

$$\delta E_x((\bar{p}_n - \zeta)^2)^{1/2} \leqslant \frac{|x|}{n} + \frac{E_x(X_n^2)^{1/2}}{n} + E(\bar{V}_n^2)^{1/2}$$
$$\leqslant (K + \sqrt{J} + \sqrt{s})/\sqrt{n}$$

for $|x| \leqslant K$, by (2.10) and (2.5). This yields (2.3) and, with (2.6), (2.2). ∎

We now consider how m_i and ζ depend on the parameters of symmetric five-operator additive models. If $v = bc + b^*c^* = 0$, $X_n = X_0$ a.s., so assume $v > 0$ and let $r = bc/v$. The quantities bc and b^*c^* determine the efficacy of success and failure, respectively, and r measures their relative magnitude. A simple computation shows that

$$m_1 = v(r - \pi_{10}) \quad \text{and} \quad m_0 = v(\pi_{01} - r).$$

Suppose that $\pi_{01} \geqslant \pi_{10}$, or, equivalently, $\pi_{11} \geqslant \pi_{00}$. This means that A_1 is more likely to be successful than A_0. The opposite case is similar. Then recurrence ($m_1 < 0$, $m_0 > 0$) occurs when $r < \pi_{10}$. Under this condition

$$\zeta = (\pi_{01} - r)/(\pi_{01} + \pi_{10} - 2r).$$

If $\pi_{01} = \pi_{10}$, $\zeta = \frac{1}{2}$. Otherwise ζ is a strictly increasing convex function that runs from $\pi_{01}/(\pi_{01} + \pi_{10}) = l$ at $r = 0$ to 1 at $r = \pi_{10}$. Thus the model predicts that asymptotic A_1 response frequency ζ will overshoot the probability matching asymptote l over the range $0 < r < \pi_{10}$.

If $\pi_{10} < r < \pi_{01}$, then $m_1 > 0$ and $m_0 > 0$, so $p_n \rightarrow 1$ a.s. according to Theorem 1.1. Thus success probability $\pi_{11} p_n + \pi_{00} q_n$ is maximized asymptotically. Finally, if $r > \pi_{01}$, $m_1 > 0$ and $m_0 < 0$, so $p_n \rightarrow 1$ or $p_n \rightarrow 0$ a.s., and both limits have positive probability.

14.3. Existence of Stationary Probabilities

If p is continuous, the Markov process X_n always possesses a stationary probability in the recurrent case. Furthermore, the moment generating functions of stationary probabilities are bounded by the function $B(\lambda)$ of Lemma 1.1. Let $\mathscr{S}$ be the set of stationary probabilities.

THEOREM 3.1.   *If* $m_0 > 0$, $m_1 < 0$, *and* p *is continuous, then* $\mathscr{S}$ *is not empty. In fact, for every stochastically and topologically closed subset Y of X, there is a* $\mu \in \mathscr{S}$ *such that* $\mu(Y) = 1$. *If* $\lambda > 0$ *and* $M_1(\lambda) < 1$, *or* $\lambda < 0$ *and* $M_0(\lambda) < 1$, $\int e^{\lambda x} \mu(dx) \leqslant B(\lambda)$ *for all* $\mu \in \mathscr{S}$.

Proof.   Let K be the transition kernel and U and T the transition operators (1.1.5) and (1.1.6) of the process. First we note that, for any $\xi \in X$, the sequence

$$\overline{K}^n(\xi, \cdot) = \overline{T}^n \delta_\xi$$

(see Section 2.2 for the notation) is conditionally weakly compact. For, by (2.10), there is a constant J such that

$$\int \overline{K}^n(\xi, dx)\, x^2 = n^{-1} \sum_{j=0}^{n-1} E_\xi(X_j^2) \leqslant J.$$

Hence

$$\overline{K}^n(\xi, I_a) \leqslant J/a^2,$$

where $I_a = (-\infty, a) \cup (a, \infty)$, for all $a > 0$ and $n \geqslant 0$. Therefore, $\overline{K}^n(\xi, \cdot)$ is uniformly tight, thus conditionally weakly compact (Parthasarathy, 1967, Theorem II.6.7).

Suppose now that Y is stochastically and topologically closed (e.g., $Y = X$). Let $\xi \in Y$ and $\mu_j = \overline{K}^{n_j}(\xi, \cdot)$ be a subsequence of $\overline{K}^n(\xi, \cdot)$ that converges weakly to a probability μ. Since Y is stochastically closed, $\mu_j(Y) = 1$ for all j, and, since Y is topologically closed, $\limsup \mu_j(Y) \leqslant \mu(Y)$. Thus $\mu(Y) = 1$. In addition, μ is stationary. For, by virtue of the continuity of p, U maps bounded continuous functions into bounded continuous functions, and this implies, via (1.1.7), that T is continuous with respect to weak convergence. Thus $T\mu_j \to T\mu$ weakly, and

$$T^{n_j}\delta_\xi/n_j - \delta_\xi/n_j = T\mu_j - \mu_j \to T\mu - \mu$$

weakly, as $j \to \infty$. But the left side converges weakly to 0, so $T\mu = \mu$, as claimed.

Suppose now that $\mu \in \mathscr{A}$, and let $\lambda > 0$ and $M_1(\lambda) < 1$, or $\lambda < 0$ and $M_0(\lambda) < 1$. For any $d > 0$, let $F(x) = \min(e^{\lambda x}, d)$. Then

$$\int F \, d\mu = \int F \, dT^n \mu = \int U^n F \, d\mu.$$

Since $U^n F(x) \leqslant d$ for all n and x, Fatou's lemma gives

$$\int F \, d\mu \leqslant \int \limsup U^n F \, d\mu.$$

But $U^n F(x) \leqslant E_x(v_n^\lambda)$, so $\int F \, d\mu \leqslant B(\lambda)$ as a consequence of (1.2). As $d \to \infty$, the left-hand side converges to $\int e^{\lambda x} \, d\mu$, so $\int e^{\lambda x} \, d\mu \leqslant B(\lambda)$. ∎

In Section 14.5 it is shown that, if p is increasing and sufficiently smooth, then stationary probabilities are approximately normal, with mean $p^{-1}(\zeta)$ and variance of the order of magnitude of the increments b_e, when these are small.

14.4. Uniqueness of the Stationary Probability

No necessary and sufficient condition is known for uniqueness of stationary probabilities of state sequences of recurrent additive models. The classical sufficient condition for uniqueness of stationary probabilities of general Markov chains is *indecomposability*, the nonexistence of disjoint stochastically closed sets (Breiman, 1968, Theorem 7.16). This criterion has the following corollary for additive models.

THEOREM 4.1. *If Q_1 or Q_0 has a positive density with respect to Lebesgue measure L, then there is at most one stationary probability.*

Proof. Suppose that $Q_i(B) = \int_B f_i(x) L(dx)$, where $f_i(x) > 0$ for all $x \in X$. Since $p(x) > 0$ and $q(x) > 0$,

$$0 = K(x, B) = p(x) Q_1(B-x) + q(x) Q_0(B-x)$$

implies that $Q_i(B-x) = 0$; thus $L(B-x) = 0$, so that $L(B) = 0$. If A and B are stochastically closed, $x \in A$, and $y \in B$, then $K(x, \tilde{A}) = 0$ and $K(y, \tilde{B}) = 0$, so $L(\tilde{A}) = 0$ and $L(\tilde{B}) = 0$. Therefore, $A \cap B \neq \emptyset$, and K is indecomposable. ∎

However, indecomposability is not necessary for uniqueness in recurrent additive models. Consider the case $Q_i(\{b_i\}) = 1$, where $b_1 = m_1 < 0$ and $b_0 = m_0 > 0$, so that X_n has the simple transition law

$$\Delta X_n = \begin{cases} b_1 & \text{with probability } p(X_n), \\ b_0 & \text{with probability } q(X_n). \end{cases} \tag{4.1}$$

Let

$$G = \{n_0 b_0 + n_1 b_1 : n_0, n_1 \text{ are integers}\}.$$

Then $x + G$ is stochastically closed for any $x \in X$, and the collection of distinct, hence disjoint, sets of this form is nondenumerable. So X_n is certainly not indecomposable. But uniqueness can obtain.

THEOREM 4.2. *If p is continuous and nondecreasing, and if b_0/b_1 is irrational, then there is a unique stationary probability.*

According to Theorem 3.1, a necessary condition for uniqueness is *irreducibility*, the nonexistence of disjoint stochastically and topologically closed subsets of X. If b_0/b_1 is rational, the sets $x + G$ are topologically closed, so uniqueness fails. On the other hand, if b_0/b_1 is irrational, X is the only stochastically and topologically closed set. For if Y is stochastically closed and $x \in Y$, then $x + G^+ \subset Y$, where

$$G^+ = \{n_0 b_0 + n_1 b_1 : n_0, n_1 \geqslant 0\}.$$

And $x + G^+$ is dense, so $Y = X$ if Y is topologically closed. Hence if b_0/b_1 is irrational, irreducibility holds as well as uniqueness. It remains to be seen whether irreducibility is sufficient for uniqueness in the general recurrent additive model with continuous nondecreasing p.

The proof of Theorem 4.2., which is due to James Pickands, III and the author, is published here for the first time.

Proof. The continuity of T ensures that $\mathscr{S}$ is weakly closed, and the inequality

$$\int \cosh \lambda x \, \mu(dx) \leqslant (B(\lambda) + B(-\lambda))/2,$$

valid for all $\mu \in \mathscr{S}$ if $\lambda > 0$ is sufficiently small according to Theorem 3.1, implies that $\mathscr{S}$ is weakly compact. Therefore, by the Krein–Milman theorem (Dunford and Schwartz, 1958, Theorem V.8.4) applied to the finite signed measures on X with the weak topology, the convex set $\mathscr{S}$ is the closed convex hull of its extremal points. Hence it suffices to show that there is a unique extremal stationary probability. A stationary probability μ is extremal if and only if it is ergodic, that is, $\bar{U}^n f \to \int f \, d\mu$ in $L_2(\mu)$ for every $f \in L_2(\mu)$ (Rosenblatt, 1967, Theorem 2).

In order to study the dependence of $\overline{U}^n f(x)$ on x, we define a collection of Markov processes $X_n(x)$ on the same probability space. Let ξ_n, $n \geq 0$, be a sequence of independent random variables, each uniformly distributed on $[0,1]$. Let $X_0(x) = x$, and, given $X_n(x)$, let

$$\Delta X_n(x) = \begin{cases} b_1 & \text{if } \xi_n \leq p_n(x), \\ b_0 & \text{if } \xi_n > p_n(x), \end{cases}$$

where $p_n(x) = p(X_n(x))$. It is easy to see that, for each $x \in X$, $X_n(x)$ has the transition law (4.1).

The processes $X_n(x)$ have the following important property: If

$$0 < x - y < b_0 + |b_1| = b,$$

then

$$X_n(x) - X_n(y) = x - y \quad \text{or} \quad x - y - b \tag{4.2}$$

for all $n \geq 0$. For this is certainly true for $n = 0$. Suppose, inductively, that $X_n(x) - X_n(y) = x - y$. Then $p_n(x) \geq p_n(y)$, since p is nondecreasing. If $\xi_n \leq p_n(y)$ or $\xi_n > p_n(x)$, $\Delta X_n(x) = \Delta X_n(y)$, so $X_{n+1}(x) - X_{n+1}(y) = x - y$. If $p_n(x) \geq \xi_n > p_n(y)$, $\Delta X_n(x) = b_1$ and $\Delta X_n(y) = b_0$, so $X_{n+1}(x) - X_{n+1}(y) = x - y - b$. The case $X_n(x) - X_n(y) = x - y - b$ is similar, so (4.2) follows.

Suppose now that f is a bounded nondecreasing diff'rentiable function on X such that $|f'| < \infty$. Then, if $0 < x - y < b$,

$$U^n f(x) - U^n f(y) = E(\Delta),$$

where

$$\Delta = f(X_n(x)) - f(X_n(y))$$
$$\leq |f'|(x-y)$$

by (4.2). Thus

$$U^n f(x) - U^n f(y) \leq |f'|(x-y)$$

and

$$\overline{U}^n f(x) - \overline{U}^n f(y) \leq |f'|(x-y) \tag{4.3}$$

for all $n \geq 0$.

Let μ_1 and μ_2 be extremal, hence ergodic, stationary probabilities. Since $\overline{U}^n f \to \int f d\mu_1$ in $L_2(\mu_1)$, there is a subsequence n' such that $\overline{U}^{n'} f \to \int f d\mu_1$ μ_1-a.s. But $\overline{U}^n f \to \int f d\mu_2$ in $L_2(\mu_2)$, so there is a subsequence n^* of n', such that $\overline{U}^{n^*} f \to \int f d\mu_i$ on a set A_i with $\mu_i(A_i) = 1$, $i = 1,2$. The support of μ_i is X. For it is topologically closed by definition and stochastically closed by Lemmas 2.2.3 and 3.4.3, and we have already noted that X is the only stochastically and topologically closed set when b_0/b_1 is irrational. It follows that A_i is dense.

If $0 < x - y < b$, $x \in A_1$, and $y \in A_2$, then letting $n \to \infty$ along the subsequence n^* in (4.3) we obtain

$$\int f d\mu_1 - \int f d\mu_2 \leqslant |f'|(x-y).$$

Since there are points y in A_2 with $x - y$ positive and arbitrarily small, $\int f d\mu_1 \leqslant \int f d\mu_2$. By symmetry, $\int f d\mu_2 \leqslant \int f d\mu_1$, so

$$\int f d\mu_1 = \int f d\mu_2 \qquad (4.4)$$

for all bounded nondecreasing differentiable functions with $|f'| < \infty$. If g is such a function, then, for any $y \in X$ and $\sigma > 0$,

$$f_\sigma(x) = g((x-y)/\sigma)$$

is too, and, if $g(\infty) = 1$ and $g(x) = 0$ for $x \leqslant 0$,

$$f_\sigma(x) \to \begin{cases} 1, & x > y, \\ 0, & x \leqslant y, \end{cases}$$

monotonically as $\sigma \to 0$. Thus, applying (4.4) to f_σ, and taking the limit as $\sigma \to 0$, we obtain $\mu_1(y, \infty) = \mu_2(y, \infty)$ for all $y \in X$, from which it follows that $\mu_1 = \mu_2$. ∎

If a recurrent additive model with p continuous has a unique stationary probability μ, then $\bar{U}^n f(x) \to \int f d\mu$ for all $x \in X$ and bounded continuous f. For we saw in the proof of Theorem 3.1 that $\{\bar{K}^n(x, \cdot)\}_{n \geqslant 0}$ is weakly conditionally compact, and that every weak subsequential limit is stationary, hence is μ. It follows easily that $\bar{K}^n(x, \cdot)$ converges weakly to μ. One wonders whether, under these conditions, $\bar{U}^n f$ converges uniformly over compact sets. This is true for $f = p$ by (B) of Theorem 2.1.

In closing this section, we note the lack of criteria for aperiodicity, that is, convergence of $K^{(n)}(x, \cdot)$ as opposed to $\bar{K}^n(x, \cdot)$. Our only result worth mentioning is negative: X_n is not aperiodic under the hypotheses of Theorem 4.2.

14.5. Slow Learning

Suppose that $b_e = \theta a_e$, where $\theta > 0$, a_e is a fixed real measurable function, and $p(x)$ and Π_i are also fixed. This section describes the limiting behavior of $X_n = X_n^\theta$ and $p_n = p(X_n)$ as $\theta \to 0$.

If

$$L_i(\omega) = E(\exp \omega a_e | A_i) < \infty$$

for $|\omega| < \varepsilon$, then $M_i(\lambda) = L_i(\theta\lambda) < \infty$ for $|\lambda| < \varepsilon/\theta$. The moments of b_e and a_e are linearly related:

$$m_i = E(b_e | A_i) = \theta E(a_e | A_i) = \theta \bar{m}_i,$$
$$s_i = E(b_e^2 | A_i) = \theta^2 E(a_e^2 | A_i) = \theta^2 \bar{s}_i,$$
$$r_i = E(|b_e|^3 | A_i) = \theta^3 E(|a_e|^3 | A_i) = \theta^3 \bar{r}_i.$$

In addition,

$$w(x) = E(\Delta X_n/\theta | X_n = x) = \bar{m}_1 p + \bar{m}_0 q,$$
$$S(x) = E((\Delta X_n/\theta)^2 | X_n = x) = \bar{s}_1 p + \bar{s}_0 q, \qquad (5.1)$$
$$\bar{r}(x) = E(|\Delta X_n/\theta|^3 | X_n = x) = \bar{r}_1 p + \bar{r}_0 q.$$

To apply Theorem 8.1.1, we take $I = I_\theta = R^1$, and note that the approximation assumption (a) is trivially fulfilled. Assuming that $p(x)$ has two bounded derivatives, as in beta models, the smoothness conditions (b) on $w(x)$ and $s(x) = S(x) - w(x)^2$ are satisfied. Finally, (c) follows from $\bar{r}(x) \leqslant \max_i \bar{r}_i$.

As a consequence of Theorem 8.1.1,

$$(X_n - f(n\theta))/\sqrt{\theta} \sim N(0, g(n\theta))$$

when $\theta \to 0$ and $n\theta$ is bounded. As usual, $f'(t) = w(f(t))$ and $f(0) = x = X_0$. If $w(x) \neq 0$, $H(f(t)) = t$ and $g(t) = G(f(t))$, where H and G are given by (12.4.5) and (12.4.8), respectively. Letting $P(t) = p(f(t))$, it follows that

$$(p_n - P(n\theta))/\sqrt{\theta} \sim N(0, p'(f(n\theta))^2 g(n\theta)).$$

Clearly $P(0) = p(x)$, and

$$P'(t) = p'(f)(\bar{m}_1 P + \bar{m}_0(1 - P)).$$

In beta models, $p' = pq$, so P satisfies the autonomous differential equation

$$P'(t) = P(1 - P)(\bar{m}_1 P + \bar{m}_0(1 - P)).$$

We mention that, if $p'(y) > 0$ for all y, and p has certain other regularities, asymptotic normality of p_n as $\theta \to 0$ can be obtained by applying Theorem 8.1.1 directly to p_n.

In the remainder of the section, we develop approximations to stationary probabilities and absorption probabilities. Suppose that $p'(x) > 0$ for all $x \in R^1$. If $\bar{m}_1$ and $\bar{m}_0$ have opposite signs, there is a unique $\xi \in R^1$ such that

$$p(\xi) = \zeta = \bar{m}_0/(\bar{m}_0 - \bar{m}_1)$$

or, equivalently, $w(\xi) = 0$. Also,

$$w'(\xi) = (\bar{m}_1 - \bar{m}_0)p'(\xi) \neq 0,$$

so that

$$\sigma^2 = S(\xi)/2|w'(\xi)|$$

is well defined (and greater than 0). Let

$$z_n = (X_n - \xi)/\sqrt{\theta}.$$

If $\bar{m}_1 < 0$ and $\bar{m}_0 > 0$, then, for every θ, X_n has at least one stationary probability μ_θ, and this distribution has finite fourth moment (Theorem 3.1). Let X_0, hence X_n, have distribution μ_θ. Since $w'(\xi) < 0$, (d) of Theorem 10.1.1 is satisfied, and the remaining hypotheses (ii.1) and (ii.2) of the second part of the theorem are easily checked. The conclusion is that

$$z_n \sim N(0, \sigma^2)$$

as $\theta \to 0$, from which

$$(p_n - \zeta)/\sqrt{\theta} \sim N(0, p'(\xi)^2 \sigma^2)$$

follows.

If $\bar{m}_0 < 0$ and $\bar{m}_1 > 0$, then, for every $\theta > 0$ and initial state x, $X_n \to \pm\infty$ a.s. by (C) of Theorem 1.1, and we wish to approximate $g_1(x) = P_x(X_n \to \infty)$. Note that $X_n \to \infty$ if and only if $z_n \to \infty$, so

$$g_1(x) = P_z(z_n \to \infty) = \phi(z),$$

where $z = (x - \xi)/\sqrt{\theta}$. By applying Theorem 11.2.1 to the process z_n and the parameter $\tau = \theta$ (not θ^2!), we shall show that

$$\sup_{x \in R^1} |g_1(x) - \Phi(z/\sigma)| \to 0$$

as $\theta \to 0$. Here Φ is the standard normal cumulative distribution function. Since ξ is a critical point of w, Lemma 8.5.1 yields

$$E(\Delta z_n | z_n = z) = \theta w'(\xi)z + o(\theta),$$

$$E((\Delta z_n)^2 | z_n = z) = \theta S(\xi) + o(\theta),$$

$$E(|\Delta z_n|^3 | z_n = z) = o(\theta),$$

where, for any $k > 0$,

$$\sup_{|z| < k} |o(\theta)|/\theta \to 0$$

as $\theta \to 0$. Thus (11.1.4) and (11.2.2) obtain, and the function $r(z)$ defined below (11.1.5) is z/σ^2. It follows that

$$B(z) = \int_0^z r(y)\,dy = z^2/2\sigma^2\,,$$

and $e^{-B(z)}$ is integrable over R^1, as Theorem 11.2.1 requires. The function $\Phi(z/\sigma)$ is the solution of

$$\psi''(z) + r(z)\psi'(z) = 0\,,$$

with limits 0 and 1 at $-\infty$ and ∞. Thus, it remains only to show that $\phi = \phi_\theta$ satisfies

$$\lim_{\substack{z \to -\infty \\ \theta \to 0}} \phi_\theta(z) = \lim_{\substack{z \to \infty \\ \theta \to 0}} 1 - \phi_\theta(z) = 0\,. \qquad (5.2)$$

Proof. The calculation that follows will put us in position to use Lemma 1.2. There is a constant $c > 0$ such that, for $|\omega| \leqslant \varepsilon/2$,

$$L_i(\omega) \leqslant 1 + \omega\overline{m}_i + c\omega^2\,.$$

Hence, if $|\lambda\theta| \leqslant \varepsilon/2$,

$$F_\lambda(e^x) - 1 \leqslant \lambda\theta(\overline{m}_1 p + \overline{m}_0 q) + c\lambda^2\theta^2$$

$$= \lambda\theta(\gamma(p-\zeta) + c\lambda\theta)\,,$$

where $\gamma = \overline{m}_1 - \overline{m}_0 > 0$. Taking $\lambda = -1/\sqrt{\theta}$, we obtain

$$F_\lambda(e^x) - 1 \leqslant -\sqrt{\theta}(\gamma(p-\zeta) - c\sqrt{\theta})$$

if $\sqrt{\theta} \leqslant \varepsilon/2$. If θ is still smaller, say $\theta \leqslant \varepsilon'$, there is a unique $x_\theta > \zeta$ such that

$$p(x_\theta) - \zeta = c\sqrt{\theta}/\gamma\,,$$

and $x \geqslant x_\theta$ implies that $F_\lambda(e^x) \leqslant 1$. Thus (1.3) with $V = e^{x_\theta}$ takes the form

$$1 - \phi_\theta(z) \leqslant \exp(-(x - x_\theta)/\sqrt{\theta}) = e^{-z}e^{z_\theta}\,,$$

where $z = (x-\xi)/\sqrt{\theta}$ and $z_\theta = (x_\theta - \xi)/\sqrt{\theta}$.
  Now

$$z_\theta = \frac{x_\theta - \xi}{p(x_\theta) - \zeta}\frac{c}{\gamma} \to \frac{1}{p'(\xi)}\frac{c}{\gamma}$$

as $\theta \to 0$. Therefore z_θ is bounded, and there is a constant K such that

$$1 - \phi_\theta(z) \leqslant Ke^{-z}$$

for all $z \in R^1$, if $\theta \leqslant \varepsilon'$. The second limit in (5.2) follows immediately, and the other holds by symmetry. ∎

15 ○ Multiresponse Linear Models

The distinctive feature of the models considered in this chapter is that the subject's response y is an element of an arbitrary measurable space $(Y, \mathcal{Y})$. The state x is the distribution of y, and the state space (X, d) is a set of probabilities on $\mathcal{Y}$, with total variation distance $d(x, x') = |x - x'|$. The response y is followed by an outcome z from a measurable space $(Z, \mathcal{Z})$. Its distribution is $\Pi(y, \cdot)$, where Π is a stochastic kernel. Thus the event $e = (y, z)$ has distribution

$$p(x, G) = \int x(dy) \int \Pi(y, dz) I_G(y, z).$$

The event space is $(E, \mathcal{G}) = (Y, \mathcal{Y}) \times (Z, \mathcal{Z})$. Occurrence of e transforms x into

$$u(x, e) = (1 - \theta_e) x + \gamma_e,$$

where γ_e is a measure on $\mathcal{Y}$ with

$$\gamma_e(Y) = \theta_e \leqslant 1,$$

225

$\gamma_.$ is a measurable mapping into $(M(Y), d)$, and

$$\lambda_e = \theta_e^{-1}\gamma_e \in X$$

if $\theta_e > 0$.

We assume that X is convex, so that $u(x, e) \in X$, and separable, so that u is jointly measurable. Both conditions are satisfied if, for example, $\mathcal{Y}$ is countably generated and X is the set of probabilities absolutely continuous with respect to a fixed σ-finite measure.

Some interesting characterizations of transformations of probabilities of the form $x \to (1-\theta)x + \theta\lambda$ are given by Blau (1961).

The linear free-responding model and Suppes' continuous response model discussed in Chapter 0 are of this type. In the free-responding model, y is an interresponse time and z is the reinforcement indicator variable, so $Y = (0, \infty)$ and $Z = \{0, 1\}$. Also, $\theta_{y1} = \theta$ and $\theta_{y0} = \theta^*$ do not depend on y, and

$$\lambda_e = \begin{cases} \tau^* & \text{if } z = 0, \\ (1-\alpha)\tau + \alpha\Lambda(y, \cdot) & \text{if } z = 1, \end{cases}$$

where τ and τ^* are probabilities on $\mathcal{Y}$, and Λ is a stochastic kernel on $Y \times \mathcal{Y}$. The probability $\Pi(y, \{1\})$ of reinforcing a y-second interresponse time is denoted $u(y)$. In Suppes' model, y and z are the predicted and "correct" points on, say, the unit circle $Y = Z$ in the complex plane, and $\lambda_e = \lambda(z, \cdot)$ does not depend on y. Generalizing Suppes' assumption that θ_e is constant, we assume that $\theta_e = \theta(z)$ depends only on z. The five-operator linear model is also a special case; take $Y = \{0, 1\}$, $Z = \{0, 1\} \times \{0, 1\}$, $\theta_{ijk} = k\theta_{ij}$, $\lambda_{ij1}(\{j\}) = 1$, and $\Pi(i; j, k) = \pi_{ij}c_{ij}$ if $k = 1$ and $\pi_{ij}(1-c_{ij})$ if $k = 0$. Of course, here the real variable $x(\{1\})$ characterizes the probability x, and it is natural to describe the model in terms of this variable, as we do in Chapter 12.

Response and outcome random variables are denoted Y_n and Z_n; thus $E_n = (Y_n, Z_n)$. Other useful notations are

$$\theta_y = \int \Pi(y, dz)\theta_{yz}$$

and

$$\gamma_y(A) = \int \Pi(y, dz)\gamma_{yz}(A).$$

15.1. Criteria for Regularity

We first give a sufficient condition for the model to be distance diminishing.

THEOREM 1.1.   If $\inf_{y \in Y} \theta_y > 0$, the model is distance diminishing.

Proof.

$$r_1 = \sup_{x \neq x'} \int p(x, de) \, \frac{d(u(x, e), u(x', e))}{d(x, x')}$$

$$= \sup_x \int p(x, de) \, (1 - \theta_e)$$

$$= 1 - \inf_x \int p(x, de) \, \theta_e .$$

But

$$\int p(x, de) \, \theta_e = \int x(dy) \, \theta_y \geqslant \inf \theta_y ,$$

so that

$$r_1 \leqslant 1 - \inf \theta_y < 1 . \quad \blacksquare$$

Theorems 1.2 and 1.3 give criteria for X_n to be regular with respect to the bounded Lipschitz functions $L(X)$. The condition $\inf \theta_y > 0$ is assumed in Theorem 1.2 and follows from the assumptions of Theorem 1.3, so both relate to distance diminishing models. Both theorems are corollaries of results in Chapter 4.

THEOREM 1.2. *If $\inf \theta_y > 0$, and if there are $a > 0$ and $\phi \in P(Y)$ such that $\lambda_e(A) \geqslant a\phi(A)$, for all $A \in \mathcal{Y}$ and $e \in E$ with $\theta_e > 0$, then X_n is regular.*

THEOREM 1.3. *If there are $a > 0$ and $v \in P(Z)$ such that $\Pi(y, B) \geqslant av(B)$, for all $y \in Y$ and $B \in \mathcal{Z}$, if $\gamma_e(A) = \gamma(z, A)$ does not depend on y [thus $\theta_e = \theta(z)$ does not either], and if $\int v(dz) \theta(z) > 0$, then X_n is regular.*

In the free-responding model,

$$\lambda_e \geqslant (1 - \alpha) \, (\tau \wedge \tau^*),$$

where $\tau \wedge \tau^*$ is the infimum of τ and τ^* (see Neveu, 1965, p. 107), so λ_e has a lower bound of the type required by Theorem 1.2 if $\alpha < 1$ and τ and τ^* are not mutually singular. The condition in Theorem 1.3 that the reinforcement function Π have a response independent component av is very natural in applications of Suppes' model. The extreme case of noncontingent outcomes, $\Pi(y, \cdot) = v$, has received much attention in the experimental literature.

Proof of Theorem 1.2. Clearly X is bounded:

$$d(x, x') \leqslant |x| + |x'| = 2 .$$

Let X' be the convex hull of $\{\lambda_e \colon \theta_e > 0\}$. Then X' is invariant (Definition

4.2.1), so, by Theorem 4.2.2, it suffices to show that the transition operator U' for the corresponding submodel is regular.

If $x \in X'$, there are nonnegative p_i with $\sum p_i = 1$, and $e(i) \in E$ with $\theta_{e(i)} > 0$, such that $x = \sum p_i \lambda_{e(i)}$. Thus

$$x(A) \geqslant \sum p_i a\phi(A) = a\phi(A),$$

so that

$$p(x, A) \geqslant av(A),$$

where

$$v(A) = \int \phi(dy) \int \Pi(y, dz) I_A(y, z).$$

Thus the submodel satisfies (a) of Section 4.1. Furthermore,

$$r_1' = \int v(de)(1 - \theta_e) = 1 - \int \phi(dy)\theta_y$$

$$\leqslant 1 - \inf\theta_y < 1.$$

Therefore U' is regular, according to Theorem 4.1.1. ∎

Proof of Theorem 1.3. The transition operator

$$Uf(x) = \int x(dy) \int \Pi(y, dz)f((1 - \theta(z))x + \gamma(z, \cdot))$$

is the same as for the (reduced) model with $X^* = X$, $E^* = Z$, $u^*(x, z) = u(x, e)$, and $p^*(x, B) = \int x(dy)\Pi(y, B)$. But

$$p^*(x, B) \geqslant av(B),$$

and

$$\int v(dz)\frac{d(u^*(x, z), u^*(x', z))}{d(x, x')} = 1 - \int v(dz)\theta(z) < 1,$$

so U is regular by Theorem 4.1.1. ∎

When $\theta_y > 0$ for all $y \in Y$,

$$\lambda_y(A) = \gamma_y(A)/\theta_y$$

is a stochastic kernel. The following lemma is needed in the next section.

LEMMA 1.1. Under the hypotheses of either Theorem 1.2 or Theorem 1.3, there is a $c > 0$ and a probability ψ on $\mathscr{Y}$ such that

$$\lambda_y(A) \geqslant c\psi(A) \tag{1.1}$$

for all y and A.

Proof. Under the hypotheses of Theorem 1.2,

$$\lambda_y(A) = \theta_y^{-1} \int_{\theta_{yz} > 0} \Pi(y, dz) \, \theta_{yz} \, \lambda_{yz}(A)$$

$$\geq a\phi(A).$$

Under the assumptions of Theorem 1.3,

$$\lambda_y(A) = \theta_y^{-1} \int \Pi(y, dz) \, \gamma(z, A) \geq c\psi(A),$$

where

$$c = a/\sup \theta_y$$

and

$$\psi(A) = \int \nu(dz) \gamma(z, A). \quad \blacksquare$$

15.2. The Distribution of Y_n and Y_∞

Let x_n be the unconditional distribution of Y_n; i.e.,

$$x_n(A) = P(Y_n \in A).$$

Then, for any bounded measurable function g on Y,

$$\int g(y) x_n(dy) = E(g(Y_n))$$

$$= E(E(g(Y_n)|X_n)) = E\left(\int g(y) X_n(dy) \right).$$

In particular, $x_n(A) = E(X_n(A))$.

Note that

$$E(X_{n+1}(A)|X_n) = \int p(X_n, de) \, ((1 - \theta_e) X_n(A) + \gamma_e(A))$$

$$= \left(1 - \int X_n(dy) \theta_y \right) X_n(A) + \int X_n(dy) \gamma_y(A).$$

Thus,

$$x_{n+1}(A) = \left(1 - \int x_n(dy) \theta_y \right) x_n(A) + \int x_n(dy) \gamma_y(A)$$

$$- \text{cov}\left(\int X_n(dy) \theta_y, X_n(A) \right), \tag{2.1}$$

which is analogous to (12.2.4). If $\theta_y = \bar{\theta}$ for all y, then $\int X_n(dy)\,\theta_y = \bar{\theta}$ a.s., so that x_{n+1} is obtained from x_n via the linear transformation

$$x_{n+1}(A) = (1-\bar{\theta})\,x_n(A) + \bar{\theta}\int x_n(dy)\,\lambda_y(A).$$

Constancy of θ_y generalizes the condition $\delta = 0$ in Chapter 12. It is satisfied in the free-responding model with $u(y) \equiv p$, for then $\theta_y \equiv \theta p + \theta^*(1-p)$. It holds also in Suppes' model if $\theta(z) \equiv \theta$ or if $\Pi(y, \cdot) = v$. In the latter case,

$$\lambda_y = \int v(dz)\,\gamma(z, \cdot)/\bar{\theta} = \bar{\lambda}$$

for all y, so

$$x_{n+1} = (1-\bar{\theta})\,x_n + \bar{\theta}\bar{\lambda}$$

or

$$x_n = \bar{\lambda} + (1-\bar{\theta})^n(x_0 - \bar{\lambda}).$$

Suppose now that the model is distance diminishing and that X_n is regular. By Theorem 6.2.1, the model is uniformly regular with $\phi_n = O(\alpha^n)$, where $\alpha < 1$. From Section 6.2, we recall that the sequence $\mathscr{E}^\infty = \{F_n\}_{n\geqslant 0}$ of coordinate functions on E^∞ is a stationary process, with respect to the asymptotic distribution r of $\mathscr{E}^N = \{E_{n+N}\}_{n\geqslant 0}$ as $N \to \infty$. Let $Y_{\infty+n}$ and $Z_{\infty+n}$ be the coordinates of F_n: $F_n = (Y_{\infty+n}, Z_{\infty+n})$, and let x_∞ be the distribution of $Y_\infty = Y_{\infty+0}$:

$$x_\infty(A) = r(Y_\infty \in A)$$

for $A \in \mathscr{Y}$. Then

$$|x_n(A) - x_\infty(A)| \leqslant \phi_n,$$

so $|x_n - x_\infty| \to 0$ geometrically as $n \to \infty$.

If the real valued measurable function g on Y is positive or integrable,

$$\int g(y)\,x_\infty(dy) = \int g(Y_\infty(e^\infty))\,r(de^\infty)$$

is denoted $\bar{g}$. For example, if $Y = (0, \infty)$, the real powers $g(y) = y^\beta$ are of special interest, while if Y is the unit circle, we might consider $g(y) = (\arg y)^k$. The asymptotic expectation $\bar{g}$ can be estimated as accurately as desired by the corresponding sample mean from a single subject. If $\int |g(y)|\,x_\infty(dy) < \infty$,

$$(1/n)\,S_n = (1/n)\sum_{j=0}^{n-1} g(Y_j) \to \bar{g}$$

a.s. as $n \to \infty$, by Theorem 6.2.3. And, if $\int g^2(y)\,x_\infty(dy) < \infty$, Theorem

6.2.4 shows that

$$(S_n - n\bar{g})/\sqrt{n} \sim N(0, \sigma^2),$$

where σ^2 is the usual sum of the autocovariances

$$\rho_j = \text{cov}(g(Y_\infty), g(Y_{\infty+j})).$$

At the end of the section, we consider a case in which $Y = (0, \infty)$, and determine the powers β for which $\int y^\beta x_\infty(dy) < \infty$.

To get information about x_∞, we return to (2.1). Letting $n \to \infty$ and canceling $x_\infty(A)$ yields

$$x_\infty(A) \int x_\infty(dy)\,\theta_y = \int x_\infty(dy)\,\gamma_y(A) - C(A), \tag{2.2}$$

where

$$C(A) = \lim_{n \to \infty} \text{cov}\left(\int X_n(dy)\,\theta_y,\, X_n(A) \right).$$

Neglecting the term $C(A)$, we obtain the nonlinear integral equation

$$x^*(A) \int x^*(dy)\,\theta_y \doteq \int x^*(dy)\,\gamma_y(A).$$

If there is a unique solution x^*, it is analogous to the approximation λ to $x_\infty = P(A_{1\infty})$ in Theorem 12.2.1. Since that approximation is good for small θ_{ij}, we expect $x_\infty \doteq x^*$ when θ_e is small.

Throughout the remainder of the section, it is assumed that $\theta_y = \bar{\theta} > 0$ for all $y \in Y$. Then $C(A) = 0$, so that

$$x_\infty(A) = \int x_\infty(dy)\,\lambda_y(A). \tag{2.3}$$

We now solve this equation under the additional condition (1.1), which, according to Lemma 1.1, is no more restrictive than our sufficient conditions for regularity. If $c = 1$ in (1.1), then $\lambda_y = \psi$ and $x_\infty = \psi$. If $c < 1$, let ξ be the stochastic kernel defined by

$$\lambda_y(A) = c\psi(A) + (1-c)\xi(y, A).$$

Substitution of this expression into (2.3) yields

$$x_\infty(A) = c\psi(A) + (1-c) \int x_\infty(dy)\,\xi(y, A), \tag{2.4}$$

which leads, on iteration, to

$$x_\infty(A) = c \sum_{j=0}^{k} (1-c)^j \int \psi(dy)\,\xi^{(j)}(y, A) + (1-c)^{k+1} \int x_\infty(dy)\,\xi^{(k+1)}(y, A).$$

Since the last term is bounded by $(1-c)^{k+1}$, and $c > 0$, passage to the limit yields

$$x_\infty(A) = c \sum_{j=0}^{\infty} (1-c)^j \int \psi(dy) \, \xi^{(j)}(y, A)$$

$$= \int \psi(dy) \, \xi'(y, A), \qquad (2.5)$$

where

$$\xi'(y, A) = c \sum_{=0}^{\infty} (1-c)^j \xi^{(j)}(y, A).$$

In the free-responding model with $u(y) \equiv p$,

$$\gamma_y = (1-p)\theta^* \tau^* + p\theta((1-\alpha)\tau + \alpha \Lambda(y, \cdot)),$$

so that we can take

$$c\psi = \bar{\theta}^{-1}((1-p)\theta^* \tau^* + p\theta(1-\alpha)\tau)$$

in (1.1), and $\xi = \Lambda$. The case $\Lambda(y, A) = \eta(A/y)$ is of special interest. Consider now the general model with $Y = (0, \infty)$ and $\xi(y, A) = \eta(A/y)$. Then

$$\xi^{(j)}(y, A) = \eta^j(A/y),$$

where $\eta^0 = \delta_1$, $\eta^1 = \eta$, and η^j is the jth convolution power of η:

$$\eta^{j+1}(A) = \int \eta(dy) \eta^j(A/y).$$

Also,

$$\xi'(y, A) = \eta'(A/y),$$

where

$$\eta'(A) = c \sum_{j=0}^{\infty} (1-c)^j \eta^j(A). \qquad (2.6)$$

The solution (2.5) takes a particularly simple form in terms of the Mellin transforms

$$\hat{x}_\infty(\beta) = \int y^\beta x_\infty(dy),$$

$\hat{\psi}(\beta)$, and $\hat{\eta}(\beta)$. Here β may be positive or negative, and $0 < \hat{x}_\infty(\beta) \leq \infty$. Since the Mellin transform of a convolution is the product of the transforms (whether or not these are finite), (2.5) yields

$$\hat{x}_\infty(\beta) = \hat{\psi}(\beta) \widehat{\eta'}(\beta).$$

And it is easy to show that (2.6) can be transformed term by term to obtain

$$\widehat{\eta'}(\beta) = c \sum_{j=0}^{\infty} (1-c)^j [\hat{\eta}(\beta)]^j.$$

Thus $\hat{x}_\infty(\beta) < \infty$ if and only if $\hat{\psi}(\beta) < \infty$ and $(1-c)\hat{\eta}(\beta) < 1$, in which case

$$\hat{x}_\infty(\beta) = \frac{c\hat{\psi}(\beta)}{1-(1-c)\hat{\eta}(\beta)}. \tag{2.7}$$

This formula can also be obtained directly, by transforming both sides of (2.4).

If $\hat{\eta}(\beta_0) < \infty$ for some $\beta_0 > 0$, then $\hat{\eta}(\beta) \to 1$ as $\beta \downarrow 0$, so $(1-c)\hat{\eta}(\beta) < 1$ for β sufficiently small. On the other hand, if $\eta(1, \infty) > 0$, as would normally be the case in the free-responding model, $\hat{\eta}(\beta) \to \infty$ as $\beta \to \infty$, so that $\hat{x}_\infty(\beta) = \infty$ for β sufficiently large. Similar considerations apply to negative β.

16 ○ The Zeaman–House–Lovejoy Models

The Zeaman–House–Lovejoy or ZHL models were described in Section 0.1. We recall that a rat is fed when he chooses the black arm (B) of a T-maze, instead of the white one (W). According to the models, he attends to brightness (br), rather than position (po), with probability v, and, given attention to brightness, he enters the black arm with probability y:

$$v = P(br), \qquad y = P(B|br).$$

In the full model, there is another variable, z, the probability of going left given attention to position, and $x = (v, y, z)$ is the state variable. Observe that, if $v = 1$ and $y = 1$, the rat attends to brightness and makes the correct response with probability 1. The consequent state transformation does not change x, so all states $x = (1, 1, z)$, $0 \leqslant z \leqslant 1$, are absorbing. But Theorem 3.4.1 implies that a distance diminishing model with compact state space has at most a finite number of absorbing states. Therefore, the full ZHL model is not distance diminishing. Furthermore, very little is known about it, beyond what follows from our study of the reduced model. The small-step-size theory of Chapter 8 is applicable, but its implications have not been worked out in detail.

234

The reduced ZHL model has state variable $x = (v, y)$ and state space $X = [0, 1] \times [0, 1]$, with Euclidean metric d. Its events, event probabilities, and state transformations are listed in Table 1, which is an amplification of Table 2 of Section 0.1. The row numbers in Table 1 provide convenient labels for events. Of course, all ϕ's and θ's are in the closed unit interval.

TABLE 1

Event Effects and Probabilities for the Reduced ZHL Model
$(\bar{v} = 1 - v)$

Event	Δv	Δy	Probability
1. $br\,B$	$\phi_1 \bar{v}$	$\theta_1 \bar{y}$	vy
2. $br\,W$	$-\phi_2 v$	$\theta_2 \bar{y}$	$v\bar{y}$
3. $po\,B$	$-\phi_3 v$	0	$\bar{v}/2$
4. $po\,W$	$\phi_4 \bar{v}$	0	$\bar{v}/2$

The relationship between stochastic processes associated with the full and reduced ZHL models is exactly what would be expected intuitively. Let

$$X_n = (V_n, Y_n, Z_n) \quad \text{and} \quad E_n = (s_n, a_n, r_n)$$

be any state and event sequences for the full model. Thus s_n is the stimulus configuration $[(B, W)$ or $(W, B)]$ on trial n, a_n is the dimension attended to, and r_n is the rat's choice (B or W). Then, by Theorem 1.2.4,

$$X_n = (V_n, Y_n) \quad \text{and} \quad E_n = (a_n, r_n)$$

are state and event sequences for the reduced model. Thus any theorem concerning V_n, Y_n, a_n, and r_n in the reduced model applies also to the full model. Bearing this in mind, we restrict our attention in the remainder of this chapter to the reduced model, and refer to it simply as "the ZHL model."

16.1. A Criterion for Absorption

THEOREM 1.1. *If $\phi_1, \phi_4, \theta_1, \theta_2 > 0$, the ZHL model is distance diminishing.*

THEOREM 1.2. *Its state sequences are absorbing, with single absorbing state $\xi = (1, 1)$.*

In particular, $X_n \to \xi$ a.s. as $n \to \infty$, by Theorem 3.4.3. Also, since

$$p(\xi, po \cup W) = 0,$$

$E(\# po \cup W) < \infty$ by Theorem 6.2.2, where $\# po \cup W$ is the total number of trials on which either a perceptual or an overt error occurs. In particular, $\# po \cup W < \infty$ a.s.; that is, subjects learn with probability 1. This conclusion may appear obvious, but no simple, direct proof is known.

Proof of Theorem 1.1. We shall use Proposition 1 of Section 2.1. The functions $p(\cdot, e)$ have bounded partial derivatives, so $m(p(\cdot, e)) < \infty$. All state transformations have the form

$$u(x, e) = \begin{pmatrix} (1-\phi)v + \gamma \\ (1-\theta)y + \psi \end{pmatrix}.$$

Thus

$$u(x, e) - u(x', e) = \begin{pmatrix} (1-\phi)(v-v') \\ (1-\theta)(y-y') \end{pmatrix},$$

$$d^2(u(x, e), u(x', e)) = (1-\phi)^2(v-v')^2 + (1-\theta)^2(y-y')^2$$
$$\leqslant (1 - (\phi \wedge \theta))^2 d^2(x, x'),$$

and

$$\iota(u(\cdot, e)) \leqslant 1 - (\phi \wedge \theta) \leqslant 1.$$

Furthermore, $\iota(u(\cdot, 1)) < 1$, since $\phi_1 > 0$ and $\theta_1 > 0$.

Let $P = \{x : v > 0 \text{ and } y > 0\}$. If $x \in P$, $p(x, 1) > 0$, so we can take $j = 1$ and $e^j = 1$ in Proposition 1. For $x \in' P$, we display, in the next paragraph, a succession $e^n = (e_0, \ldots, e_{n-1})$ of events such that $u(x, e^n) \in P$ and $p_n(x, e^n) > 0$. Then, if $j = n+1$ and $e^j = (e_0, \ldots, e_{n-1}, 1)$,

$$\iota(u(\cdot, e^j)) \leqslant \iota(u(\cdot, e^n)) \iota(u(\cdot, 1)) < 1,$$

and

$$p_j(x, e^j) = p_n(x, e^n) p(u(x, e^n), 1) > 0,$$

as Proposition 1 requires.

If $\phi_2 < 1$, e^n can be chosen as follows (+ indicates positivity):

v	y	e^n
0	+	4
+	0	2
0	0	4, 2

If $\phi_2 = 1$, then each 2 must be followed by 4 to restore positivity of v. ∎

Proof of Theorem 1.2. Let

$$\lambda = \begin{cases} u(x, e'') & \text{if } x \in' P, \\ x & \text{if } x \in P, \end{cases}$$

where e'' and P are as in the previous proof, and let $\sigma_n(x)$ be the set of possible values of X_n when $X_0 = x$. Then $\lambda \in P \cap \sigma_n(x)$ ($n = 0$ if $x \in P$). But $u(\cdot, 1)$ maps $P \cap \sigma_m(x)$ into $P \cap \sigma_{m+1}(x)$, so induction yields

$$\lambda_k = u(\lambda, 1^{(k)}) \in P \cap \sigma_{n+k}(x)$$

for all $k \geqslant 1$, where $1^{(k)} = (1, 1, \ldots, 1)$ (k times).

It follows that

$$d(\sigma_{n+k}(x), \xi) \leqslant d(\lambda_k, \xi)$$
$$\leqslant \iota(u(\cdot, 1^{(k)})) d(\lambda, \xi),$$

since $u(\xi, 1^{(k)}) = \xi$; hence

$$d(\sigma_{n+k}(x), \xi) \leqslant \iota(u(\cdot, 1))^k d(\lambda, \xi) \to 0$$

as $k \to \infty$. An application of Theorem 3.6.2 completes the proof. ∎

16.2. Expected Total Errors

Throughout this section we suppose, following Zeaman and House (1963), that

$$\phi_1 = \phi_2 = \phi_3 = \phi_4 = \phi > 0$$

and

$$\theta_1 = \theta_2 = \theta > 0.$$

Theorem 2.1 gives the expected total numbers of overt and perceptual errors under these conditions.

THEOREM 2.1. *For any* $0 \leqslant v, y \leqslant 1$,

$$E_x(\#W) = \bar{v}/\phi + 2\bar{y}/\theta \tag{2.1}$$

and

$$E_x(\#po) = 2\bar{v}/\phi + 2\bar{y}/\theta, \tag{2.2}$$

where $\bar{v} = 1 - v$.

Proof. Events 2, 3, and 4 have probability 0 at ξ, so, as a consequence of Theorem 6.2.2, $g_k(x) = E_x(\#k)$ is the unique Lipschitz function such that

$$g_k(x) = p(x, k) + Ug_k(x) \qquad (2.3)$$

and $g_k(\xi) = 0$. This characterization is now used to establish formulas for these expectations. Table 1 gives

$$Uy - y = E(\Delta y | x)$$
$$= \theta(\bar{y}vy + \bar{y}v\bar{y}) = \theta\bar{y}v; \qquad (2.4)$$

hence

$$\bar{y} - U\bar{y} = \theta\bar{y}v$$

and

$$\bar{y}/\theta = \bar{y}v + U\bar{y}/\theta. \qquad (2.5)$$

Since $\bar{y}v = p(x, 2)$, and $\bar{y}/\theta$ is Lipschitz and vanishes at ξ,

$$g_2(x) = \bar{y}/\theta. \qquad (2.6)$$

Returning to Table 1,

$$Uv - v = E(\Delta v | x)$$
$$= \phi(\bar{v}vy - v^2\bar{y} - v\bar{v}/2 + \bar{v}^2/2).$$

Rewriting y in the first term on the right as $1 - \bar{y}$, we get

$$Uv - v = \phi(-v\bar{y} + \bar{v}/2), \qquad (2.7)$$

from which it follows that

$$\bar{v}/\phi = -v\bar{y} + \bar{v}/2 + U\bar{v}/\phi.$$

When (2.5) is added to this equation, the result is

$$\bar{v}/\phi + \bar{y}/\theta = \bar{v}/2 + U(\bar{v}/\phi + \bar{y}/\theta).$$

But $p(x, 3) = p(x, 4) = \bar{v}/2$, and $\bar{v}/\phi + \bar{y}/\theta$ is Lipschitz and vanishes at ξ, so

$$g_3(x) = g_4(x) = \bar{v}/\phi + \bar{y}/\theta. \qquad (2.8)$$

Formulas (2.1) and (2.2) follow from (2.6) and (2.8) on noting that

$$E_x(\#W) = g_2(x) + g_4(x)$$

and

$$E_x(\#po) = g_3(x) + g_4(x). \quad \blacksquare$$

We now consider reversal of the correct response. If, on trial n and thereafter, food is placed in the white arm, (2.1) implies that the expected total number of (overt) errors on the new problem, given X_n, is $\overline{V}_n/\phi + 2Y_n/\theta$. Thus the unconditional expected number of errors is

$$\Psi_n = E(\overline{V}_n)/\phi + 2E(Y_n)/\theta.$$

The change in Ψ_n as the result of one additional trial before reversal is then

$$\Delta\Psi_n = -E(\Delta V_n)/\phi + 2E(\Delta Y_n)/\theta.$$

In view of (2.4) and (2.7),

$$\Delta\Psi_n = E(3V_n \overline{Y}_n - \overline{V}_n/2). \tag{2.9}$$

This formula is needed for the study of the overlearning reversal effect in the next section.

16.3. The Overlearning Reversal Effect

To apply Theorem 8.1.1 to the ZHL model, we simply assume that the parameters $\phi_j = \gamma_j \theta$ and $\theta_j = \eta_j \theta$ depend linearly on a parameter $\theta > 0$. Then $I_\theta = I = X$ is the closed unit square, $\mathscr{L}(\Delta X_n/\theta | X_n = x)$ does not depend on θ,

$$w(x) = E(\Delta X_n/\theta | X_n = x)$$

and

$$S(x) = E((\Delta X_n/\theta)^2 | X_n = x)$$

have polynomial coordinate functions, and $\Delta X_n/\theta$ is bounded, so it is easy to see that all of the assumptions of the theorem hold. Let $X_0 = x$ a.s., and let f satisfy

$$f'(t) = w(f(t)) \tag{3.1}$$

with $f(0) = x$. The theorem says that, for any $T < \infty$,

$$E(X_n) - f(n\theta) = O(\theta) \tag{3.2}$$

and

$$E(|X_n - E(X_n)|^2) = O(\theta) \tag{3.3}$$

uniformly over $x \in X$ and $n\theta \leqslant T$. Furthermore, X_n is approximately normally distributed when θ is small and $n\theta$ is bounded.

We now revert to the special case $\theta_1 = \theta_2 = \theta$ and $\phi_j = \phi$, $1 \leqslant j \leqslant 4$, considered in the last section, and assume that $\phi = \gamma\theta$, where $\gamma > 0$. This parameter is thus the ratio of the perceptual and response learning rates. We will study the asymptotic behavior of $f(t)$, and then use the information obtained to show which values of γ produce an overlearning reversal effect when θ is small.

Let $v(t)$ and $y(t)$ be the coordinate functions of $f(t)$: $f(t) = (v(t), y(t))$. It follows from (2.4) and (2.7) that the coordinate equations of (3.1) are

$$v'(t) = \gamma(\bar{v}/2 - v\bar{y}) \tag{3.4}$$

and

$$y'(t) = v\bar{y}. \tag{3.5}$$

Since $f(t) \in X$, $0 \leqslant v(t)$, $y(t) \leqslant 1$. The values $v = 1$ and $y = 1$ are associated with perfect learning. It is clear from (3.5) that $y(t)$ is nondecreasing. Thus, if $y(0) = 1$, $y(t) \equiv 1$, and (3.4) gives $\bar{v}(t) = \bar{v}(0)e^{-\gamma t/2}$. Throughout the remainder of the section, it is assumed that $y(0) < 1$.

According to Lemma 3.1, $v(t)$ and $y(t)$ both converge to 1 as $t \to \infty$. It should be noted that $v(t)$ need not be monotonic. By (3.4), $v'(0) \geqslant 0$ if $v(0) \leqslant v$, and $v'(0) < 0$ if $v(0) > v$, where

$$v = 1/(1 + 2\bar{y}(0)).$$

In the former case, $v'(t) > 0$ for all $t > 0$. In the latter, there is an $s > 0$ such that $v'(t) < 0$ for $t < s$, $v'(s) = 0$, and $v'(t) > 0$ for $t > s$. Since these facts are not used below, their proofs are omitted.

LEMMA 3.1.   For any $\gamma > 0$,

$$\bar{y}(t) \sim \alpha e^{-t} \tag{3.6}$$

as $t \to \infty$, where

$$\alpha = \bar{y}(0) \exp 2(\bar{y}(0) + \bar{v}(0)/\gamma).$$

If $\gamma < 2$,

$$\bar{v}(t) \sim \beta e^{-\gamma t/2} \tag{3.7}$$

for some $\beta > 0$. If $\gamma = 2$,

$$\bar{v}(t) \sim 2\alpha t e^{-t}, \tag{3.8}$$

and, if $\gamma > 2$,

$$\bar{v}(t) \sim \frac{2\gamma\alpha}{\gamma - 2} e^{-t}. \tag{3.9}$$

Proof.   Equations (3.4) and (3.5) are equivalent to

$$\bar{v}'(t) = \gamma(v\bar{y} - \bar{v}/2) \tag{3.10}$$

and

$$\bar{y}'(t) = -v\bar{y}. \tag{3.11}$$

Thus, if $\Sigma(t) = \bar{v}/\gamma + \bar{y}$,

$$\Sigma'(t) = -\bar{v}/2. \tag{3.12}$$

Therefore, $\Sigma(t) \geqslant 0$ is nonincreasing, so that

$$\Sigma(\infty) = \lim_{t \to \infty} \Sigma(t)$$

exists. Since $y(\infty)$ exists, $v(\infty)$ does too. Integrating both sides of (3.12), we obtain

$$\Sigma(0) - \Sigma(t) = \int_0^t \bar{v}(s) \, ds/2;$$

hence

$$\Sigma(0) - \Sigma(\infty) = \int_0^\infty \bar{v}(s) \, ds/2.$$

Finiteness of the integral implies $v(\infty) = 1$.

It follows from (3.11) that

$$\bar{y}(t) = \bar{y}(0) \exp - \int_0^t v(s) \, ds$$

$$= \bar{y}(0) \exp(-t) \exp \int_0^t \bar{v}(s) \, ds.$$

Thus,

$$\bar{y}(t) \sim \bar{y}(0) \exp 2(\Sigma(0) - \Sigma(\infty)) \exp(-t).$$

In particular, $y(\infty) = 1$, so $\Sigma(\infty) = 0$, and (3.6) is proved.

Solving (3.10) for $\bar{v}$ in terms of $q = \gamma v \bar{y}$, we obtain

$$\bar{v}(t) = e^{-\gamma t/2} \left(\bar{v}(0) + \int_0^t e^{\gamma s/2} q(s) \, ds \right). \tag{3.13}$$

If $\gamma < 2$, (3.6) implies that $e^{\gamma s/2} q(s)$ is integrable over the whole positive axis. Furthermore,

$$\beta = \bar{v}(0) + \int_0^\infty e^{\gamma s/2} q(s) \, ds > 0.$$

For this is certainly true if $\bar{v}(0) > 0$, and, if $\bar{v}(0) = 0$, then $q(s) > 0$ for s sufficiently small, which implies positivity of β. Thus (3.7) obtains.

If $\gamma = 2$, $e^{\gamma s/2} q(s) \to 2\alpha$ as $s \to \infty$; hence

$$\bar{v}(t)\, e^t/t = \bar{v}(0)/t + \int_0^t e^{\gamma s/2} q(s)\, ds/t$$

$$\to 2\alpha$$

when $t \to \infty$, as required for (3.8).

Finally, if $\gamma > 2$,

$$\int_0^t e^{\gamma s/2} q(s)\, ds = \int_0^t e^{(\gamma - 2)s/2} \left[e^s q(s) \right] ds$$

$$\sim \gamma\alpha \int_0^t e^{(\gamma - 2)s/2}\, ds$$

$$\sim \frac{2\gamma\alpha}{\gamma - 2}\, e^{(\gamma - 2)t/2}.$$

This estimate and (3.13) yield (3.9). ▮

Throughout what follows, the initial value $x = (v, y)$ of $X_n = X_n^\theta$ and $f(t)$ is fixed and independent of θ, with $y < 1$. At the end of the last section, we considered $\Psi_n = \Psi_n^\theta$, the expected number of errors following a reversal before trial n, and obtained the expression (2.9) for the change in this quantity due to one additional trial before reversal. This expression and Lemma 3.1 are the basis for Theorem 3.1.

THEOREM 3.1. *If $\gamma < 3$ ($\gamma > 3$), there is a T_0 with the following property. For any $T > T_0$, there is an $\varepsilon = \varepsilon_T > 0$ such that, if $\theta < \varepsilon$, then $\Delta\Psi_n^\theta < 0$ ($\Delta\Psi_n^\theta > 0$), for all $T_0 \leqslant n\theta \leqslant T$.*

The theorem is concerned with large values of n ($n \geqslant T_0/\theta$), or, loosely speaking, with overtraining. It says that, when θ is small, overtraining facilitates reversal (the overlearning reversal effect) if $\gamma < 3$, but retards reversal if $\gamma > 3$. This is consonant with the intuition that, when the perceptual learning rate $\phi = \gamma\theta$ is small relative to the response learning rate θ, the gain in attention to the relevant stimulus dimension with overtraining should more than compensate for the slight further strengthening of incorrect stimulus–response associations. It is, perhaps, surprising that the overlearning reversal effect is predicted for values of γ almost as large as 3. Of course, to obtain an experimentally measurable effect of overtraining, it is necessary to give a reasonable number k of overtraining trials. The change in expected total errors due to overtraining is then

$$\Psi_{n+k}^\theta - \Psi_n^\theta = \sum_{j=0}^{k-1} \Delta\Psi_{n+j}^\theta.$$

Proof. According to (2.9), $\Delta \Psi_n^\theta = E(P(X_n))$, where P is the polynomial

$$P(x) = 3v\bar{y} - \bar{v}/2.$$

Clearly

$$|\Delta \Psi_n^\theta - P(f(n\theta))| \leqslant |E(P(X_n)) - P(\mu_n)| + |P(\mu_n) - P(f(n\theta))|,$$

where $\mu_n = E(X_n)$. Since the first partial derivatives of P are bounded over X,

$$|P(\mu_n) - P(f(n\theta))| \leqslant C|\mu_n - f(n\theta)| \leqslant C\theta$$

by (3.2). And, since the second partial derivatives of P are bounded,

$$|E(P(X_n)) - P(\mu_n)| \leqslant CE(|X_n - \mu_n|^2) \leqslant C\theta$$

by (3.3). Thus, for any $T < \infty$, there is a $C = C_T$ such that

$$|\Delta \Psi_n^\theta - P(f(n\theta))| \leqslant C\theta \tag{3.14}$$

for all $n\theta \leqslant T$.

Let

$$p(t) = P(f(t)) = 3v(t)\,\bar{y}(t) - \bar{v}(t)/2.$$

It follows easily from Lemma 3.1 that, as $t \to \infty$,

$$
\begin{aligned}
p(t)e^{\gamma t/2} &\to -\beta/2 && \text{if} \quad \gamma < 2, \\
p(t)e^t/t &\to -\alpha && \text{if} \quad \gamma = 2, \\
p(t)e^t &\to 2\alpha(\gamma - 3)/(\gamma - 2) && \text{if} \quad \gamma > 2.
\end{aligned}
$$

Therefore, if $\gamma < 3$, there is a T_0 such that $p(t) < 0$, for $t \geqslant T_0$. And, if $\gamma > 3$, there is a T_0 such that $p(t) > 0$, for $t \geqslant T_0$. Suppose that $\gamma < 3$, and let $T > T_0$. Since $-p(t)$ is continuous and strictly positive on $[T_0, T]$,

$$S = \min_{T_0 \leqslant t \leqslant T} -p(t) > 0.$$

If $T_0 \leqslant n\theta \leqslant T$, then

$$\Delta \Psi_n^\theta - p(n\theta) \leqslant C\theta$$

by (3.14); hence

$$\Delta \Psi_n^\theta - p(n\theta) < S \leqslant -p(n\theta),$$

if $\theta < \varepsilon = S/C$. Thus $\Delta \Psi_n^\theta < 0$, as was to be shown. The analogous assertion for $\gamma > 3$ is proved similarly. ∎

17 ○ Other Learning Models

17.1. Suppes' Continuous Pattern Model

Suppes proposed two models for simple learning experiments with continua of responses, such as the continuous prediction experiment described in Section 0.1. His linear model was considered in Chapter 15. The other is an analog of the pattern model for two-choice experiments (Suppes, 1960). This section treats the ergodic theory of a slight generalization of the latter model.

There is a set S of N *stimulus patterns* s, and a measurable *response space* $(Y, \mathcal{Y})$. The state x of learning is a vector $(x_s, s \in S)$ of points in Y. As a trial begins, the subject samples a single stimulus pattern s with probability $1/N$, and makes a response y according to a distribution $\lambda_s(x_s, dy)$. If, for example, Y is a circle, x_s might be the mode of this distribution. Given y, the outcome or "correct response" z has distribution $\pi(y, dz)$. Conditioning is effective $(k=1)$ with probability $c(y, z)$, and ineffective $(k=0)$ otherwise. The event variable is $e = (s, y, z, k)$. If conditioning is effective, x_s is changed to z, while x_t, $t \neq s$, remains unchanged:

$$u(x, e)_s = z,$$

$$u(x, e)_t = x_t \quad \text{for} \quad t \neq s.$$

If conditioning is ineffective, $u(x, e) = x$. For this model, the distribution $p(x, de)$ of e given x is

$$p(x; s, dy, dz, k) = (1/N) \lambda_s(x_s, dy) \pi(y, dz) \begin{cases} c(y, z) & \text{if} \quad k = 1, \\ 1 - c(y, z) & \text{if} \quad k = 0. \end{cases}$$

Naturally, we assume that $\lambda_s(\cdot, A)$, $\pi(\cdot, D)$, and c are measurable.

Let K and U be the transition kernel and transition operator for a state sequence X_n, and let $B(X)$ be the set of bounded measurable scalar valued functions on X. Event, response, and outcome sequences are denoted E_n, Y_n, and Z_n, respectively. The following result is analogous to Theorem 15.1.3 for multiresponse linear models.

THEOREM 1.1. *If $c(y, z)$ and $\pi(y, D)$ have lower bounds of the form $c(y, z) \geqslant c(z)$ and $\pi(y, D) \geqslant \mu(D)$, where $c(z)$ is a nonnegative measurable function, μ is a measure, and $a = \int c(z) \mu(dz) > 0$, then U is regular with respect to $B(X)$.*

The conclusion is equivalent to $K^{(n)}(x, B) \to K^\infty(B)$ as $n \to \infty$, uniformly over x and B. The limit K^∞ is the unique stationary probability of K.

Proof. Note that $u(x, e) = u^*(x, e^*)$ depends on x and $e^* = (s, z, k)$, but not on y. The functions u^* and

$$p^*(x, A^*) = p(x, e^* \in A^*)$$

define a (reduced) model with states $x^* = x$ and events e^*. If $f \in B(X)$,

$$Uf(x) = \int p(x, de) f(u(x, e))$$

$$= \int p(x, de) f(u^*(x, e^*))$$

$$= \int p^*(x, de^*) f(u^*(x, e^*))$$

$$= U^*f(x).$$

Thus $U = U^*$, and it suffices to show that U^* is regular. This is accomplished via Theorem 4.1.2.

To begin,
$$p^*(x; s, D, k) = p(x; s, Y, D, k)$$

$$= (1/N) \int \lambda_s(x_s, dy) \int_D \pi(y, dz) \left[kc(y,z) + (1-k)(1-c(y,z)) \right]$$

$$\geq (1/N) \int \lambda_s(x_s, dy) \int_D \mu(dz) kc(z)$$

$$= (1/N) \int_D \mu(dz) c(z) k$$

$$= av(s, D, k). \tag{1.1}$$

This function v has a unique extension to a probability on the event space $(E^*, \mathscr{G}^*)$, and it follows from (1.1) that

$$p^*(x, A^*) \geq av(A^*)$$

for all $A^* \in \mathscr{G}^*$, as hypothesis (a) of Theorem 4.1.2 requires.

Let $e_n^* = (s_n, z_n, k_n)$, $e^N = (e_0^*, \ldots, e_{N-1}^*)$, and

$$G = \{ e^N : s_m \neq s_n \text{ for } m \neq n, \text{ and } k_n = 1 \text{ for all } n \}.$$

If $e^N \in G$,

$$u^*(x, e^N)_{s_n} = z_n$$

for $n \leq N-1$, so $u^*(x, e^N) = u^*(e^N)$ does not depend on x. Finally,

$$v^N(e^N) = \prod_{n=0}^{N-1} v(s_n, Y, 1) = 1/N^N,$$

so

$$v^N(G) = N!/N^N > 0,$$

and (b') of Theorem 4.1.2 obtains. ∎

When U is regular on $B(X)$, the model is uniformly regular (Theorem 6.2.1), so that $\{E_{j+n}\}_{n \geq 0}$ possesses an asymptotic distribution r as $j \to \infty$. If g is a measurable real valued function on Y^{2m},

$$g_j = g(Y_j, Z_j, \ldots, Y_{j+m-1}, Z_{j+m-1}),$$

and

$$\int g^2 \, dr = \int_{E^\infty} g^2(y_0, z_0, \ldots, y_{m-1}, z_{m-1}) r(de^\infty) < \infty,$$

then

$$(1/n) S_n = (1/n) \sum_{j=0}^{n-1} g_j \to \bar{g} = \int g \, dr$$

a.s. as $n \to \infty$ (Theorem 6.2.3), and S_n is asymptotically normally distributed with mean $n\bar{g}$ and variance proportional to n (Theorem 6.2.4). Finally, by Theorem 6.1.2, the results of Chapter 5 apply to g_j when $m = 1$ and g is bounded.

17.2. Successive Discrimination

In Chapter 16 we considered the ZHL model for simultaneous discrimination learning, in which the two values of the relevant stimulus dimension are present on each trial. In this section we discuss a similar model for successive discrimination, where only one value appears per trial. Suppose, for example, that a stimulus card overhead at the choice point of a T-maze may be black or white. When it is black (an s_0 trial), the rat is fed if he goes to the left side (A_0 response), while, if it is white (s_1), he is fed if he goes to the right (A_1). The two trial types are randomly interspersed and equiprobable.

Bush (1965) developed some suggestions of L. B. Wyckoff, Jr., into the model described next, which, following Bush, we call the *Wyckoff model*. The state x has four coordinates, v, y_1, y_0, and z. The variable v gives the rat's probability of observing or attending to the stimulus card (a), while y_i is the probability of making the correct A_i response on an s_i trial, given a. Finally, z is the probability of A_1 on either type trial, given inattention ($\tilde{a}$). To summarize:

$$P(s_i) = \tfrac{1}{2},$$

$$P(a) = v,$$

$$P(A_i|s_i a) = y_i,$$

$$P(A_1|\tilde{a}) = z.$$

Events e are of the form $s_i a A_j$ or $s_i \tilde{a} A_j$.

It remains only to indicate how various events affect x. The probability v of attention increases if the rat attends and gets food or does not attend and does not get food, and decreases otherwise. The variable y_i increases on $s_i a$ trials, regardless of the subject's response, and otherwise does not change. The $\tilde{a}$-trial probability z of going right changes only on $\tilde{a}$ trials, increasing or decreasing depending on whether food is on the right or left, just as in models for simple learning. All of these changes are effected by simple linear operators. Thus, for example, the possible values of Δv after $\tilde{a}$ and their probabilities of occurrence are

$$-\phi_{11}v \quad \text{if} \quad s_1\tilde{a}A_1 \quad \text{with probability} \quad \bar{v}z/2,$$

$$-\phi_{00}v \quad \text{if} \quad s_0\tilde{a}A_0 \quad \text{with probability} \quad \bar{v}\bar{z}/2,$$

$$\phi_{10}\bar{v} \quad \text{if} \quad s_1\tilde{a}A_0 \quad \text{with probability} \quad \bar{v}\bar{z}/2,$$

$$\phi_{01}\bar{v} \quad \text{if} \quad s_0\tilde{a}A_1 \quad \text{with probability} \quad \bar{v}z/2,$$

where $\bar{v} = 1 - v$.

Under the natural lateral symmetry conditions $\phi_{11} = \phi_{00} = \phi_3$ and $\phi_{10} = \phi_{01} = \phi_4$, the two events involving correct (C) responses, as well as the two events involving incorrect (I) responses, can be combined into two new events, $\tilde{a}C$ and $\tilde{a}I$, which produce Δv's of $-\phi_3 v$ and $\phi_4\bar{v}$, respectively. The probability $\bar{v}/2$ of these new events does not depend on z. Relabeling the four events involving a to indicate whether the subject's choice was correct or not, we obtain the reduced model described in Table 1. The fact that there are four parameters in lines 1–4 instead of eight reflects lateral symmetry conditions like those that made the reduction possible. The new state variable is, of course, $x = (v, y_1, y_0)$.

TABLE 1

EVENT EFFECTS AND PROBABILITIES FOR THE REDUCED WYCKOFF MODEL ($\bar{v} = 1 - v$)

Event	Δv	Δy_1	Δy_0	Probability
1. s_1aC	$\phi_1\bar{v}$	$\theta\bar{y}_1$	0	$vy_1/2$
2. s_1aI	$-\phi_2 v$	$\theta^*\bar{y}_1$	0	$v\bar{y}_1/2$
3. s_0aC	$\phi_1\bar{v}$	0	$\theta\bar{y}_0$	$vy_0/2$
4. s_0aI	$-\phi_2 v$	0	$\theta^*\bar{y}_0$	$v\bar{y}_0/2$
5. $\tilde{a}C$	$-\phi_3 v$	0	0	$\bar{v}/2$
6. $\tilde{a}I$	$\phi_4\bar{v}$	0	0	$\bar{v}/2$

Our subsequent discussion focuses on this model, whose properties are quite analogous to those of the reduced ZHL model. Since the proofs are also similar, they are omitted. If $\phi_1, \phi_4, \theta, \theta^* > 0$, the Wyckoff model is distance diminishing and absorbing, with single absorbing state $(1, 1, 1)$. Thus $V_n \to 1$ and $Y_{in} \to 1$ a.s. as $n \to \infty$, where V_n and Y_{in} are the values of v and y_i on trial n. The expected total numbers $E(\#I)$ and $E(\#\tilde{a})$ of overt and perceptual errors are finite. Under the additional conditions $\phi_j = \phi$,

$1 \leqslant j \leqslant 4$, and $\theta = \theta^*$,

$$E_x(\#I) = \bar{v}/\phi + 2(\bar{y}_1 + \bar{y}_0)/\theta$$

and

$$E_x(\#\tilde{a}) = 2\bar{v}/\phi + 2(\bar{y}_1 + \bar{y}_0)/\theta.$$

Let $\phi = \gamma\theta$, where $\gamma > 0$ is fixed. If $n\theta$ is bounded, then $\mathrm{var}(V_n) = O(\theta)$, $\mathrm{var}(Y_{in}) = O(\theta)$,

$$E(V_n) = v(n\theta) + O(\theta),$$

and

$$E(Y_{in}) = y_i(n\theta) + O(\theta),$$

where

$$v'(t) = (\gamma/2)\,(\bar{v} - v(\bar{y}_1 + \bar{y}_0)),$$
$$y_i'(t) = \bar{y}_i v/2,$$

$V_0 = v(0)$, and $Y_{i0} = y_i(0)$ a.s. Introducing $\bar{y} = \bar{y}_0 + \bar{y}_1$ into the equation for v' and the sum of the equations for y_1' and y_0', we obtain

$$\bar{v}'(t) = (\gamma/2)\,(v\bar{y} - \bar{v})$$

and

$$\bar{y}'(t) = -v\bar{y}/2.$$

These equations are similar to (16.3.10) and (16.3.11), and can be put to the same use. When θ is small, an overlearning reversal effect is predicted for $\gamma < \frac{3}{2}$ but not for $\gamma > \frac{3}{2}$. More precisely, Theorem 16.3.1 holds with $\frac{3}{2}$ in place of 3.

17.3. Signal Detection: Forced-Choice

This section and the next treat learning models for two types of signal detection experiments. In the *forced-choice* paradigm, the subject must specify which of two temporal intervals or spatial locations a signal occurred in. In *yes–no* experiments, the subject must state whether or not there was a signal in a single observation interval. When there is feedback concerning correctness of responses, it is natural to assume that the subject can make use of it to improve his performance. In this way we are led to consider learning models for signal detection. The model of Atkinson and Kinchla (1965, see also Atkinson, Bower, and Crothers, 1965, Chapter 5) for forced-choice experiments is discussed below. Friedman, Carterette, Nakatani, and

Ahumada (1968) have considered a similar model for the yes–no paradigm. Kac's (1962, 1969) yes–no model, a predecessor of the forced-choice model of Dorfman and Biderman (1971), is taken up in the next section.

Suppose that a signal occurs in temporal interval S_1 with probability $\eta\gamma$, and in S_2 with probability $\eta(1-\gamma)$. If $\eta < 1$, then, unbeknown to the subject, there is no signal in either interval (S_0) with probability $1-\eta$. On an S_i trial, $i = 1$ or 2, a *detection* occurs with probability σ and produces sensory state s_i; otherwise sensory state s_0 results. This state always occurs on S_0 trials. When the subject is in state s_1 or s_2, he makes the appropriate response (A_1 or A_2). In state s_0, he makes response A_1 with probability x. It is this bias parameter that undergoes a learning process. After his response, the subject is told that the signal occurred in the first (O_1) or second (O_2) interval. On signal trials this feedback is correct, but, on S_0 trials, O_1 and O_2 occur with probabilities π and $1-\pi$.

Events in this model are of the form $e = S_i s_j A_k O_l$, and their conditional probabilities given x are easily derived from the above specifications. For example,

$$p(x, e) = \begin{cases} \eta\gamma\sigma & \text{if} \quad e = S_1 s_1 A_1 O_1, \\ (1-\eta)\,x(1-\pi) & \text{if} \quad e = S_0 s_0 A_1 O_2. \end{cases}$$

The response bias parameter x changes only when detection fails to occur, increasing after O_1 and decreasing after O_2. Linear state transformations are assumed:

$$u(x, e) = \begin{cases} (1-\theta_1)x + \theta_1 & \text{if} \quad s_0 O_1, \\ (1-\theta_2)x & \text{if} \quad s_0 O_2, \\ x & \text{otherwise}, \end{cases}$$

where $0 < \theta_i \leqslant 1$. Note that

$$p(x, s_0 O_1) = \eta\gamma(1-\sigma) + (1-\eta)\pi = g_1$$

and

$$p(x, s_0 O_2) = \eta(1-\gamma)(1-\sigma) + (1-\eta)(1-\pi) = g_2$$

do not depend on x.

Let X_n be the value of x on trial n. Clearly,

$$E(\Delta X_n | X_n) = \theta_1(1-X_n)g_1 - \theta_2 X_n g_2,$$

so

$$\Delta E(X_n) = \theta_1 g_1 (1 - E(X_n)) - \theta_2 g_2 E(X_n),$$

and, letting $n \to \infty$,

$$x_\infty = \lim_{n \to \infty} E(X_n) = \theta_1 g_1 / (\theta_1 g_1 + \theta_2 g_2).$$

The asymptotic probabilities of appropriate and inappropriate A_1 responses ("hits" and "false alarms") are

$$h = \lim_{n \to \infty} P(A_{1n} | S_{1n}) = \sigma + (1 - \sigma) x_\infty$$

and

$$f = \lim_{n \to \infty} P(A_{1n} | S_{2n}) = (1 - \sigma) x_\infty.$$

Thus, however, η, γ, π, and θ_i may vary, (f, h) is confined to the line $h = \sigma + f$, which is the *receiver operating characteristic* or *ROC* curve predicted by the model. Given a single subject's data for an n trial block, the natural estimators of f and h are the proportions F_n and H_n of A_1 responses on S_2 and S_1 trials.

It is not difficult to show that, if $\sigma < 1$ or $\eta < 1$, this model is distance diminishing, and the process X_n is regular. Thus, according to the corollary to Theorem 6.1.1, the results of Chapter 5 apply to functions $g(E_n)$ of an event sequence E_n. To illustrate one of these results, we show that (F_n, H_n) is asymptotically normally distributed, with mean (f, h) and covariance matrix proportional to $1/n$, as $n \to \infty$.

Clearly

$$F_n = \overline{S_2 A_1} / \overline{S}_2 \qquad \text{and} \qquad H_n = \overline{S_1 A_1} / \overline{S}_1, \tag{3.1}$$

where

$$\overline{S}_1 = (1/n) \sum_{j=0}^{n-1} S_{1j},$$

and S_{1j} is 1 or 0 depending on whether or not S_1 occurs on trial j. Now S_{1j}, S_{2j}, and the comparable indicators for $S_1 A_1$ and $S_2 A_1$ are functions of E_j. It follows from the multivariate central limit theorem described in Section 5.7 that

$$\overline{Y}_n = (\overline{S}_2, \overline{S_2 A_1}, \overline{S}_1, \overline{S_1 A_1})$$

is asymptotically multivariate normal, with mean

$$y = (\eta(1 - \gamma), \eta(1 - \gamma) f, \eta \gamma, \eta \gamma h)$$

and covariance matrix Σ / n, where Σ is given by the series (5.7.2). But the

function, call it Ψ, from $\overline{Y}_n$ to (F_n, H_n) [see (3.1)] is continuously differentiable with $\Psi(y) = (f, h)$, provided that $\eta > 0$ and $0 < \gamma < 1$. Hence

$$\sqrt{n}(F_n - f, H_n - h) \sim N(0, \Lambda),$$

where

$$\Lambda = \Psi'(y)^* \Sigma \Psi'(y),$$

$\Psi'(y)$ is the derivative of Ψ at y, and $*$ indicates transposition.

17.4. Signal Detection: Yes–No

Suppose that, on every trial, the subject has an internal response y to the
stimulus (signal or noise) that is present. If there is a signal (S_1), this variable
has distribution function F_1; otherwise (S_0), its distribution function is F_0.
The sequence of trial types is independent, and $P(S_i) = p_i > 0$. The subject
declares that the signal was present (A_1) if y exceeds a criterion x, and that
it was absent (A_0) if $y \leqslant x$. He is then told whether he was right or wrong.

Kac (1962, 1969) considered the possibility that the criterion x in such a
system undergoes a learning process. Specifically, he assumed that x is
incremented by $\varDelta > 0$ if there is a false alarm $(S_0 A_1)$ and decremented by $\varDelta$
in the case of a missed signal $(S_1 A_0)$. Dropping the assumption of equal
changes, we arrive at a learning model with state x, events $e = S_i A_j$, state
transformations

$$u(x, e) - x = \begin{cases} \varDelta_1 < 0 & \text{if } e = S_1 A_0, \\ \varDelta_0 > 0 & \text{if } e = S_0 A_1, \\ 0 & \text{otherwise,} \end{cases}$$

and event probabilities

$$p(x, S_i A_0) = p_i F_i(x)$$

and

$$p(x, S_i A_1) = p_i (1 - F_i(x)).$$

In view of the form of the state transformations, it is not surprising that
Kac's model behaves much like the recurrent additive models of Chapter 14.
The exposition that follows skips a number of proofs that are similar to
ones in that chapter. It is, of course, part of the intuitive background of
the detection problem that the signal should tend to produce a larger internal
response than the noise, e.g., $\int y \, dF_1 > \int y \, dF_0$, but none of our results
depend on this condition. Continuity and strict monotonicity of F_0 and F_1
suffice for everything except slow learning.

State sequences in this model oscillate, in the sense that

$$\limsup_{n \to \infty} X_n = \infty \qquad \text{and} \qquad \liminf_{n \to \infty} X_n = -\infty$$

a.s. If $v = e^x$ and $\lambda \in R^1$, there are constants $C(\lambda) < 1$ and $B(\lambda)$ such that

$$E_x(v_n^\lambda) \leqslant v^\lambda C^n(\lambda) + B(\lambda) \tag{4.1}$$

for all $n \geqslant 0$. Taking $\lambda = \pm 1$ and adding, we see that, for any fixed x, $E_x(X_n^2)$ is a bounded sequence.

The counterpart of (A) of Theorem 14.2.1 is especially interesting. Let a_{0n} and a_{1n} be the proportions of false alarms and missed signals in an n trial block:

$$a_{in} = \sum_{m=0}^{n-1} S_{im} A_{i'm} \bigg/ \sum_{m=0}^{n-1} S_{im}, \qquad i' = 1 - i,$$

and put $a_n = (a_{0n}, a_{1n})$. Let L be the line

$$L = \{(a_0, a_1) : \Delta_0 p_0 a_0 + \Delta_1 p_1 a_1 = 0\},$$

and let $d(a, L)$ be the distance from a point a in the plane to L.

THEOREM 4.1. *As $n \to \infty$, $d(a_n, L) \to 0$ a.s.*

Proof. Let $X_0 = x$ a.s. Clearly

$$\Delta X_m = \sum_i \Delta_i S_{im} A_{i'm},$$

so

$$X_n/n - x/n = \sum_i \Delta_i \sum_{m=0}^{n-1} S_{im} A_{i'm}/n. \tag{4.2}$$

Since $E(X_n^2)$ is bounded, $X_n/n \to 0$ a.s. By the strong law of large numbers,

$$p_i n \bigg/ \sum_{m=0}^{n-1} S_{im} \to 1$$

a.s., as $n \to \infty$. Hence, multiplying the ith term on the right in (4.2) by this ratio, we get

$$\sum_i \Delta_i p_i a_{in} \to 0$$

a.s., and $d(a_n, L)$ is proportional to this sum. ∎

Let K be the transition kernel of X_n, and let

$$\bar{K}^n(x, B) = (1/n) \sum_{j=0}^{n-1} K^{(j)}(x, B).$$

THEOREM 4.2. *For any* $x \in R^1$, *$\overline{K}^n(x, \cdot)$ converges to a stationary prob-ability $K^\infty(x, \cdot)$. There is a unique stationary probability if and only if Δ_0/Δ_1 is irrational.*

It follows from (4.1) that

$$\int K^\infty(x, dy) e^{\lambda y} \leqslant B(\lambda)$$

for all x and λ. Additional information about K^∞ when Δ_0/Δ_1 is rational is developed in the course of the proof.

Proof. Suppose that Δ_1/Δ_0 is irrational. Since $p_i > 0$ and F_i is strictly increasing,

$$\sigma(x) = p_1 F_1(x) + p_0(1 - F_0(x)) > 0$$

and

$$\tilde{p}(x) = p_1 F_1(x)/\sigma(x)$$

is strictly increasing. It is also continuous, with $\tilde{p}(-\infty) = 0$ and $\tilde{p}(\infty) = 1$. Thus the Markov process $\tilde{X}_n$ with transitions

$$\Delta \tilde{X}_n = \begin{cases} \Delta_1 & \text{with probability} \quad \tilde{p}(\tilde{X}_n), \\ \Delta_0 & \text{with probability} \quad 1 - \tilde{p}(\tilde{X}_n), \end{cases}$$

has a unique stationary probability, according to Theorem 14.4.2. If $\tilde{K}$ is its transition kernel, then

$$K(x, B) = \sigma(x) \tilde{K}(x, B) + (1 - \sigma(x)) \delta_x(B).$$

It follows that $\mu \to \tilde{\mu}$, where

$$\tilde{\mu}(A) = \int_A \mu(dx) \sigma(x) \bigg/ \int_{R^1} \mu(dx) \sigma(x),$$

is a one-to-one mapping of stationary probabilities of K into stationary probabilities of $\tilde{K}$. Thus K has at most one stationary probability. The argument in the second to last paragraph of Section 14.4 then yields weak convergence of $\overline{K}^n(x, \cdot)$ to the unique stationary probability μ.

If Δ_0/Δ_1 is rational, let j and k be relatively prime positive integers such that $\Delta_0/|\Delta_1| = j/k$, and let

$$\varepsilon = \Delta_0/j = |\Delta_1|/k.$$

It is not difficult to show that

$$G^+ = \{n_0 \Delta_0 + n_1 \Delta_1 : n_0, n_1 \geqslant 0\}$$

$$= \varepsilon Z, \tag{4.3}$$

where Z is the set of all integers. Clearly $C_x = x + G^+$ is stochastically closed, so the restriction K_x of K to C_x is the transition kernel for a denumerable Markov chain. As a consequence of (4.3), any two states communicate, so

$$\lim_{n \to \infty} \overline{K}_x^n(y, z) = \pi(z)$$

for all $y, z \in C_x$ (Parzen, 1962, Theorem 8A, p. 249). But

$$\overline{K}_x^n(y, \{z : |z| \leqslant k\}) \to 1$$

as $k \to \infty$, uniformly in n, from which it follows that $\sum_{z \in C_x} \pi(z) = 1$, and

$$\lim_{n \to \infty} \overline{K}_x^n(y, A) = \sum_{z \in A} \pi(z) = \pi(A),$$

for any $A \subset C_x$. The distribution π is the unique stationary probability of K_x, and $\pi(z) > 0$ for all $z \in C_x$ (Parzen, 1962, Theorem 8B, p. 249, and Theorem 8C, p. 251). Therefore

$$\lim_{n \to \infty} \overline{K}^n(x, B) = \pi(B \cap C_x) = K^\infty(x, B)$$

for all Borel sets B, $K^\infty(x, \cdot)$ is the unique stationary probability of K with support C_x, and $K^\infty(x + \varepsilon, \cdot) = K^\infty(x, \cdot)$. ∎

To study slow learning, we fix $\rho = \Delta_1 / \Delta_0 < 0$, and let $\Delta_0 = \theta \to 0$. The moments

$$w(x) = E(\Delta X_n / \theta | X_n = x)$$
$$= \rho p_1 F_1(x) + p_0(1 - F_0(x))$$

and

$$S(x) = E((\Delta X_n / \theta)^2 | X_n = x)$$
$$= \rho^2 p_1 F_1(x) + p_0(1 - F_0(x))$$

do not depend on θ, so (a) of Section 8.1 is satisfied, with $I_\theta = R^1$. If F_i has two bounded derivatives, $w(x)$ and $s(x) = S(x) - w^2(x)$ satisfy the smoothness condition (b). Finally, $|\Delta X_n / \theta|$ is bounded by the maximum of 1 and ρ, so (c) holds, and Theorem 8.1.1 is applicable. Thus, if $X_0^\theta = x$ does not depend on θ,

$$(X_n^\theta - f(n\theta)) / \sqrt{\theta} \sim N(0, g(t)) \tag{4.4}$$

as $\theta \to 0$ and $n\theta \to t$, where

$$f'(t) = w(f(t)),$$
$$g'(t) = 2w'(f(t))g(t) + s(f(t)),$$

$f(0) = x$, and $g(0) = 0$.

It follows that $\mathscr{L}(X_n^\theta) \to \delta_{f(t)}$. Kac (1962) gave two interesting heuristic derivations of this result, describing the limit function via the equation

$$\int_x^{f(t)} (1/w(u))\,du = t,$$

which we mentioned in Section 12.4 [see (12.4.5)].

Since $w(x)$ is continuous and strictly decreasing, with $w(-\infty) = p_0 > 0$ and $w(\infty) = \rho p_1 < 0$, there is a unique ξ such that $w(\xi) = 0$. As $t \to \infty$, $f(t) \to \xi$, and, if $w'(\xi) < 0$ (i.e., $F_1'(\xi) > 0$ or $F_0'(\xi) > 0$),

$$g(t) \to \sigma^2 = S(\xi)/2|w'(\xi)|.$$

In view of (4.4), one expects the limiting distributions $K^\infty(x, \cdot) = K_\theta^\infty(x, \cdot)$ to be asymptotically normal, with mean ξ and variance $\theta\sigma^2$, as $\theta \to 0$. It follows from Theorem 10.1.1 that this is the case.

18 ○ Diffusion Approximation in a Genetic Model and a Physical Model

This chapter treats diffusion approximation in a population genetic model of S. Wright and in the Ehrenfest model for heat exchange. Since sequences of states in these models are finite Markov chains, their "small step size" theory has much in common with that of stimulus sampling models (Section 13.3).

18.1. Wright's Model

Our description of this model is based on Ewens (1969, Section 4.8). The reader should also consult that volume for references to the extensive literature on diffusion approximation in population genetics. The work of Karlin and McGregor (1964a,b) is of particular interest.

Consider a diploid population of $2M$ individuals. At a certain chromosomal locus there are two alleles, A_1 and A_2. The number i of A_1 genes in the population thus ranges from 0 to $2M$, and the proportion, $x = i/2M$, from 0 to 1. The A_1 gene frequencies i (or x) in successive generations are assumed to form a Markov chain, with transition probabilities

$$p_{ij} = \binom{2M}{j} \pi_i^j (1 - \pi_i)^{2M - j},$$

where

$$\pi_i = (1-u)\pi_i^* + v(1-\pi_i^*)$$

and

$$\pi_i^* = \frac{(1+s_1)x^2 + (1+s_2)x(1-x)}{(1+s_1)x^2 + 2(1+s_2)x(1-x) + (1-x)^2}.$$

The constant u represents the probability that an A_1 gene mutates to A_2, while v is the probability that A_2 mutates to A_1. The genotypes A_1A_1, A_1A_2, and A_2A_2 have fitness $1+s_1$, $1+s_2$, and 1, respectively, so s_1 and s_2 control selective pressures.

Let X_n be the proportion of A_1 genes in generation n. The standard formulas for the mean and variance of the binomial distribution give

$$E(X_{n+1}|X_n = x) = \pi_i$$

and

$$\mathrm{var}(X_{n+1}|X_n = x) = \pi_i(1-\pi_i)/2M. \qquad (1.1)$$

Thus

$$E(\Delta X_n|X_n = x) = \pi_i - x \qquad (1.2)$$

and, since $\pi_i(1-\pi_i) = x(1-x) + O(|\pi_i - x|)$,

$$\mathrm{var}(\Delta X_n|X_n = x) = x(1-x)/2M + O(|\pi_i - x|/2M). \qquad (1.3)$$

The theory of Part II has a number of implications for the behavior of $X_n = X_n^M$ as $M \to \infty$ and the parameters u, v, and $s_i \to 0$. In order to study small values of u, v, and s_i, we let $u = \bar{u}\rho$, $v = \bar{v}\rho$, and $s_i = \bar{s}_i\rho$, where $\bar{u} \geqslant 0$, $\bar{v} \geqslant 0$, and $\bar{s}_i$ are fixed, and $\rho \to 0$. Under these conditions, it is shown later that

$$E(\Delta X_n|X_n = x) = \rho w(x) + O(\rho^2), \qquad (1.4)$$

where

$$w(x) = \bar{v} - (\bar{u}+\bar{v})x + x(1-x)(\bar{s}_2 + (\bar{s}_1 - 2\bar{s}_2)x).$$

Also,

$$\mathrm{var}(\Delta X_n|X_n = x) = x(1-x)/2M + O(\rho/2M). \qquad (1.5)$$

It remains only to specify the relative magnitudes of ρ and $1/2M$. We will consider two possibilities: $\rho = 1/(2M)^{1/2}$ and $\rho = 1/2M$. These will be referred to as the cases of large and small drift, respectively. The results described next follow immediately from the indicated theorem in Part II. The hypotheses of these theorems are verified at the end of the section.

LARGE DRIFT: TRANSIENT BEHAVIOR.   Let

$$I_M = \{i/2M : 0 \leqslant i \leqslant 2M\},$$

and, for any $0 \leqslant x \leqslant 1$, let $f(t) = f(t, x)$ and $g(t) = g(t, x)$ be the solutions of the differential equations

$$f'(t) = w(f(t))$$

and

$$g'(t) = 2w'(f(t))g(t) + f(t)(1 - f(t)),$$

with $f(0) = x$ and $g(0) = 0$. Suppose that X_0^M is concentrated at a point $x_M \in I_M$, and that $x_M \to x$ as $M \to \infty$. Let $v_n^M = f(n/(2M)^{1/2}, x_M)$. By Theorem 8.1.1,

$$(2M)^{1/2}(X_n^M - v_n^M) \sim N(0, g(t, x)) \qquad (1.6)$$

as $M \to \infty$ and $n/(2M)^{1/2} \to t$. In particular, the deterministic approximation v_n^M to X_n^M should be highly satisfactory when M is large and $n/(2M)^{1/2}$ is bounded.

LARGE DRIFT: STEADY-STATE BEHAVIOR.   Assume that $\bar{v} = w(0) > 0$ and $\bar{u} = -w(1) > 0$, that w has a unique root λ in $(0, 1)$, and that $w'(\lambda) < 0$. As $t \to \infty$, $f(t) \to \lambda$ and

$$g(t) \to \sigma^2 = \lambda(1 - \lambda)/2|w'(\lambda)|.$$

The process X_n^M has no absorbing states, and the asymptotic distribution

$$\mathscr{L}_\infty^M = \lim_{n \to \infty} \mathscr{L}((2M)^{1/2}(X_n^M - \lambda))$$

does not depend on the distribution of X_0^M. Theorem 10.1.1 shows that

$$\lim_{M \to \infty} \mathscr{L}_\infty^M = N(0, \sigma^2),$$

just as (1.6) suggests. Theorem 10.3.1 gives a formula for a constant γ such that

$$\lim_{n \to \infty} E(X_n^M) = \lambda + \gamma/(2M)^{1/2} + o(1/(2M)^{1/2}).$$

SMALL DRIFT: TRANSIENTS.   Suppose now that $\rho = 1/2M$, and assume, once again, that $X_0^M = x_M \to x$ as $M \to \infty$. According to Theorem 9.1.1, there is a unique transition probability $P(t; x, A)$ such that

$$\int (y-x) P(\tau; x, dy) = \tau w(x) + o(\tau),$$

$$\int (y-x)^2 P(\tau; x, dy) = \tau x(1-x) + o(\tau),$$

$$\int |y-x|^3 P(\tau; x, dy) = o(\tau),$$

where the o's are uniform over $0 \leqslant x \leqslant 1$. As $M \to \infty$ and $n/2M \to t$,

$$\mathcal{L}(X_n^M) \to P(t; x, \cdot).$$

Kimura (1964) discusses the eigenfunction expansion (9.3.9) of the density of $P(t; x, \cdot)$.

SMALL DRIFT: ABSORPTION PROBABILITIES.   If $\bar{u} = 0$ and $\bar{v} = 0$, both 0 and 1 are absorbing states for X_n^M, and the process is eventually absorbed at one or the other a.s. Let

$$\phi_M(x) = P_x(X_n^M \text{ is absorbed at } 1).$$

The function w reduces to

$$w(x) = x(1-x)(\bar{s}_2 + (\bar{s}_1 - 2\bar{s}_2) x),$$

so that

$$r(x) = 2w(x)/x(1-x) = 2(\bar{s}_2 + (\bar{s}_1 - 2\bar{s}_2) x).$$

Let ψ be the solution of

$$\psi''(x) + r(x) \psi'(x) = 0$$

with $\psi(0) = 0$ and $\psi(1) = 1$. By Theorem 11.1.1,

$$\max_{x \in I_M} |\phi_M(x) - \psi(x)| \to 0$$

as $M \to \infty$.

Proofs.   To check the hypotheses of the theorems cited above, we must obtain suitable estimates of $\pi_i - x$ and $E(|\Delta X_n|^3 | X_n = x)$. Note first that

$$\pi_i - x = v - (u+v) x + (1-u-v)(\pi_i^* - x). \tag{1.7}$$

Also,

$$\pi_i^* = x \frac{1 + s_1 x + s_2(1-x)}{1 + s_1 x^2 + 2s_2 x(1-x)},$$

so that

$$\pi_i^* - x = x(1-x)\frac{s_1 x + s_2(1-2x)}{1 + s_1 x^2 + 2s_2 x(1-x)} \tag{1.8}$$

and

$$\pi_i^* - x = x(1-x)(s_1 x + s_2(1-2x))(1 + O(\rho)). \tag{1.9}$$

Combining (1.2), (1.7), and (1.9), we obtain (1.4), and of course,

$$\pi_i - x = O(\rho), \tag{1.10}$$

an estimate that will be used repeatedly. All O's in this section are uniform over x.

Since the conditional distribution of $2MX_{n+1}$ given x is binomial,

$$(2M)^4 E((X_{n+1} - \pi_i)^4 | X_n = x)$$
$$= 2M\pi_i(1-\pi_i)(3(2M-1)\pi_i(1-\pi_i) + \pi_i^3 + (1-\pi_i)^3).$$

Thus

$$E((X_{n+1} - \pi_i)^4 | X_n = x) \leqslant \pi_i(1-\pi_i)/(2M)^2. \tag{1.11}$$

Since $|y+z|^p \leqslant 2^{p-1}(|y|^p + |z|^p)$ for $p \geqslant 1$, and $\rho \leqslant 1/(2M)^{1/2}$ for large or small drift, (1.10) and (1.11) yield

$$E(|\Delta X_n|^4 | X_n = x) = O((2M)^{-2}).$$

Therefore,

$$E(|\Delta X_n|^3 | X_n = x) = O((2M)^{-3/2}). \tag{1.12}$$

Consider first the case of large drift, and let $\theta = \rho = 1/(2M)^{1/2}$. It follows easily from (1.4), (1.5), and (1.12) that Theorem 8.1.1 applies, with $s(x) = x(1-x)$. When $\bar{u} > 0$, $\bar{v} > 0$, w has a unique root λ in $(0, 1)$, and $w'(\lambda) < 0$, the conditions of Theorem 10.1.1 are also met. An expansion

$$E(\Delta X_n | X_n = x) = \rho w(x) + \rho^2 v(x) + O(\rho^3)$$

of the type required by Theorem 10.3.1 can be obtained from (1.7) and (1.8).

We turn now to small drift, and let $\tau = \rho = 1/2M$. By (1.5) and (1.10),

$$E((\Delta X_n)^2 | X_n = x) = x(1-x)/2M + O((2M)^{-2}), \tag{1.13}$$

which, together with (1.4) and (1.12), shows that Theorem 9.1.1 applies, with $a(x) = w(x)$ and $b(x) = x(1-x)$. For Theorem 11.1.1, it suffices to show that the errors $O(h)$ in (1.4), (1.12), and (1.13) are $O(x(1-x)h)$ when $\bar{u} = \bar{v} = 0$. In the case of (1.4), this follows from (1.9), which also yields the refinement

$$\pi_i - x = \pi_i^* - x = O(x(1-x)\rho) \tag{1.14}$$

of (1.10). This and (1.3) give

$$E((\Delta X_n)^2 | X_n = x) = x(1-x)/2M + O(x(1-x)(2M)^{-2}).$$

Applying the Schwartz inequality to $Y^3 = YY^2$, where $Y = |X_{n+1} - \pi_i|$, and using (1.1) and (1.11), we obtain

$$E(|X_{n+1} - \pi_i|^3 | X_n = x) \leqslant \pi_i(1-\pi_i)(2M)^{-\frac{3}{2}}.$$

But $\pi_i(1-\pi_i) = O(x(1-x))$, so using (1.14) once again,

$$E(|\Delta X_n|^3 | X_n = x) = O(x(1-x)(2M)^{-\frac{3}{2}}). \quad \blacksquare$$

18.2. The Ehrenfest Model

There are $2M$ balls, distributed between two urns, I and II. The number in urn I on trial n is $J_n = J_n^M$. On any trial, a ball is selected at random, and shifted to the other urn. Thus,

$$\Delta J_n = \begin{cases} 1 & \text{with probability} \quad 1 - J_n/2M, \\ -1 & \text{with probability} \quad J_n/2M. \end{cases}$$

The physical significance of this model is discussed by Kac (1947, 1969), who also gives an explicit expression for its higher-order transition probabilities [1947, Eq. (62)]. We note that J_n has the same transition probabilities as the number of stimulus elements conditioned to response A_1 in the pattern model with $\pi_{01} = \pi_{10} = c_{01} = c_{10} = 1$.

It is easy to see that Theorem 8.1.1 is applicable to $X_n = (J_n - M)/M$, with $\theta = 1/M$. Clearly, $\Delta X_n/\theta = \Delta J_n$, so

$$w(x) = E(\Delta J_n | X_n = x) = -x$$

and

$$s(x) = \text{var}(\Delta J_n | X_n = x) = 1 - x^2.$$

Let $J_0^M = j_M$ a.s., where $(j_M - M)/M \to x$, and let

$$g(t,x) = ((1 - e^{-2t})/2) - x^2 t e^{-2t}.$$

It follows from the theorem that

$$((J_n^M - M) - (j_M - M)e^{-n/M})/\sqrt{M} \sim N(0, g(t,x))$$

as $M \to \infty$ and $n/M \to t$. Consequently, if $(j_M - M)/\sqrt{M} \to z$,

$$(J_n^M - M)/\sqrt{M} \sim N(ze^{-t}, (1 - e^{-2t})/2).$$

This was noted by Kac (1947, p. 384).

○ References

R. C. Atkinson, G. H. Bower, and E. J. Crothers, 1965. *An Introduction to Mathematical Learning Theory*. Wiley, New York.

R. C. Atkinson and W. K. Estes, 1963. Stimulus sampling theory, in *Handbook of Mathematical Psychology* (R. D. Luce, R. R. Bush, and E. Galanter, Eds.), Vol. II, pp. 121–268. Wiley, New York.

R. C. Atkinson and R. A. Kinchla, 1965. A learning model for forced-choice detection experiments, *British Journal of Mathematical and Statistical Psychology* **18**, 183–206.

G. Birkhoff and G. C. Rota, 1969. *Ordinary Differential Equations*, 2nd ed. Ginn (Blaisdell), Boston, Massachusetts.

M. E. Bitterman, 1965. Phyletic differences in learning, *American Psychologist* **20**, 396–410.

J. H. Blau, 1961. Transformation of probabilities, *Proceedings of the American Mathematical Society* **12**, 511–518.

G. H. Bower, 1959. Choice-point behavior, in *Studies in Mathematical Learning Theory* (R. R. Bush and W. K. Estes, Eds.), pp. 109–124. Stanford Univ. Press, Stanford, California.

L. Breiman, 1968. *Probability*. Addison-Wesley, Reading, Massachusetts.

R. R. Bush, 1959. Sequential properties of linear models, in *Studies in Mathematical Learning Theory* (R. R. Bush and W. K. Estes, Eds.), pp. 215–227. Stanford Univ. Press, Stanford, California.

R. R. Bush, 1965. Identification learning, in *Handbook of Mathematical Psychology* (R. D. Luce, R. R. Bush, and E. Galanter, Eds.), Vol. III, pp. 161–203. Wiley, New York.

R. R. Bush and F. Mosteller, 1955. *Stochastic Models for Learning*. Wiley, New York.

R. R. Bush and F. Mosteller, 1959. A comparison of eight models, in *Studies in Mathematical Learning Theory* (R. R. Bush and W. K. Estes, Eds.), pp. 293–307. Stanford Univ. Press, Stanford, California.

A. B. Chia, 1970. Spectral representations of multi-element pattern models, *Journal of Mathematical Psychology* 7, 150–162.

K. L. Chung, 1967. *Markov Chains*, 2nd ed. Springer-Verlag, New York.

W. Doeblin and R. Fortet, 1937. Sur des chaînes à liaisons complètes, *Bulletin de la Société Mathématique de France* 65, 132–148.

D. D. Dorfman and M. Biderman, 1971. A learning model for a continuum of sensory states, *Journal of Mathematical Psychology* 8, 264–285.

R. M. Dudley, 1966. Convergence of Baire measures, *Studia Mathematica* 27, 251–268.

N. Dunford and J. T. Schwartz, 1958. *Linear Operators*, Part I. Wiley (Interscience), New York.

J. Elliott, 1955. Eigenfunction expansions associated with certain singular differential operators, *Transactions of the American Mathematical Society* 78, 406–425.

W. K. Estes, 1959. Component and pattern models with Markovian interpretations, in *Studies in Mathematical Learning Theory* (R. R. Bush and W. K. Estes, Eds.), pp. 9–52. Stanford Univ. Press, Stanford, California.

W. K. Estes, 1964. Probability learning, in *Categories of Human Learning* (A. W. Melton, Ed.), pp. 89–128. Academic Press, New York.

W. K. Estes, 1970. *Learning Theory and Mental Development*. Academic Press, New York.

W. K. Estes and P. Suppes, 1959a. Foundations of linear models, in *Studies in Mathematical Learning Theory* (R. R. Bush and W. K. Estes, Eds.), pp. 137–179. Stanford Univ. Press, Stanford, California.

W. K. Estes and P. Suppes, 1959b. Foundations of statistical learning theory, II. The stimulus sampling model, Technical Report No. 26, Institute for Mathematical Studies in the Social Sciences, Stanford, California.

W. J. Ewens, 1969. *Population Genetics*. Methuen, London.

W. Feller, 1968. *An Introduction to Probability Theory and Its Applications*, Vol. I, 3rd ed. Wiley, New York.

W. Feller, 1971. *An Introduction to Probability Theory and Its Applications*, Vol. II, 2nd ed. Wiley, New York.

M. Fréchet, 1952. *Recherches Théoriques Modernes sur le Calcul des Probabilités*, Vol. II, 2nd ed. Méthode des fonctiones arbitraires. Théorie des événements en chaîne dans le cas d'un nombre fini d'états possibles. Gauthier-Villars, Paris.

M. P. Friedman, E. C. Carterette, L. Nakatani, and A. Ahumada, 1968. Comparison of some learning models for response bias in signal detection, *Perception and Psychophysics* 3, 5–11.

I. I. Gikhman and A. V. Skorokhod, 1969. *Introduction to the Theory of Random Processes*. Saunders, Philadelphia.

P. R. Halmos, 1950. *Measure Theory*. Van Nostrand-Reinhold, Princeton, New Jersey.

E. J. Hannan, 1970. *Multiple Time Series*. Wiley, New York.

E. Hille, 1969. *Lectures on Ordinary Differential Equations*. Addison-Wesley, Reading, Massachusetts.

H. S. Hoffman, 1965. Theory construction through computer simulation, in *Classical Conditioning* (W. F. Prokasy, Ed.), pp. 107–117. Appleton, New York.

I. A. Ibragimov, 1962. Some limit theorems for stationary processes, *Theory of Probability and Its Applications* 7, 349–382.

C. T. Ionescu Tulcea, 1959. On a class of operators occurring in the theory of chains of infinite order, *Canadian Journal of Mathematics* 11, 112–121.

C. T. Ionescu Tulcea and G. Marinescu, 1950. Théorie ergodique pour des classes d'opérations non complètement continues, *Annals of Mathematics* **52**, 140–147.

M. Iosifescu, 1963. Random systems with complete connections with an arbitrary set of states, *Revue de Mathématiques Pures et Appliquées* **8**, 611–645.

M. Iosifescu and R. Theodorescu, 1969. *Random Processes and Learning.* Springer-Verlag, New York.

R. Isaac, 1962. Markov processes and unique stationary probability measures, *Pacific Journal of Mathematics* **12**, 273–286.

B. Jamison, 1964. Asymptotic behavior of successive iterates of continuous functions under a Markov operator, *Journal of Mathematical Analysis and Applications* **9**, 203–214.

B. Jamison, 1965. Ergodic decompositions induced by certain Markov operators, *Transactions of the American Mathematical Society* **117**, 451–468.

B. Jamison and R. Sine, 1969. Irreducible almost periodic Markov operators, *Journal of Mathematics and Mechanics* **18**, 1043–1057.

M. Kac, 1947. Random walk and the theory of Brownian motion, *American Mathematical Monthly* **54**, 369–391.

M. Kac, 1962. A note on learning signal detection, *IRE Transactions on Information Theory* **8**, 126–128.

M. Kac, 1969. Some mathematical models in science, *Science* **166**, 695–699.

S. Karlin and J. McGregor, 1964a. On some stochastic models in genetics, in *Stochastic Models in Medicine and Biology* (J. Gurland, Ed.), pp. 245–271. Univ. of Wisconsin Press, Madison, Wisconsin.

S. Karlin and J. McGregor, 1964b. Direct product branching processes and related Markov chains, *Proceedings of the National Academy of Sciences* **51**, 598–602.

J. G. Kemeny and J. L. Snell, 1960. *Finite Markov Chains.* Van Nostrand-Reinhold, Princeton, New Jersey.

A. Khintchine, 1948. *Asymptotische Gesetze der Wahrscheinlichkeitsrechnung.* Chelsea, New York.

M. Kimura, 1964. Diffusion models in population genetics, *Journal of Applied Probability* **1**, 177–232.

W. Kintsch, 1970. *Learning, Memory, and Conceptual Processes.* Wiley, New York.

J. Lamperti, 1966. *Probability.* Benjamin, New York.

M. Loève, 1963. *Probability Theory*, 3rd ed. Van Nostrand-Reinhold, Princeton, New Jersey.

E. Lovejoy, 1966. Analysis of the overlearning reversal effect, *Psychological Review* **73**, 87–103.

E. Lovejoy, 1968. *Attention in Discrimination Learning.* Holden-Day, San Francisco.

R. D. Luce, 1959. *Individual Choice Behavior.* Wiley, New York.

P. Mandl, 1968. *Analytical Treatment of One-Dimensional Markov Processes.* Springer-Verlag, New York.

H. P. McKean, Jr., 1956. Elementary solutions for certain parabolic partial differential equations, *Transactions of the American Mathematical Society* **82**, 519–548.

J. L. Myers, 1970. Sequential choice behavior, in *The Psychology of Learning and Motivation* (G. H. Bower, Ed.), Vol. 4, pp. 109–170. Academic Press, New York.

E. D. Neimark and W. K. Estes, 1967. *Stimulus Sampling Theory.* Holden-Day, San Francisco.

J. Neveu, 1965. *Mathematical Foundations of the Calculus of Probability.* Holden-Day, San Francisco.

M. F. Norman, 1964. Incremental learning on random trials, *Journal of Mathematical Psychology* **1**, 336–350.

M. F. Norman, 1966. An approach to free-responding on schedules that prescribe reinforcement probability as a function of inter-response time, *Journal of Mathematical Psychology* **3**, 235–268.

M. F. Norman, 1968a. Some convergence theorems for stochastic learning models with distance diminishing operators, *Journal of Mathematical Psychology* **5**, 61–101.

M. F. Norman, 1968b. Mathematical learning theory, in *Mathematics of the Decision Sciences* (G. B. Dantzig and A. F. Veinott, Eds.), Part 2, pp. 283–313. American Mathematical Society, Providence, Rhode Island.

M. F. Norman, 1968c. Slow learning, *British Journal of Mathematical and Statistical Psychology* **21**, 141–159.

M. F. Norman, 1968d. On the linear model with two absorbing barriers, *Journal of Mathematical Psychology* **5**, 225–241.

M. F. Norman, 1970a. A uniform ergodic theorem for certain Markov operators on Lipschitz functions on bounded metric spaces, *Zeitschrift für Wahrscheinlichkeitstheorie und verwandte Gebiete* **15**, 51–56.

M. F. Norman, 1970b. Limit theorems for additive learning models, *Journal of Mathematical Psychology* **7**, 1–11.

M. F. Norman, 1971a. Slow learning with small drift in two-absorbing-barrier models, *Journal of Mathematical Psychology* **8**, 1–21.

M. F. Norman, 1971b. Statistical inference with dependent observations: extensions of classical procedures, *Journal of Mathematical Psychology* **8**, 444–451.

M. F. Norman and N. V. Graham, 1968. A central limit theorem for families of stochastic processes indexed by a small average step size parameter, and some applications to learning models, *Psychometrika* **33**, 441–449.

M. F. Norman and J. I. Yellott, Jr., 1966. Probability matching, *Psychometrika* **31**, 43–60.

K. R. Parthasarathy, 1967. *Probability Measures on Metric Spaces*. Academic Press, New York.

E. Parzen, 1958. On asymptotically efficient consistent estimates of the spectral density function of a stationary time series, *Journal of the Royal Statistical Society, Series B* **20**, 303–322.

E. Parzen, 1962. *Stochastic Processes*. Holden-Day, San Francisco.

B. Rosén, 1967a. On the central limit theorem for sums of dependent random variables, *Zeitschrift für Wahrscheinlichkeitstheorie und verwandte Gebiete* **7**, 48–82.

B. Rosén, 1967b. On asymptotic normality of sums of dependent random vectors, *Zeitschrift für Wahrscheinlichkeitstheorie und verwandte Gebiete* **7**, 95–102.

M. Rosenblatt, 1964a. Equicontinuous Markov operators, *Theory of Probability and its Applications* **9**, 205–222.

M. Rosenblatt, 1964b. Almost periodic transition operators acting on the continuous functions on a compact space, *Journal of Mathematics and Mechanics* **13**, 837–847.

M. Rosenblatt, 1967. Transition probability operators, in *Proceedings of the Fifth Berkeley Symposium on Mathematical Statistics and Probability* (L. M. Le Cam and J. Neyman, Eds.), Vol. II, Part 2, pp. 473–483. Univ. of California Press, Berkeley, California.

H. Rouanet and S. Rosenberg, 1964. Stochastic models for the response continuum in a determinate situation: comparisons and extensions, *Journal of Mathematical Psychology* **1**, 215–232.

H. L. Royden, 1968. *Real Analysis*, 2nd ed. Macmillan, New York.

R. J. Serfling, 1968. Contributions to central limit theory for dependent variables, *Annals of Mathematical Statistics* **39**, 1158–1175.

R. J. Serfling, 1970a. Moment inequalities for the maximum cumulative sum, *Annals of Mathematical Statistics* **41**, 1227–1234.

R. J. Serfling, 1970b. Convergence properties of S_n under moment restrictions, *Annals of Mathematical Statistics* **41**, 1235–1248.

S. Sternberg, 1963. Stochastic learning theory, in *Handbook of Mathematical Psychology* (R. D. Luce, R. R. Bush, and E. Galanter, Eds.), Vol. II, pp. 1–120. Wiley, New York.

P. Suppes, 1959. A linear model for a continuum of responses, in *Studies in Mathematical Learning Theory* (R. R. Bush and W. K. Estes, Eds.), pp. 400–414. Stanford Univ. Press, Stanford, California.

P. Suppes, 1960. Stimulus-sampling theory for a continuum of responses, in *Mathematical Methods in the Social Sciences, 1959* (K. J. Arrow, S. Karlin, and P. Suppes, Eds.), pp. 348–365. Stanford Univ. Press, Stanford, California.

P. Suppes and R. W. Frankmann, 1961. Test of stimulus sampling theory for a continuum of responses with unimodal noncontingent determinate reinforcement, *Journal of Experimental Psychology* **61**, 122–132.

P. Suppes, H. Rouanet, M. Levine, and R. W. Frankmann, 1964. Empirical comparison of models for a continuum of responses with noncontingent bimodal reinforcement, in *Studies in Mathematical Psychology* (R. C. Atkinson, Ed.), pp. 358–379. Stanford Univ. Press, Stanford, California.

N. S. Sutherland and N. J. Mackintosh, 1971. *Mechanisms of Animal Discrimination Learning*. Academic Press, New York.

M. Tatsuoka and F. Mosteller, 1959. A commuting-operator model, in *Studies in Mathematical Learning Theory* (R. R. Bush and W. K. Estes, Eds.), pp. 228–247. Stanford Univ. Press, Stanford, California.

J. Theios, 1963. Simple conditioning as two-stage all-or-none learning, *Psychological Review* **70**, 403–417.

W. Vervaat, 1969. Upper bounds for the distance in total variation between the binomial or negative binomial and the Poisson distribution, *Statistica Neerlandica* **23**, 79–86.

S. Weinstock, A. J. North, A. L. Brody, and J. LoGuidice, 1965. Probability learning in a T-maze with noncorrection, *Journal of Comparative and Physiological Psychology* **60**, 76–81.

S. S. Wilks, 1962. *Mathematical Statistics*. Wiley, New York.

J. I. Yellott, Jr., 1969. Probability learning with noncontingent success, *Journal of Mathematical Psychology* **6**, 541–575.

D. Zeaman and B. J. House, 1963. The role of attention in retardate discrimination learning, in *Handbook of Mental Deficiency* (N. R. Ellis, Ed.), pp. 159–223. McGraw-Hill, New York.

○ List of Symbols

These symbols are used in the same or similar ways in two or more chapters. The definitions given on the pages indicated do not cover all local variations in meaning.

a.s., 21
$a(x)$, 16, 138
A_i, A_{in}, 2, 175
$\bar{A}_{1n}$, 16, 180
$b(x)$, 17, 138
$B(X)$, 22
$\mathcal{B}$, 21, 24
c_{ij}, 4, 175
C_k, 4, 175
$C(X)$, 51
$d(x, y)$, 13, 30
δ, 179, 200
δ_x, 22
$\delta p_j(x, y, \cdot)$, 31
e^n, 26

E, E_n, 12, 24
$\mathcal{E}$, 24
$\mathcal{E}^N$, 25
$f(t)$, 15, 118
$g(t)$, 119
$\mathcal{G}$, 24
γ, 158
H_n^θ, 116
I, 116, 138
I_θ, 116
$I_B(x)$, 24
$\iota(w)$, 35
J, 116
$K(x, B)$, 21
$K_\tau(x, B)$, 138

$K^{(n)}(x, B)$, 23
$\overline{K}^n(x, B)$, 38
L, 37
$L(X)$, 34
l, 3, 179, 181
$\mathscr{L}(\cdot)$, 114
λ, 16, 152, 181
$m(f)$, 34
$M(X)$, 22
$N(0, \sigma^2)$, 74
$N(0, \Sigma)$, 95
$o(\cdot)$, 126, 138, 164
$\mathrm{osc}(f)$, 22
$O(\cdot)$, 75
O_j, 2, 175
Ω, 21, 24
$p(x, A)$, 12, 24
$p_k(x, A)$, $p_\infty(x, A)$, 25
P, 21, 24
P_x, 22
$P(t; x, A)$, 139
$P(X)$, 22
$\phi(x)$, 16, 165
π_{ij}, 2, 175
Π_{ij}, 175
$\psi(x)$, 17, 164
r_j, 31
$r(V)$, 37
R_j, 31
R^N, 116
ρ_u, 74
$s(x)$, 117

S, 25
$S(x)$, 117
$S(x, \theta)$, 116
σ^2, 74, 153
$\sigma_n(x)$, 61
$T\mu$, 22
τ, 138
θ, 5, 111, 116, 195
$u(x, e)$, 12, 24
$u(x, e^n)$, 26
U, 22
U_τ, 144
U^n, 23
$\overline{U}^n$, U^∞, 37
$v(x)$, 158
V, 37, 45
$w(x)$, 15, 117
$w'(x)$, 117
$w(x, \theta)$, 116
x_n, 15, 179
x_∞, 16, 180
X, X_n, 12, 21, 24
X_n', 13, 26
X_n^θ, 14, 116
$\mathscr{X}$, 21, 24
$\#$, 185
$\wedge$, $\vee$, 75
(μ, f), 23
$|f|$, $|\mu|$, 22
$\|f\|$, 34, 37, 142
x^*, $|x|$, x^2, 117

○ Index

271